# How to Raise a Boring Girlfriend

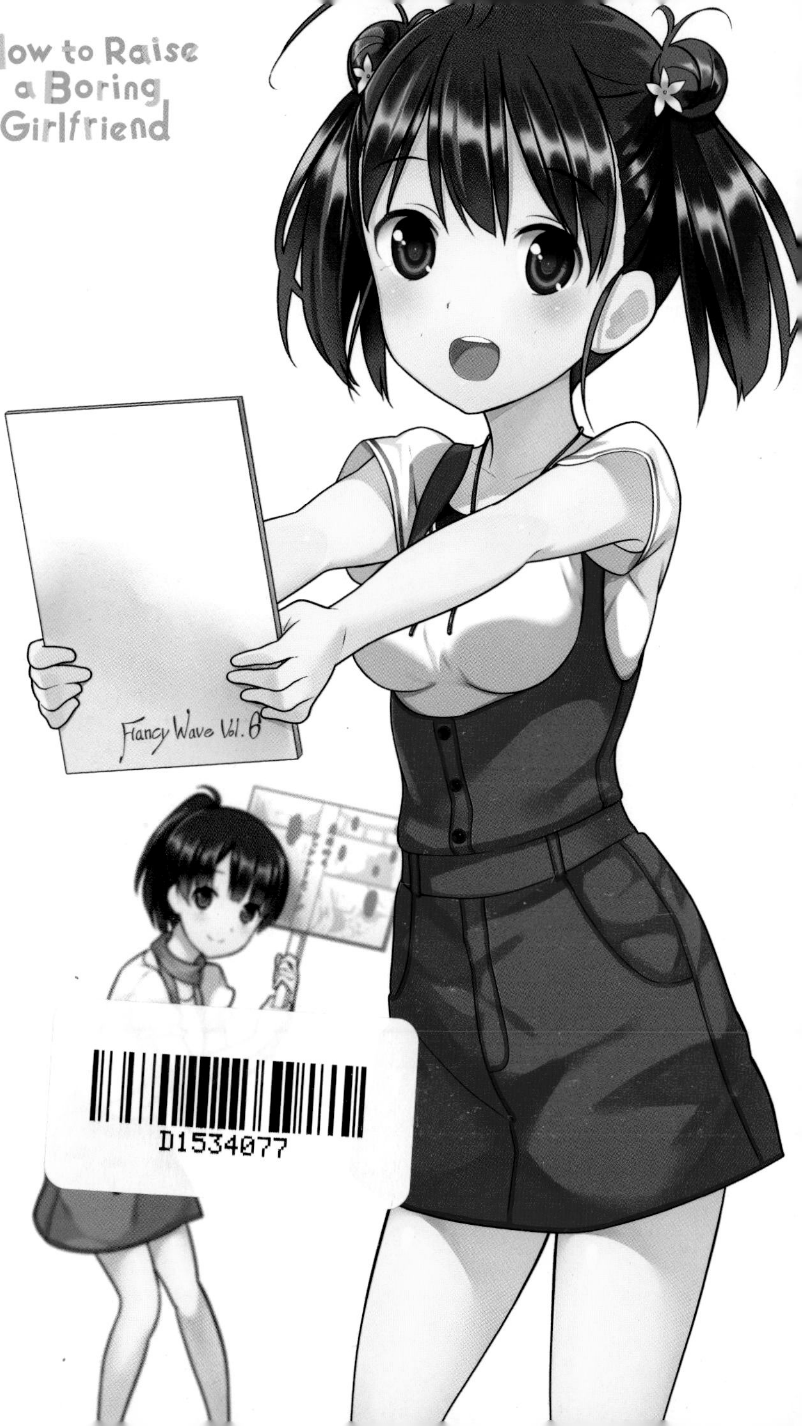
Francy Wave Vol. 6

# contents

# How to Raise a Boring Girlfriend

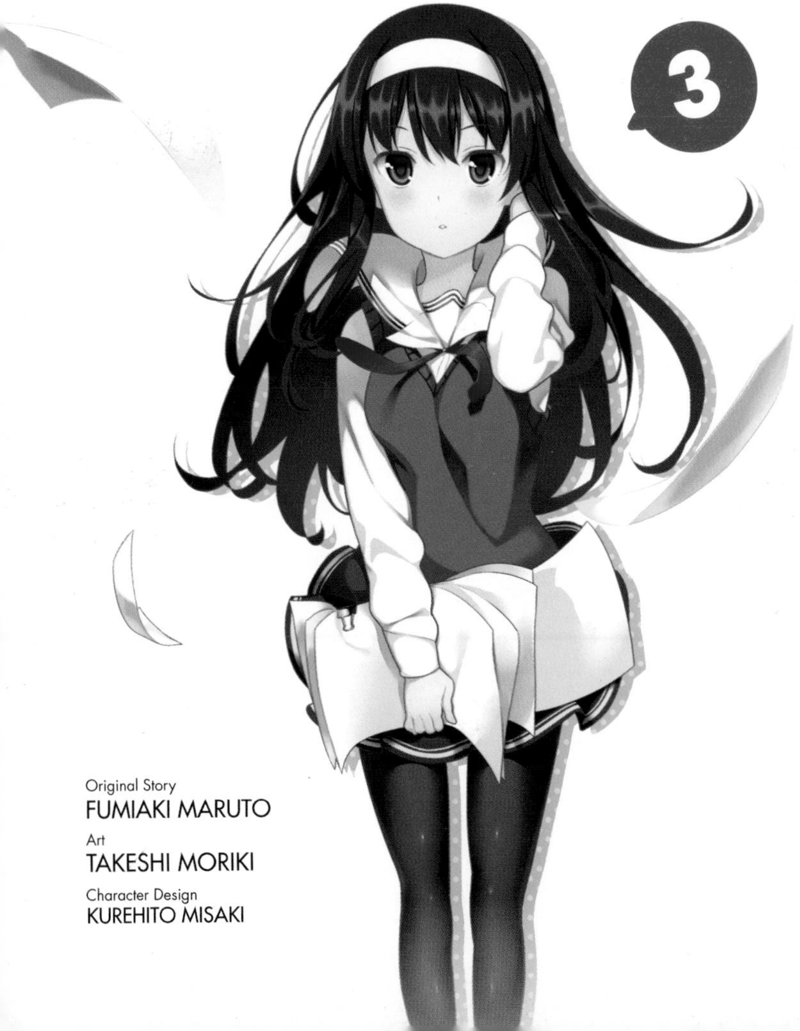
3

Original Story
FUMIAKI MARUTO
Art
TAKESHI MORIKI
Character Design
KUREHITO MISAKI

**How to Raise a Boring Girlfriend**

Volume Three

Presented by
Fumiaki Maruto &
Takeshi Moriki

Character Design by
Kurehito Misaki

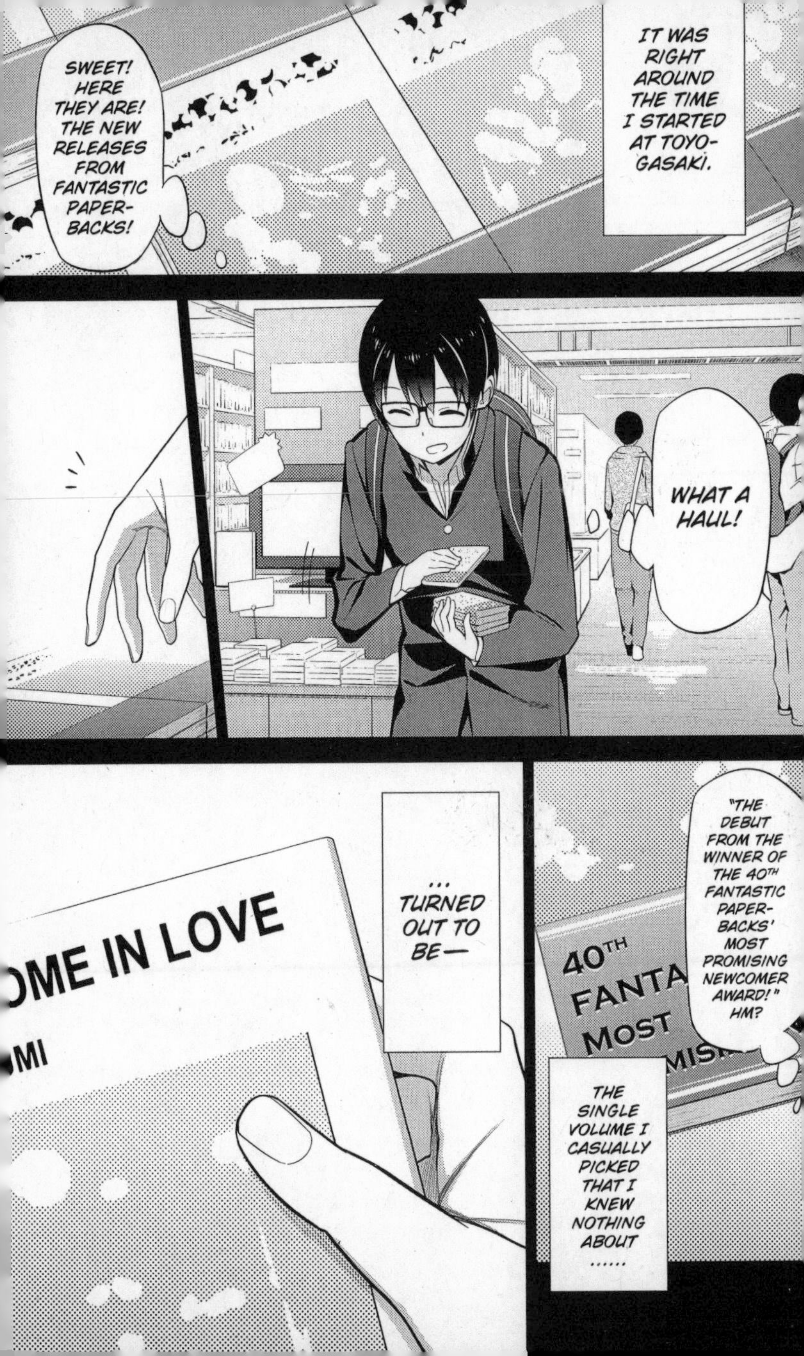
IT WAS RIGHT AROUND THE TIME I STARTED AT TOYOGASAKI.
SWEET! HERE THEY ARE! THE NEW RELEASES FROM FANTASTIC PAPERBACKS!
WHAT A HAUL!
"THE DEBUT FROM THE WINNER OF THE 40TH FANTASTIC PAPERBACKS' MOST PROMISING NEWCOMER AWARD!" HM?
THE SINGLE VOLUME I CASUALLY PICKED THAT I KNEW NOTHING ABOUT ......
... TURNED OUT TO BE—

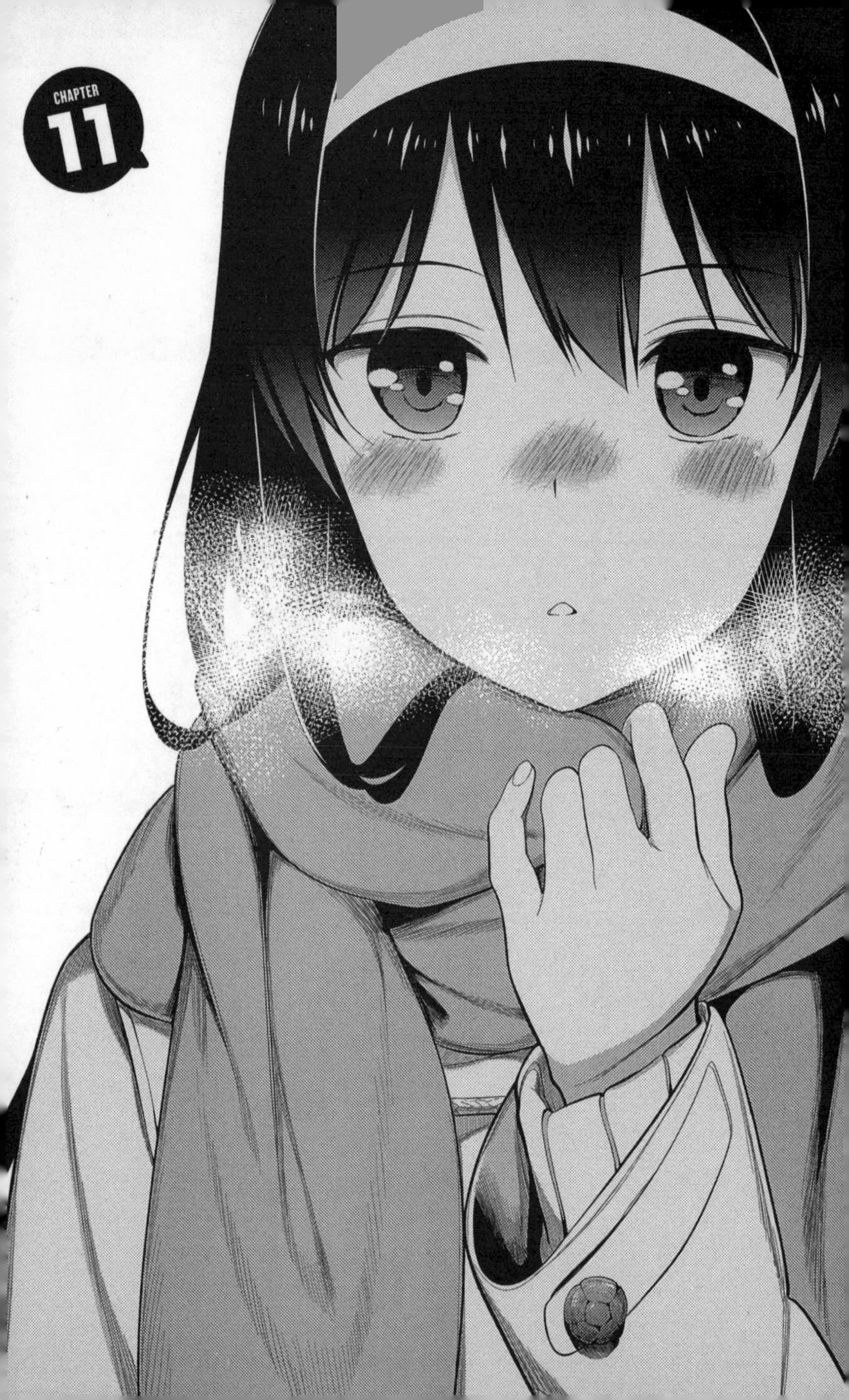
CHAPTER
11

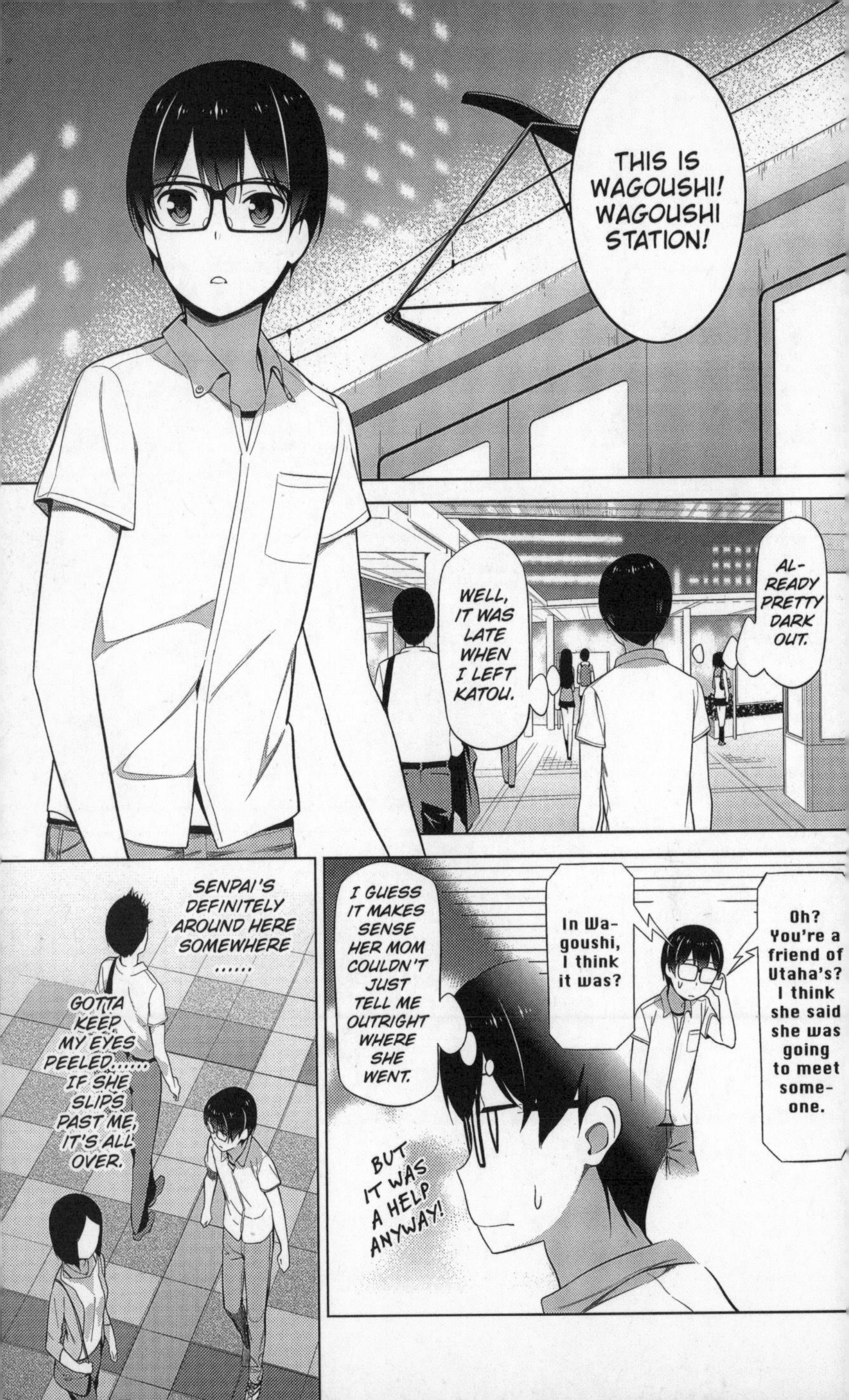
THIS IS WAGOUSHI! WAGOUSHI STATION!
AL-READY PRETTY DARK OUT.
WELL, IT WAS LATE WHEN I LEFT KATOU.
Oh? You're a friend of Utaha's? I think she said she was going to meet some-one.
In Wa-goushi, I think it was?
I GUESS IT MAKES SENSE HER MOM COULDN'T JUST TELL ME OUTRIGHT WHERE SHE WENT.
BUT IT WAS A HELP ANYWAY!
SENPAI'S DEFINITELY AROUND HERE SOMEWHERE ......
GOTTA KEEP MY EYES PEELED...... IF SHE SLIPS PAST ME, IT'S ALL OVER.

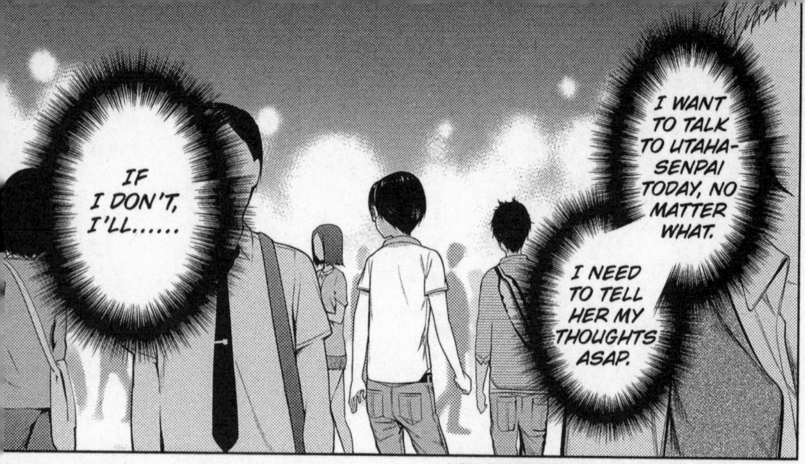
I WANT TO TALK TO UTAHA-SENPAI TODAY, NO MATTER WHAT.
I NEED TO TELL HER MY THOUGHTS ASAP.
IF I DON'T, I'LL......

SIGN: CHOUBUNDOU BOOKSTORE

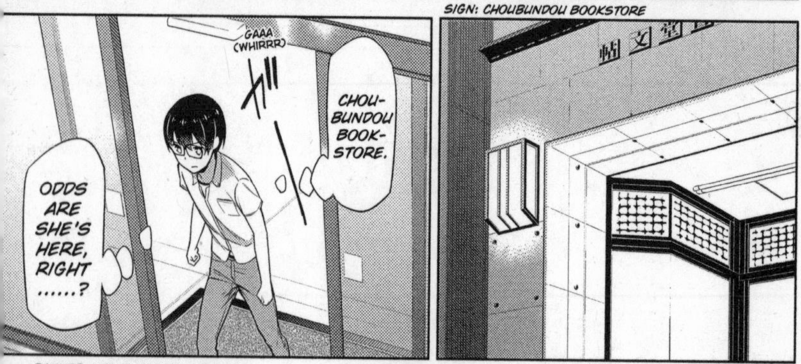
GAAA (WHIRRR)
CHOU-BUNDOU BOOK-STORE.
ODDS ARE SHE'S HERE, RIGHT......?

BANNER: UTAKO KASUMI SIGNING

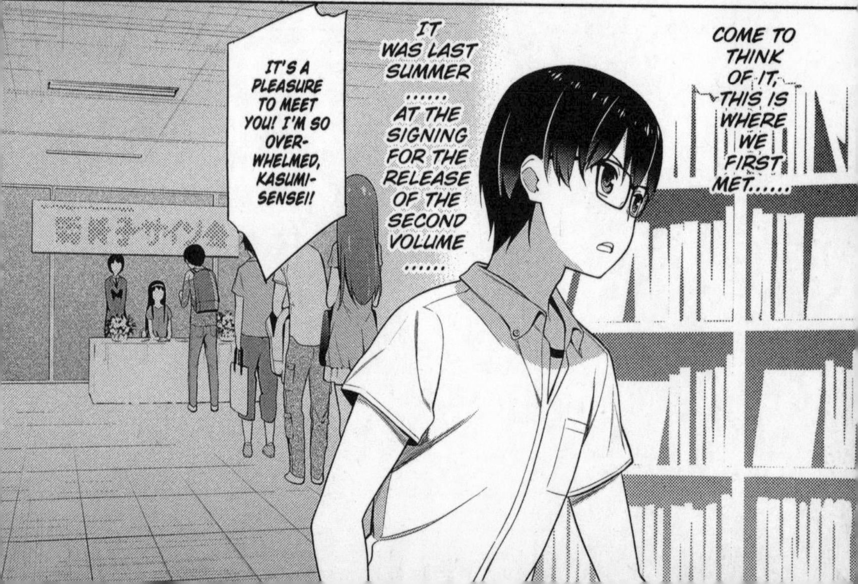
COME TO THINK OF IT, THIS IS WHERE WE FIRST MET......
IT WAS LAST SUMMER...... AT THE SIGNING FOR THE RELEASE OF THE SECOND VOLUME......
IT'S A PLEASURE TO MEET YOU! I'M SO OVER-WHELMED, KASUMI-SENSEI!

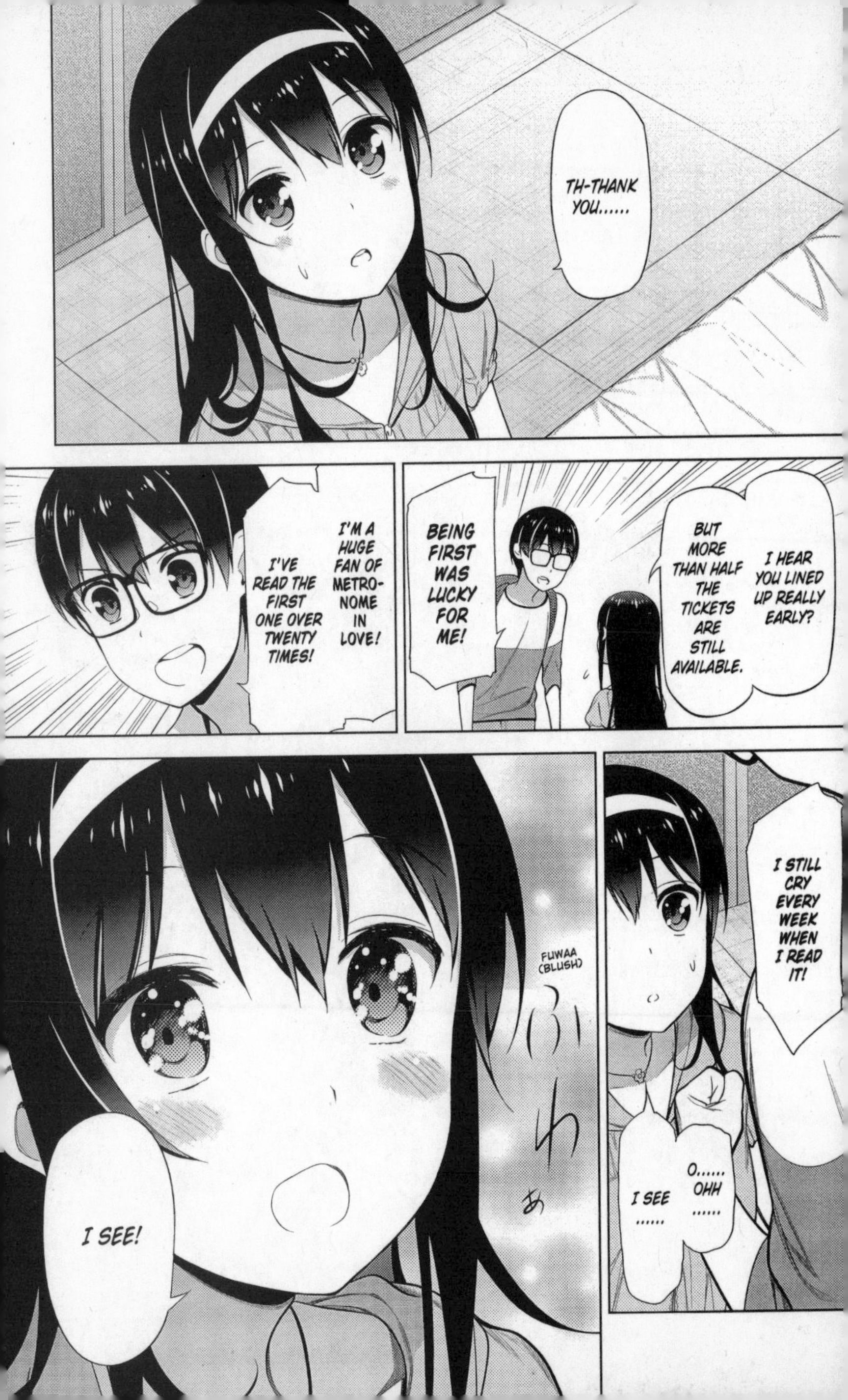
TH-THANK YOU......
I HEAR YOU LINED UP REALLY EARLY?
BUT MORE THAN HALF THE TICKETS ARE STILL AVAILABLE.
BEING FIRST WAS LUCKY FOR ME!
I'M A HUGE FAN OF METRO-NOME IN LOVE!
I'VE READ THE FIRST ONE OVER TWENTY TIMES!
I STILL CRY EVERY WEEK WHEN I READ IT!
O...... OHH ......
I SEE ......
FUWAA (BLUSH)
I SEE!

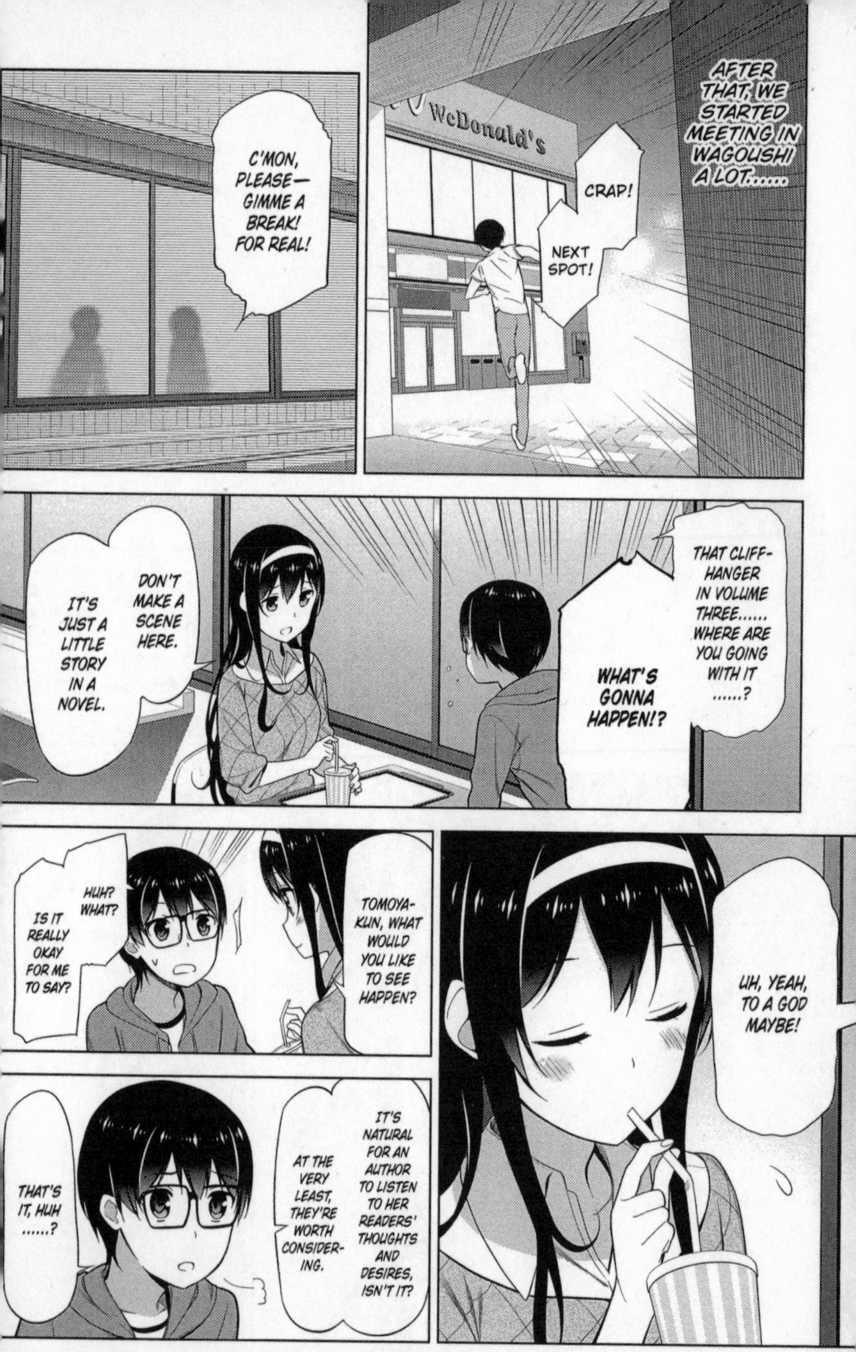
AFTER THAT, WE STARTED MEETING IN WAGOUSHI A LOT......
WcDonald's
CRAP!
NEXT SPOT!
C'MON, PLEASE—GIMME A BREAK! FOR REAL!
THAT CLIFF-HANGER IN VOLUME THREE...... WHERE ARE YOU GOING WITH IT ......?
WHAT'S GONNA HAPPEN!?
DON'T MAKE A SCENE HERE.
IT'S JUST A LITTLE STORY IN A NOVEL.
UH, YEAH, TO A GOD MAYBE!
TOMOYA-KUN, WHAT WOULD YOU LIKE TO SEE HAPPEN?
HUH? WHAT?
IS IT REALLY OKAY FOR ME TO SAY?
IT'S NATURAL FOR AN AUTHOR TO LISTEN TO HER READERS' THOUGHTS AND DESIRES, ISN'T IT?
AT THE VERY LEAST, THEY'RE WORTH CONSIDER-ING.
THAT'S IT, HUH ......?

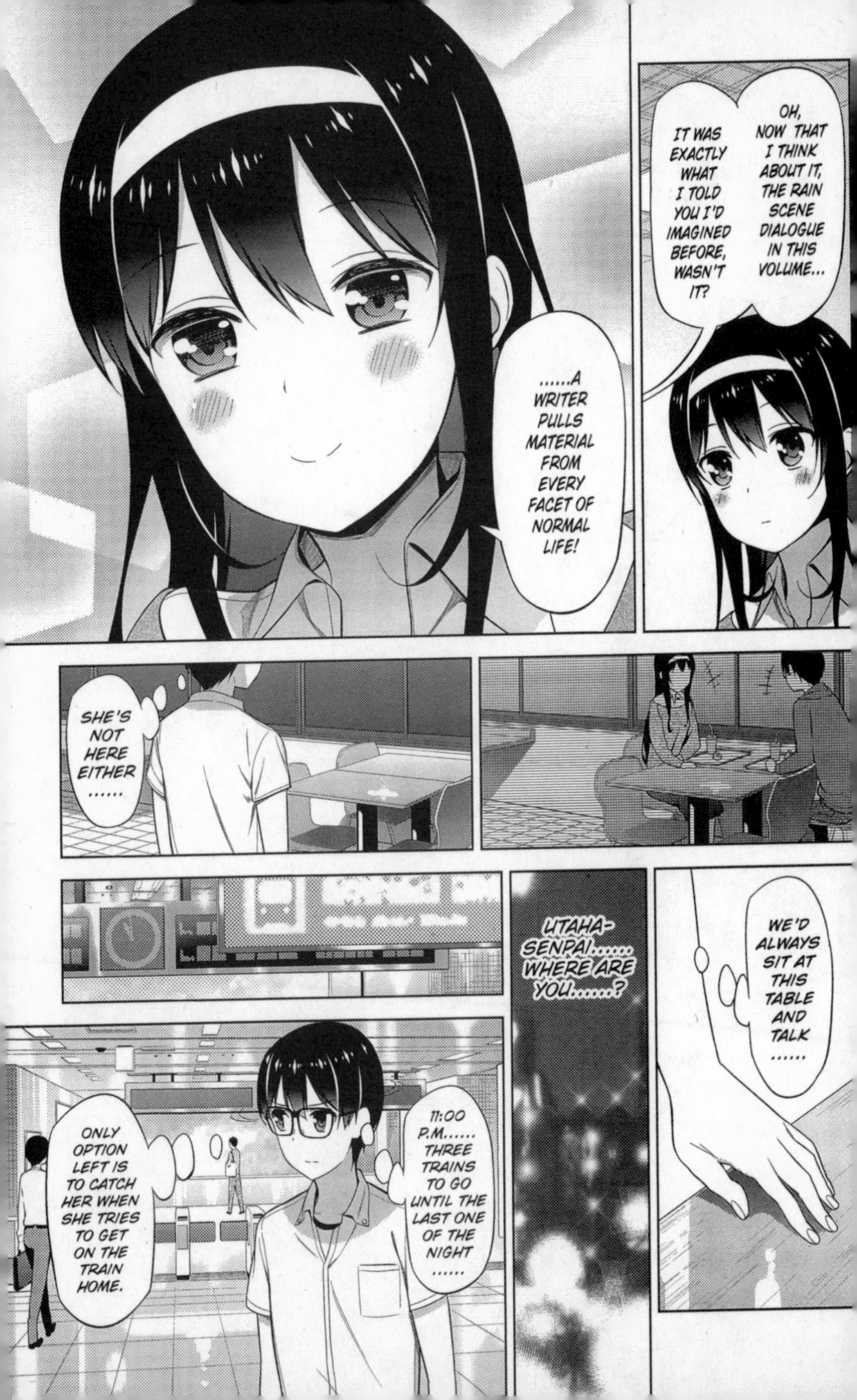
OH, NOW THAT I THINK ABOUT IT, THE RAIN SCENE DIALOGUE IN THIS VOLUME...
IT WAS EXACTLY WHAT I TOLD YOU I'D IMAGINED BEFORE, WASN'T IT?
......A WRITER PULLS MATERIAL FROM EVERY FACET OF NORMAL LIFE!
SHE'S NOT HERE EITHER ......
WE'D ALWAYS SIT AT THIS TABLE AND TALK ......
UTAHA-SENPAI...... WHERE ARE YOU......?
11:00 P.M...... THREE TRAINS TO GO UNTIL THE LAST ONE OF THE NIGHT ......
ONLY OPTION LEFT IS TO CATCH HER WHEN SHE TRIES TO GET ON THE TRAIN HOME.

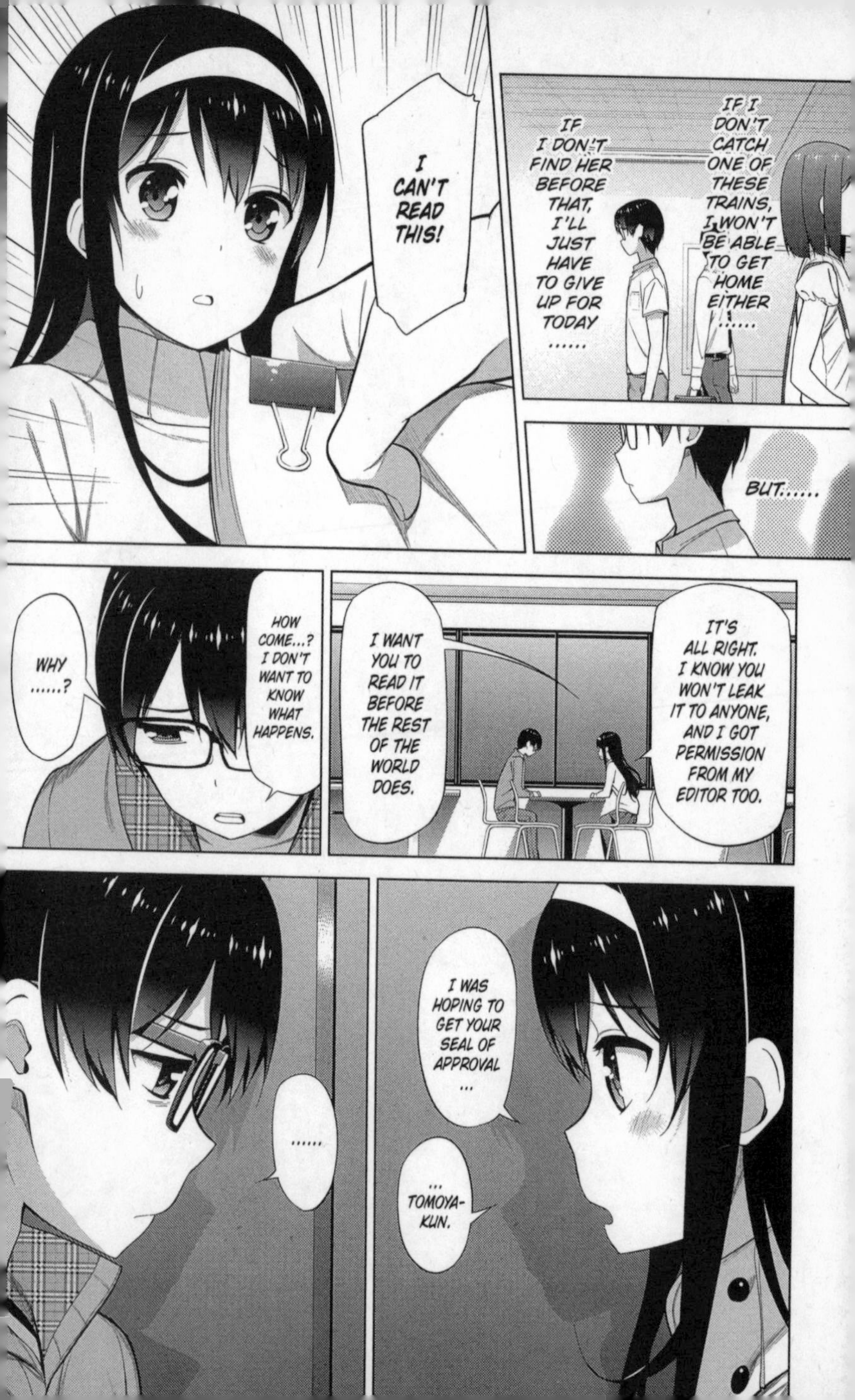
IF I DON'T CATCH ONE OF THESE TRAINS, I WON'T BE ABLE TO GET HOME EITHER ......
IF I DON'T FIND HER BEFORE THAT, I'LL JUST HAVE TO GIVE UP FOR TODAY ......
BUT......
I CAN'T READ THIS!
IT'S ALL RIGHT. I KNOW YOU WON'T LEAK IT TO ANYONE, AND I GOT PERMISSION FROM MY EDITOR TOO.
I WANT YOU TO READ IT BEFORE THE REST OF THE WORLD DOES.
HOW COME...? I DON'T WANT TO KNOW WHAT HAPPENS.
WHY ......?
I WAS HOPING TO GET YOUR SEAL OF APPROVAL ...
... TOMOYA-KUN.
......

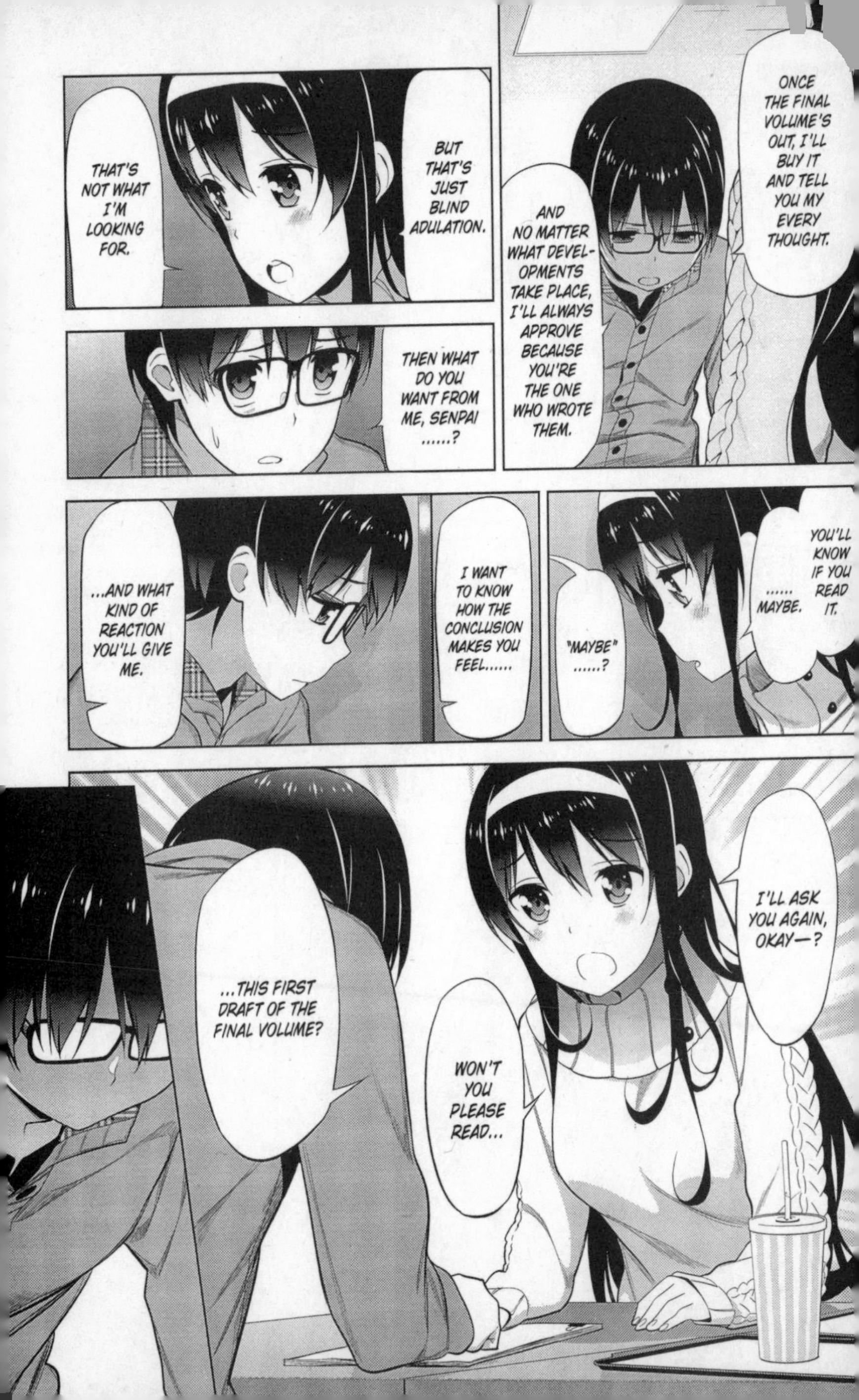
ONCE THE FINAL VOLUME'S OUT, I'LL BUY IT AND TELL YOU MY EVERY THOUGHT.
AND NO MATTER WHAT DEVEL-OPMENTS TAKE PLACE, I'LL ALWAYS APPROVE BECAUSE YOU'RE THE ONE WHO WROTE THEM.
BUT THAT'S JUST BLIND ADULATION.
THAT'S NOT WHAT I'M LOOKING FOR.
THEN WHAT DO YOU WANT FROM ME, SENPAI ......?
YOU'LL KNOW IF YOU READ IT.
...... MAYBE.
"MAYBE" ......?
I WANT TO KNOW HOW THE CONCLUSION MAKES YOU FEEL......
...AND WHAT KIND OF REACTION YOU'LL GIVE ME.
I'LL ASK YOU AGAIN, OKAY—?
WON'T YOU PLEASE READ...
...THIS FIRST DRAFT OF THE FINAL VOLUME?

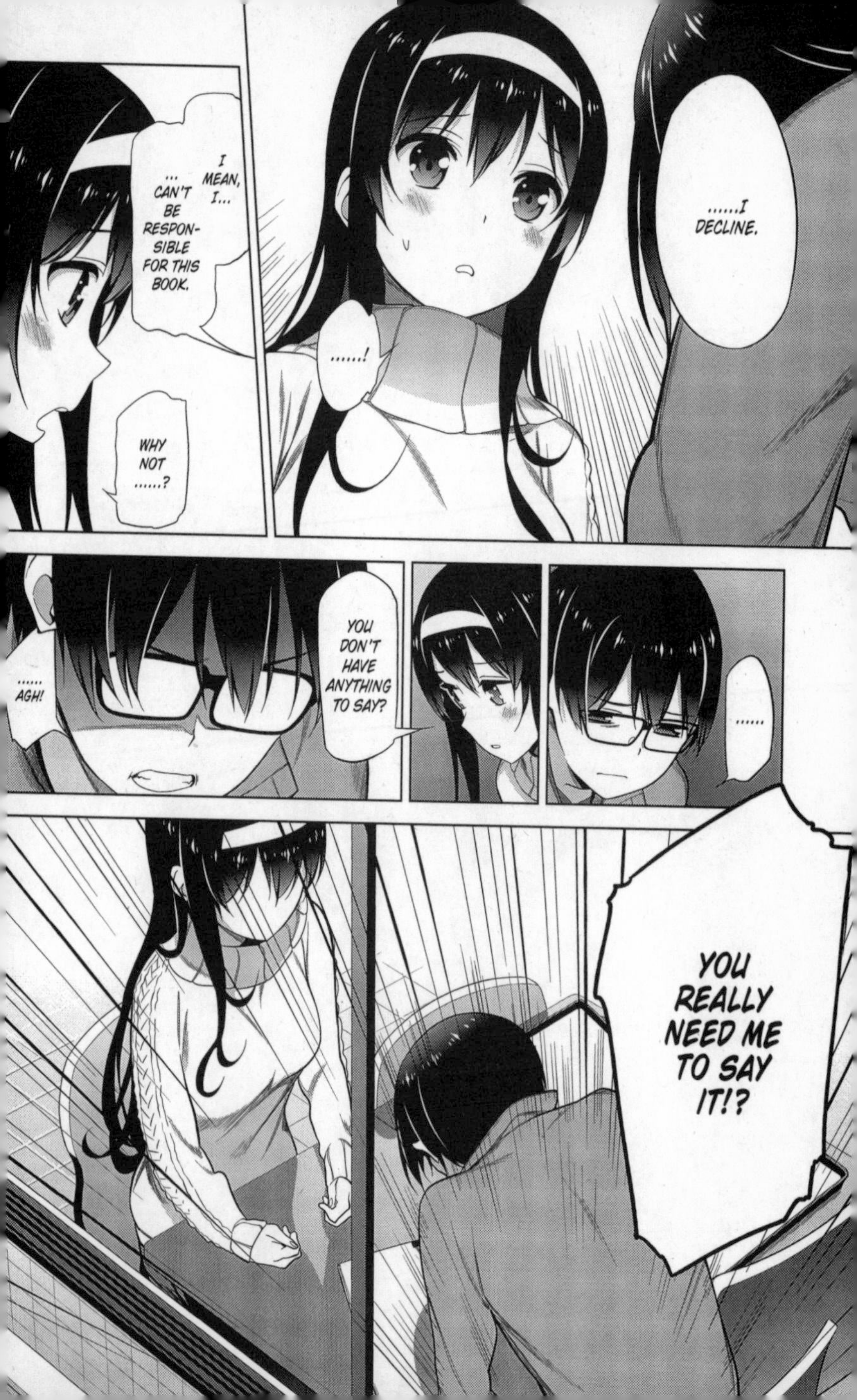
......I DECLINE.
......!
I MEAN, I...
... CAN'T BE RESPONSIBLE FOR THIS BOOK.
WHY NOT ......?
......
YOU DON'T HAVE ANYTHING TO SAY?
...... AGH!
YOU REALLY NEED ME TO SAY IT!?

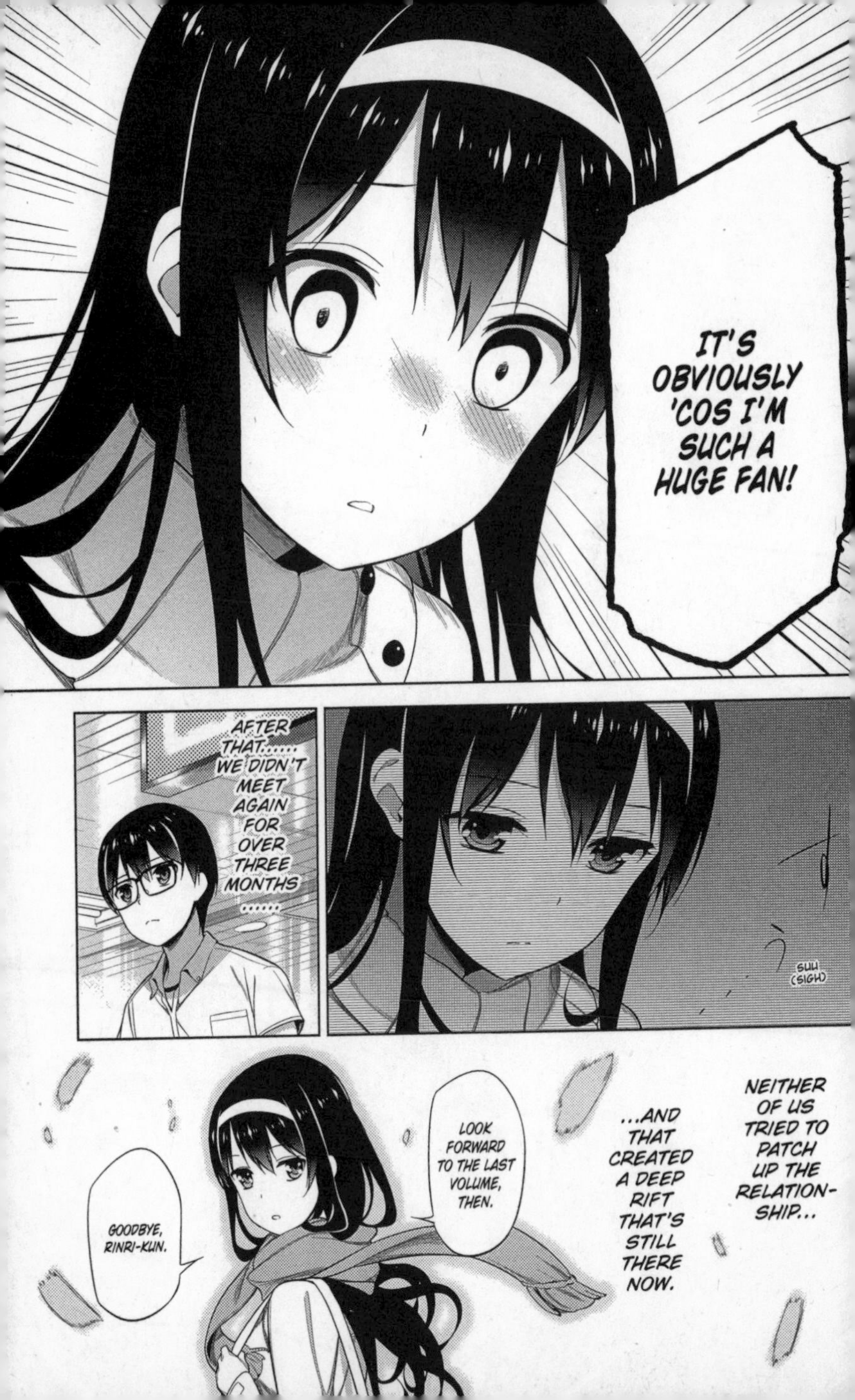
IT'S OBVIOUSLY 'COS I'M SUCH A HUGE FAN!
SUU (SIGH)
AFTER THAT...... WE DIDN'T MEET AGAIN FOR OVER THREE MONTHS ......
NEITHER OF US TRIED TO PATCH UP THE RELATION-SHIP...
...AND THAT CREATED A DEEP RIFT THAT'S STILL THERE NOW.
LOOK FORWARD TO THE LAST VOLUME, THEN.
GOODBYE, RINRI-KUN.

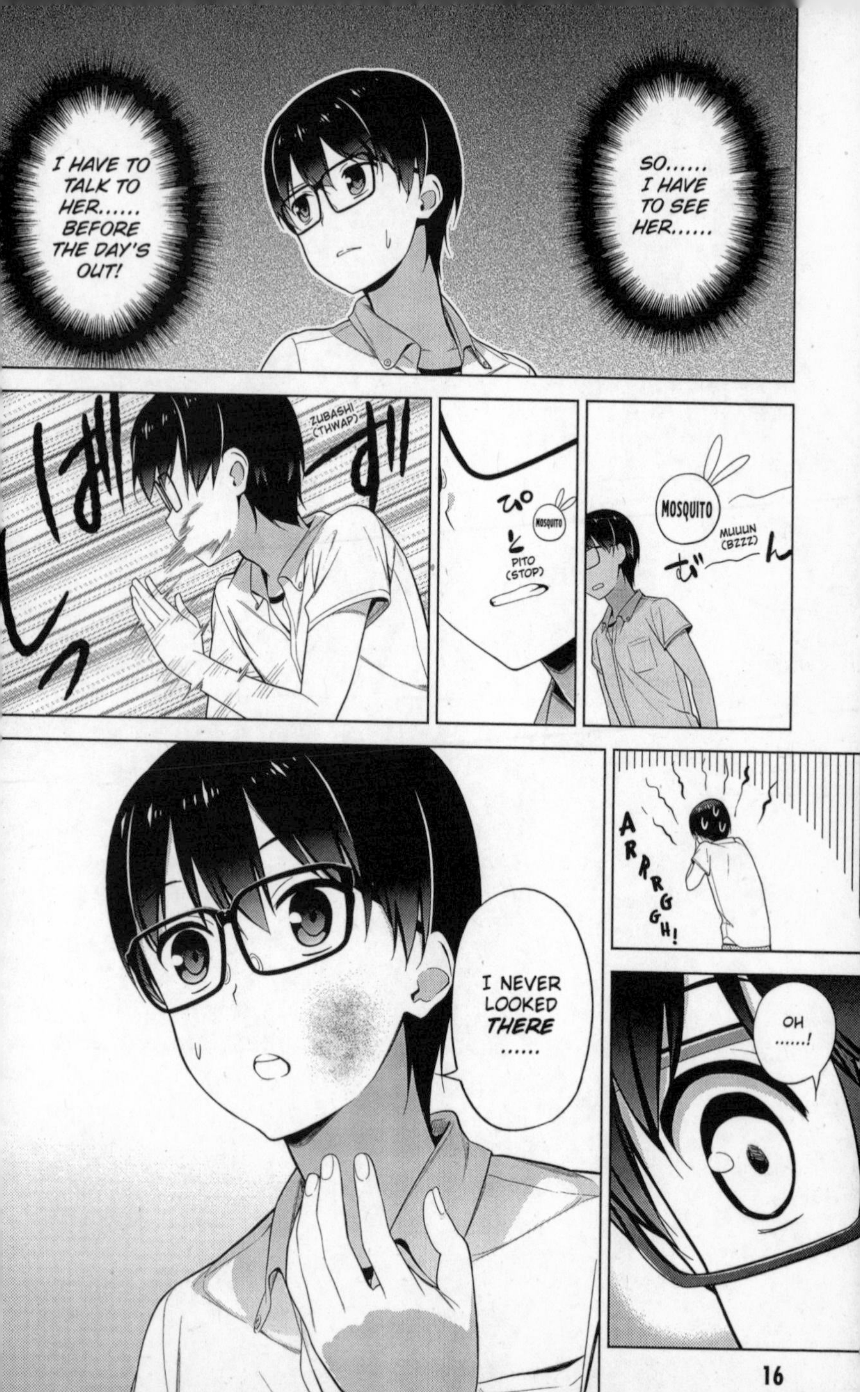

SO...... I HAVE TO SEE HER......
I HAVE TO TALK TO HER...... BEFORE THE DAY'S OUT!
MOSQUITO
むーん
MUUUN (BZZZ)
ぴと
PITO (STOP)
MOSQUITO
ZUBASHI (THWAP)
ARRRGGH!
OH ......!
I NEVER LOOKED THERE ......

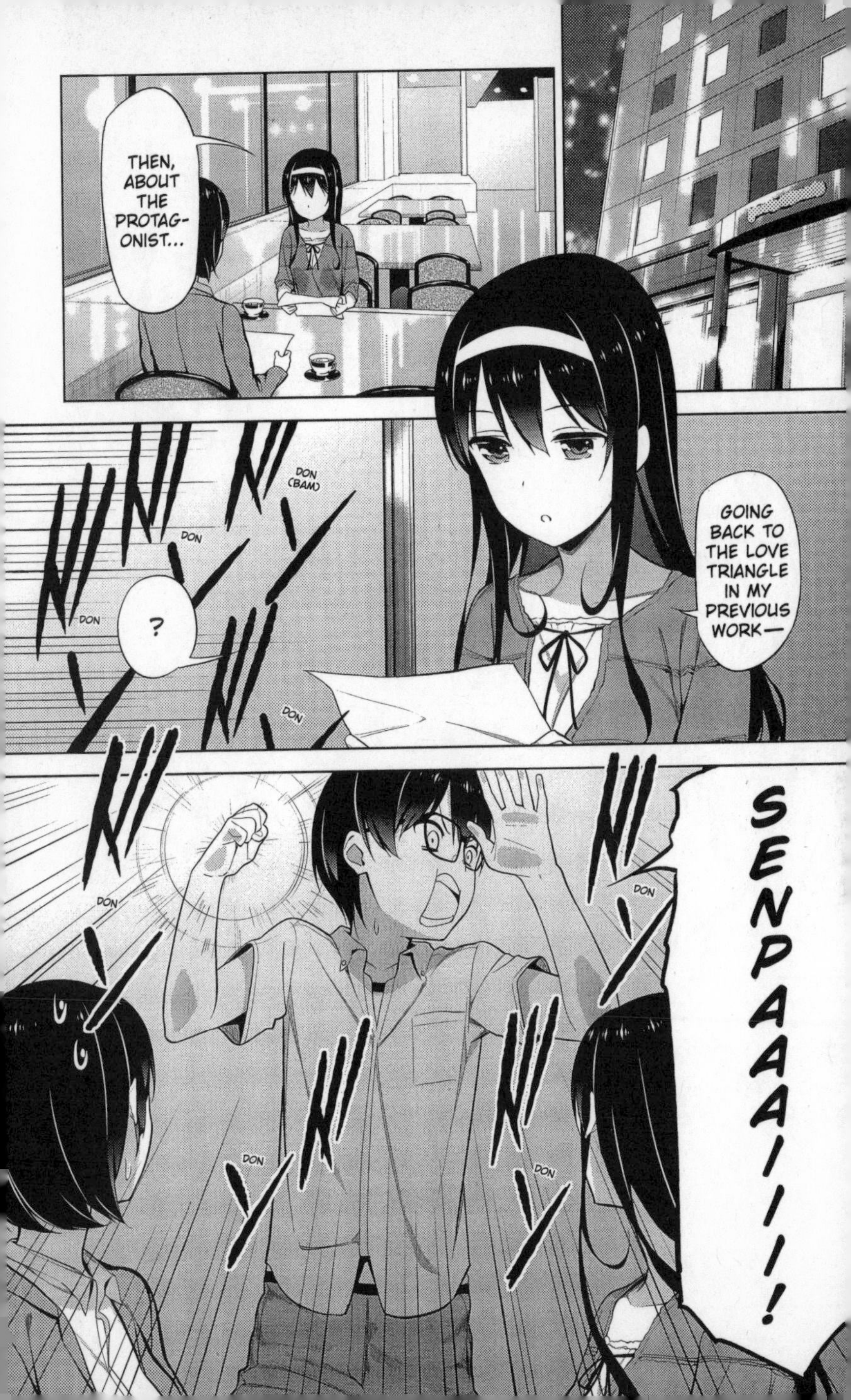
THEN, ABOUT THE PROTAG-ONIST...
GOING BACK TO THE LOVE TRIANGLE IN MY PREVIOUS WORK—
DON (BAM)
DON
?
DON
DON
SENPAAAAI!!!
DON
DON
DON
DON

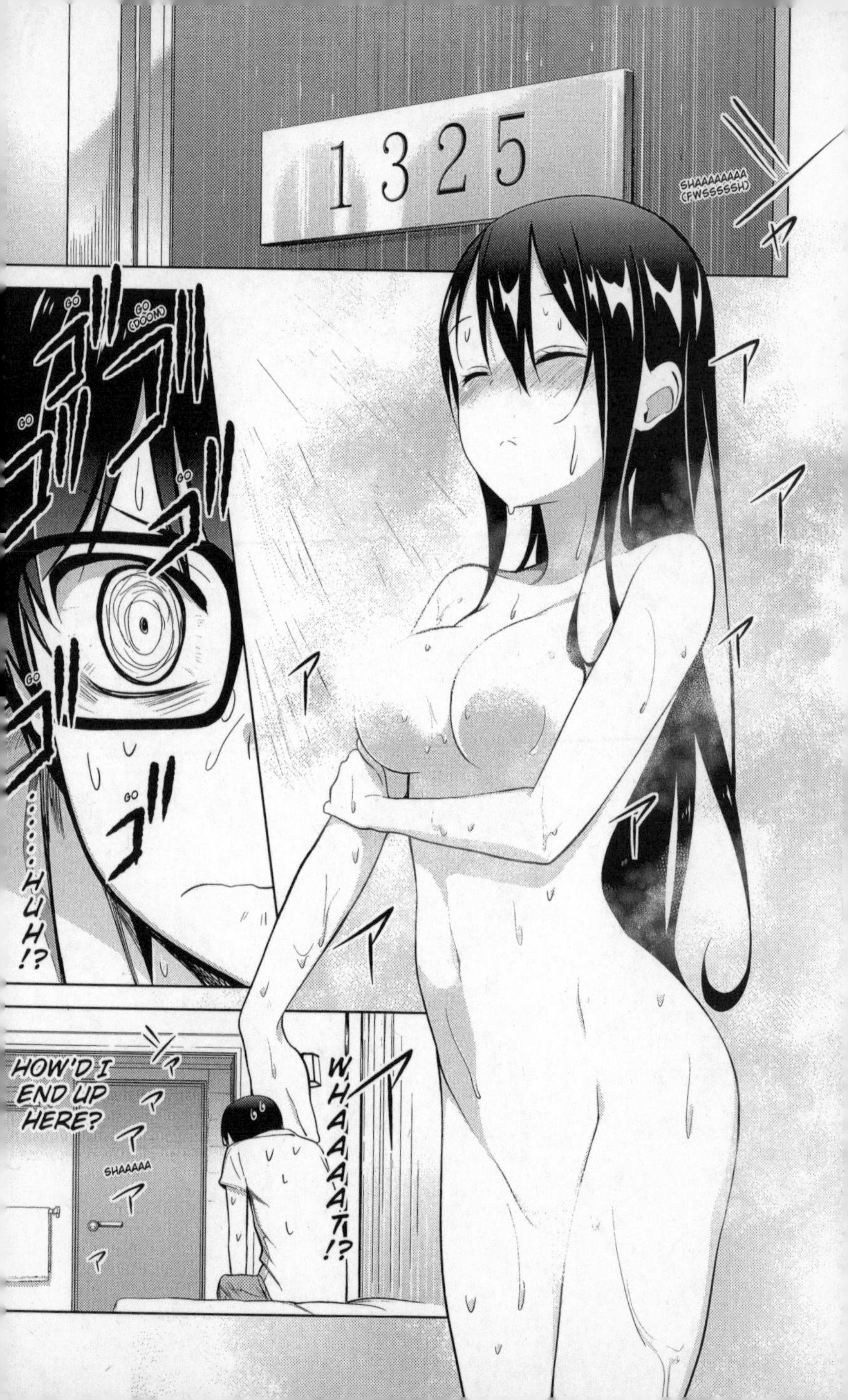
1325
SHAAAAAAAA (FWSSSSSH)
GO
GO (DOON)
GO
GO
GO
GO
......HUH!?
WHAAAAAT!?
HOW'D I END UP HERE?
SHAAAAA

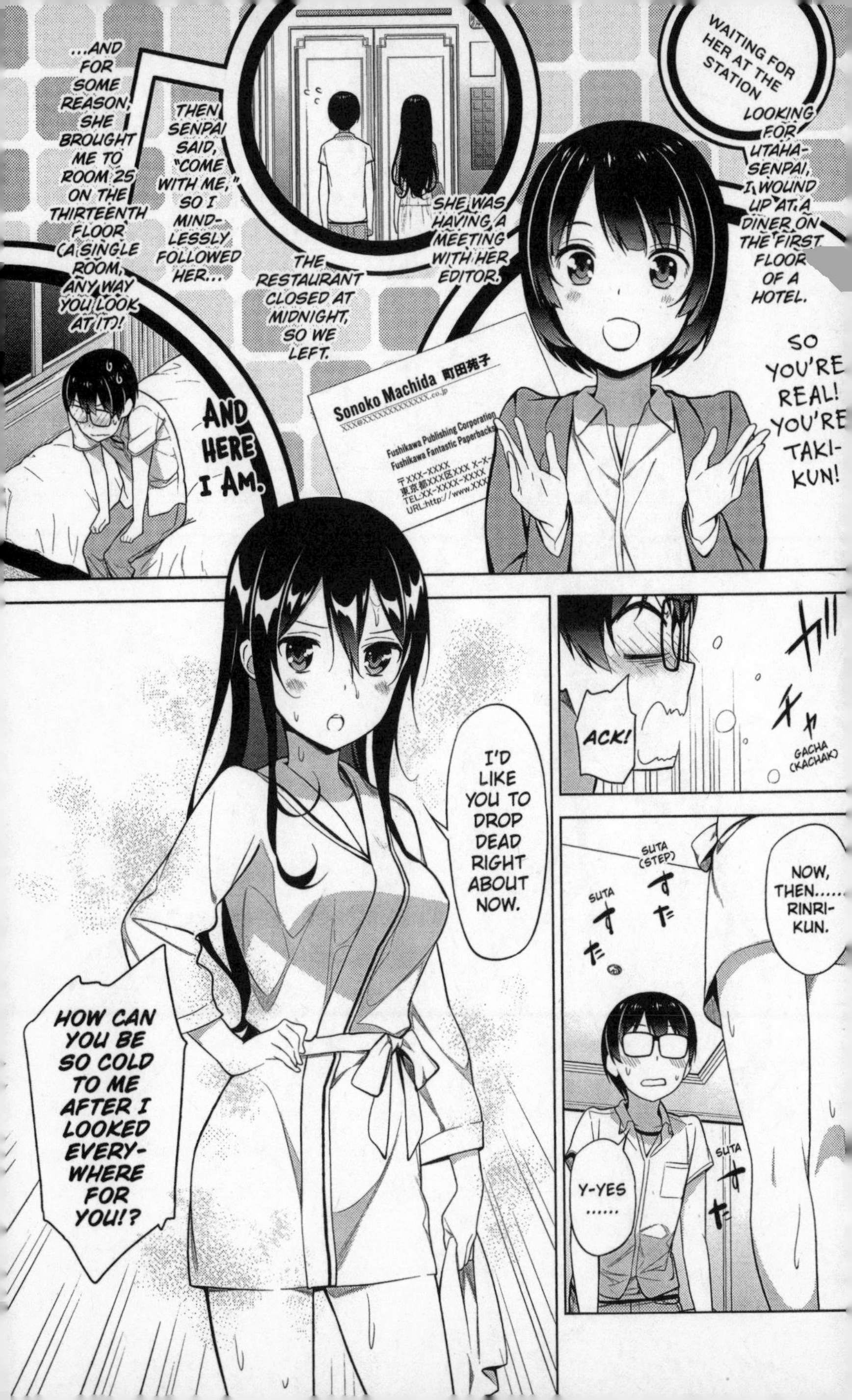
WAITING FOR HER AT THE STATION
LOOKING FOR UTAHA-SENPAI, I WOUND UP AT A DINER ON THE FIRST FLOOR OF A HOTEL.
SO YOU'RE REAL! YOU'RE TAKI-KUN!
Sonoko Machida 町田苑子
XXX@XXXXXXXXXXXX.co.jp
Fushikawa Publishing Corporation
Fushikawa Fantastic Paperbacks
〒XXX-XXXX
東京都XXX区XXX X-X-
TEL:XX-XXXX-XXXX
URL:http://www.XXX
SHE WAS HAVING A MEETING WITH HER EDITOR.
THE RESTAURANT CLOSED AT MIDNIGHT, SO WE LEFT.
THEN SENPAI SAID, "COME WITH ME," SO I MINDLESSLY FOLLOWED HER...
...AND FOR SOME REASON, SHE BROUGHT ME TO ROOM 25 ON THE THIRTEENTH FLOOR (A SINGLE ROOM, ANY WAY YOU LOOK AT IT)!
AND HERE I AM.
ガチャ
GACHA (KACHAK)
ACK!
NOW, THEN...... RINRI-KUN.
すた
SUTA (STEP)
すた
SUTA
Y-YES ......
すた
SUTA
I'D LIKE YOU TO DROP DEAD RIGHT ABOUT NOW.
HOW CAN YOU BE SO COLD TO ME AFTER I LOOKED EVERYWHERE FOR YOU!?

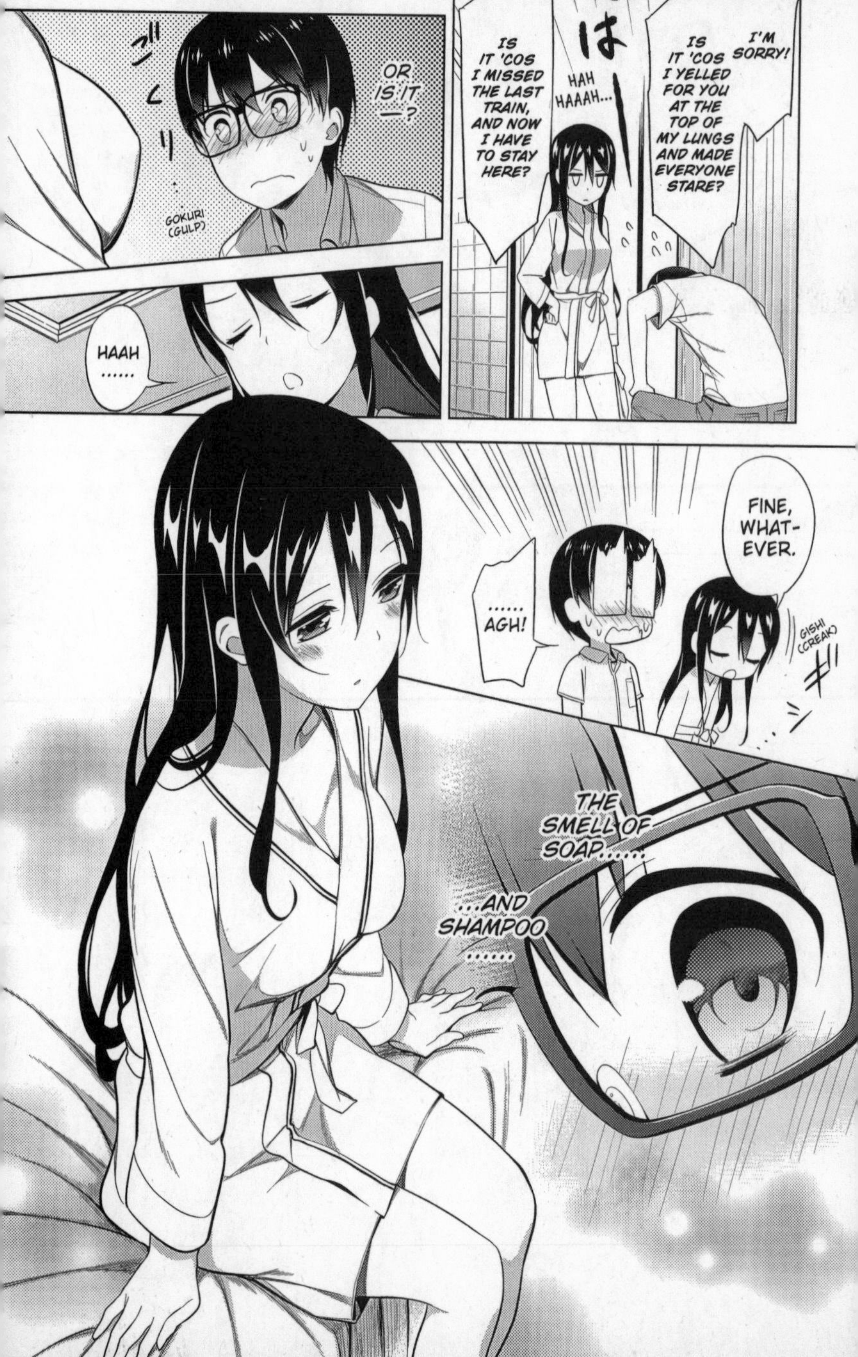
I'M SORRY!
IS IT 'COS I YELLED FOR YOU AT THE TOP OF MY LUNGS AND MADE EVERYONE STARE?
はは
HAH HAAAH...
IS IT 'COS I MISSED THE LAST TRAIN, AND NOW I HAVE TO STAY HERE?
OR IS IT —?
ごくり
GOKURI (GULP)
HAAAH ......
FINE, WHAT-EVER.
GISHI (CREAK)
......AGH!
THE SMELL OF SOAP......
...AND SHAMPOO ......

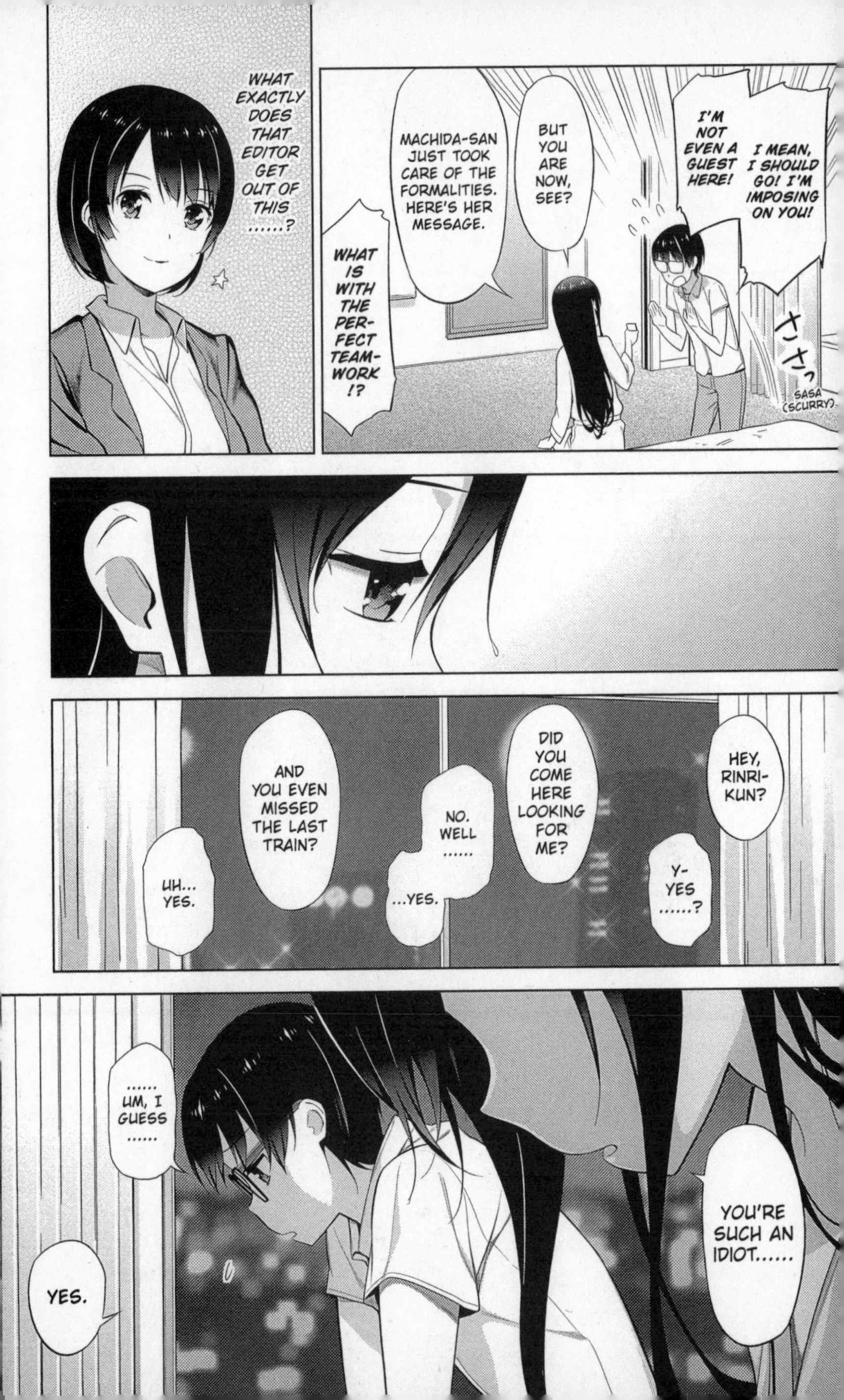
I MEAN, I SHOULD GO! I'M IMPOSING ON YOU!
I'M NOT EVEN A GUEST HERE!
ささっ
SASA (SCURRY)
BUT YOU ARE NOW, SEE?
MACHIDA-SAN JUST TOOK CARE OF THE FORMALITIES. HERE'S HER MESSAGE.
WHAT IS WITH THE PER-FECT TEAM-WORK!?
WHAT EXACTLY DOES THAT EDITOR GET OUT OF THIS ......?
HEY, RINRI-KUN?
Y-YES ......?
DID YOU COME HERE LOOKING FOR ME?
NO. WELL ......
...YES.
AND YOU EVEN MISSED THE LAST TRAIN?
UH... YES.
YOU'RE SUCH AN IDIOT......
...... UM, I GUESS ......
YES.

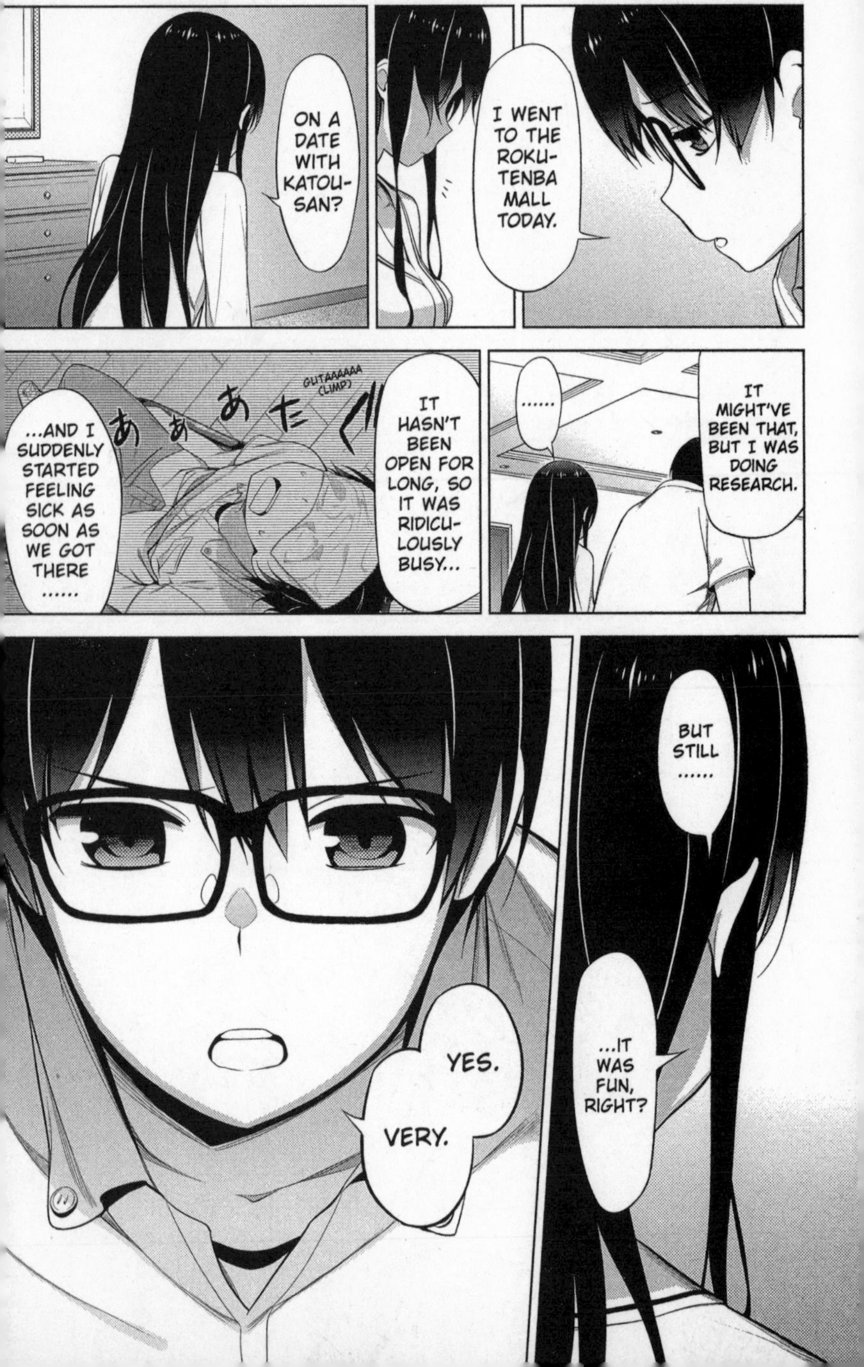
I WENT TO THE ROKU-TENBA MALL TODAY.
ON A DATE WITH KATOU-SAN?
IT MIGHT'VE BEEN THAT, BUT I WAS DOING RESEARCH.
......
IT HASN'T BEEN OPEN FOR LONG, SO IT WAS RIDICULOUSLY BUSY...
GUTAAAAAA (LIMP)
...AND I SUDDENLY STARTED FEELING SICK AS SOON AS WE GOT THERE ......
BUT STILL ......
...IT WAS FUN, RIGHT?
YES.
VERY.

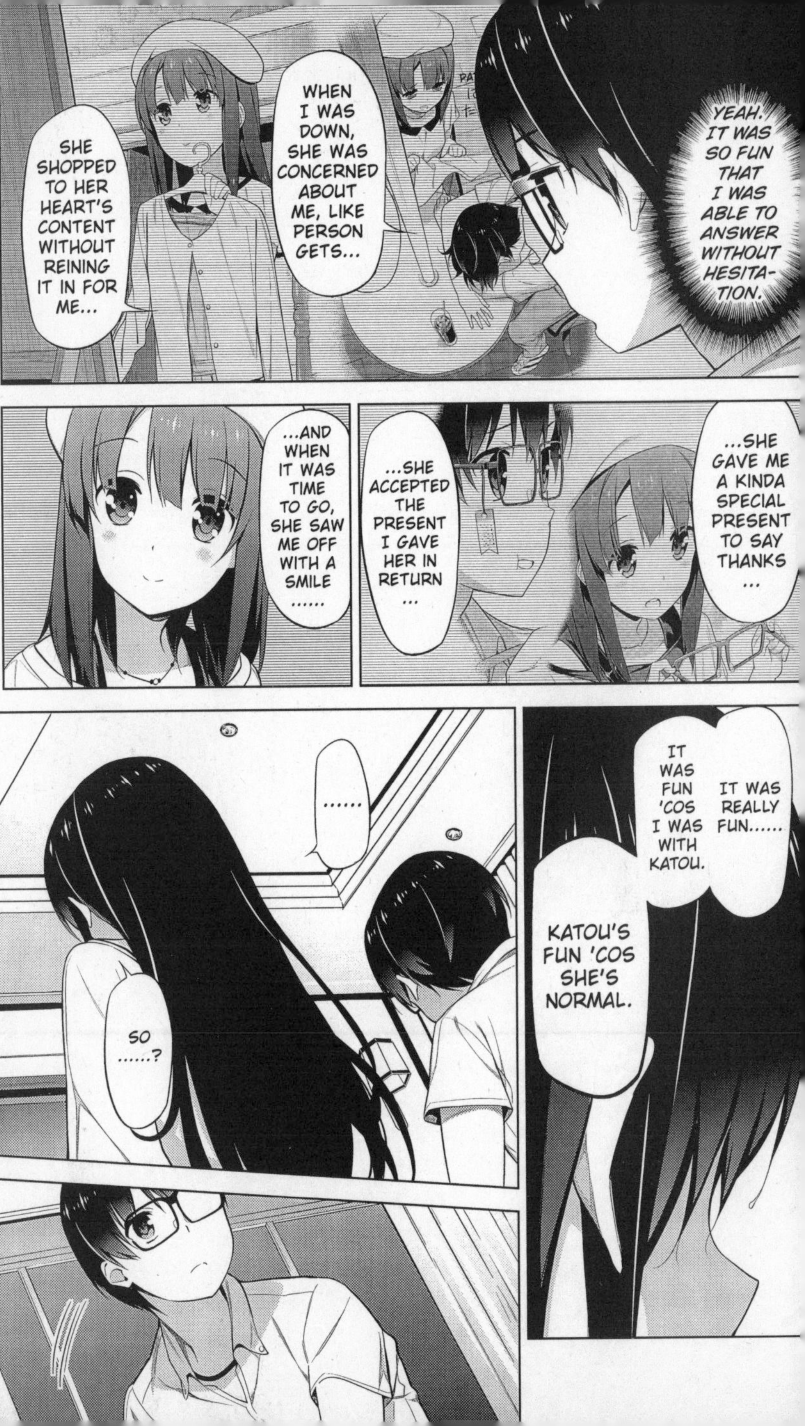
YEAH. IT WAS SO FUN THAT I WAS ABLE TO ANSWER WITHOUT HESITATION.
WHEN I WAS DOWN, SHE WAS CONCERNED ABOUT ME, LIKE PERSON GETS...
SHE SHOPPED TO HER HEART'S CONTENT WITHOUT REINING IT IN FOR ME...
...SHE GAVE ME A KINDA SPECIAL PRESENT TO SAY THANKS ...
...SHE ACCEPTED THE PRESENT I GAVE HER IN RETURN ...
...AND WHEN IT WAS TIME TO GO, SHE SAW ME OFF WITH A SMILE ......
IT WAS REALLY FUN......
IT WAS FUN 'COS I WAS WITH KATOU.
KATOU'S FUN 'COS SHE'S NORMAL.
......
SO ......?

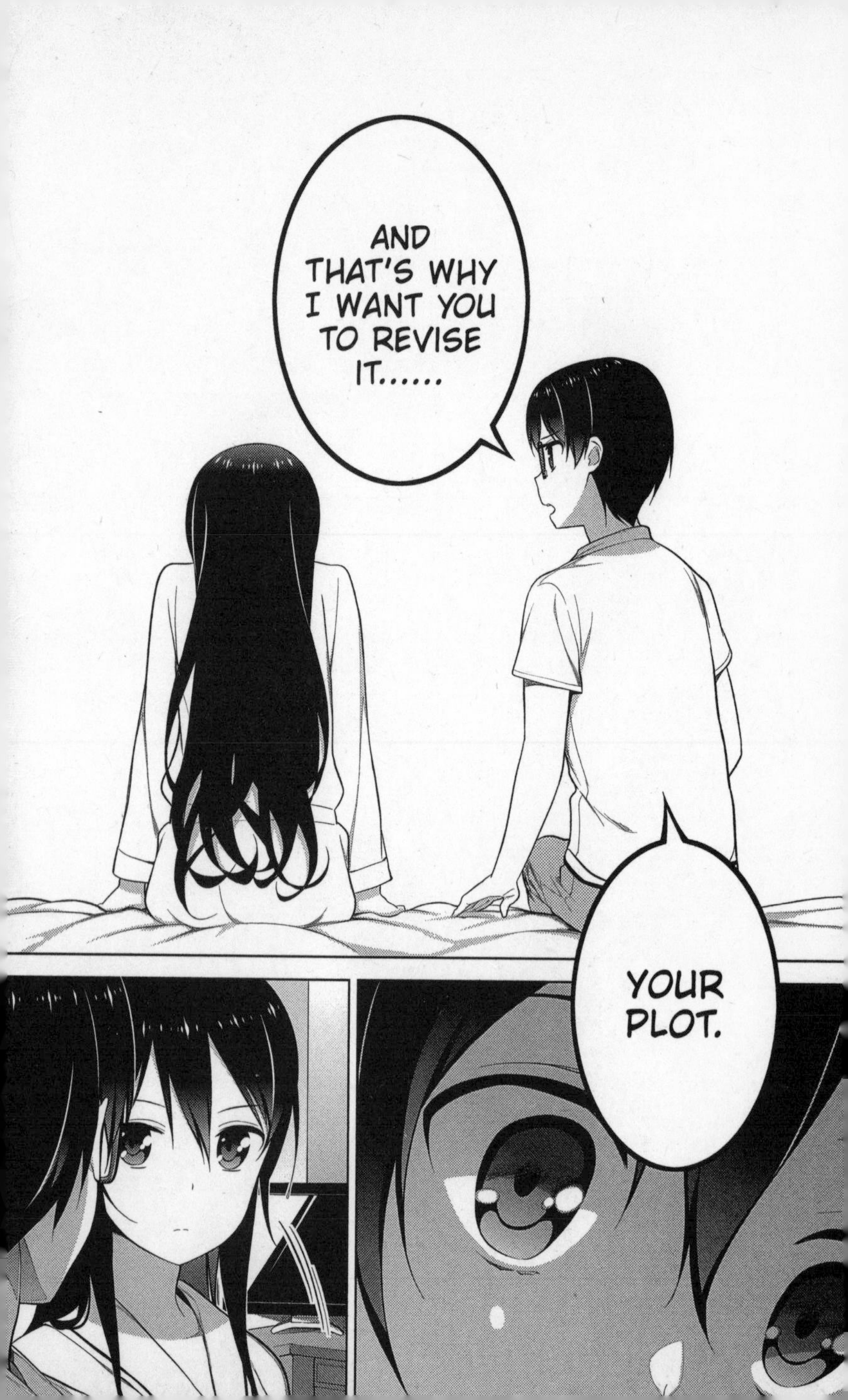
AND THAT'S WHY I WANT YOU TO REVISE IT......
YOUR PLOT.

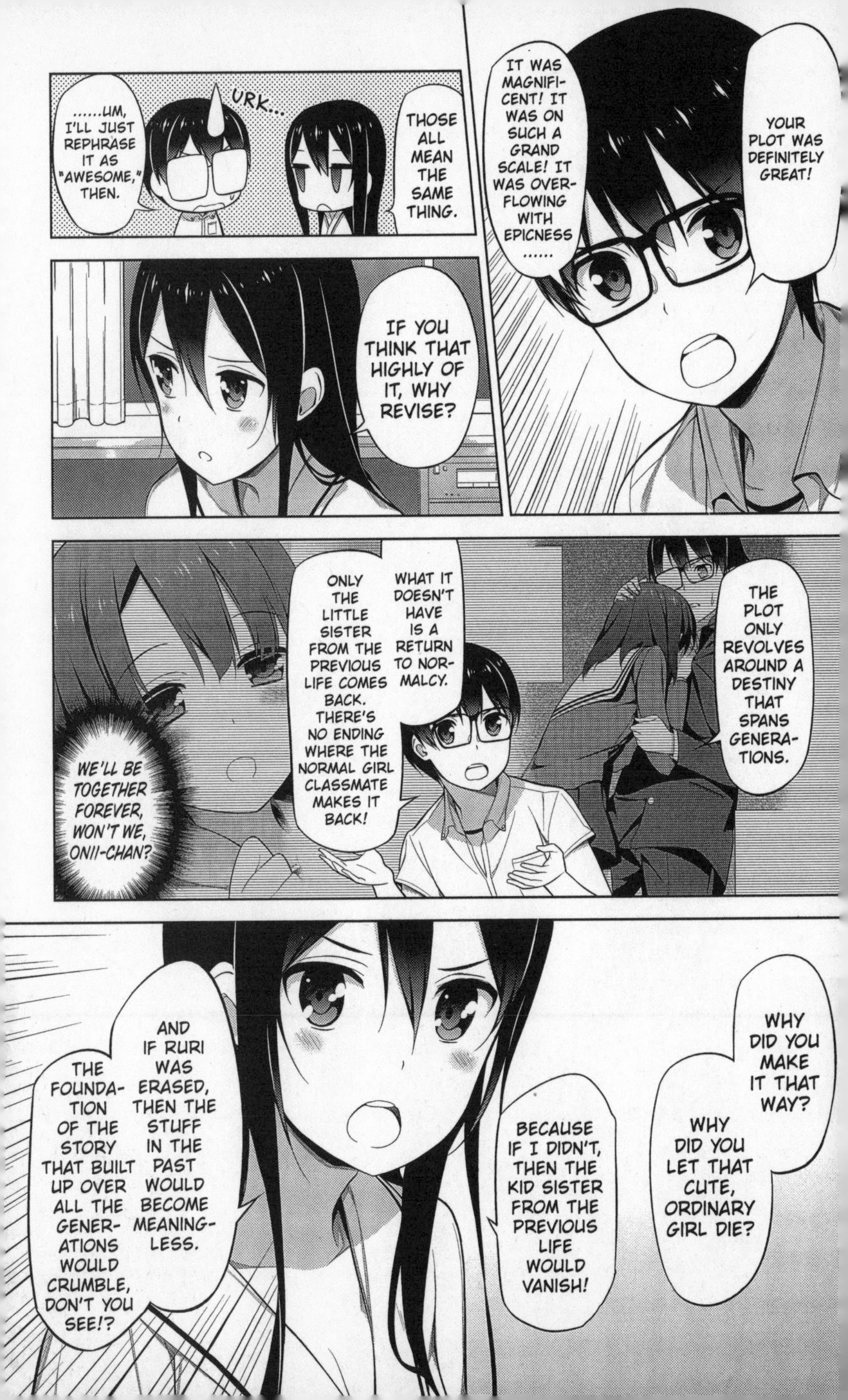
YOUR PLOT WAS DEFINITELY GREAT!
IT WAS MAGNIFICENT! IT WAS ON SUCH A GRAND SCALE! IT WAS OVERFLOWING WITH EPICNESS ......
THOSE ALL MEAN THE SAME THING.
URK...
......UM, I'LL JUST REPHRASE IT AS "AWESOME," THEN.
IF YOU THINK THAT HIGHLY OF IT, WHY REVISE?
THE PLOT ONLY REVOLVES AROUND A DESTINY THAT SPANS GENERATIONS.
WHAT IT DOESN'T HAVE IS A RETURN TO NORMALCY.
ONLY THE LITTLE SISTER FROM THE PREVIOUS LIFE COMES BACK. THERE'S NO ENDING WHERE THE NORMAL GIRL CLASSMATE MAKES IT BACK!
WE'LL BE TOGETHER FOREVER, WON'T WE, ONII-CHAN?
WHY DID YOU MAKE IT THAT WAY?
WHY DID YOU LET THAT CUTE, ORDINARY GIRL DIE?
BECAUSE IF I DIDN'T, THEN THE KID SISTER FROM THE PREVIOUS LIFE WOULD VANISH!
AND IF RURI WAS ERASED, THEN THE STUFF IN THE PAST WOULD BECOME MEANINGLESS.
THE FOUNDATION OF THE STORY THAT BUILT UP OVER ALL THE GENERATIONS WOULD CRUMBLE, DON'T YOU SEE!?

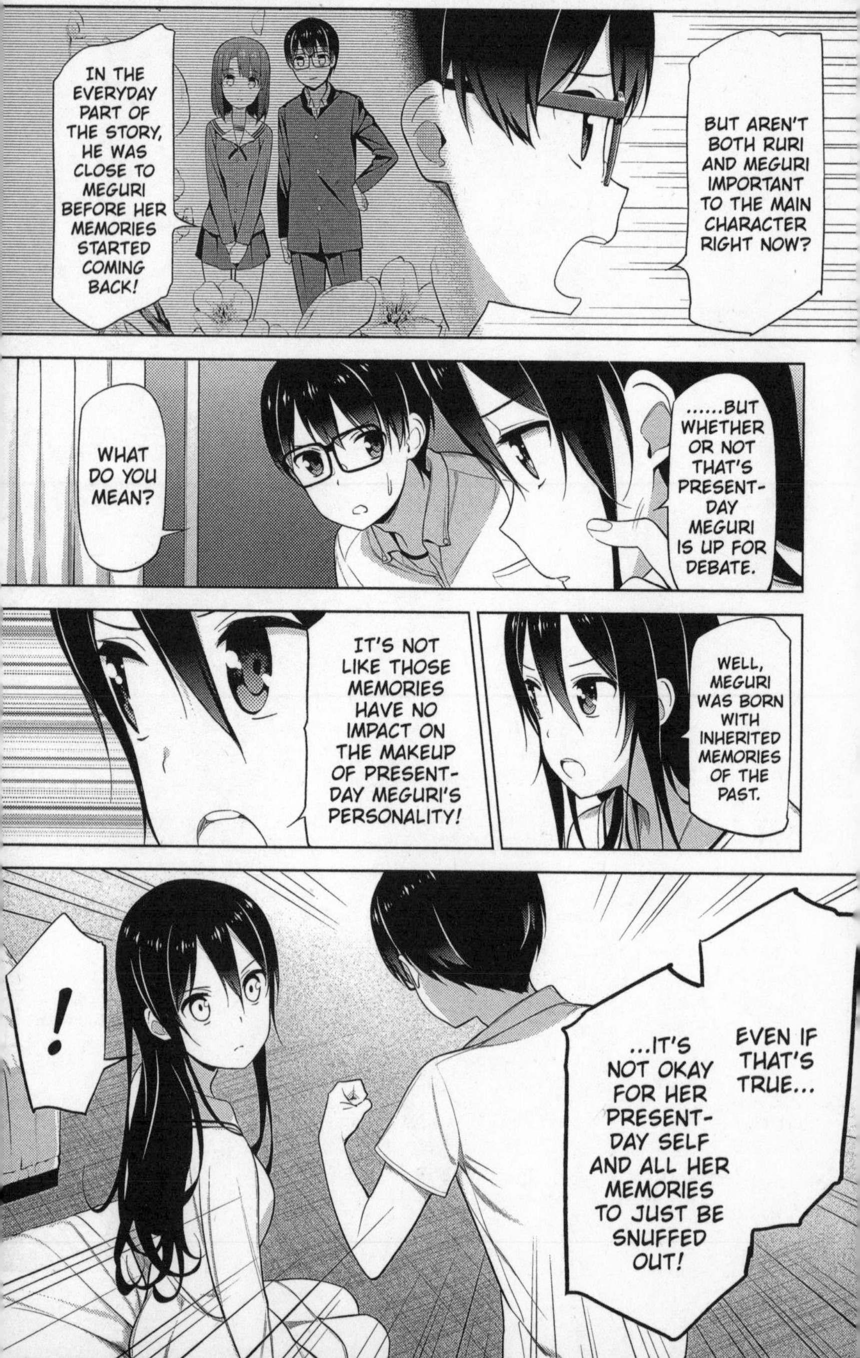
BUT AREN'T BOTH RURI AND MEGURI IMPORTANT TO THE MAIN CHARACTER RIGHT NOW?
IN THE EVERYDAY PART OF THE STORY, HE WAS CLOSE TO MEGURI BEFORE HER MEMORIES STARTED COMING BACK!
......BUT WHETHER OR NOT THAT'S PRESENT-DAY MEGURI IS UP FOR DEBATE.
WHAT DO YOU MEAN?
WELL, MEGURI WAS BORN WITH INHERITED MEMORIES OF THE PAST.
IT'S NOT LIKE THOSE MEMORIES HAVE NO IMPACT ON THE MAKEUP OF PRESENT-DAY MEGURI'S PERSONALITY!
EVEN IF THAT'S TRUE...
...IT'S NOT OKAY FOR HER PRESENT-DAY SELF AND ALL HER MEMORIES TO JUST BE SNUFFED OUT!
!

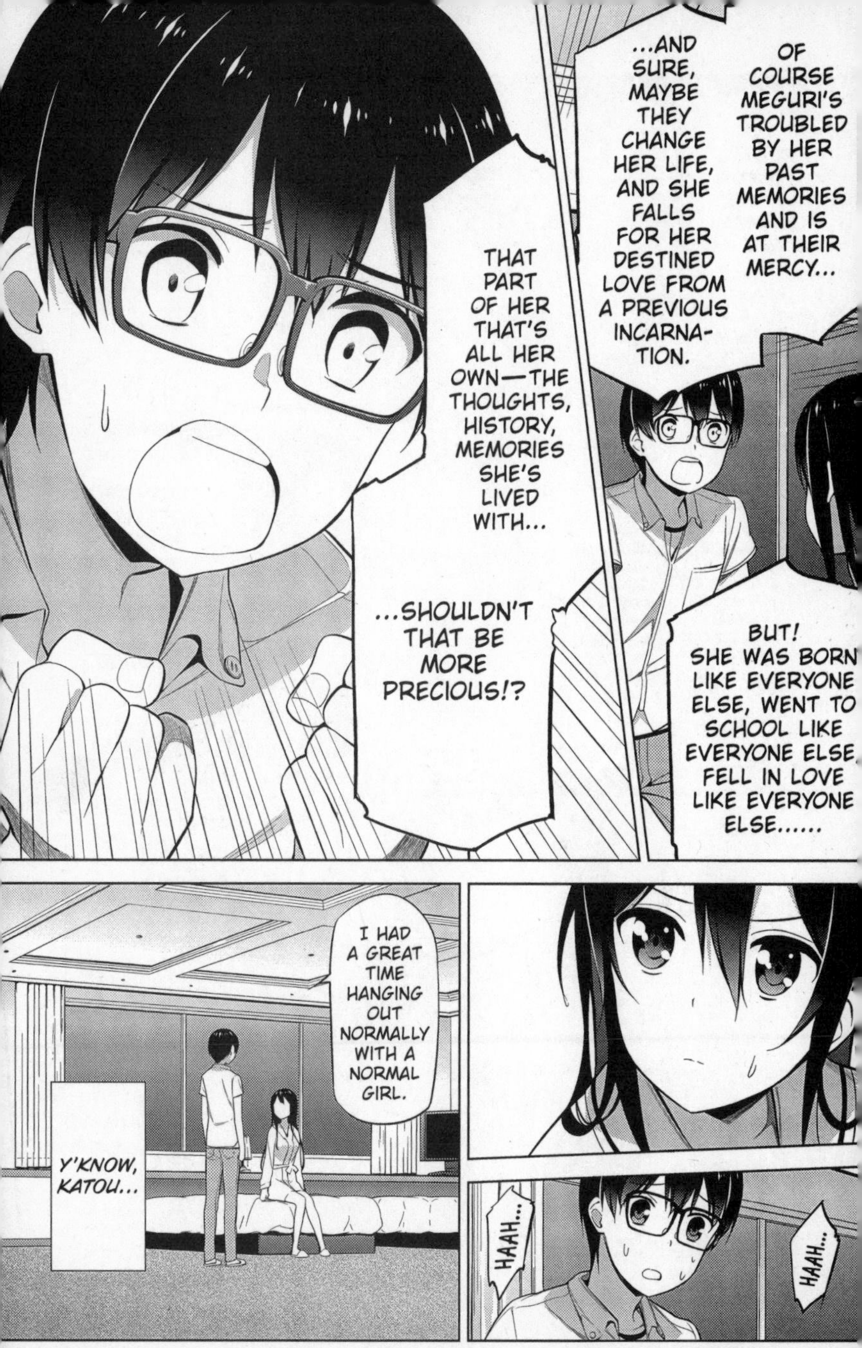
OF COURSE MEGURI'S TROUBLED BY HER PAST MEMORIES AND IS AT THEIR MERCY...
...AND SURE, MAYBE THEY CHANGE HER LIFE, AND SHE FALLS FOR HER DESTINED LOVE FROM A PREVIOUS INCARNA-TION.
BUT! SHE WAS BORN LIKE EVERYONE ELSE, WENT TO SCHOOL LIKE EVERYONE ELSE FELL IN LOVE LIKE EVERYONE ELSE......
THAT PART OF HER THAT'S ALL HER OWN—THE THOUGHTS, HISTORY, MEMORIES SHE'S LIVED WITH...
...SHOULDN'T THAT BE MORE PRECIOUS!?
HAAH...
HAAH...
I HAD A GREAT TIME HANGING OUT NORMALLY WITH A NORMAL GIRL.
Y'KNOW, KATOU...

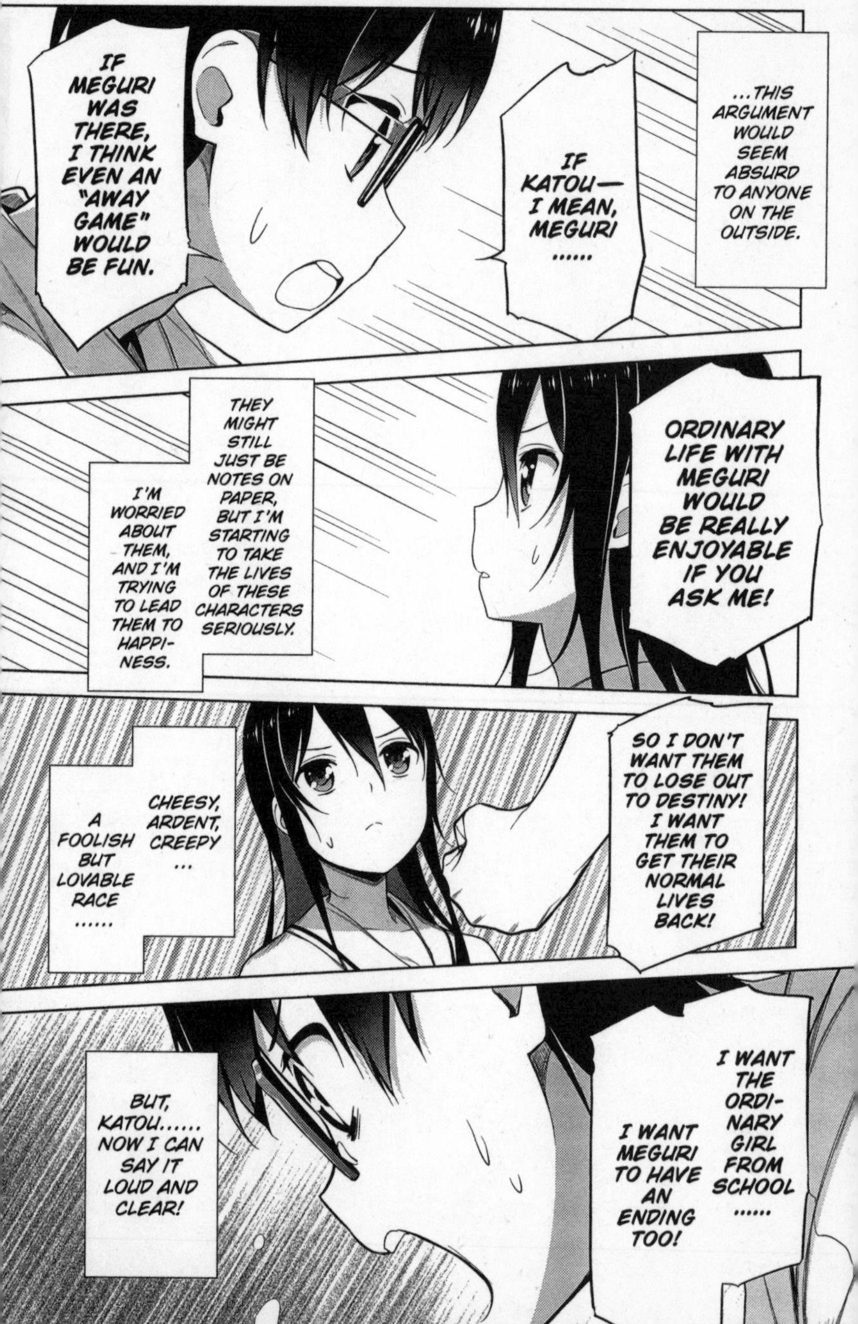
...THIS ARGUMENT WOULD SEEM ABSURD TO ANYONE ON THE OUTSIDE.
IF KATOU— I MEAN, MEGURI ......
IF MEGURI WAS THERE, I THINK EVEN AN "AWAY GAME" WOULD BE FUN.
ORDINARY LIFE WITH MEGURI WOULD BE REALLY ENJOYABLE IF YOU ASK ME!
THEY MIGHT STILL JUST BE NOTES ON PAPER, BUT I'M STARTING TO TAKE THE LIVES OF THESE CHARACTERS SERIOUSLY.
I'M WORRIED ABOUT THEM, AND I'M TRYING TO LEAD THEM TO HAPPI-NESS.
SO I DON'T WANT THEM TO LOSE OUT TO DESTINY! I WANT THEM TO GET THEIR NORMAL LIVES BACK!
CHEESY, ARDENT, CREEPY ...
A FOOLISH BUT LOVABLE RACE ......
I WANT THE ORDI-NARY GIRL FROM SCHOOL ......
I WANT MEGURI TO HAVE AN ENDING TOO!
BUT, KATOU...... NOW I CAN SAY IT LOUD AND CLEAR!

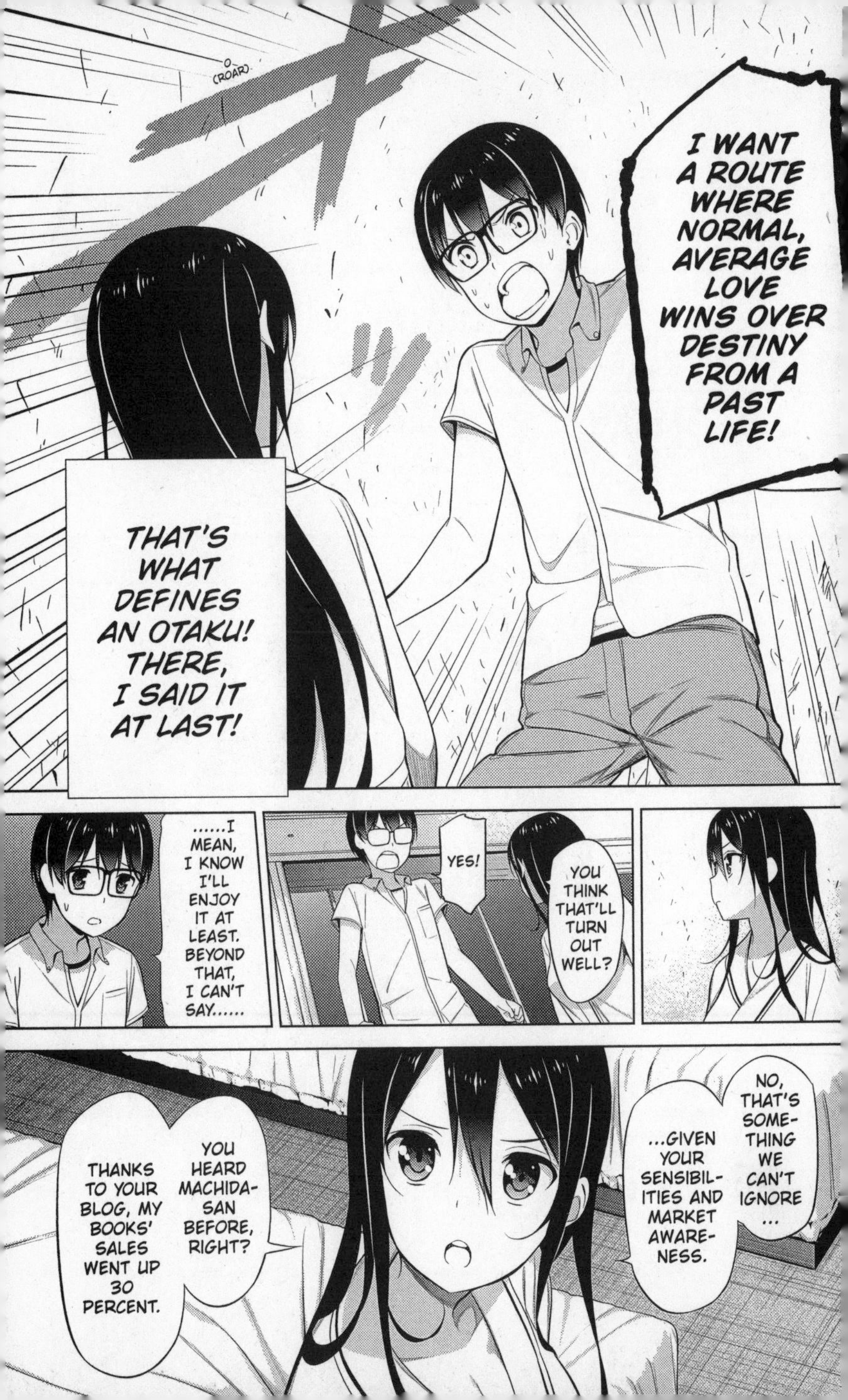
I WANT A ROUTE WHERE NORMAL, AVERAGE LOVE WINS OVER DESTINY FROM A PAST LIFE!
O (ROAR)
THAT'S WHAT DEFINES AN OTAKU! THERE, I SAID IT AT LAST!
YOU THINK THAT'LL TURN OUT WELL?
YES!
......I MEAN, I KNOW I'LL ENJOY IT AT LEAST. BEYOND THAT, I CAN'T SAY......
NO, THAT'S SOME-THING WE CAN'T IGNORE ...
...GIVEN YOUR SENSIBIL-ITIES AND MARKET AWARE-NESS.
YOU HEARD MACHIDA-SAN BEFORE, RIGHT?
THANKS TO YOUR BLOG, MY BOOKS' SALES WENT UP 30 PERCENT.

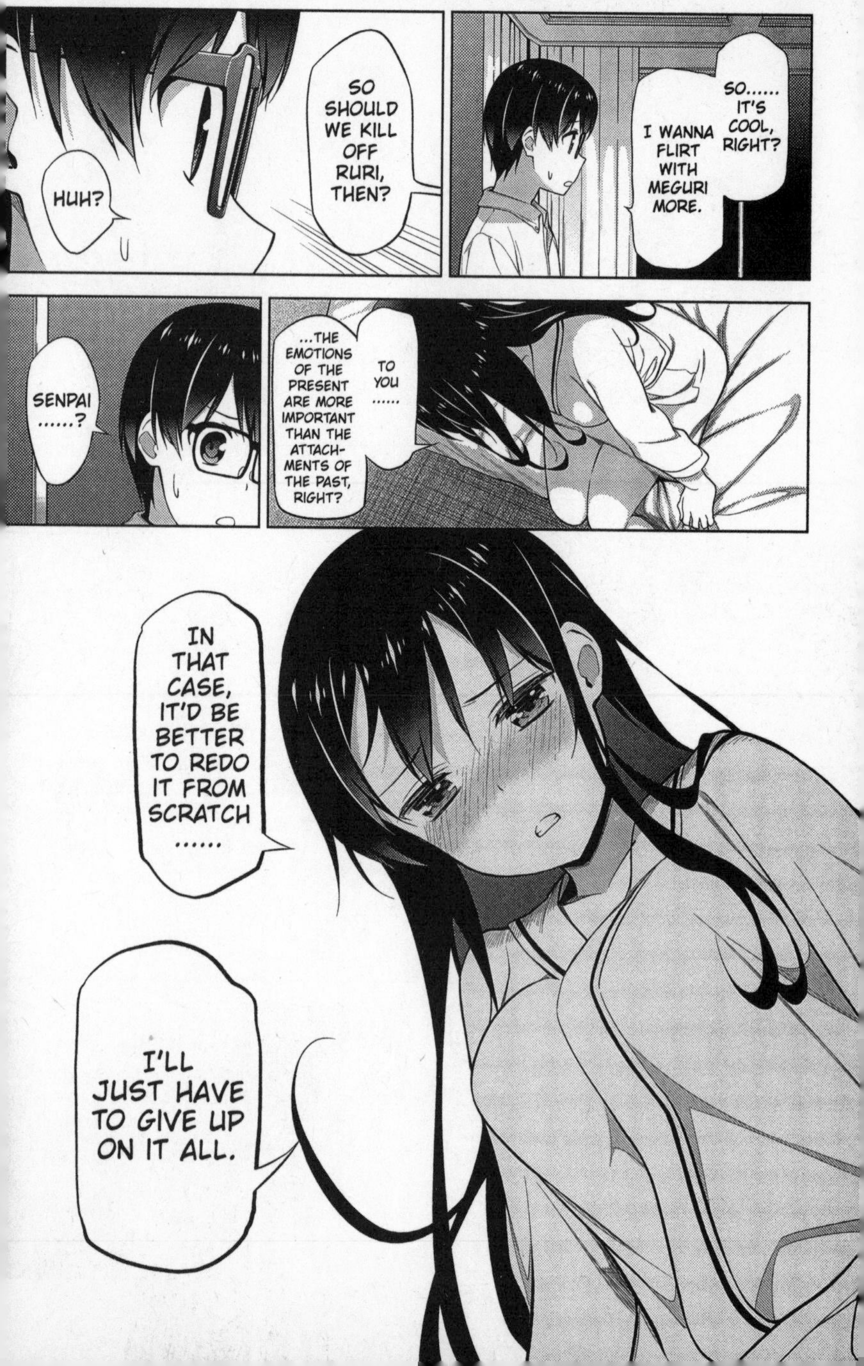
SO...... IT'S COOL, RIGHT?
I WANNA FLIRT WITH MEGURI MORE.
SO SHOULD WE KILL OFF RURI, THEN?
HUH?
TO YOU ......
...THE EMOTIONS OF THE PRESENT ARE MORE IMPORTANT THAN THE ATTACHMENTS OF THE PAST, RIGHT?
SENPAI ......?
IN THAT CASE, IT'D BE BETTER TO REDO IT FROM SCRATCH ......
I'LL JUST HAVE TO GIVE UP ON IT ALL.

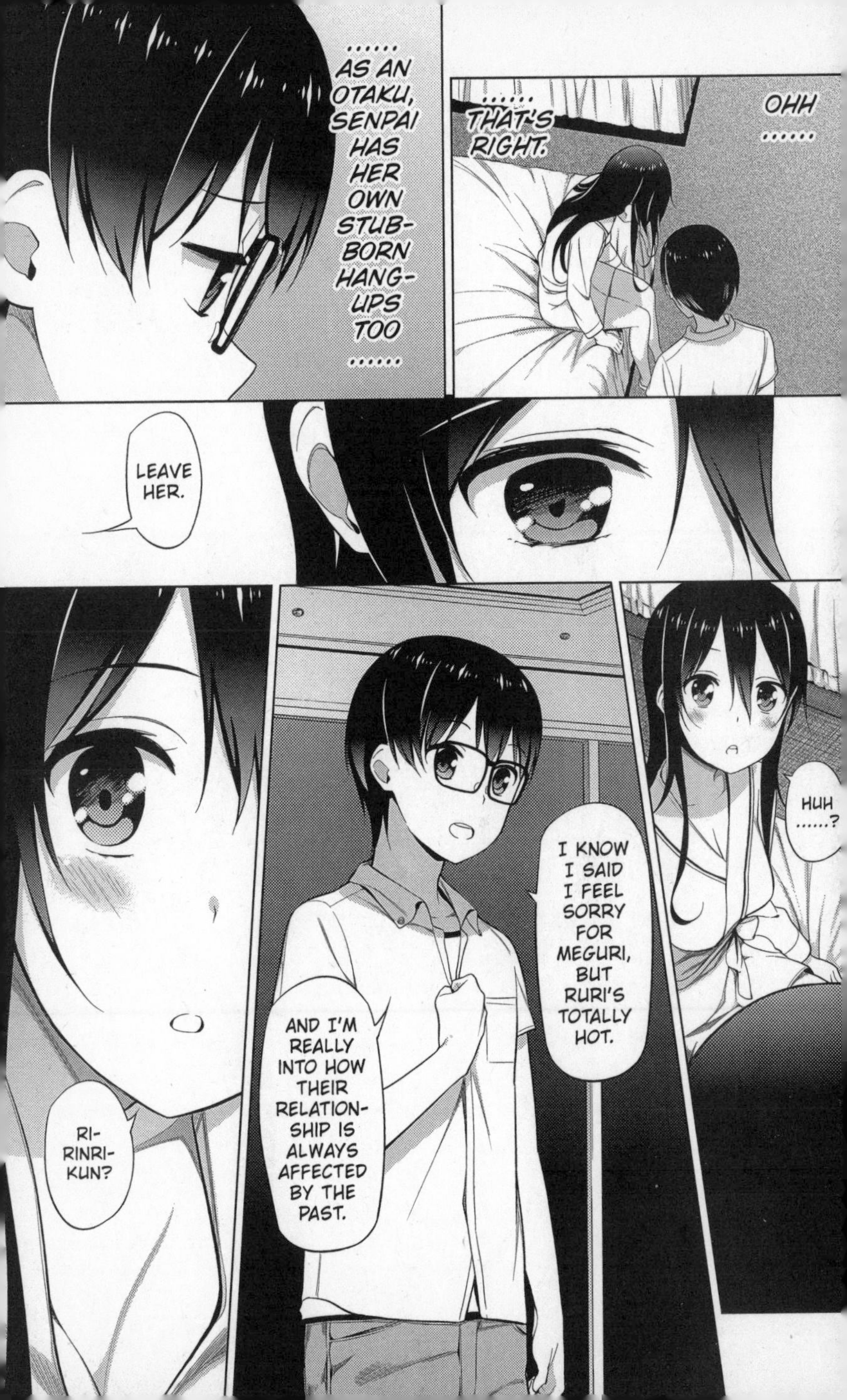
OHH ......
...... THAT'S RIGHT.
...... AS AN OTAKU, SENPAI HAS HER OWN STUB-BORN HANG-UPS TOO ......
LEAVE HER.
HUH ......?
I KNOW I SAID I FEEL SORRY FOR MEGURI, BUT RURI'S TOTALLY HOT.
AND I'M REALLY INTO HOW THEIR RELATION-SHIP IS ALWAYS AFFECTED BY THE PAST.
RI-RINRI-KUN?

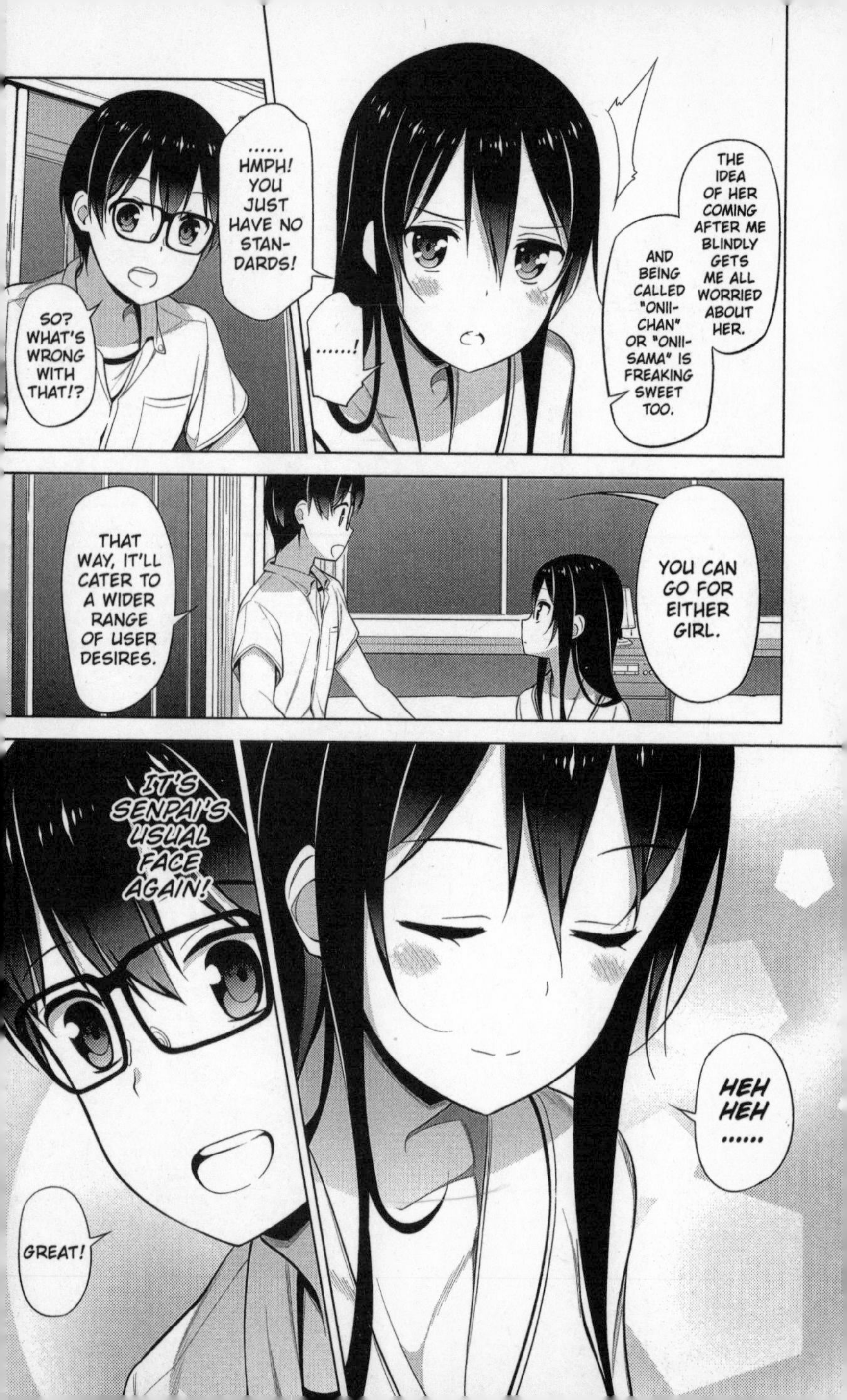
THE IDEA OF HER COMING AFTER ME BLINDLY GETS ME ALL WORRIED ABOUT HER.
AND BEING CALLED "ONII-CHAN" OR "ONII-SAMA" IS FREAKING SWEET TOO.
......!
......HMPH! YOU JUST HAVE NO STAN-DARDS!
SO? WHAT'S WRONG WITH THAT!?
YOU CAN GO FOR EITHER GIRL.
THAT WAY, IT'LL CATER TO A WIDER RANGE OF USER DESIRES.
HEH HEH ......
IT'S SENPAI'S USUAL FACE AGAIN!
GREAT!

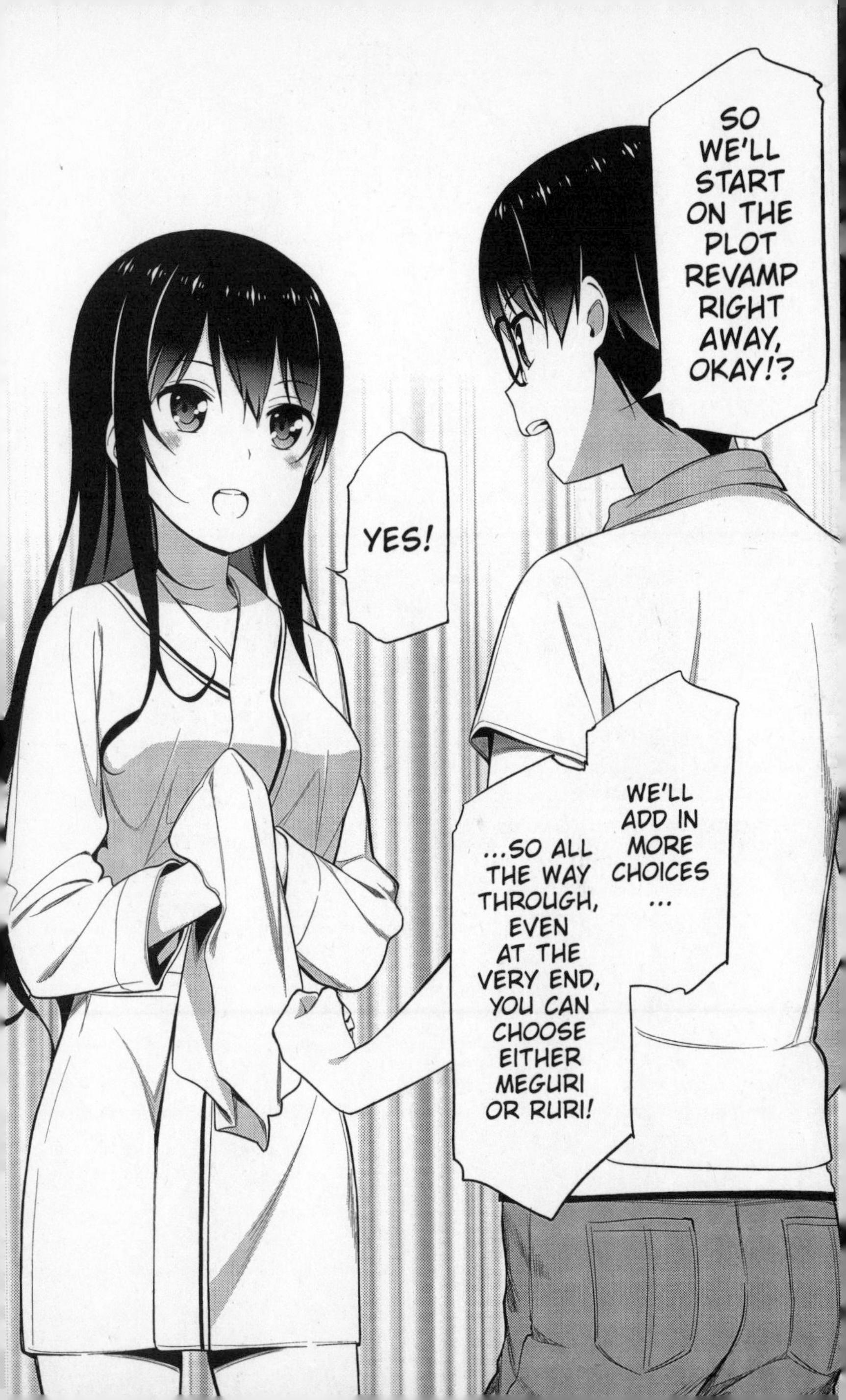
SO WE'LL START ON THE PLOT REVAMP RIGHT AWAY, OKAY!?
YES!
WE'LL ADD IN MORE CHOICES...
...SO ALL THE WAY THROUGH, EVEN AT THE VERY END, YOU CAN CHOOSE EITHER MEGURI OR RURI!

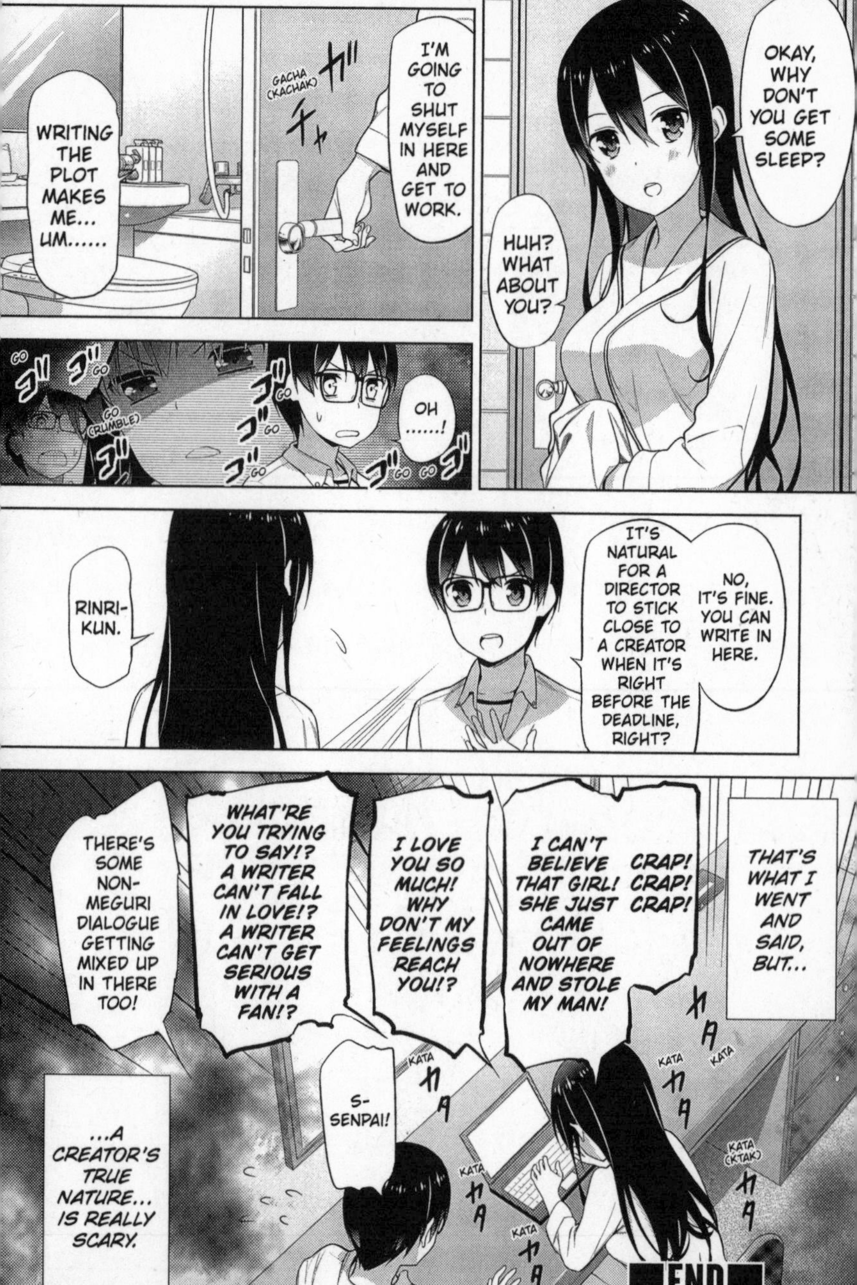
OKAY, WHY DON'T YOU GET SOME SLEEP?
HUH? WHAT ABOUT YOU?
I'M GOING TO SHUT MYSELF IN HERE AND GET TO WORK.
GACHA (KACHAK)
WRITING THE PLOT MAKES ME... UM......
GO GO GO (RUMBLE)
OH ......!
GO GO GO GO
NO, IT'S FINE. YOU CAN WRITE IN HERE.
IT'S NATURAL FOR A DIRECTOR TO STICK CLOSE TO A CREATOR WHEN IT'S RIGHT BEFORE THE DEADLINE, RIGHT?
RINRI-KUN.
THAT'S WHAT I WENT AND SAID, BUT...
CRAP! CRAP! CRAP!
I CAN'T BELIEVE THAT GIRL! SHE JUST CAME OUT OF NOWHERE AND STOLE MY MAN!
I LOVE YOU SO MUCH! WHY DON'T MY FEELINGS REACH YOU!?
WHAT'RE YOU TRYING TO SAY!? A WRITER CAN'T FALL IN LOVE!? A WRITER CAN'T GET SERIOUS WITH A FAN!?
THERE'S SOME NON-MEGURI DIALOGUE GETTING MIXED UP IN THERE TOO!
KATA KATA
KATA (KTAK)
KATA
S-SENPAI!
KATA KATA
...A CREATOR'S TRUE NATURE... IS REALLY SCARY.
END

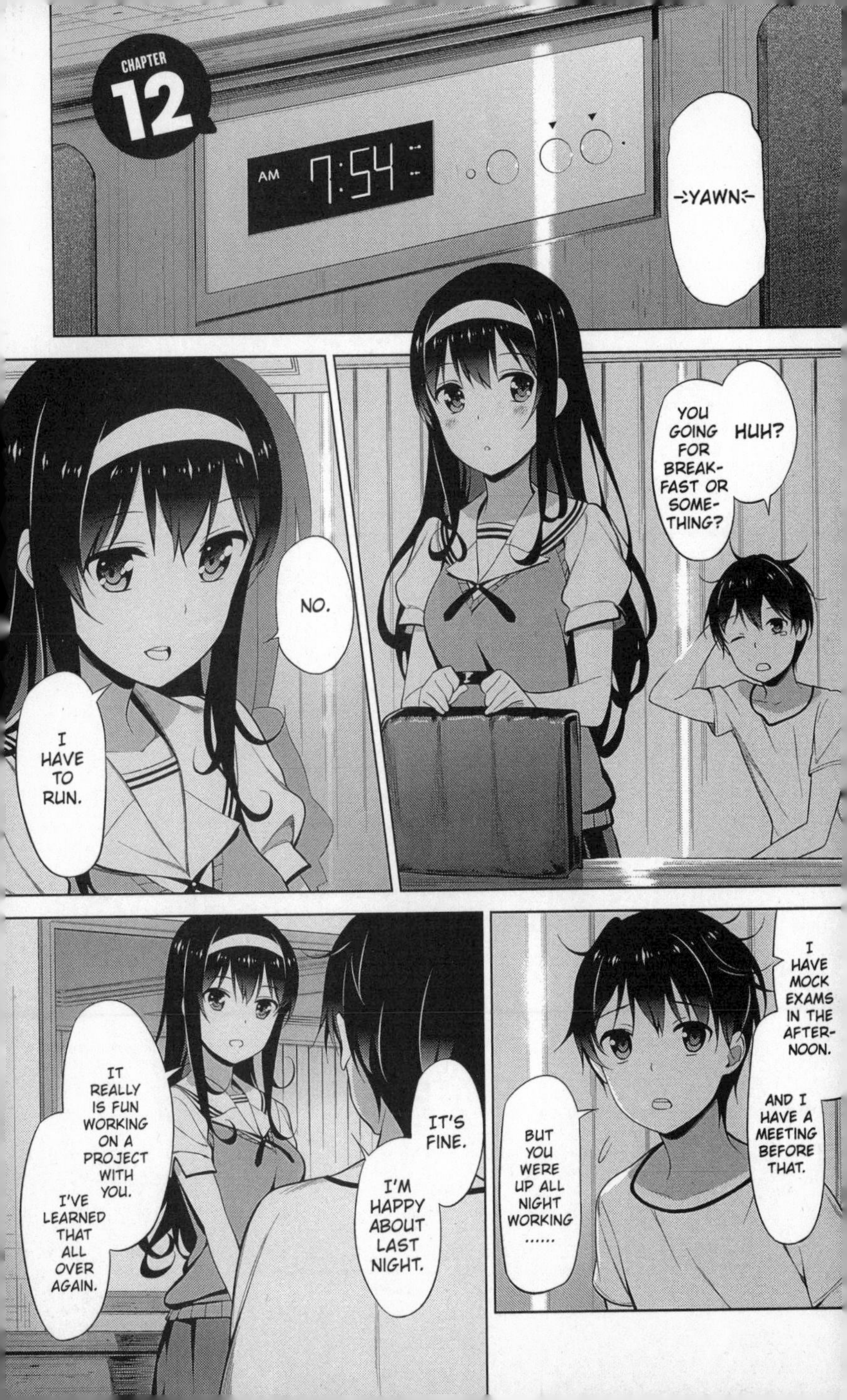
CHAPTER 12
AM 7:54
-YAWN-
HUH?
YOU GOING FOR BREAK-FAST OR SOME-THING?
NO.
I HAVE TO RUN.
I HAVE MOCK EXAMS IN THE AFTER-NOON.
AND I HAVE A MEETING BEFORE THAT.
BUT YOU WERE UP ALL NIGHT WORKING......
IT'S FINE.
I'M HAPPY ABOUT LAST NIGHT.
IT REALLY IS FUN WORKING ON A PROJECT WITH YOU.
I'VE LEARNED THAT ALL OVER AGAIN.

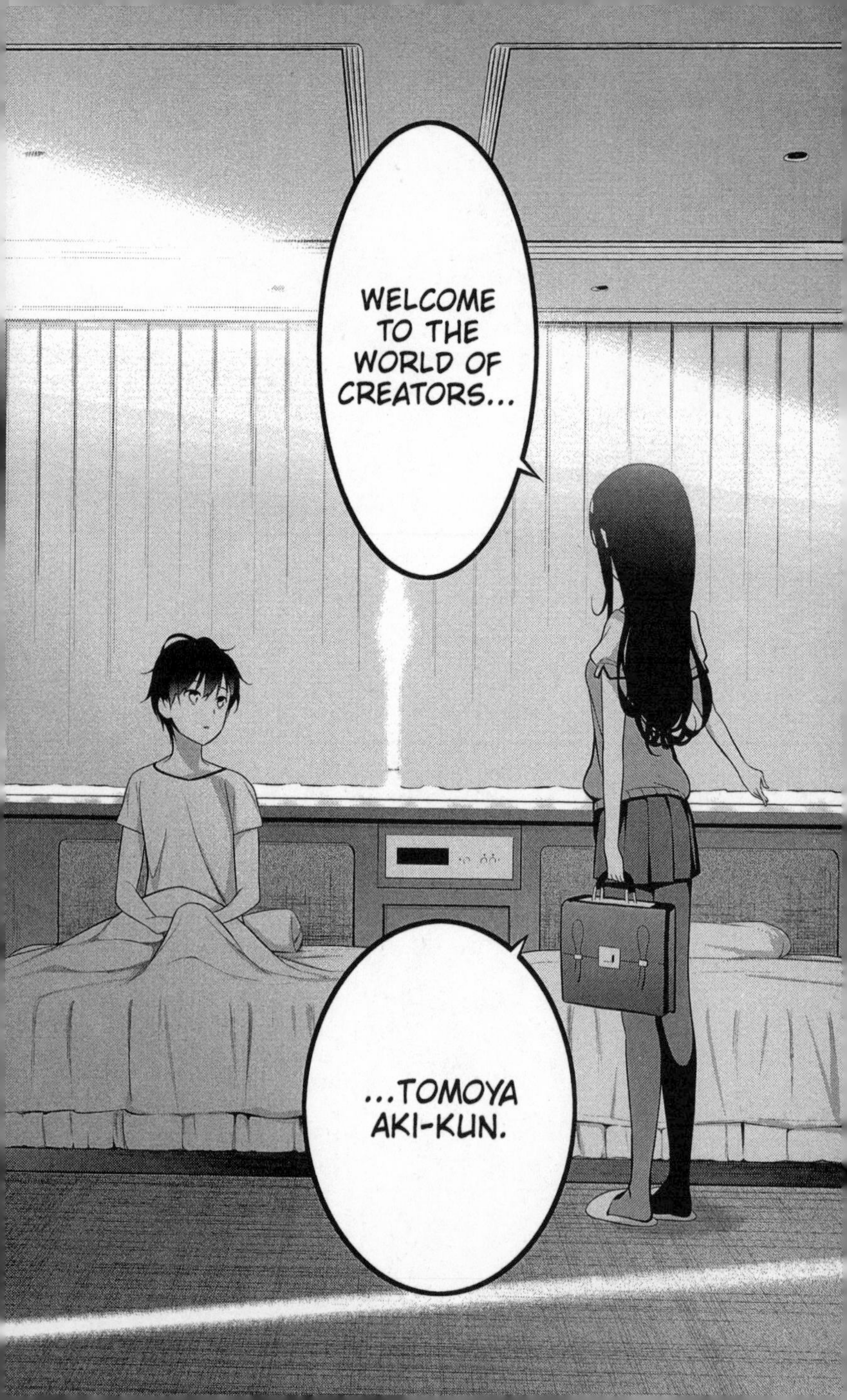
WELCOME TO THE WORLD OF CREATORS...
...TOMOYA AKI-KUN.

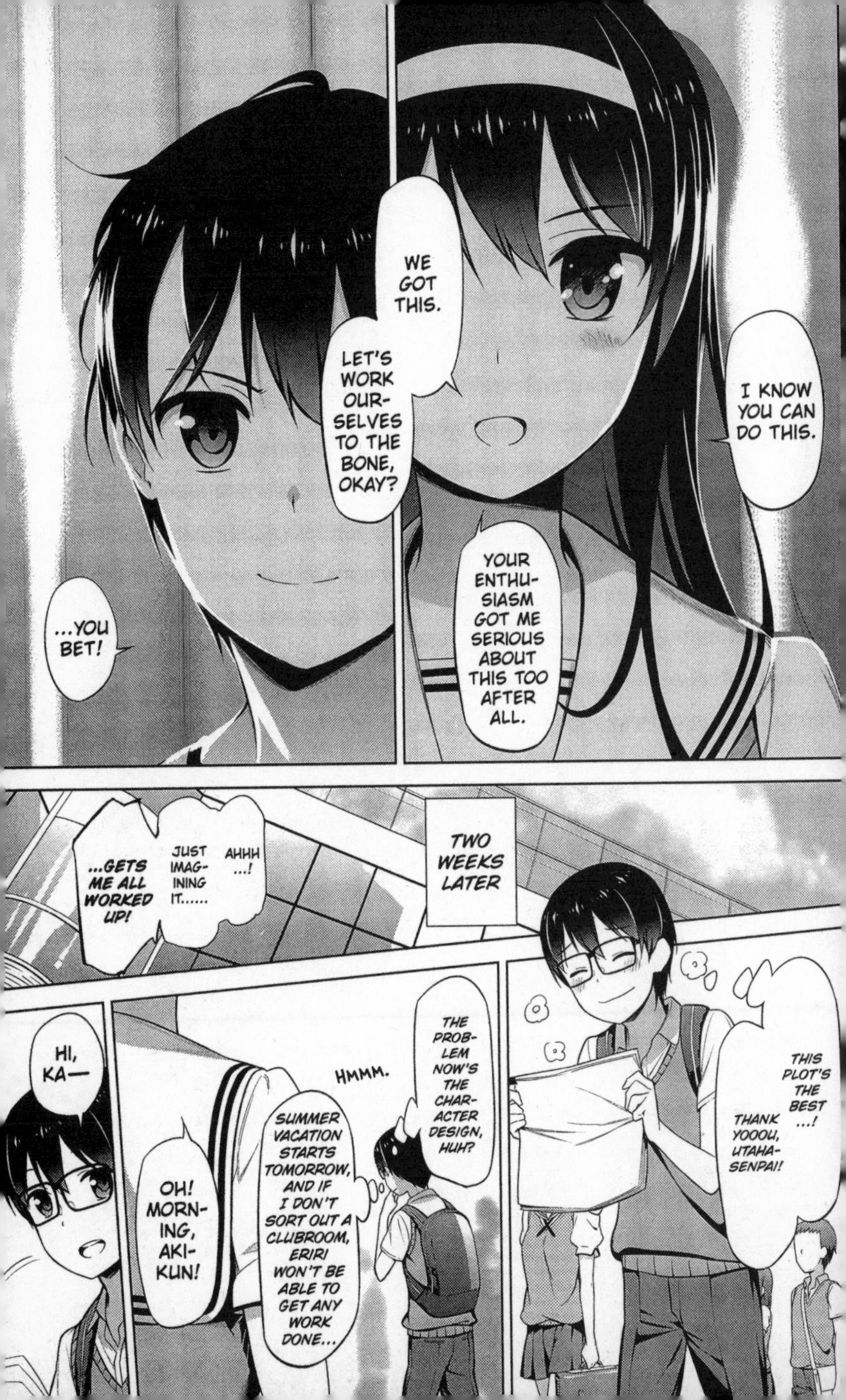
I KNOW YOU CAN DO THIS.
YOUR ENTHUSIASM GOT ME SERIOUS ABOUT THIS TOO AFTER ALL.
WE GOT THIS.
LET'S WORK OURSELVES TO THE BONE, OKAY?
...YOU BET!
TWO WEEKS LATER
AHHH...!
JUST IMAGINING IT......
...GETS ME ALL WORKED UP!
THIS PLOT'S THE BEST...!
THANK YOOOU, UTAHA-SENPAI!
THE PROBLEM NOW'S THE CHARACTER DESIGN, HUH?
HMMM.
SUMMER VACATION STARTS TOMORROW, AND IF I DON'T SORT OUT A CLUBROOM, ERIRI WON'T BE ABLE TO GET ANY WORK DONE...
HI, KA—
OH! MORNING, AKI-KUN!

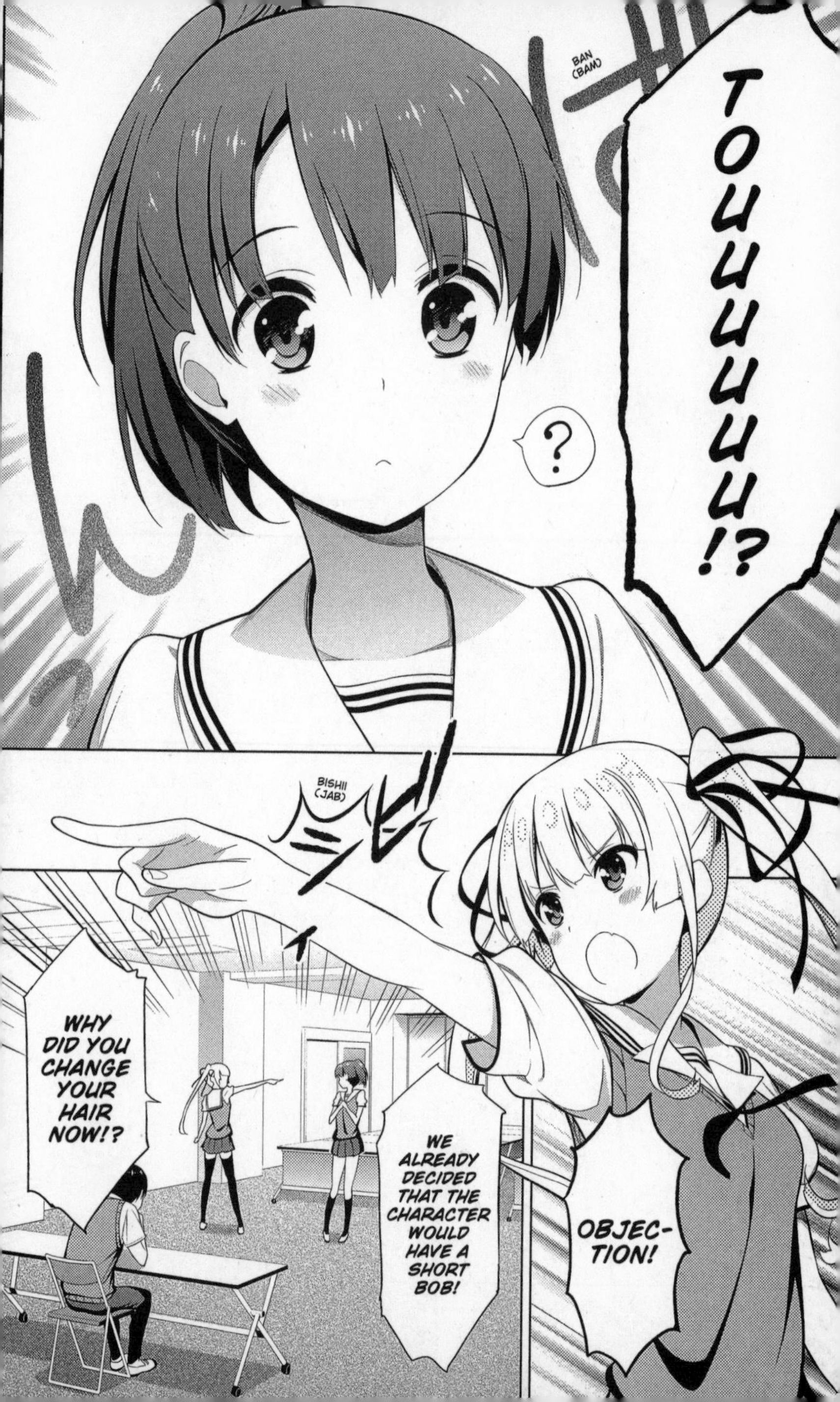
TOUUUUUUU!?
BAN (BAM)
?
BISHII (JAB)
OBJECTION!
WE ALREADY DECIDED THAT THE CHARACTER WOULD HAVE A SHORT BOB!
WHY DID YOU CHANGE YOUR HAIR NOW!?

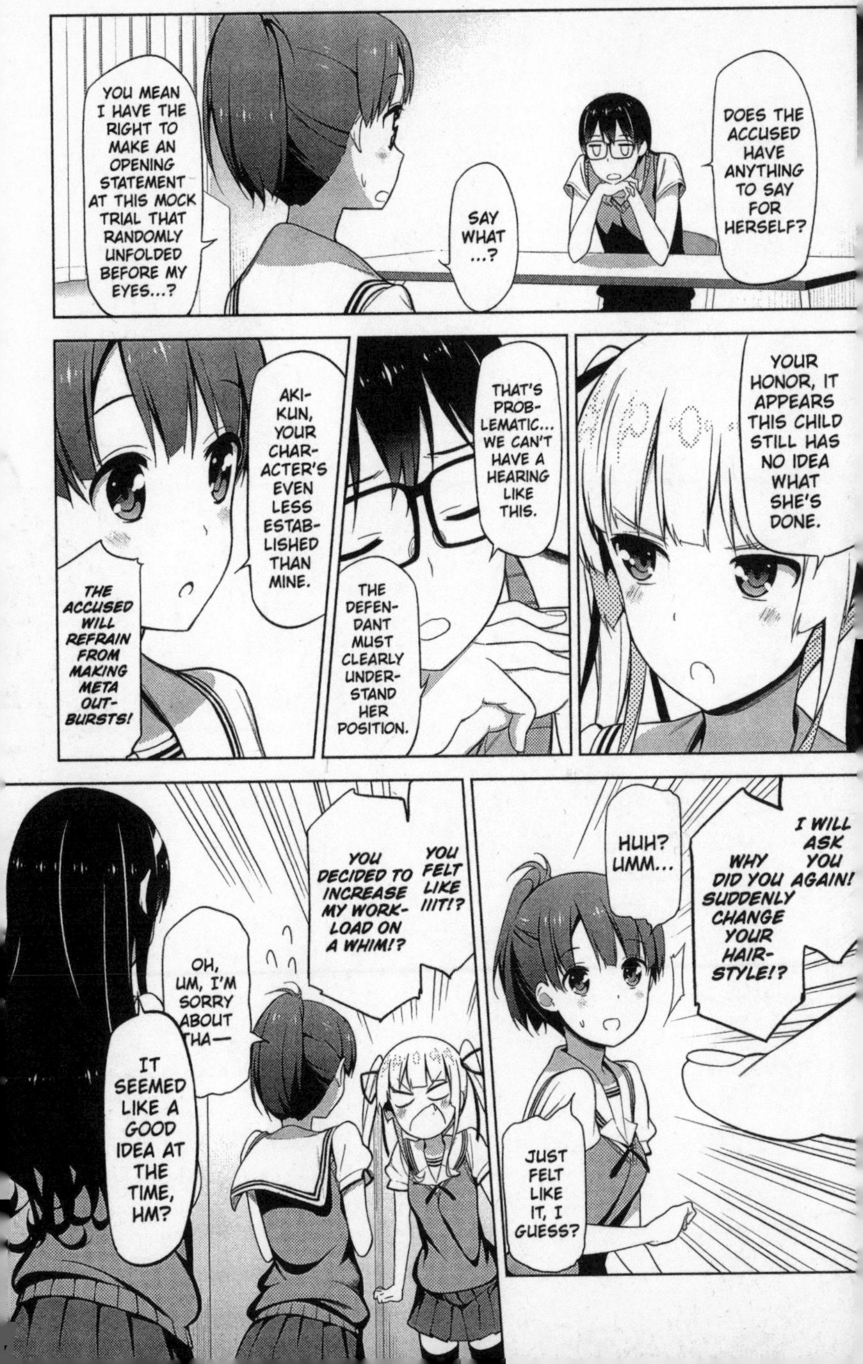

DOES THE ACCUSED HAVE ANYTHING TO SAY FOR HERSELF?
SAY WHAT ...?
YOU MEAN I HAVE THE RIGHT TO MAKE AN OPENING STATEMENT AT THIS MOCK TRIAL THAT RANDOMLY UNFOLDED BEFORE MY EYES...?
YOUR HONOR, IT APPEARS THIS CHILD STILL HAS NO IDEA WHAT SHE'S DONE.
THAT'S PROBLEMATIC... WE CAN'T HAVE A HEARING LIKE THIS.
THE DEFENDANT MUST CLEARLY UNDERSTAND HER POSITION.
AKI-KUN, YOUR CHARACTER'S EVEN LESS ESTABLISHED THAN MINE.
THE ACCUSED WILL REFRAIN FROM MAKING META OUTBURSTS!
I WILL ASK YOU AGAIN!
WHY DID YOU SUDDENLY CHANGE YOUR HAIRSTYLE!?
HUH? UMM...
JUST FELT LIKE IT, I GUESS?
YOU FELT LIKE IIIT!?
YOU DECIDED TO INCREASE MY WORKLOAD ON A WHIM!?
OH, UM, I'M SORRY ABOUT THA—
IT SEEMED LIKE A GOOD IDEA AT THE TIME, HM?

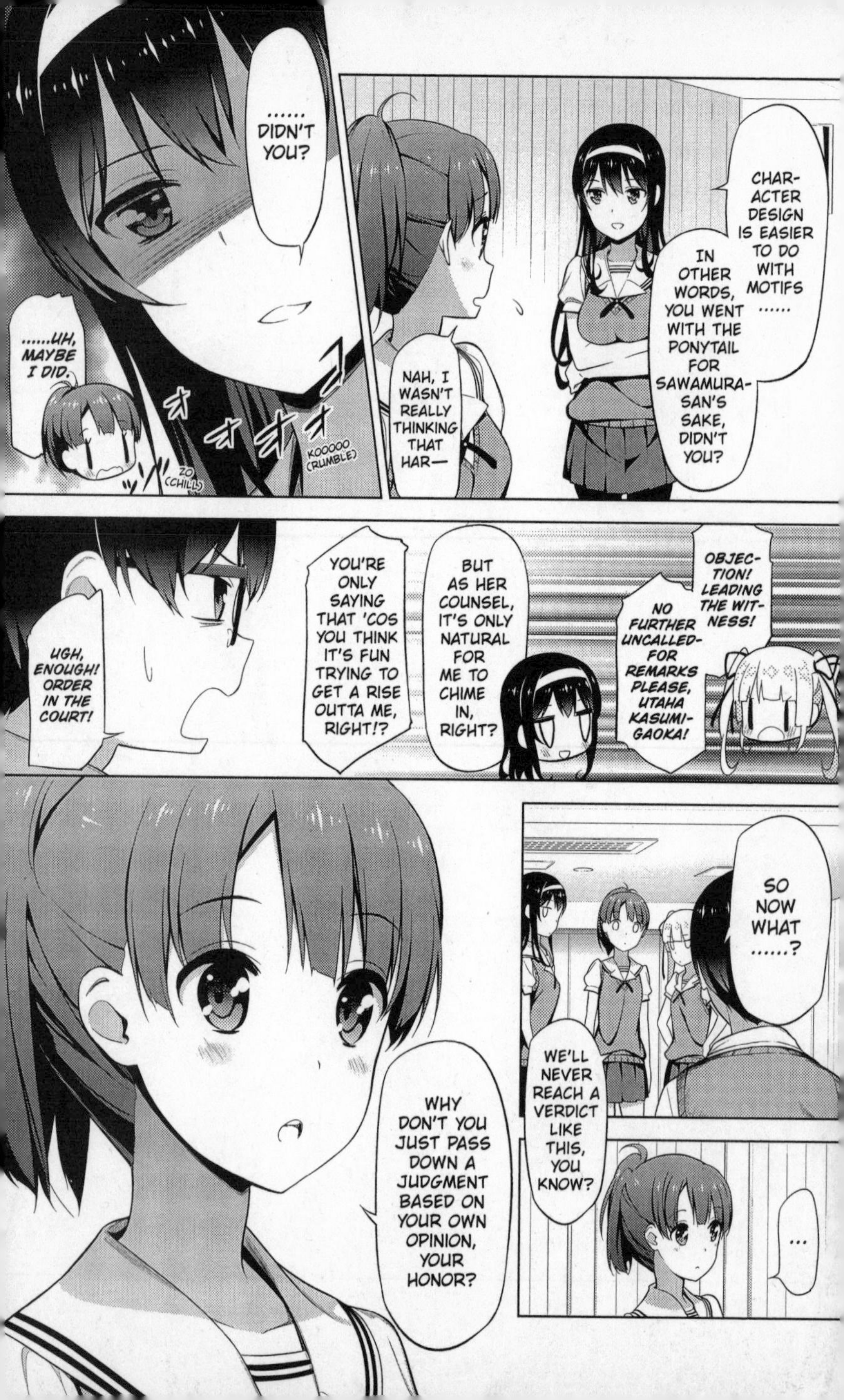
CHARACTER DESIGN IS EASIER TO DO WITH MOTIFS......
IN OTHER WORDS, YOU WENT WITH THE PONYTAIL FOR SAWAMURA-SAN'S SAKE, DIDN'T YOU?
NAH, I WASN'T REALLY THINKING THAT HAR—
......DIDN'T YOU?
KOOOOO (RUMBLE)
ZO (CHILL)
......UH, MAYBE I DID.
OBJECTION! LEADING THE WITNESS!
NO FURTHER UNCALLED-FOR REMARKS PLEASE, UTAHA KASUMIGAOKA!
BUT AS HER COUNSEL, IT'S ONLY NATURAL FOR ME TO CHIME IN, RIGHT?
YOU'RE ONLY SAYING THAT 'COS YOU THINK IT'S FUN TRYING TO GET A RISE OUTTA ME, RIGHT!?
UGH, ENOUGH! ORDER IN THE COURT!
SO NOW WHAT......?
WE'LL NEVER REACH A VERDICT LIKE THIS, YOU KNOW?
...
WHY DON'T YOU JUST PASS DOWN A JUDGMENT BASED ON YOUR OWN OPINION, YOUR HONOR?

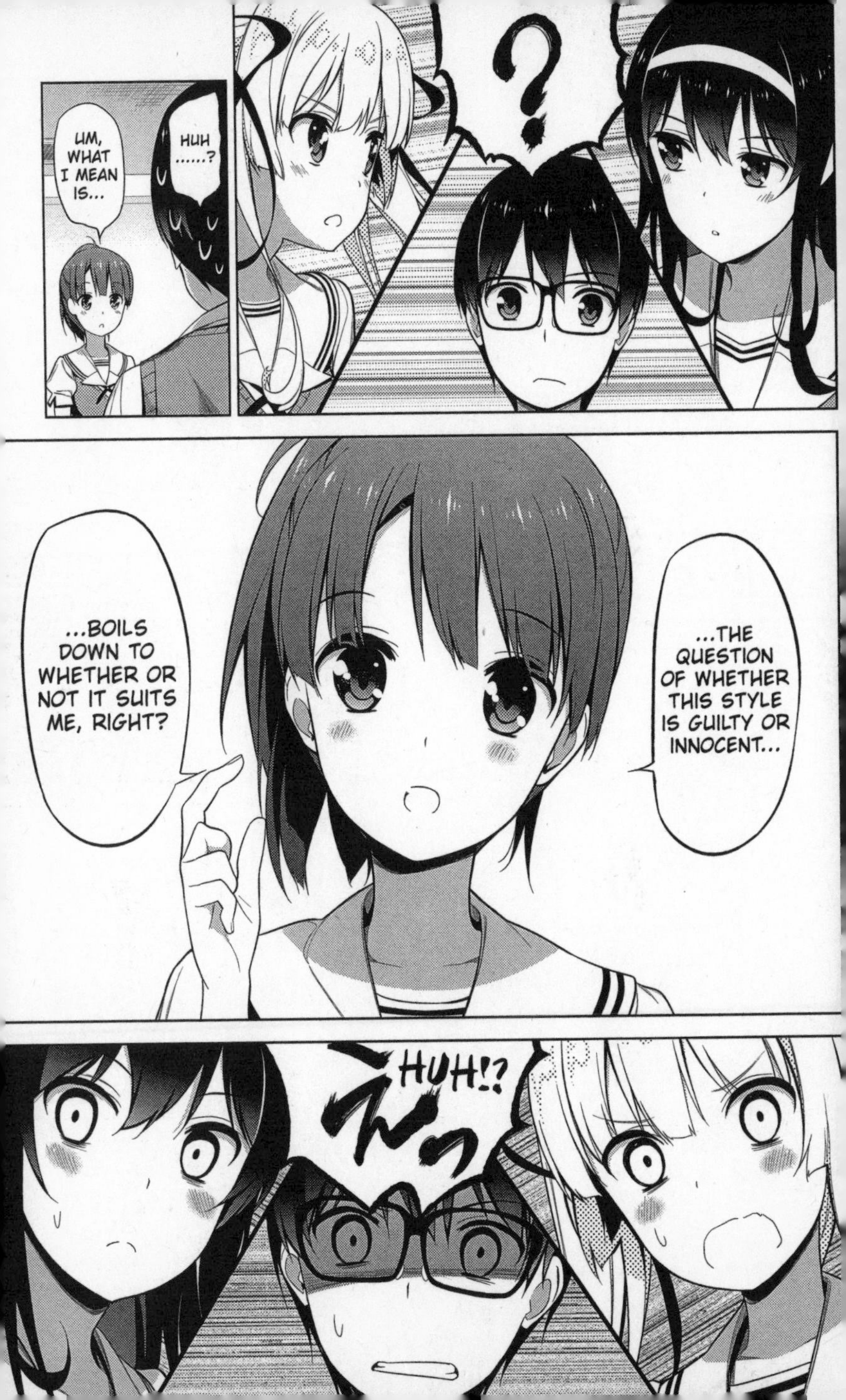
HUH ......?
UM, WHAT I MEAN IS...
...THE QUESTION OF WHETHER THIS STYLE IS GUILTY OR INNOCENT...
...BOILS DOWN TO WHETHER OR NOT IT SUITS ME, RIGHT?
HUH!?

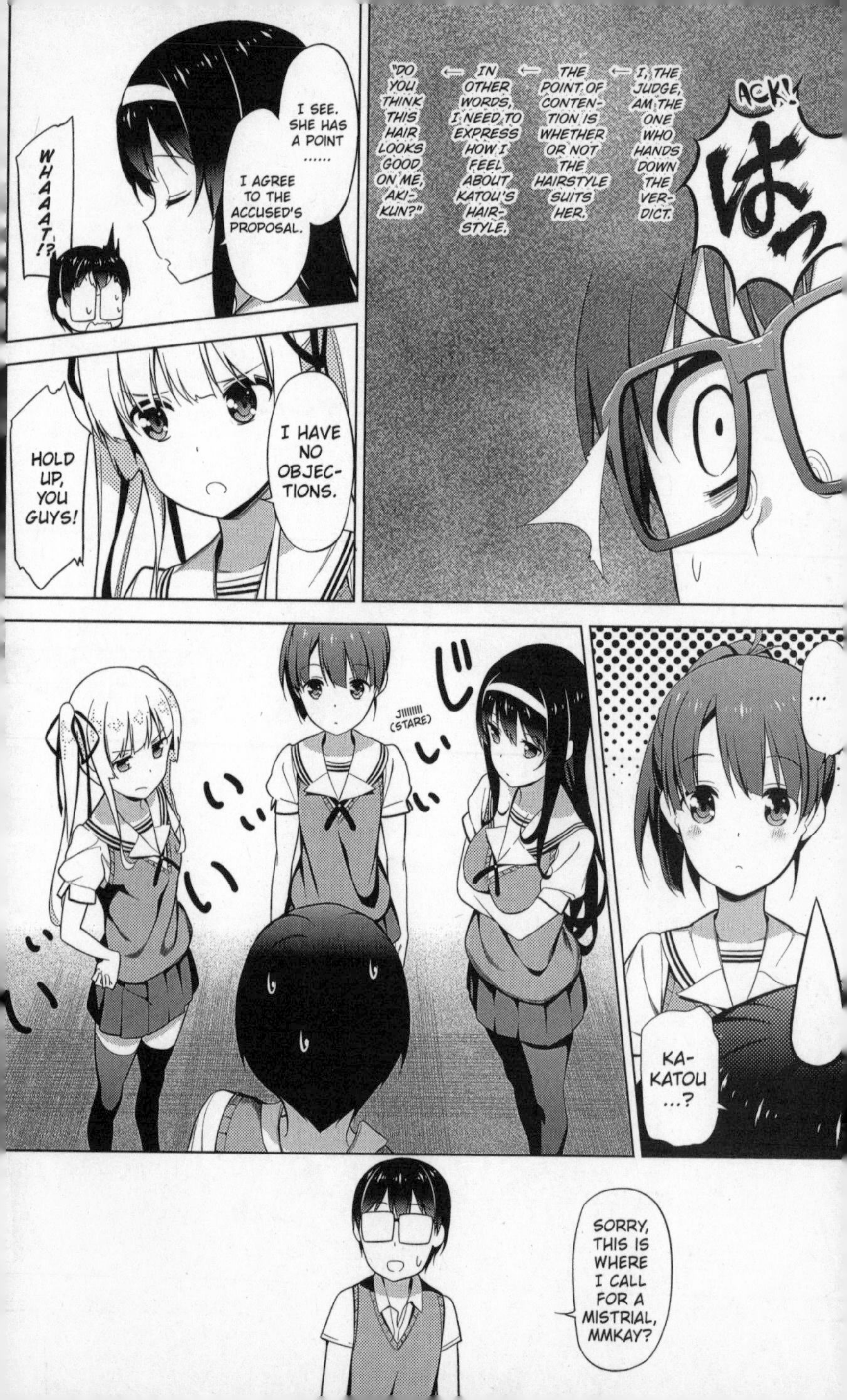
ACK!
はっ
I, THE JUDGE, AM THE ONE WHO HANDS DOWN THE VERDICT.
THE POINT OF CONTENTION IS WHETHER OR NOT THE HAIRSTYLE SUITS HER.
IN OTHER WORDS, I NEED TO EXPRESS HOW I FEEL ABOUT KATOU'S HAIRSTYLE.
"DO YOU THINK THIS HAIR LOOKS GOOD ON ME, AKI-KUN?"
I SEE. SHE HAS A POINT ......
I AGREE TO THE ACCUSED'S PROPOSAL.
WHAAAAT!?
I HAVE NO OBJECTIONS.
HOLD UP, YOU GUYS!
...
KA-KATOU ...?
JIIIIIII (STARE)
SORRY, THIS IS WHERE I CALL FOR A MISTRIAL, MMKAY?

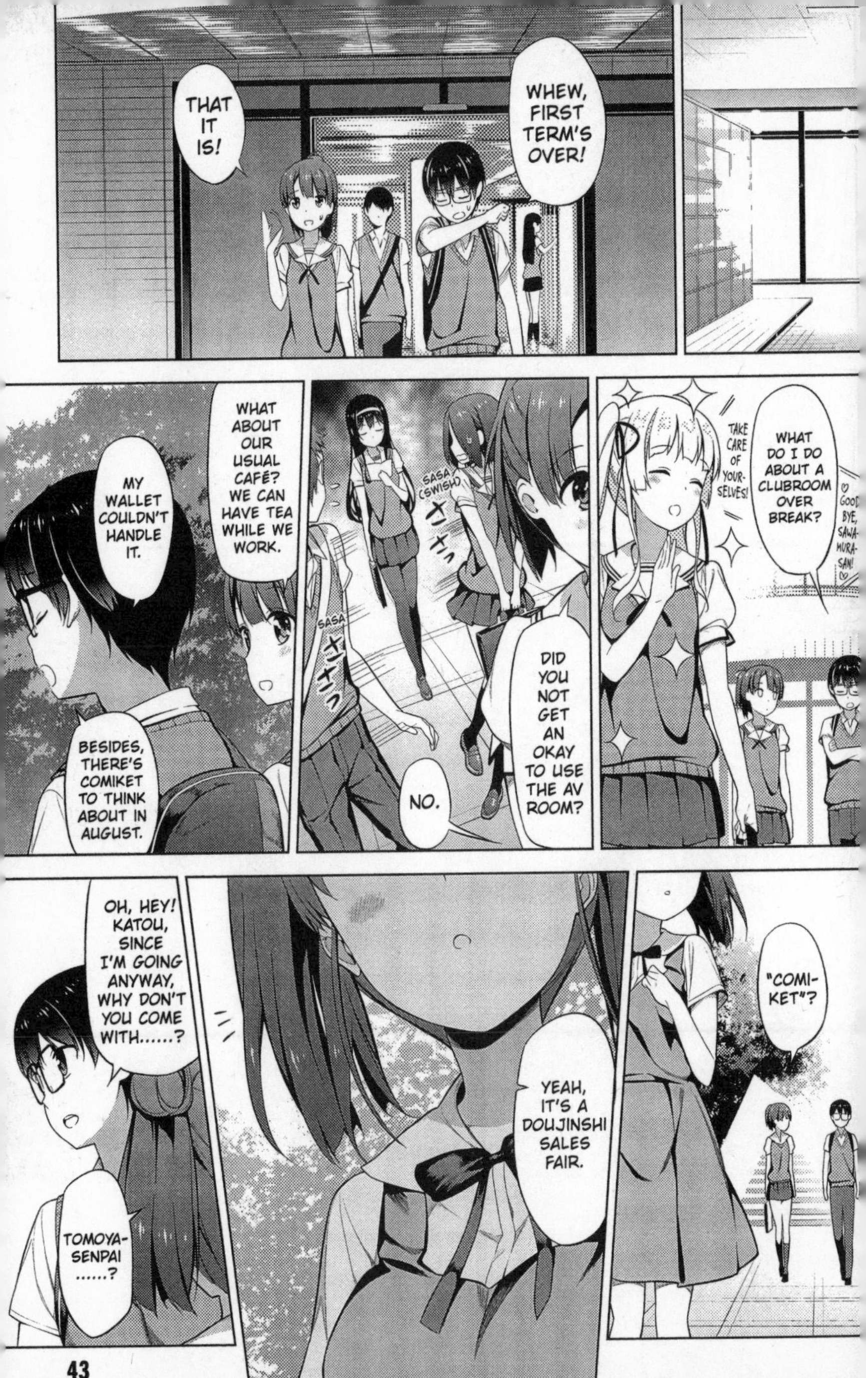
WHEW, FIRST TERM'S OVER!
THAT IT IS!
GOOD BYE, SAWAMURA-SAN!
WHAT DO I DO ABOUT A CLUBROOM OVER BREAK?
TAKE CARE OF YOURSELVES!
SASA (SWISH)
DID YOU NOT GET AN OKAY TO USE THE AV ROOM?
SASA
NO.
WHAT ABOUT OUR USUAL CAFÉ? WE CAN HAVE TEA WHILE WE WORK.
MY WALLET COULDN'T HANDLE IT.
BESIDES, THERE'S COMIKET TO THINK ABOUT IN AUGUST.
"COMI-KET"?
YEAH, IT'S A DOUJINSHI SALES FAIR.
OH, HEY! KATOU, SINCE I'M GOING ANYWAY, WHY DON'T YOU COME WITH......?
TOMOYA-SENPAI ......?

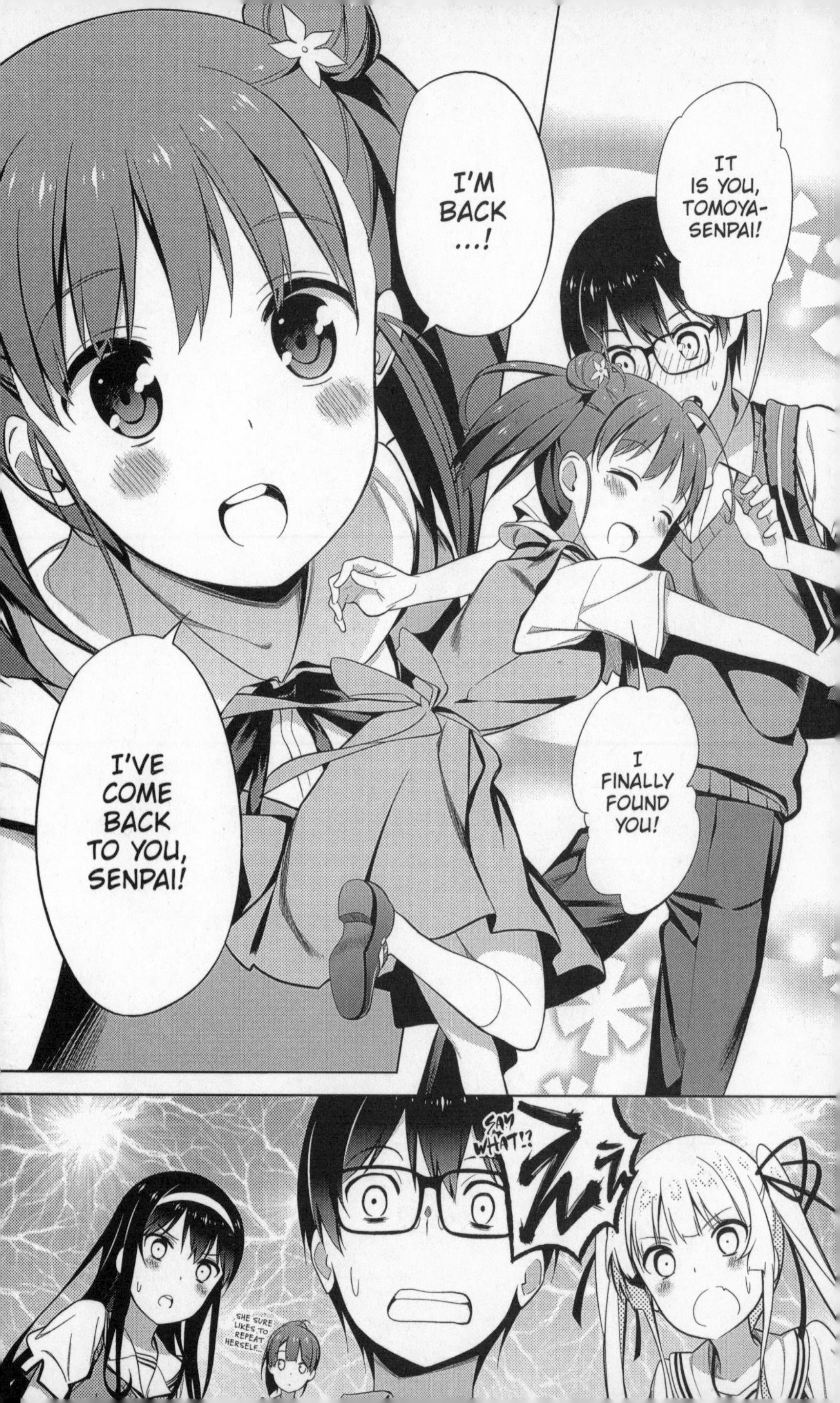
IT IS YOU, TOMOYA-SENPAI!
I'M BACK ...!
I FINALLY FOUND YOU!
I'VE COME BACK TO YOU, SENPAI!
SAY WHAT!?
SHE SURE LIKES TO REPEAT HERSELF...

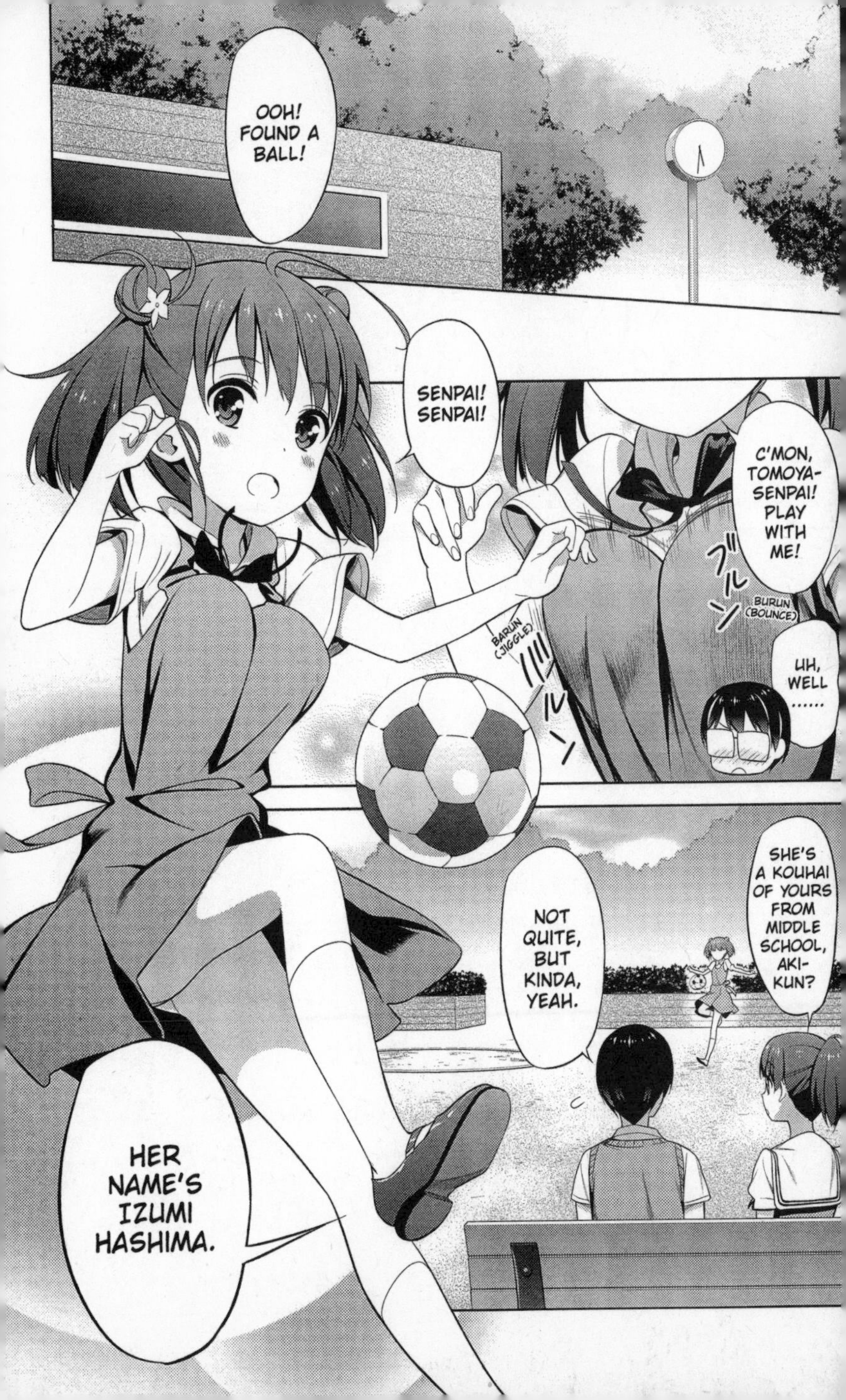
OOH! FOUND A BALL!
C'MON, TOMOYA-SENPAI! PLAY WITH ME!
ブルン
BURUN (BOUNCE)
ブルン
BARUN (JIGGLE)
UH, WELL ......
SHE'S A KOUHAI OF YOURS FROM MIDDLE SCHOOL, AKI-KUN?
NOT QUITE, BUT KINDA, YEAH.
SENPAI! SENPAI!
HER NAME'S IZUMI HASHIMA.

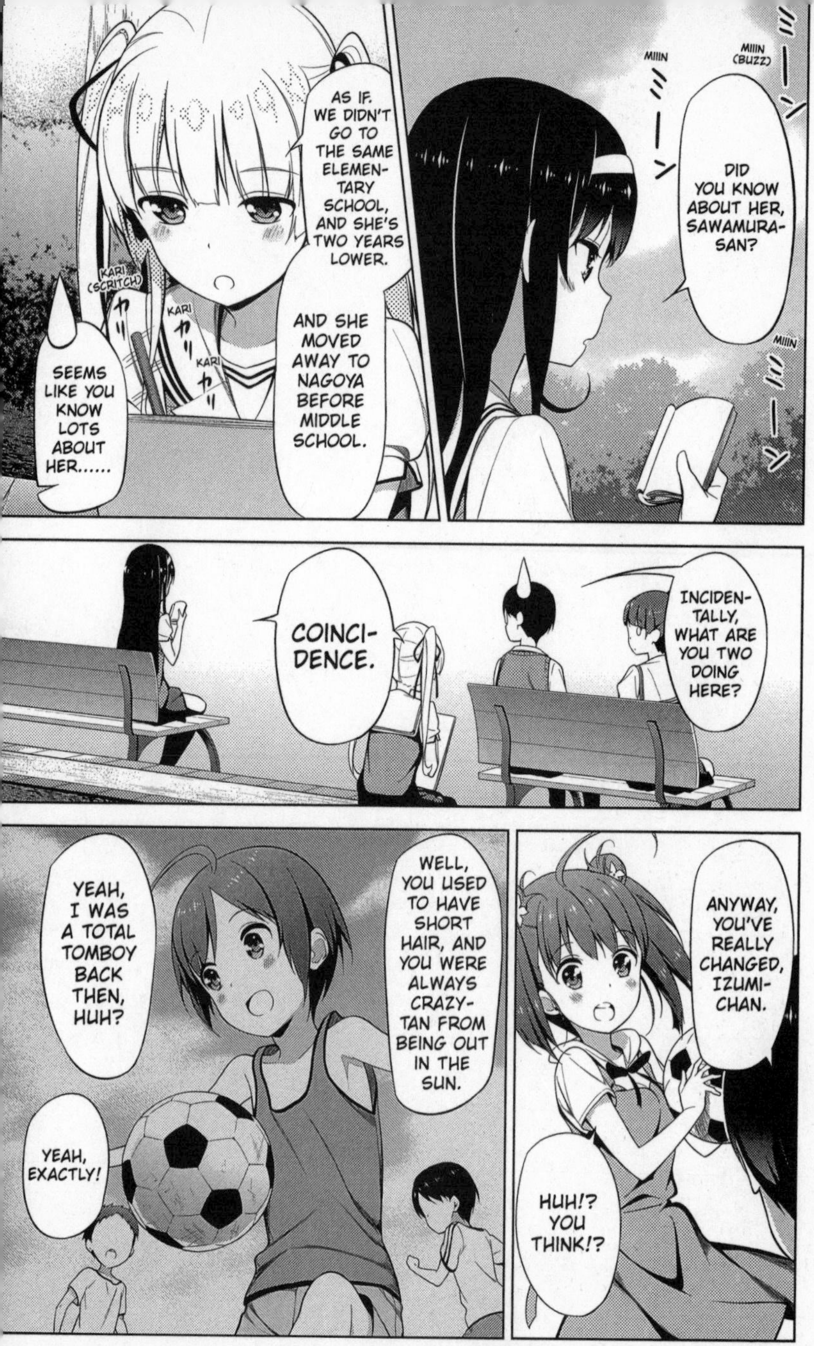
MIIN
MIIN (BUZZ)
DID YOU KNOW ABOUT HER, SAWAMURA-SAN?
MIIN
AS IF. WE DIDN'T GO TO THE SAME ELEMENTARY SCHOOL, AND SHE'S TWO YEARS LOWER.
AND SHE MOVED AWAY TO NAGOYA BEFORE MIDDLE SCHOOL.
KARI (SCRITCH)
KARI
KARI
SEEMS LIKE YOU KNOW LOTS ABOUT HER......
INCIDENTALLY, WHAT ARE YOU TWO DOING HERE?
COINCIDENCE.
ANYWAY, YOU'VE REALLY CHANGED, IZUMI-CHAN.
HUH!? YOU THINK!?
WELL, YOU USED TO HAVE SHORT HAIR, AND YOU WERE ALWAYS CRAZY-TAN FROM BEING OUT IN THE SUN.
YEAH, I WAS A TOTAL TOMBOY BACK THEN, HUH?
YEAH, EXACTLY!

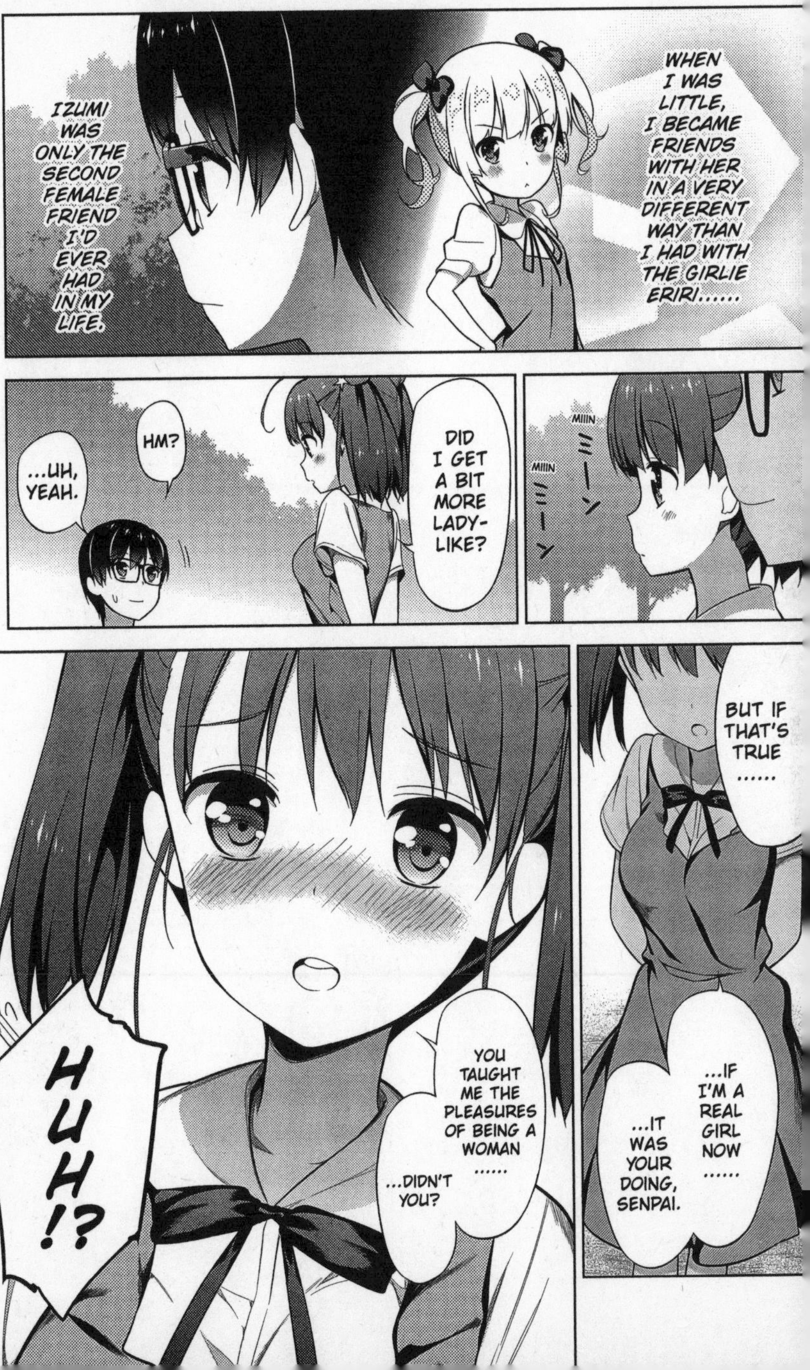
WHEN I WAS LITTLE, I BECAME FRIENDS WITH HER IN A VERY DIFFERENT WAY THAN I HAD WITH THE GIRLIE ERIRI......
IZUMI WAS ONLY THE SECOND FEMALE FRIEND I'D EVER HAD IN MY LIFE.
MIIIN
ミーン
MIIIN
ミーン
DID I GET A BIT MORE LADY-LIKE?
HM?
...UH, YEAH.
BUT IF THAT'S TRUE......
...IF I'M A REAL GIRL NOW......
...IT WAS YOUR DOING, SENPAI.
YOU TAUGHT ME THE PLEASURES OF BEING A WOMAN......
...DIDN'T YOU?
HUH!?

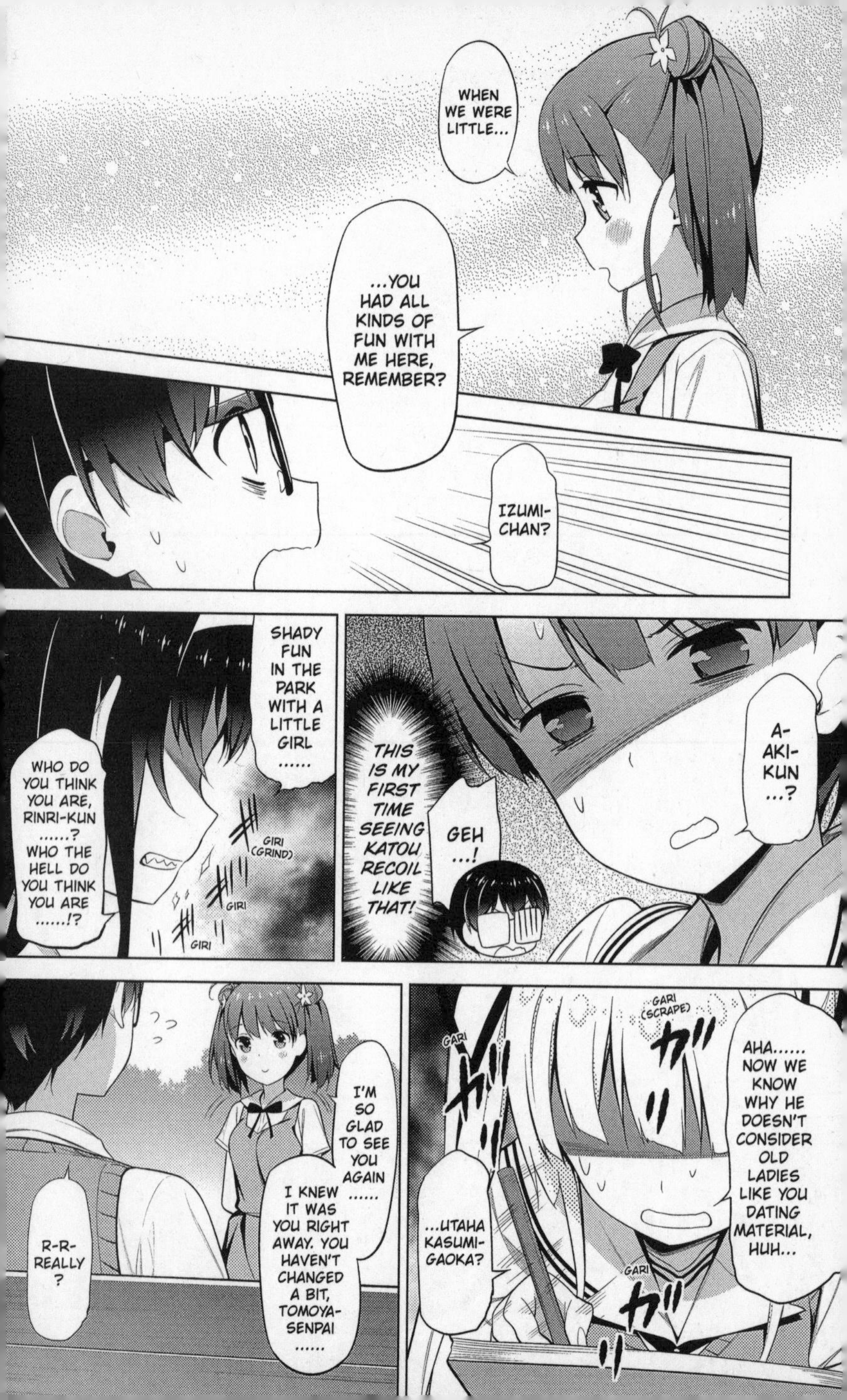
WHEN WE WERE LITTLE...
...YOU HAD ALL KINDS OF FUN WITH ME HERE, REMEMBER?
IZUMI-CHAN?
A-AKI-KUN...?
GEH...!
THIS IS MY FIRST TIME SEEING KATOU RECOIL LIKE THAT!
SHADY FUN IN THE PARK WITH A LITTLE GIRL ......
GIRI (GRIND)
GIRI
GIRI
WHO DO YOU THINK YOU ARE, RINRI-KUN ......? WHO THE HELL DO YOU THINK YOU ARE ......!?
GARI (SCRAPE)
GARI
AHA...... NOW WE KNOW WHY HE DOESN'T CONSIDER OLD LADIES LIKE YOU DATING MATERIAL, HUH...
...UTAHA KASUMIGAOKA?
GARI
I'M SO GLAD TO SEE YOU AGAIN ......
I KNEW IT WAS YOU RIGHT AWAY. YOU HAVEN'T CHANGED A BIT, TOMOYA-SENPAI ......
R-R-REALLY?

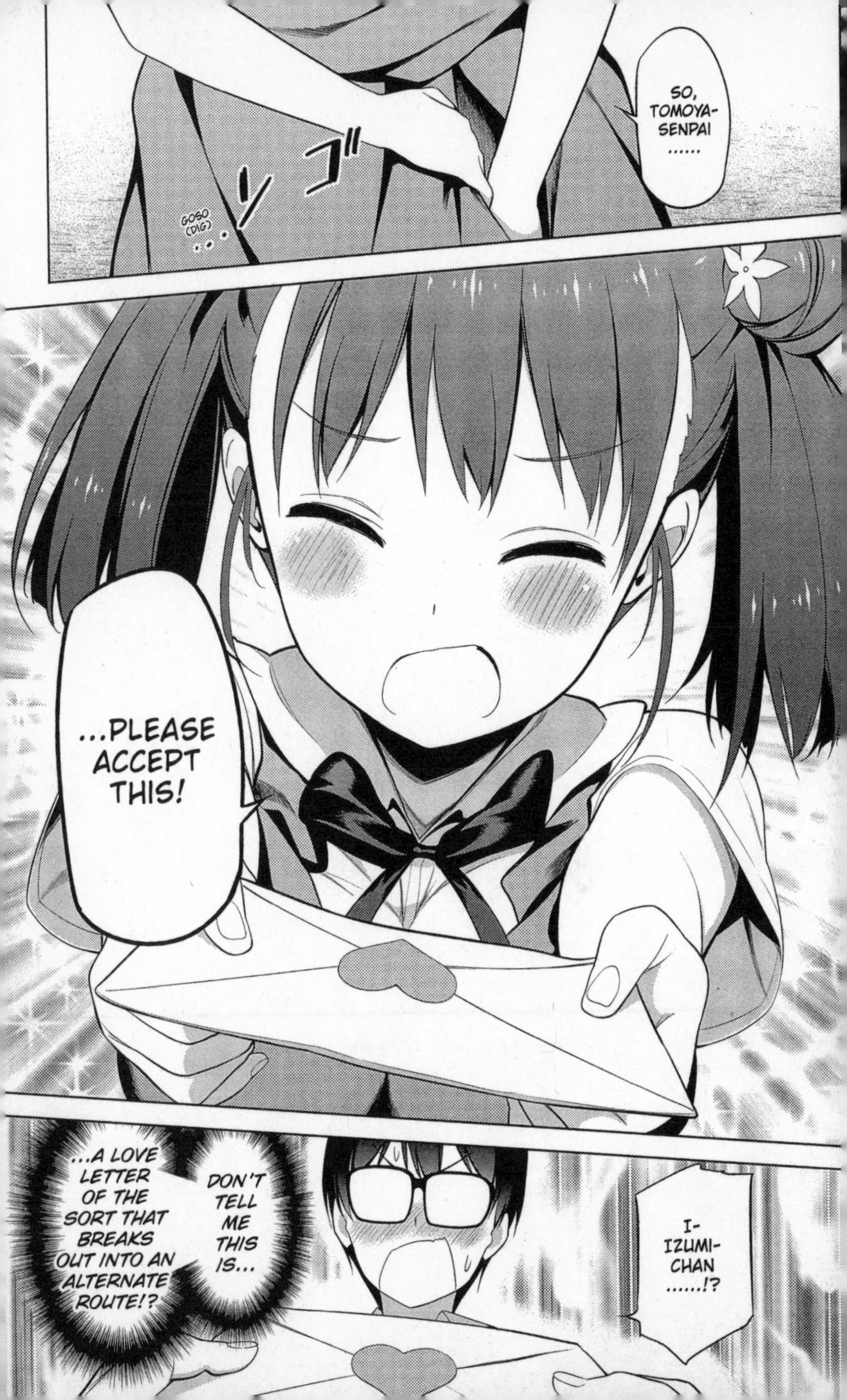
SO, TOMOYA-SENPAI ......
GOSO (DIG)
...PLEASE ACCEPT THIS!
I- IZUMI-CHAN ......!?
DON'T TELL ME THIS IS...
...A LOVE LETTER OF THE SORT THAT BREAKS OUT INTO AN ALTERNATE ROUTE!?

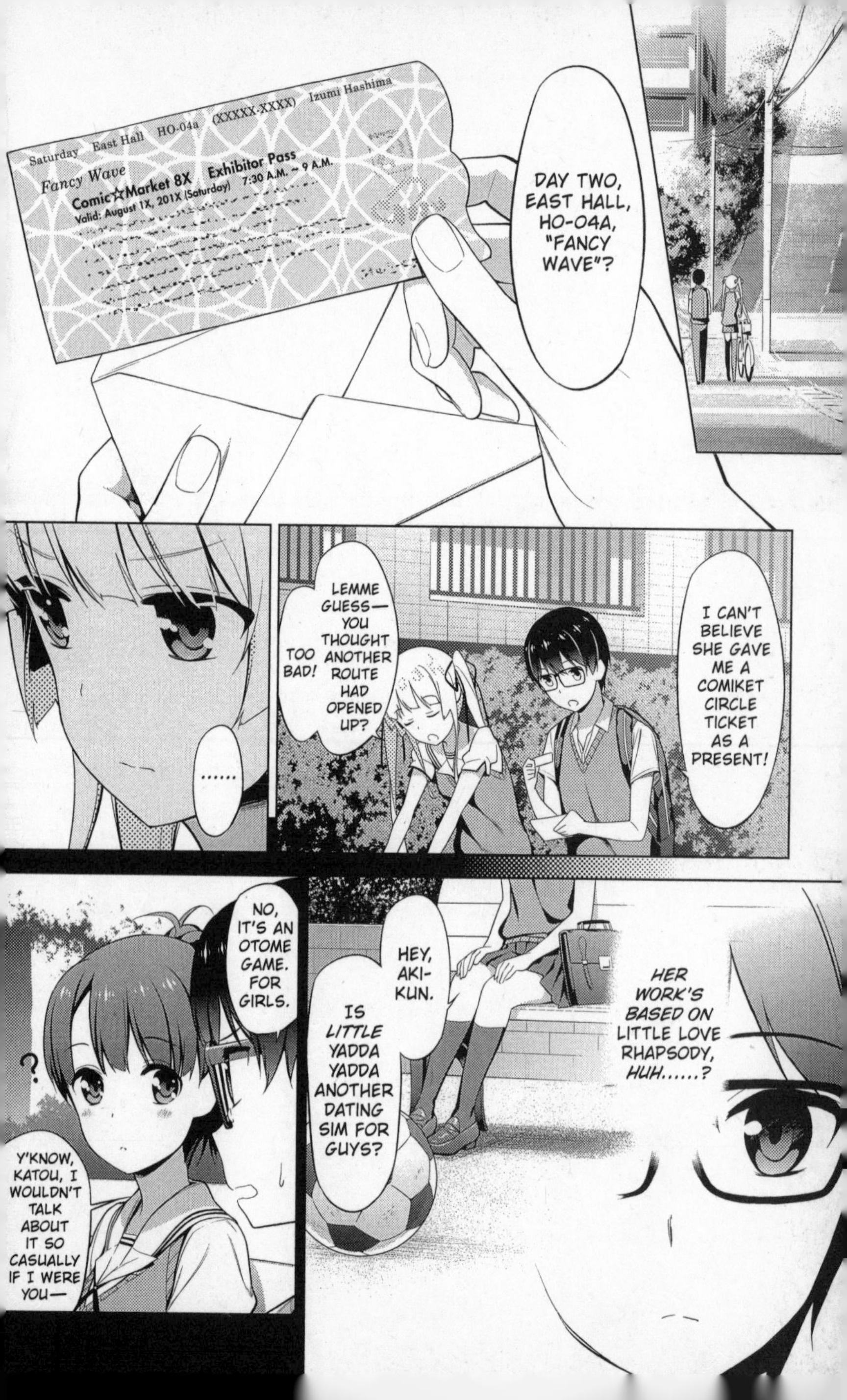
DAY TWO, EAST HALL, HO-04A, "FANCY WAVE"?
Saturday East Hall HO-04a (XXXXX-XXXX) Izumi Hashima
Fancy Wave
Comic☆Market 8X Exhibitor Pass
Valid: August 1X, 201X (Saturday) 7:30 A.M. ~ 9 A.M.
I CAN'T BELIEVE SHE GAVE ME A COMIKET CIRCLE TICKET AS A PRESENT!
LEMME GUESS—YOU THOUGHT ANOTHER ROUTE HAD OPENED UP?
TOO BAD!
......
HER WORK'S BASED ON LITTLE LOVE RHAPSODY, HUH......?
HEY, AKI-KUN.
IS LITTLE YADDA YADDA ANOTHER DATING SIM FOR GUYS?
NO, IT'S AN OTOME GAME. FOR GIRLS.
?
Y'KNOW, KATOU, I WOULDN'T TALK ABOUT IT SO CASUALLY IF I WERE YOU—

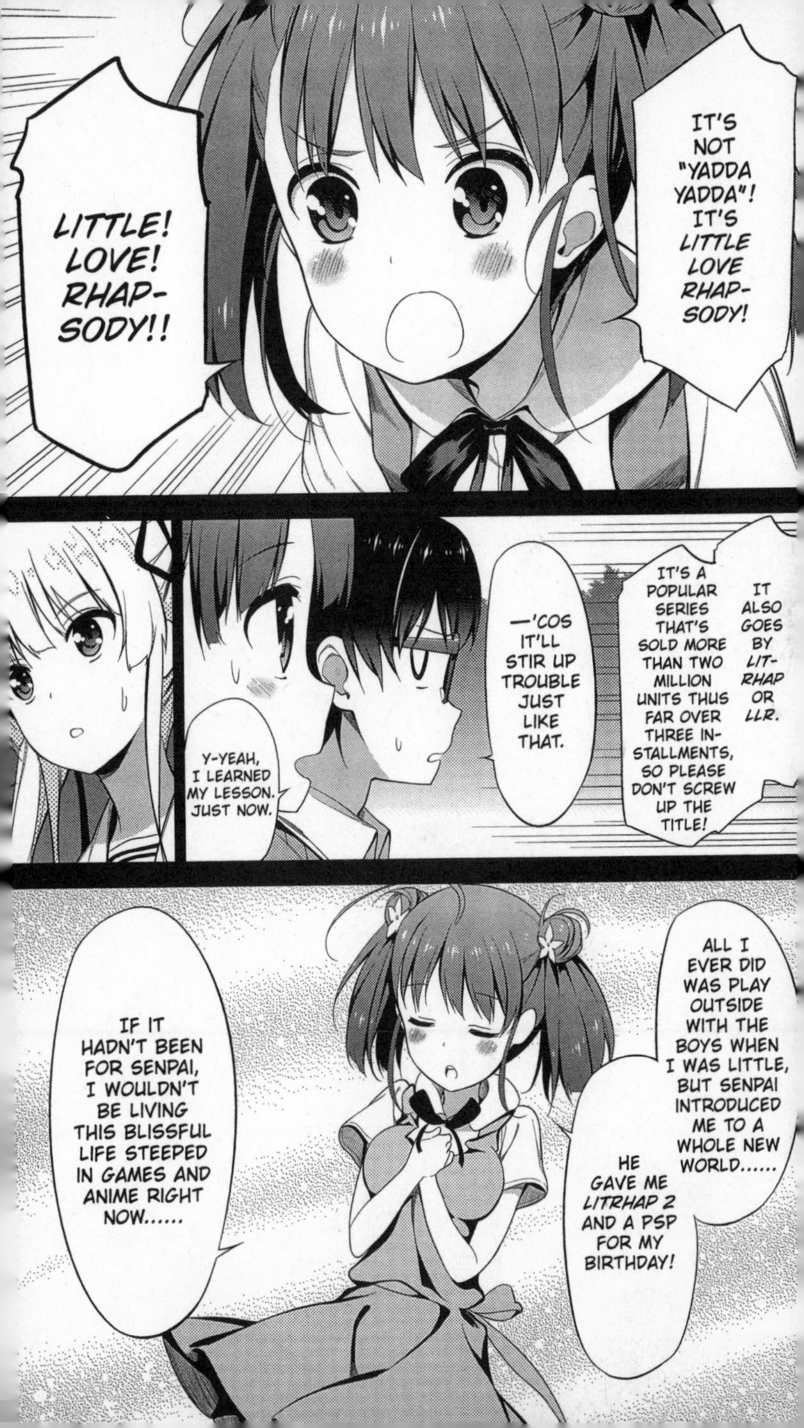
IT'S NOT "YADDA YADDA"! IT'S *LITTLE LOVE RHAPSODY*!
*LITTLE! LOVE! RHAPSODY!!*
IT'S A POPULAR SERIES THAT'S SOLD MORE THAN TWO MILLION UNITS THUS FAR OVER THREE INSTALLMENTS, SO PLEASE DON'T SCREW UP THE TITLE!
IT ALSO GOES BY *LITRHAP* OR *LLR*.
—'COS IT'LL STIR UP TROUBLE JUST LIKE THAT.
Y-YEAH, I LEARNED MY LESSON. JUST NOW.
ALL I EVER DID WAS PLAY OUTSIDE WITH THE BOYS WHEN I WAS LITTLE, BUT SENPAI INTRODUCED ME TO A WHOLE NEW WORLD......
HE GAVE ME *LITRHAP 2* AND A PSP FOR MY BIRTHDAY!
IF IT HADN'T BEEN FOR SENPAI, I WOULDN'T BE LIVING THIS BLISSFUL LIFE STEEPED IN GAMES AND ANIME RIGHT NOW......

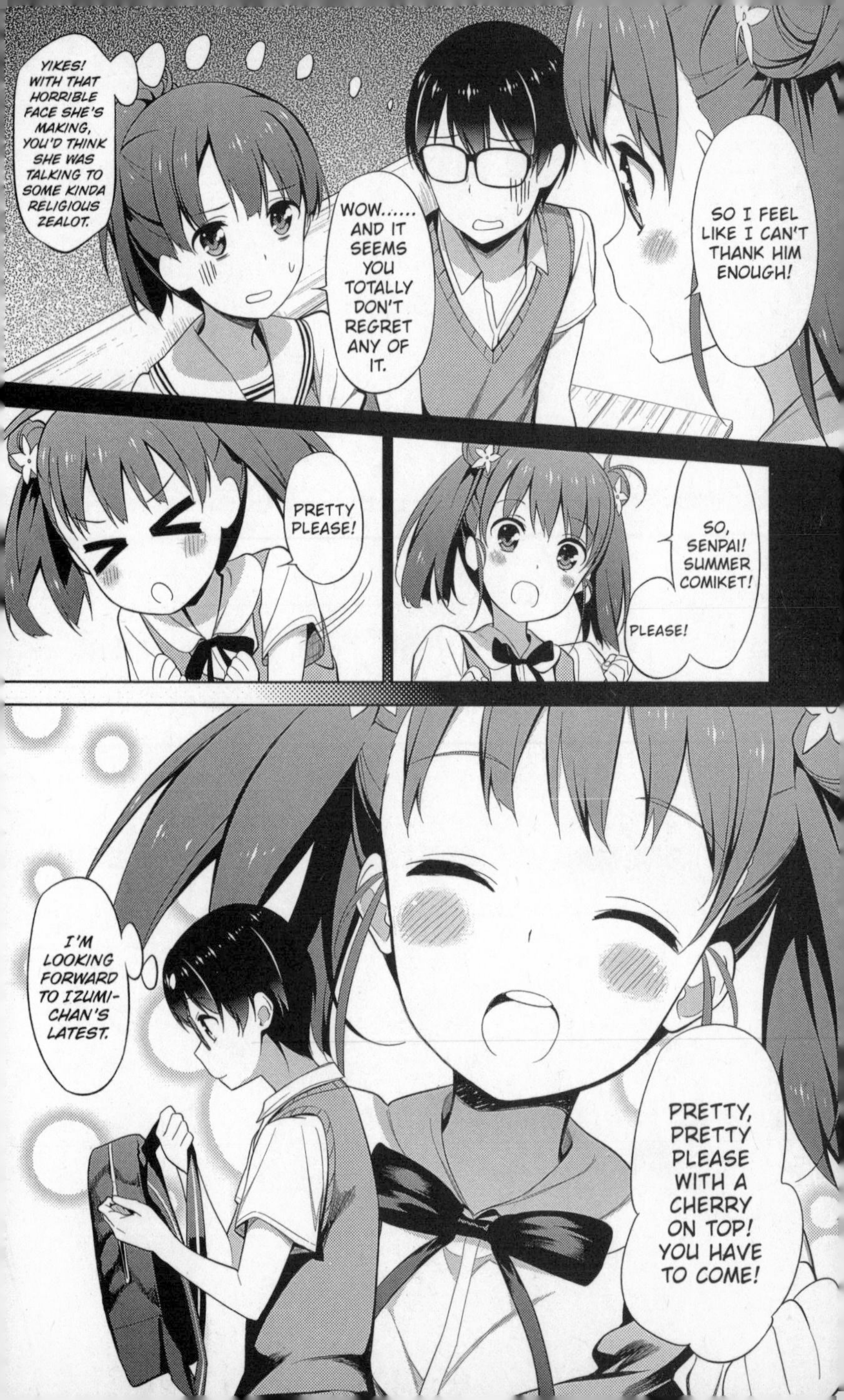
SO I FEEL LIKE I CAN'T THANK HIM ENOUGH!
WOW...... AND IT SEEMS YOU TOTALLY DON'T REGRET ANY OF IT.
YIKES! WITH THAT HORRIBLE FACE SHE'S MAKING, YOU'D THINK SHE WAS TALKING TO SOME KINDA RELIGIOUS ZEALOT.
SO, SENPAI! SUMMER COMIKET!
PLEASE!
PRETTY PLEASE!
PRETTY, PRETTY PLEASE WITH A CHERRY ON TOP! YOU HAVE TO COME!
I'M LOOKING FORWARD TO IZUMI-CHAN'S LATEST.

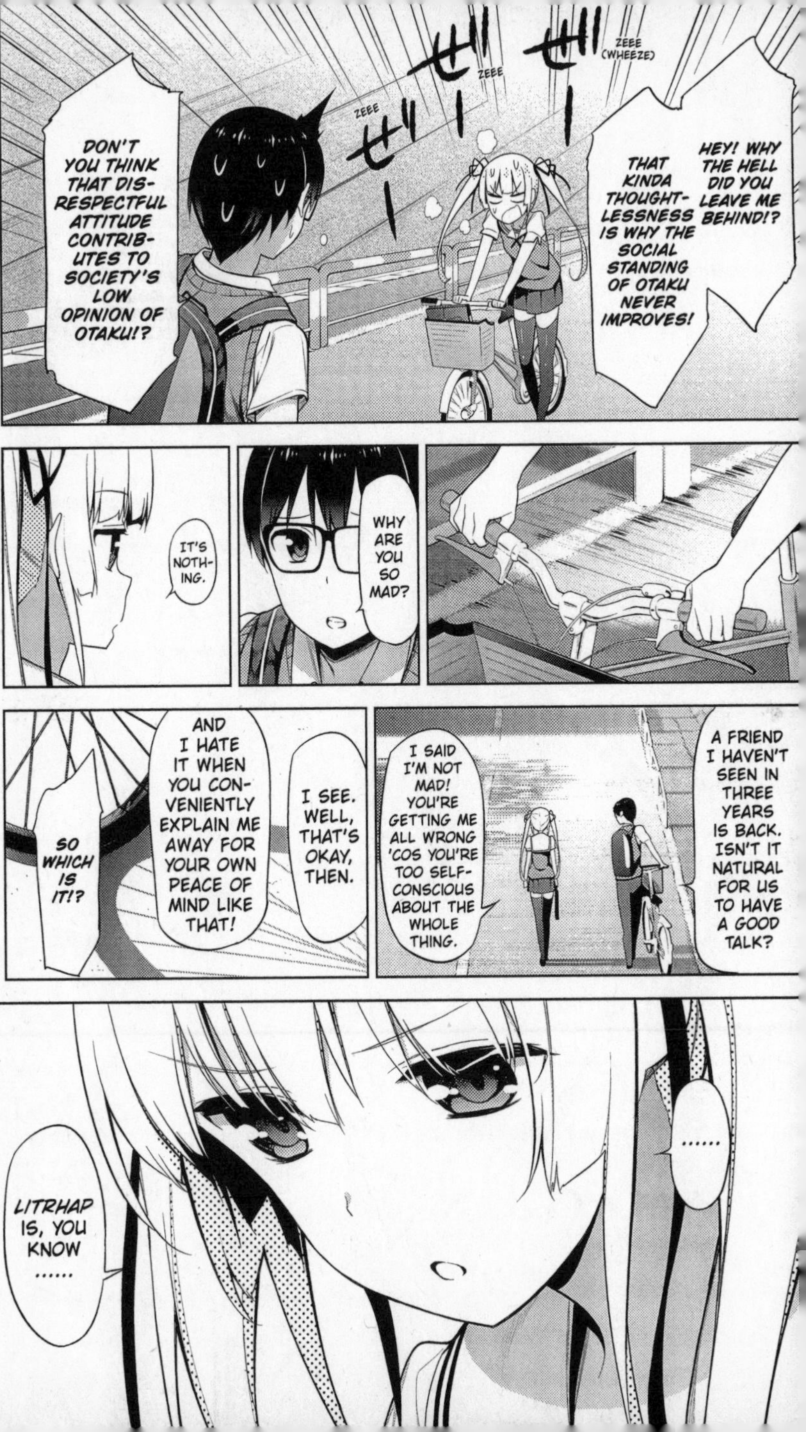

HEY! WHY THE HELL DID YOU LEAVE ME BEHIND!?
ZEEE (WHEEZE)
ZEEE
ZEEE
THAT KINDA THOUGHT-LESSNESS IS WHY THE SOCIAL STANDING OF OTAKU NEVER IMPROVES!
DON'T YOU THINK THAT DIS-RESPECTFUL ATTITUDE CONTRIB-UTES TO SOCIETY'S LOW OPINION OF OTAKU!?
WHY ARE YOU SO MAD?
IT'S NOTH-ING.
A FRIEND I HAVEN'T SEEN IN THREE YEARS IS BACK. ISN'T IT NATURAL FOR US TO HAVE A GOOD TALK?
I SAID I'M NOT MAD! YOU'RE GETTING ME ALL WRONG 'COS YOU'RE TOO SELF-CONSCIOUS ABOUT THE WHOLE THING.
I SEE. WELL, THAT'S OKAY, THEN.
AND I HATE IT WHEN YOU CON-VENIENTLY EXPLAIN ME AWAY FOR YOUR OWN PEACE OF MIND LIKE THAT!
SO WHICH IS IT!?
......
LITRHAP IS, YOU KNOW ......

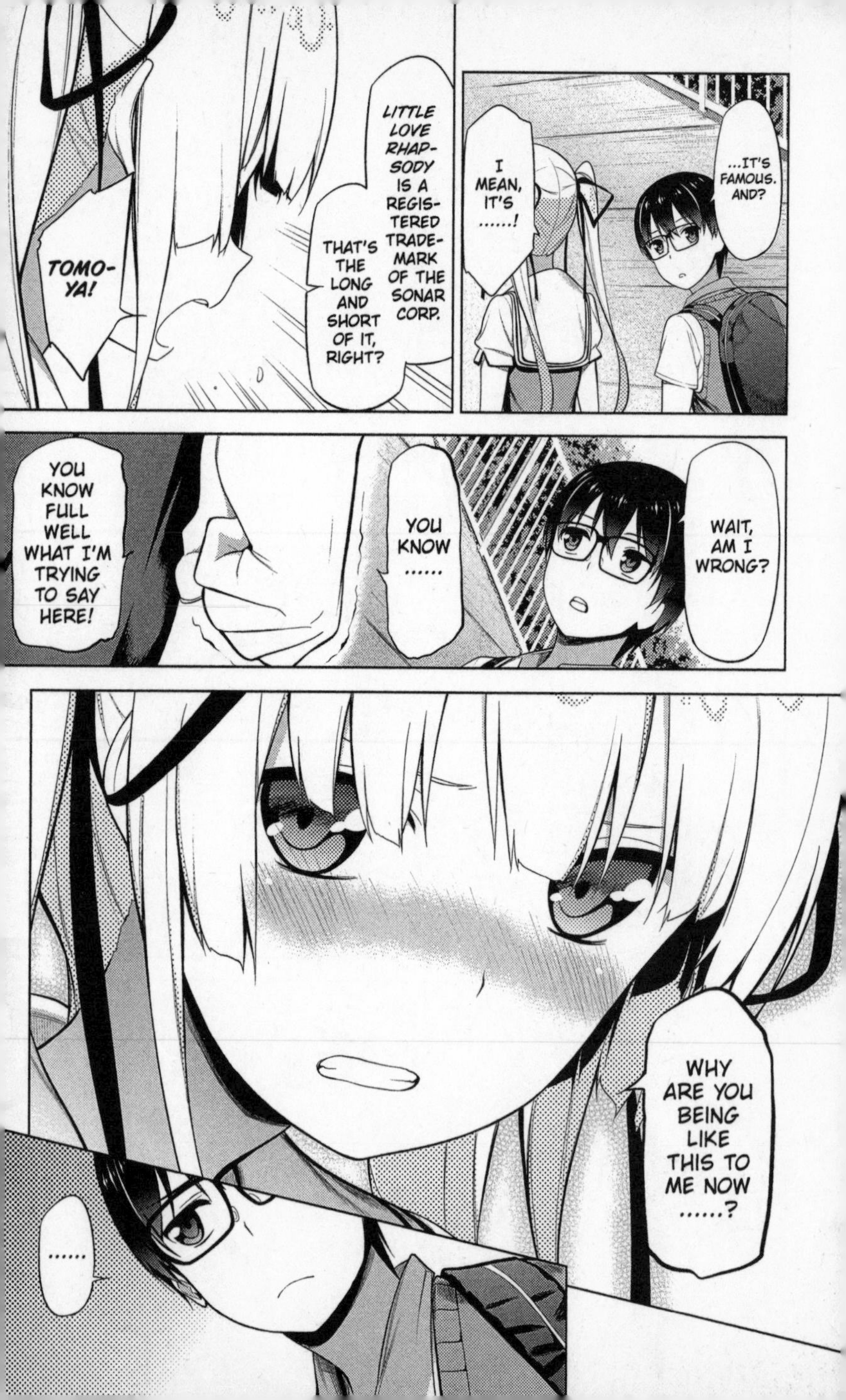
...IT'S FAMOUS. AND?
I MEAN, IT'S ......!
LITTLE LOVE RHAPSODY IS A REGISTERED TRADEMARK OF THE SONAR CORP.
THAT'S THE LONG AND SHORT OF IT, RIGHT?
TOMOYA!
WAIT, AM I WRONG?
YOU KNOW ......
YOU KNOW FULL WELL WHAT I'M TRYING TO SAY HERE!
WHY ARE YOU BEING LIKE THIS TO ME NOW ......?
......

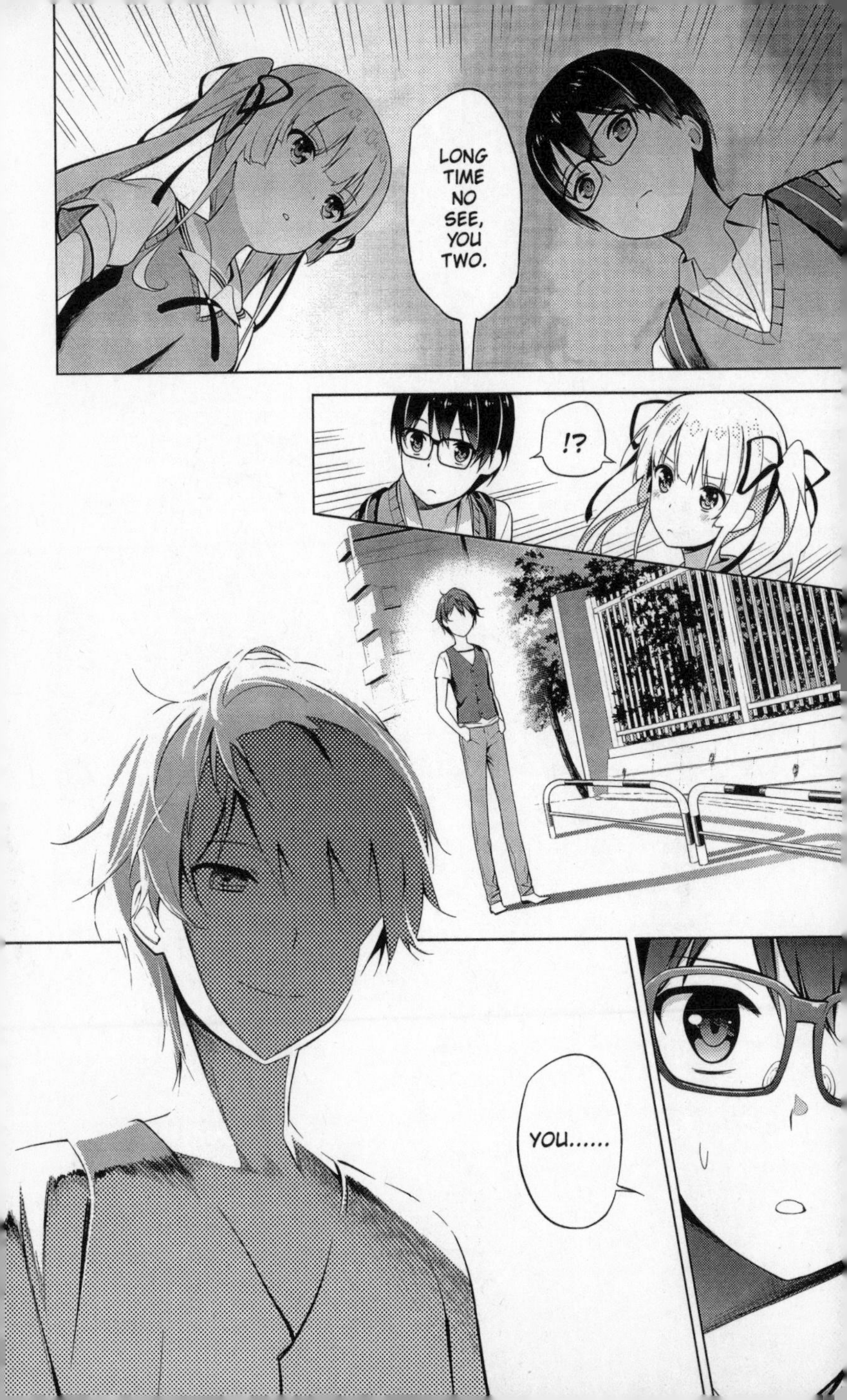
LONG TIME NO SEE, YOU TWO.
!?
YOU......

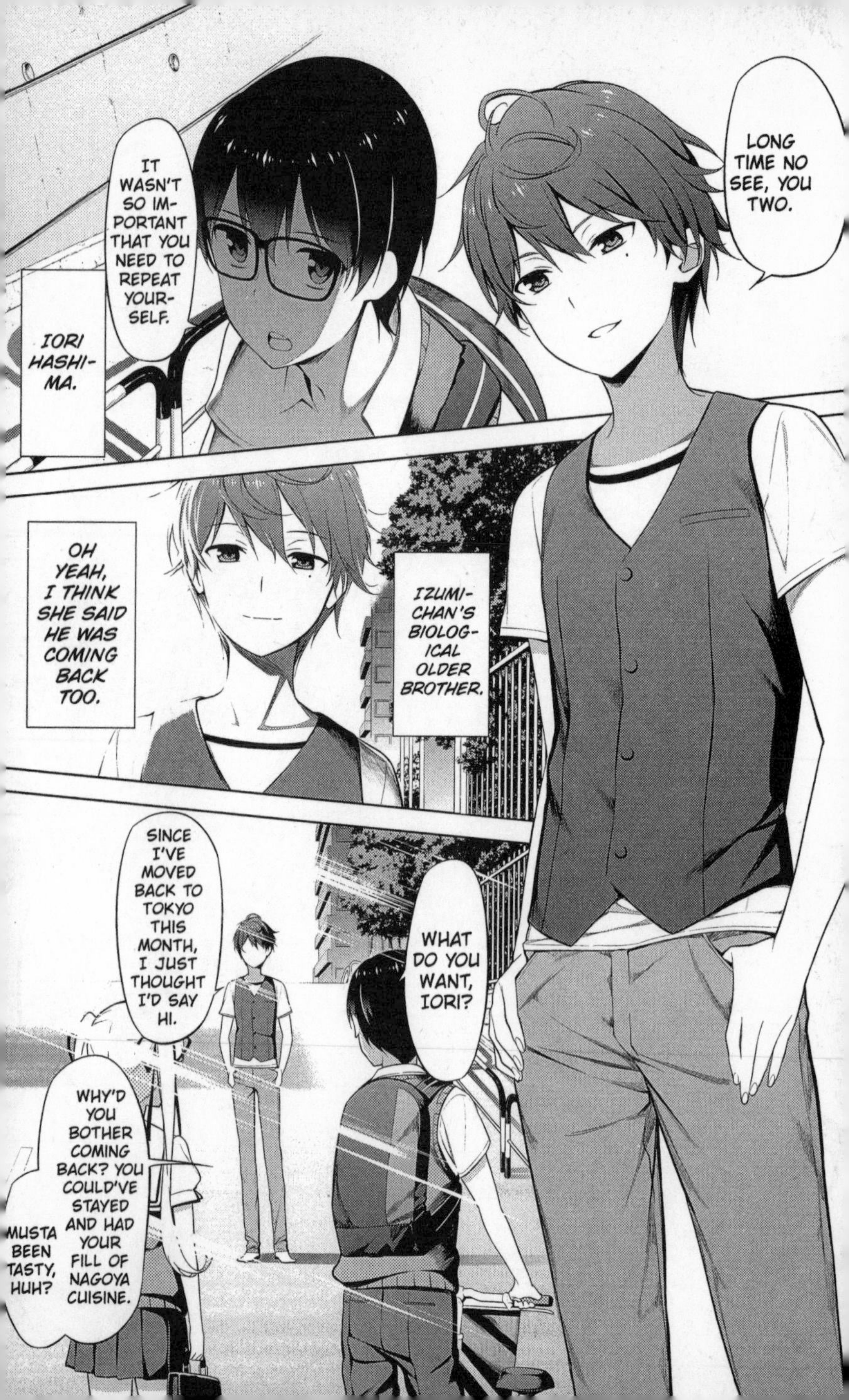
LONG TIME NO SEE, YOU TWO.
IT WASN'T SO IM-PORTANT THAT YOU NEED TO REPEAT YOUR-SELF.
IORI HASHI-MA.
IZUMI-CHAN'S BIOLOG-ICAL OLDER BROTHER.
OH YEAH, I THINK SHE SAID HE WAS COMING BACK TOO.
WHAT DO YOU WANT, IORI?
SINCE I'VE MOVED BACK TO TOKYO THIS MONTH, I JUST THOUGHT I'D SAY HI.
WHY'D YOU BOTHER COMING BACK? YOU COULD'VE STAYED AND HAD YOUR FILL OF NAGOYA CUISINE.
MUSTA BEEN TASTY, HUH?

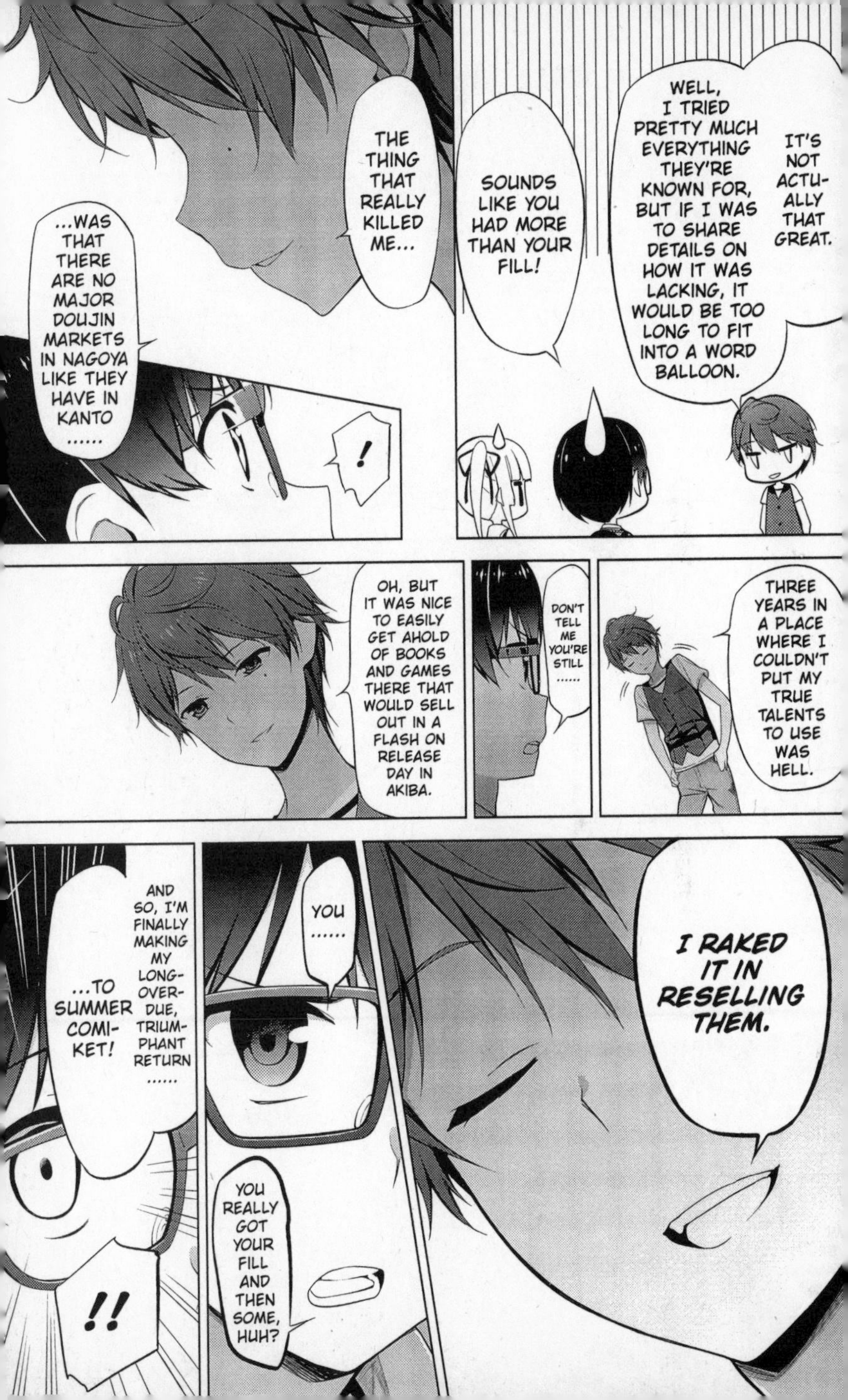
IT'S NOT ACTUALLY THAT GREAT.
WELL, I TRIED PRETTY MUCH EVERYTHING THEY'RE KNOWN FOR, BUT IF I WAS TO SHARE DETAILS ON HOW IT WAS LACKING, IT WOULD BE TOO LONG TO FIT INTO A WORD BALLOON.
SOUNDS LIKE YOU HAD MORE THAN YOUR FILL!
THE THING THAT REALLY KILLED ME...
...WAS THAT THERE ARE NO MAJOR DOUJIN MARKETS IN NAGOYA LIKE THEY HAVE IN KANTO ......
!
THREE YEARS IN A PLACE WHERE I COULDN'T PUT MY TRUE TALENTS TO USE WAS HELL.
DON'T TELL ME YOU'RE STILL ......
OH, BUT IT WAS NICE TO EASILY GET AHOLD OF BOOKS AND GAMES THERE THAT WOULD SELL OUT IN A FLASH ON RELEASE DAY IN AKIBA.
I RAKED IT IN RESELLING THEM.
YOU ......
YOU REALLY GOT YOUR FILL AND THEN SOME, HUH?
AND SO, I'M FINALLY MAKING MY LONG-OVERDUE, TRIUMPHANT RETURN ......
...TO SUMMER COMIKET!
!!

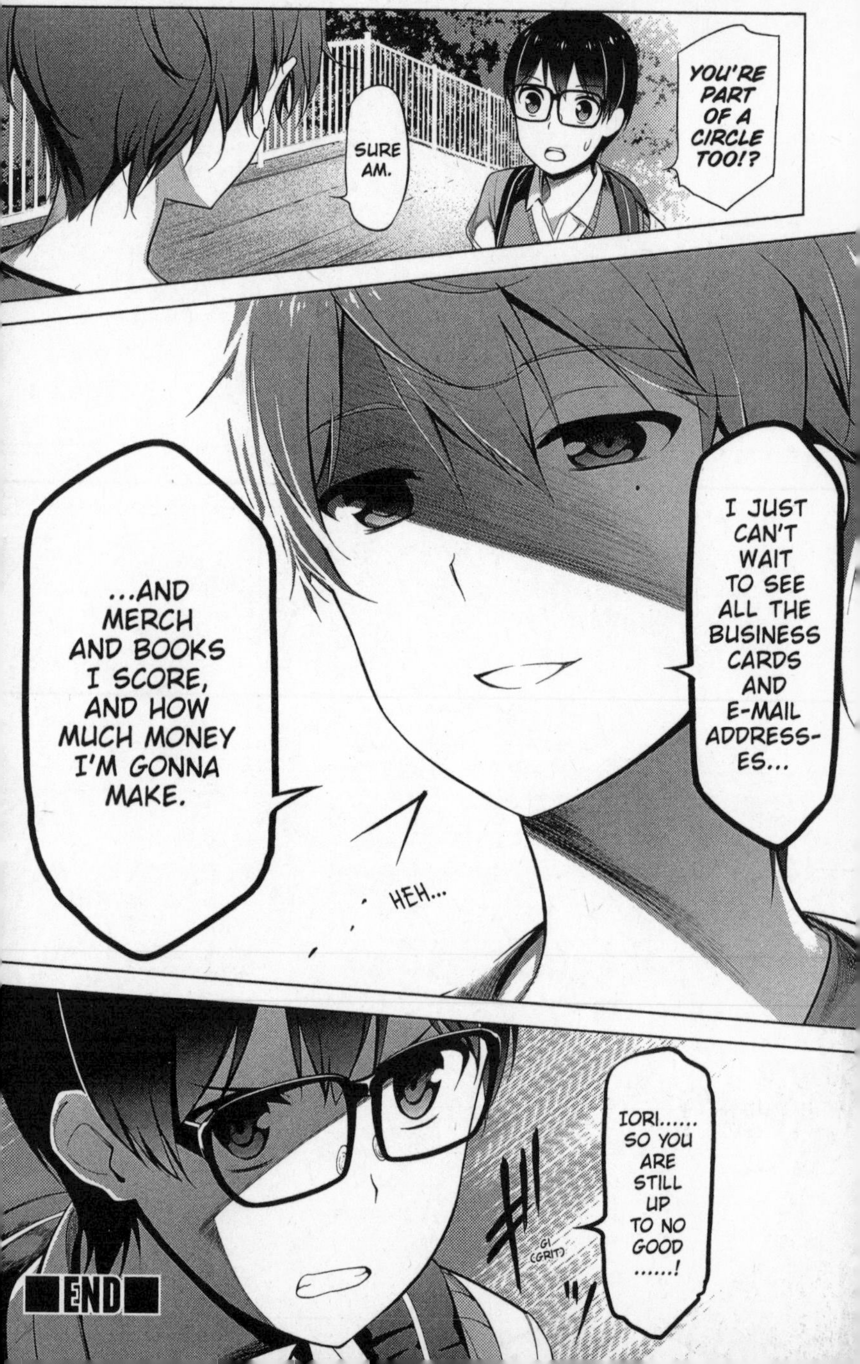
YOU'RE PART OF A CIRCLE TOO!?
SURE AM.
I JUST CAN'T WAIT TO SEE ALL THE BUSINESS CARDS AND E-MAIL ADDRESS-ES...
...AND MERCH AND BOOKS I SCORE, AND HOW MUCH MONEY I'M GONNA MAKE.
HEH...
IORI...... SO YOU ARE STILL UP TO NO GOOD ......!
GI (GRIT)
END

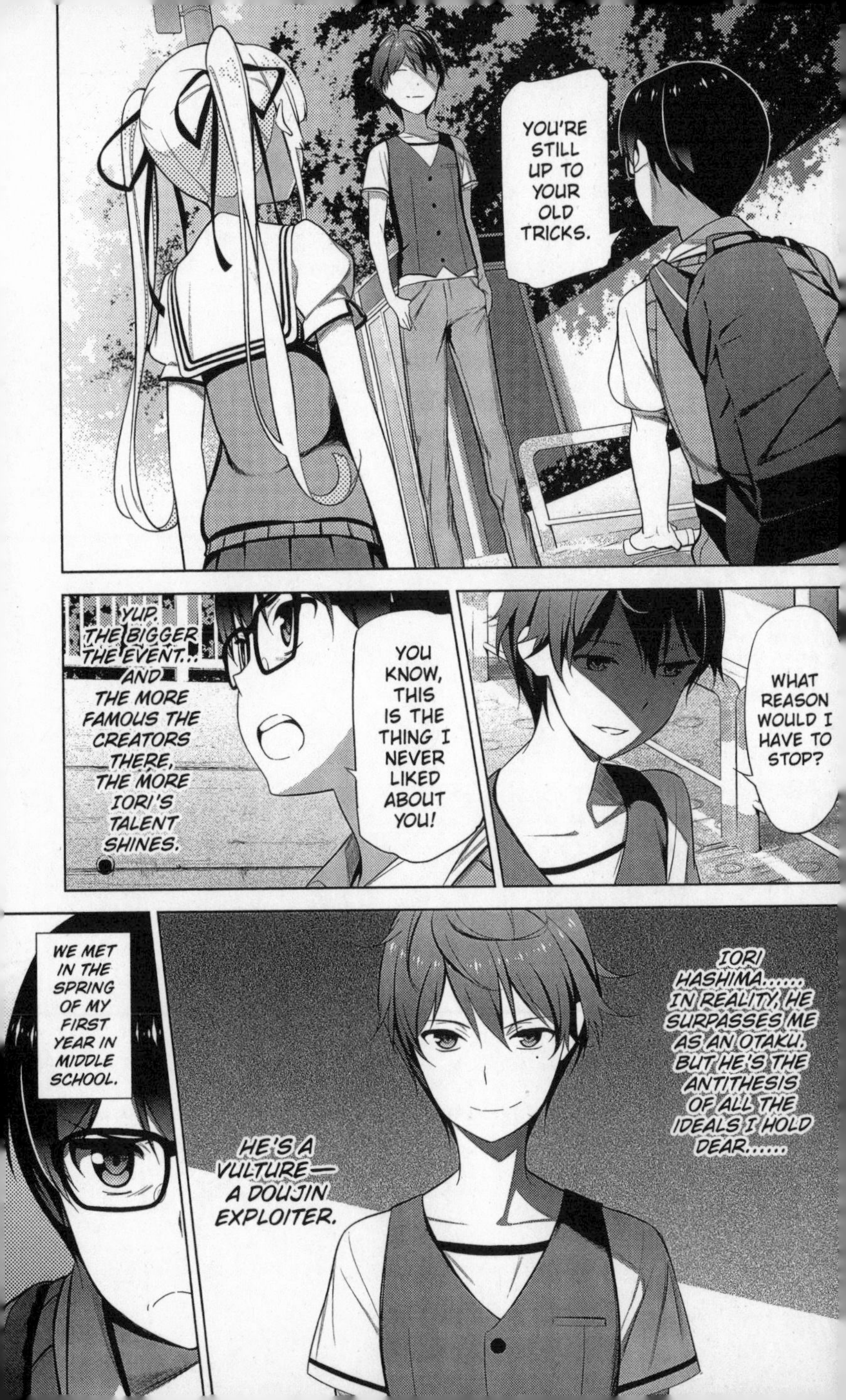

YOU'RE STILL UP TO YOUR OLD TRICKS.
WHAT REASON WOULD I HAVE TO STOP?
YOU KNOW, THIS IS THE THING I NEVER LIKED ABOUT YOU!
YUP. THE BIGGER THE EVENT... AND THE MORE FAMOUS THE CREATORS THERE, THE MORE IORI'S TALENT SHINES.
IORI HASHIMA...... IN REALITY, HE SURPASSES ME AS AN OTAKU. BUT HE'S THE ANTITHESIS OF ALL THE IDEALS I HOLD DEAR......
HE'S A VULTURE— A DOUJIN EXPLOITER.
WE MET IN THE SPRING OF MY FIRST YEAR IN MIDDLE SCHOOL.

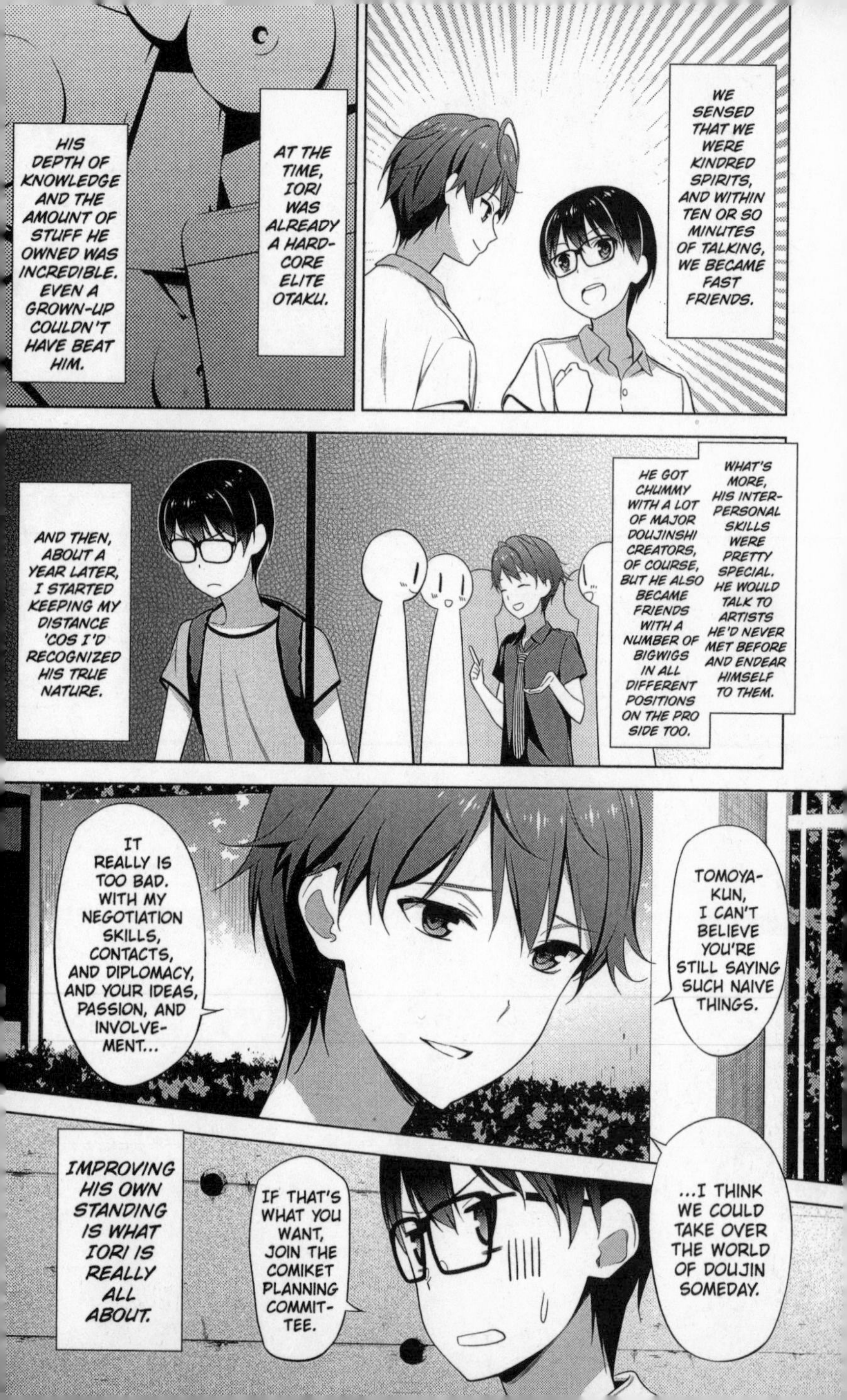
WE SENSED THAT WE WERE KINDRED SPIRITS, AND WITHIN TEN OR SO MINUTES OF TALKING, WE BECAME FAST FRIENDS.
AT THE TIME, IORI WAS ALREADY A HARD-CORE ELITE OTAKU.
HIS DEPTH OF KNOWLEDGE AND THE AMOUNT OF STUFF HE OWNED WAS INCREDIBLE. EVEN A GROWN-UP COULDN'T HAVE BEAT HIM.
WHAT'S MORE, HIS INTER-PERSONAL SKILLS WERE PRETTY SPECIAL. HE WOULD TALK TO ARTISTS HE'D NEVER MET BEFORE AND ENDEAR HIMSELF TO THEM.
HE GOT CHUMMY WITH A LOT OF MAJOR DOUJINSHI CREATORS, OF COURSE, BUT HE ALSO BECAME FRIENDS WITH A NUMBER OF BIGWIGS IN ALL DIFFERENT POSITIONS ON THE PRO SIDE TOO.
AND THEN, ABOUT A YEAR LATER, I STARTED KEEPING MY DISTANCE 'COS I'D RECOGNIZED HIS TRUE NATURE.
TOMOYA-KUN, I CAN'T BELIEVE YOU'RE STILL SAYING SUCH NAIVE THINGS.
IT REALLY IS TOO BAD. WITH MY NEGOTIATION SKILLS, CONTACTS, AND DIPLOMACY, AND YOUR IDEAS, PASSION, AND INVOLVE-MENT...
...I THINK WE COULD TAKE OVER THE WORLD OF DOUJIN SOMEDAY.
IF THAT'S WHAT YOU WANT, JOIN THE COMIKET PLANNING COMMIT-TEE.
IMPROVING HIS OWN STANDING IS WHAT IORI IS REALLY ALL ABOUT.

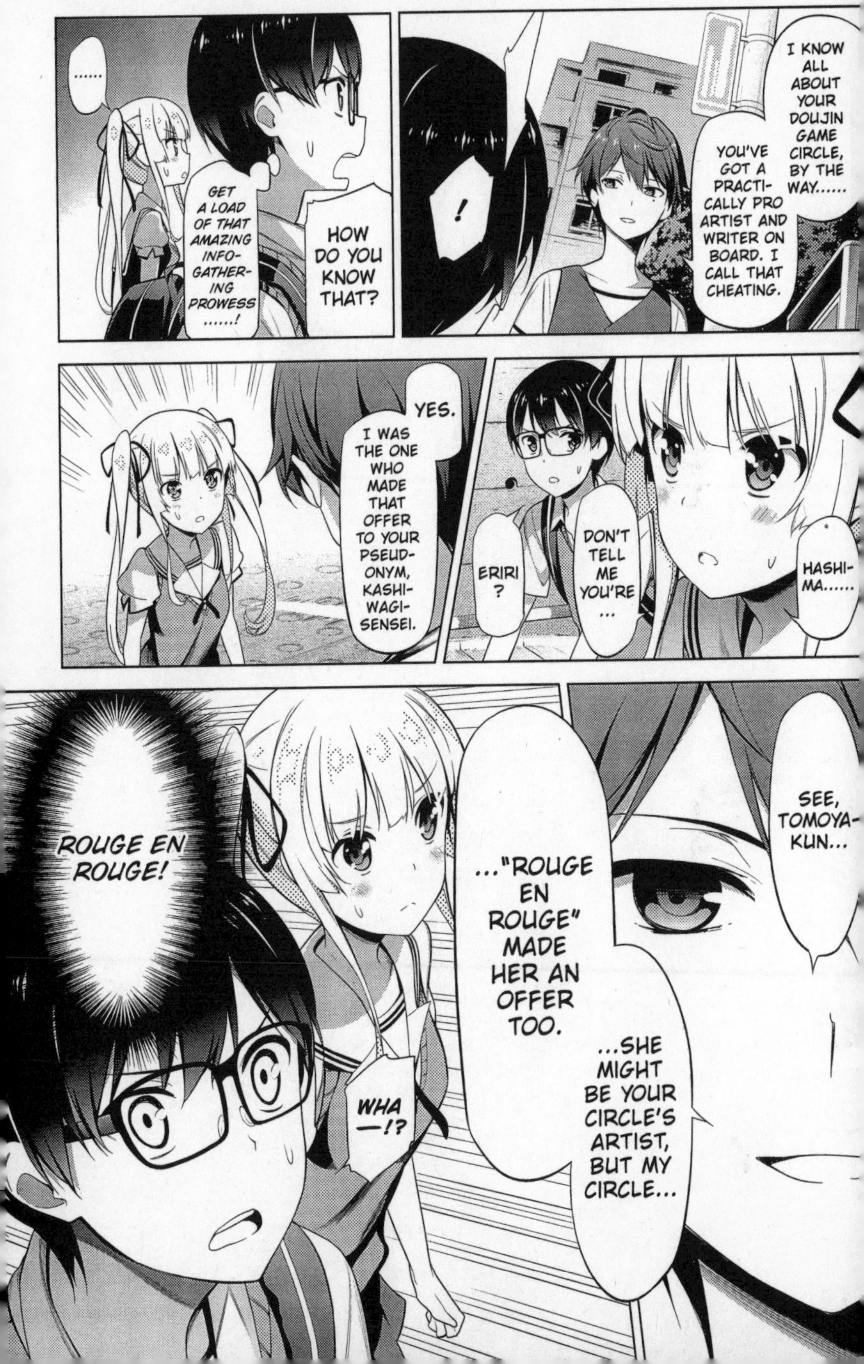
I KNOW ALL ABOUT YOUR DOUJIN GAME CIRCLE, BY THE WAY......
YOU'VE GOT A PRACTICALLY PRO ARTIST AND WRITER ON BOARD. I CALL THAT CHEATING.
!
HOW DO YOU KNOW THAT?
GET A LOAD OF THAT AMAZING INFO-GATHERING PROWESS......!
......
HASHIMA......
DON'T TELL ME YOU'RE...
ERIRI?
YES.
I WAS THE ONE WHO MADE THAT OFFER TO YOUR PSEUDONYM, KASHIWAGI-SENSEI.
SEE, TOMOYA-KUN...
..."ROUGE EN ROUGE" MADE HER AN OFFER TOO.
...SHE MIGHT BE YOUR CIRCLE'S ARTIST, BUT MY CIRCLE...
WHA—!?
ROUGE EN ROUGE!

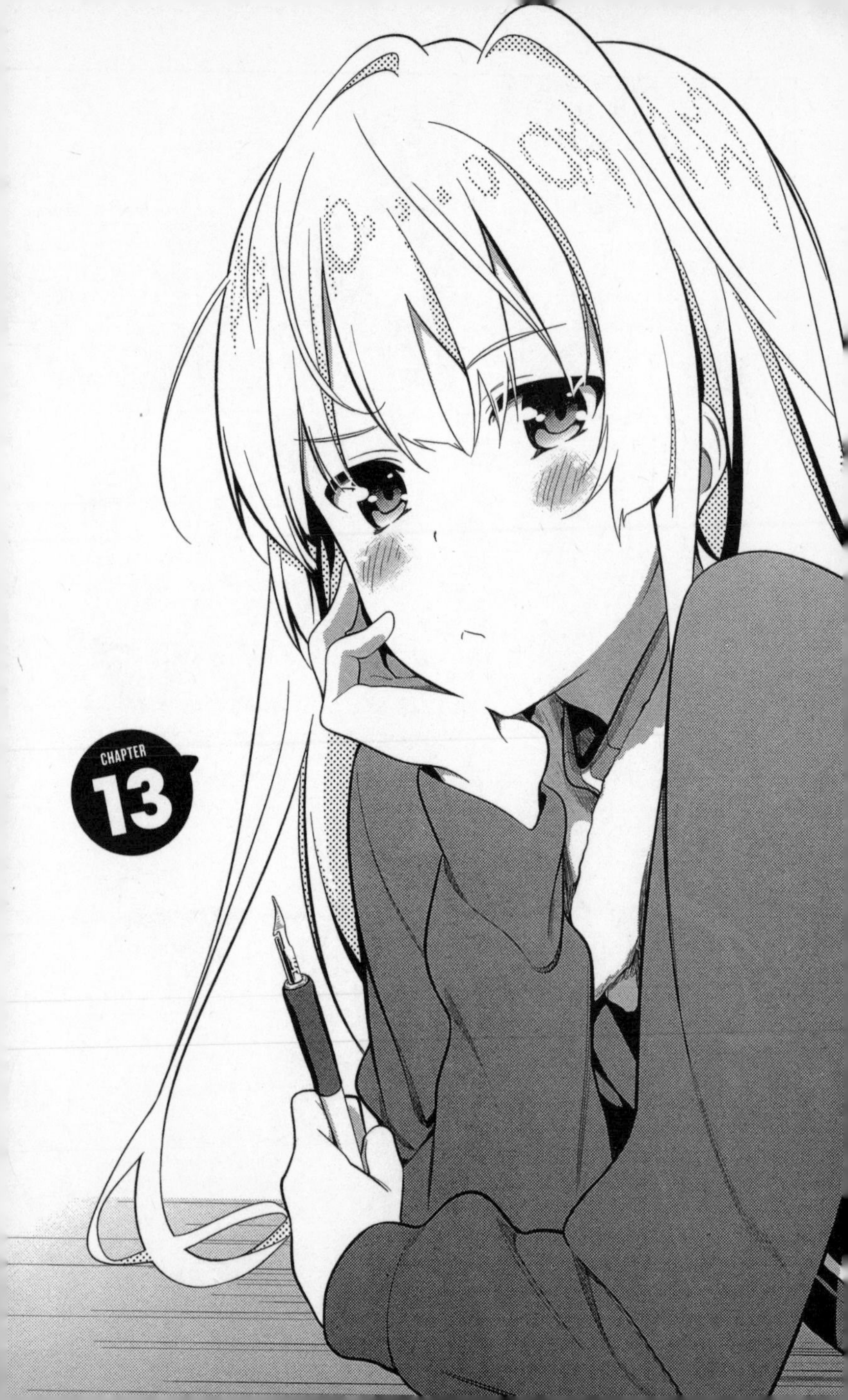
CHAPTER
13

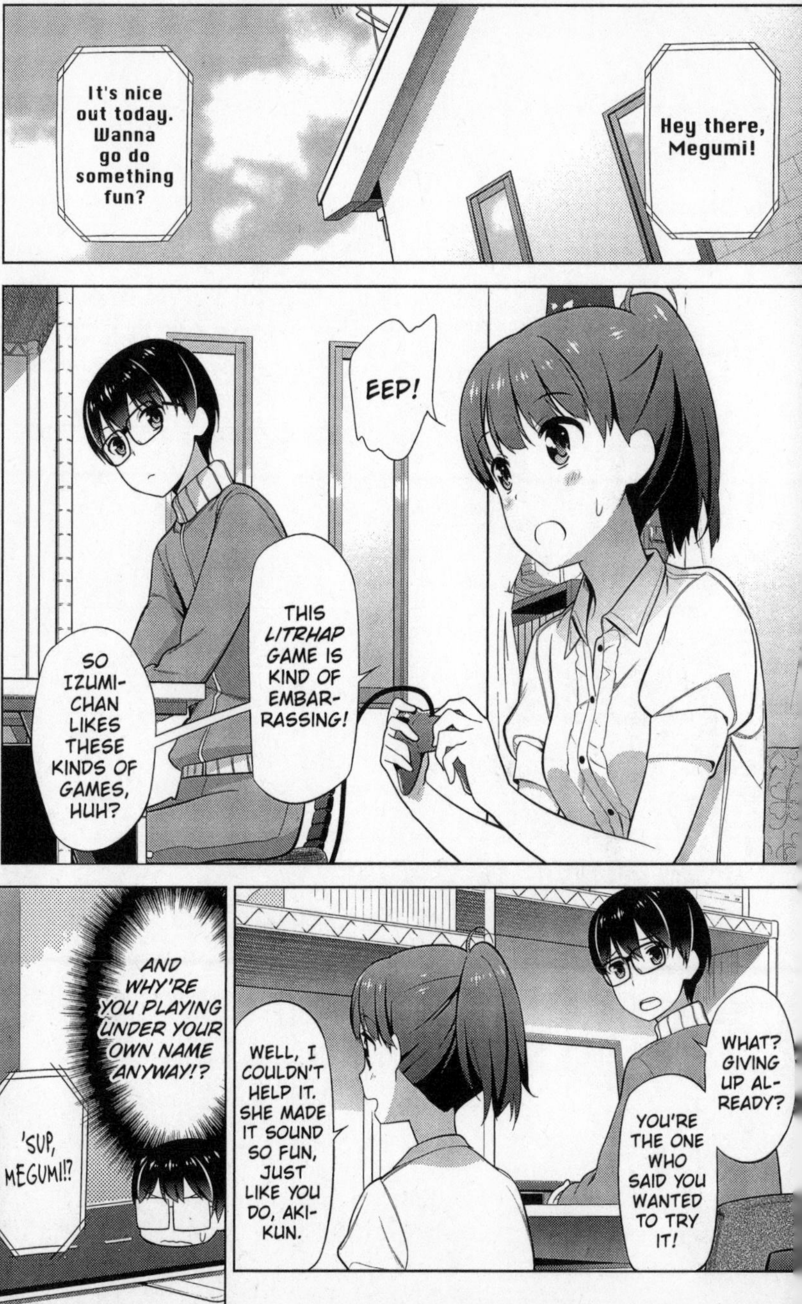
Hey there, Megumi!
It's nice out today. Wanna go do something fun?
EEP!
THIS *LITRHAP* GAME IS KIND OF EMBARRASSING!
SO IZUMI-CHAN LIKES THESE KINDS OF GAMES, HUH?
WHAT? GIVING UP ALREADY?
YOU'RE THE ONE WHO SAID YOU WANTED TO TRY IT!
WELL, I COULDN'T HELP IT. SHE MADE IT SOUND SO FUN, JUST LIKE YOU DO, AKI-KUN.
AND WHY'RE YOU PLAYING UNDER YOUR OWN NAME ANYWAY!?
'SUP, MEGUMI!?

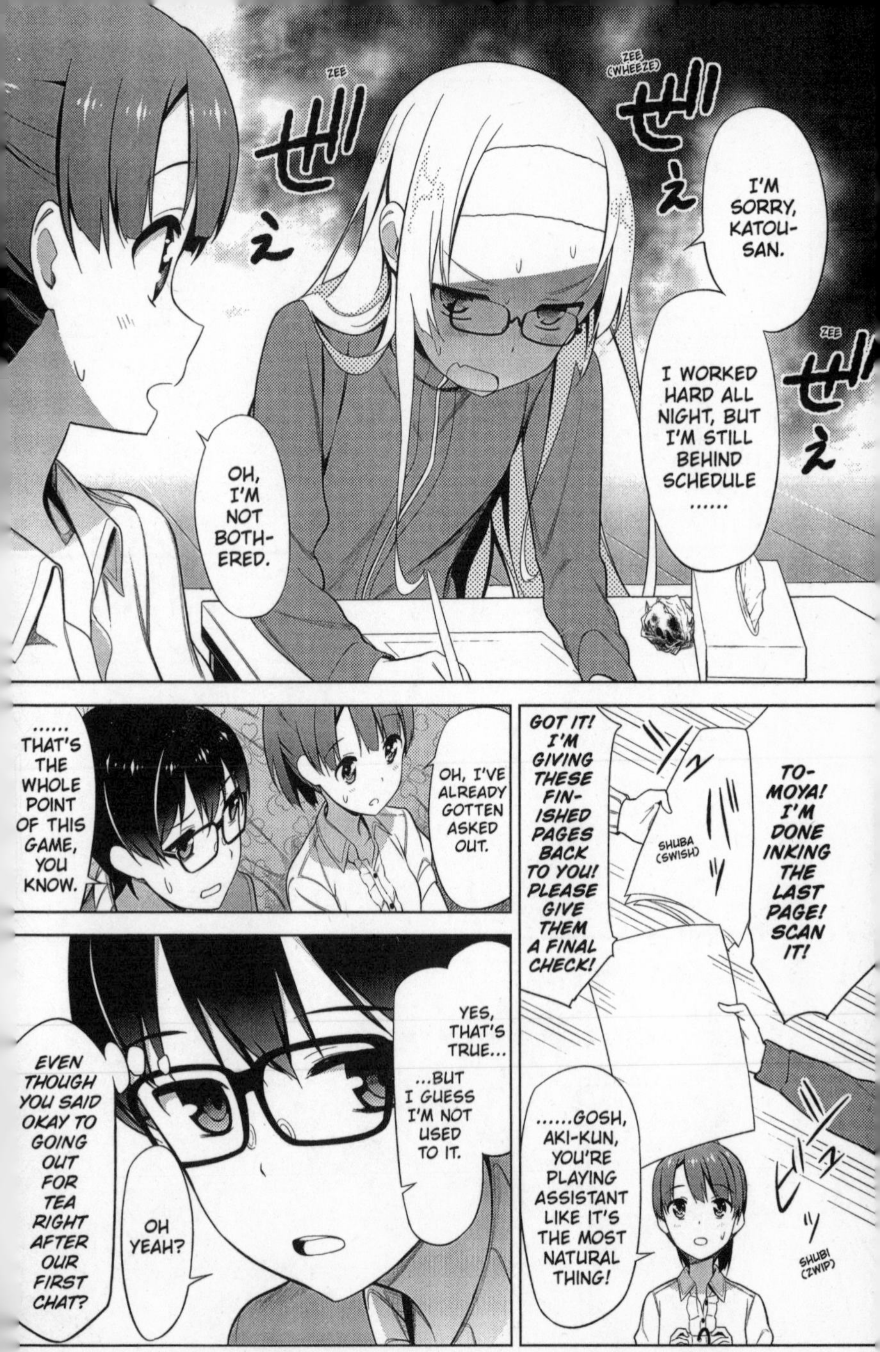
ZEE (WHEEZE)
ぜぇ
I'M SORRY, KATOU-SAN.
ZEE
ぜぇ
I WORKED HARD ALL NIGHT, BUT I'M STILL BEHIND SCHEDULE ......
ZEE
ぜぇ
OH, I'M NOT BOTHERED.
TO-MOYA! I'M DONE INKING THE LAST PAGE! SCAN IT!
SHUBA (SWISH)
GOT IT! I'M GIVING THESE FIN-ISHED PAGES BACK TO YOU! PLEASE GIVE THEM A FINAL CHECK!
SHUBI (ZWIP)
......GOSH, AKI-KUN, YOU'RE PLAYING ASSISTANT LIKE IT'S THE MOST NATURAL THING!
OH, I'VE ALREADY GOTTEN ASKED OUT.
...... THAT'S THE WHOLE POINT OF THIS GAME, YOU KNOW.
YES, THAT'S TRUE...
...BUT I GUESS I'M NOT USED TO IT.
OH YEAH?
EVEN THOUGH YOU SAID OKAY TO GOING OUT FOR TEA RIGHT AFTER OUR FIRST CHAT?

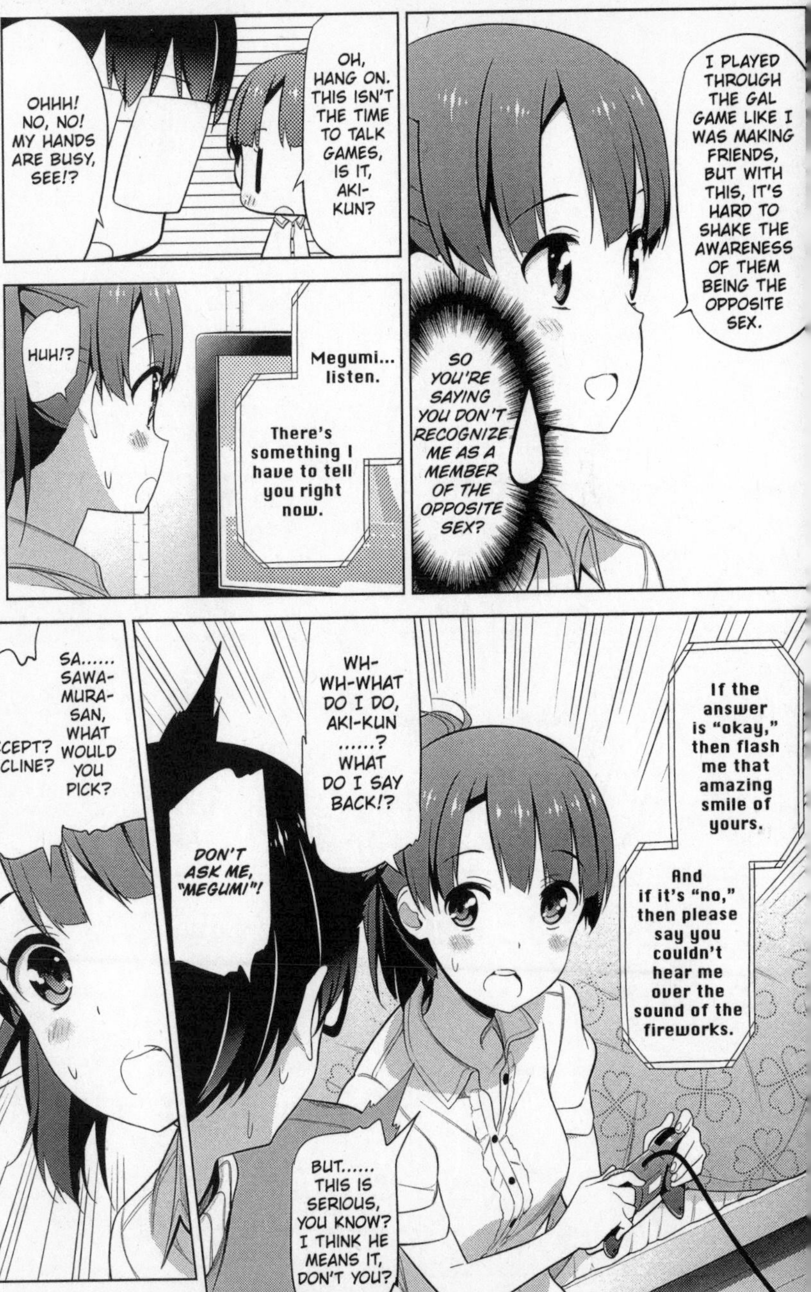
I PLAYED THROUGH THE GAL GAME LIKE I WAS MAKING FRIENDS, BUT WITH THIS, IT'S HARD TO SHAKE THE AWARENESS OF THEM BEING THE OPPOSITE SEX.
SO YOU'RE SAYING YOU DON'T RECOGNIZE ME AS A MEMBER OF THE OPPOSITE SEX?
OH, HANG ON. THIS ISN'T THE TIME TO TALK GAMES, IS IT, AKI-KUN?
OHHH! NO, NO! MY HANDS ARE BUSY, SEE!?
Megumi... listen.
There's something I have to tell you right now.
HUH!?
If the answer is "okay," then flash me that amazing smile of yours.
And if it's "no," then please say you couldn't hear me over the sound of the fireworks.
WH-WH-WHAT DO I DO, AKI-KUN ......? WHAT DO I SAY BACK!?
DON'T ASK ME, "MEGUMI"!
BUT...... THIS IS SERIOUS, YOU KNOW? I THINK HE MEANS IT, DON'T YOU?
SA...... SAWAMURA-SAN, WHAT WOULD YOU PICK?
ACCEPT? DECLINE?

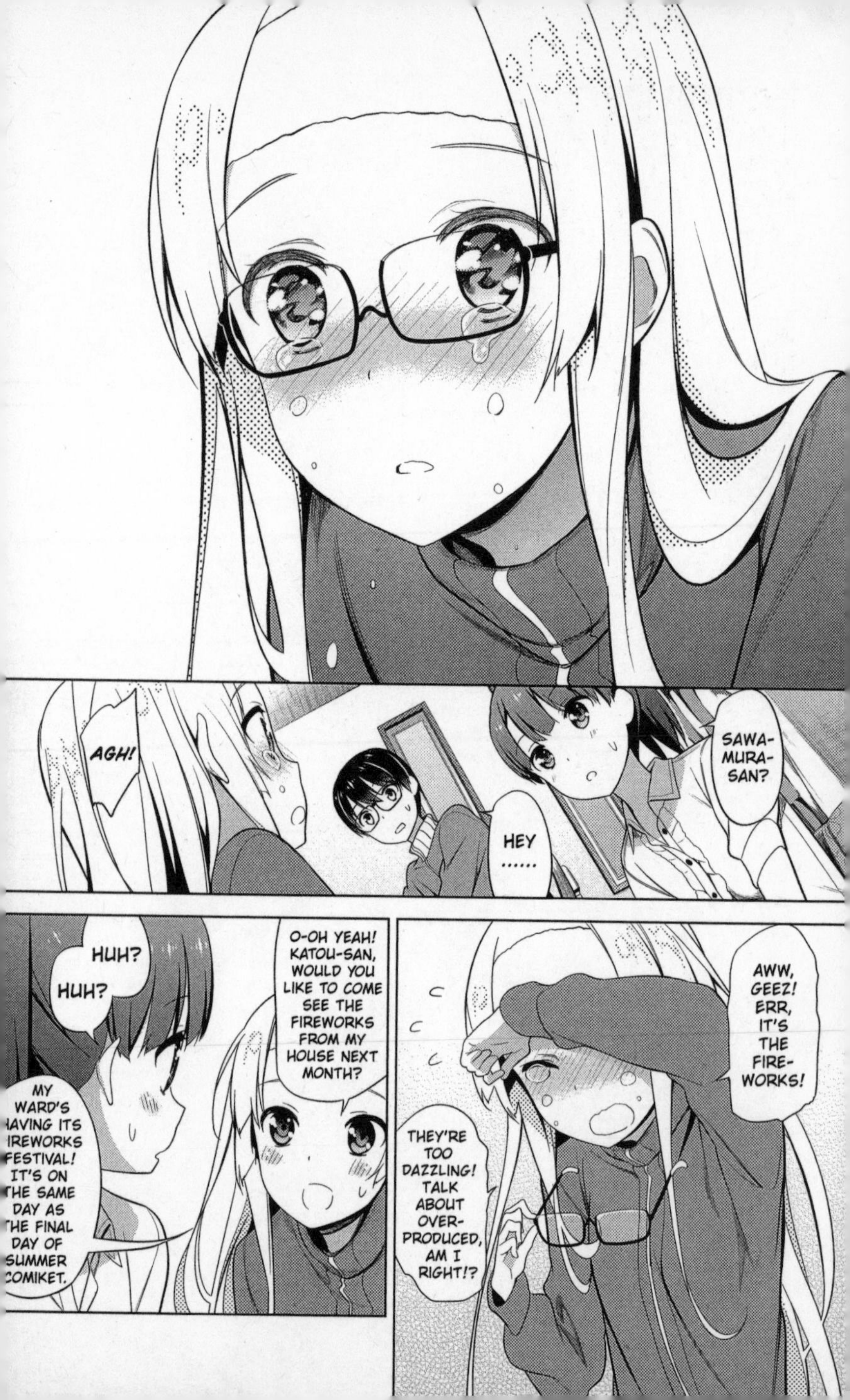
SAWA-MURA-SAN?
HEY ......
AGH!
AWW, GEEZ! ERR, IT'S THE FIRE-WORKS!
THEY'RE TOO DAZZLING! TALK ABOUT OVER-PRODUCED, AM I RIGHT!?
O-OH YEAH! KATOU-SAN, WOULD YOU LIKE TO COME SEE THE FIREWORKS FROM MY HOUSE NEXT MONTH?
HUH? HUH?
MY WARD'S AVING ITS IREWORKS FESTIVAL! IT'S ON HE SAME DAY AS THE FINAL HE FINAL DAY OF SUMMER COMIKET.

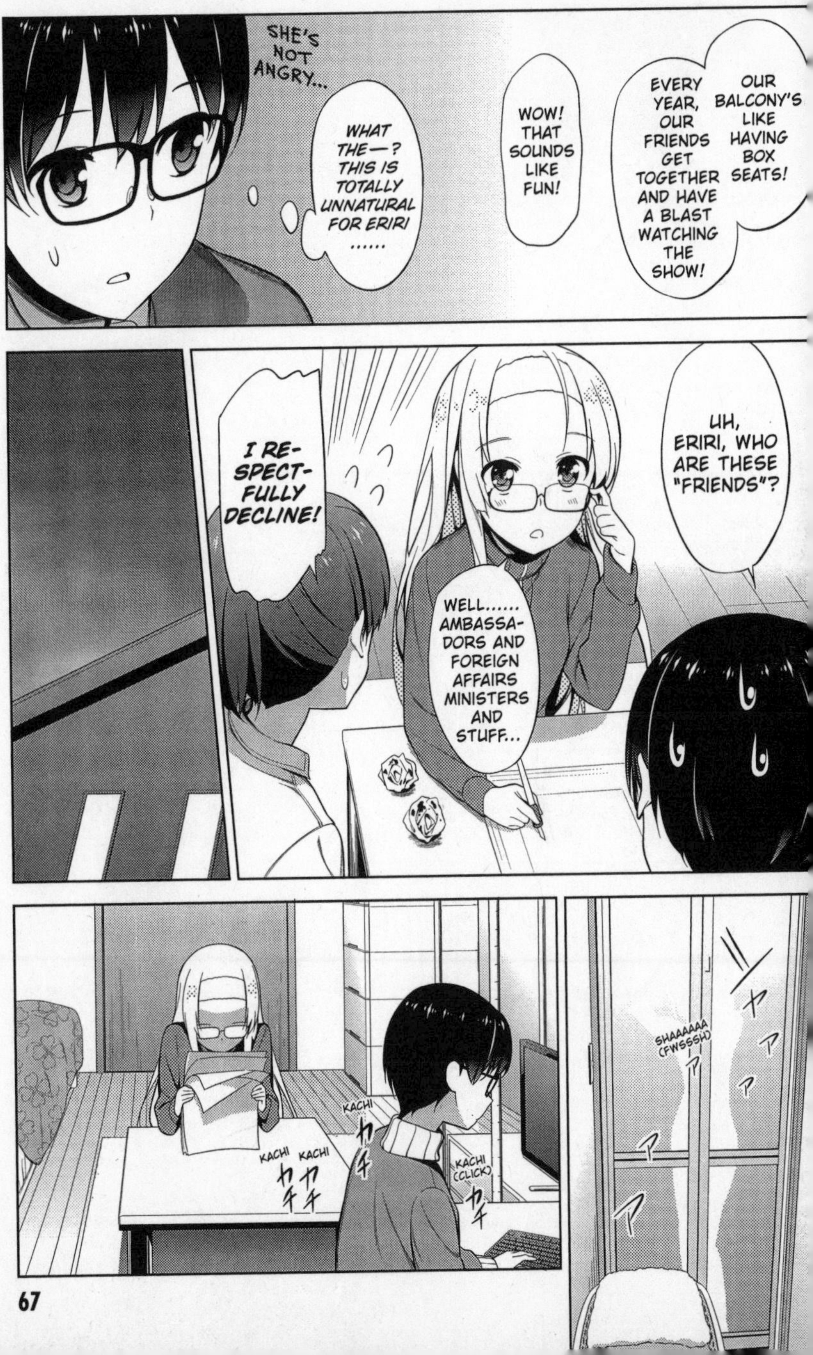
OUR BALCONY'S LIKE HAVING BOX SEATS!
EVERY YEAR, OUR FRIENDS GET TOGETHER AND HAVE A BLAST WATCHING THE SHOW!
WOW! THAT SOUNDS LIKE FUN!
WHAT THE—? THIS IS TOTALLY UNNATURAL FOR ERIRI ......
SHE'S NOT ANGRY...
UH, ERIRI, WHO ARE THESE "FRIENDS"?
WELL...... AMBASSADORS AND FOREIGN AFFAIRS MINISTERS AND STUFF...
I RE-SPECT-FULLY DECLINE!
SHAAAAAA (FWSSSH)
KACHI (CLICK)
KACHI
KACHI KACHI

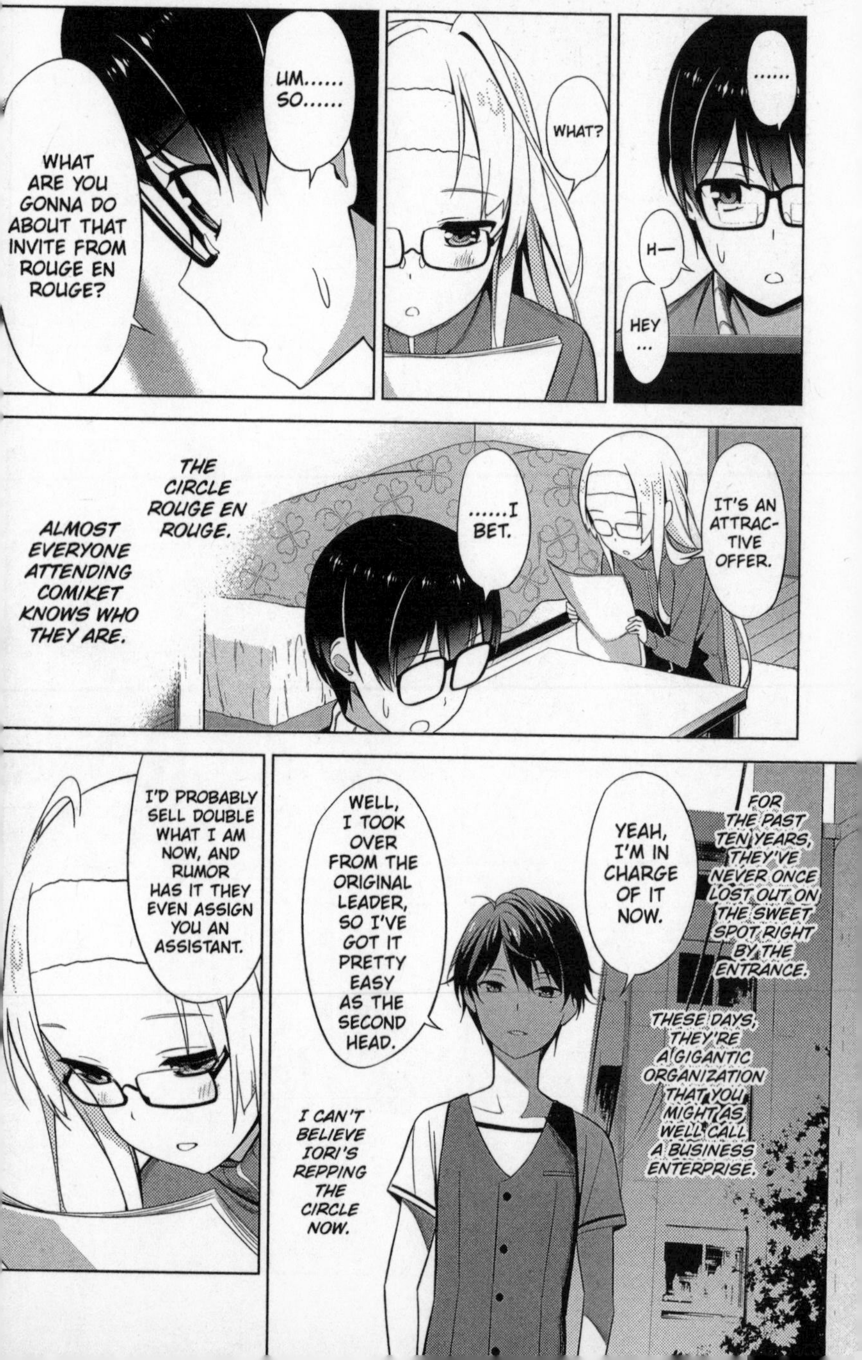
......
H—
HEY ...
WHAT?
UM...... SO......
WHAT ARE YOU GONNA DO ABOUT THAT INVITE FROM ROUGE EN ROUGE?
IT'S AN ATTRACTIVE OFFER.
......I BET.
THE CIRCLE ROUGE EN ROUGE.
ALMOST EVERYONE ATTENDING COMIKET KNOWS WHO THEY ARE.
FOR THE PAST TEN YEARS, THEY'VE NEVER ONCE LOST OUT ON THE SWEET SPOT RIGHT BY THE ENTRANCE.
YEAH, I'M IN CHARGE OF IT NOW.
WELL, I TOOK OVER FROM THE ORIGINAL LEADER, SO I'VE GOT IT PRETTY EASY AS THE SECOND HEAD.
THESE DAYS, THEY'RE A GIGANTIC ORGANIZATION THAT YOU MIGHT AS WELL CALL A BUSINESS ENTERPRISE.
I CAN'T BELIEVE IORI'S REPPING THE CIRCLE NOW.
I'D PROBABLY SELL DOUBLE WHAT I AM NOW, AND RUMOR HAS IT THEY EVEN ASSIGN YOU AN ASSISTANT.

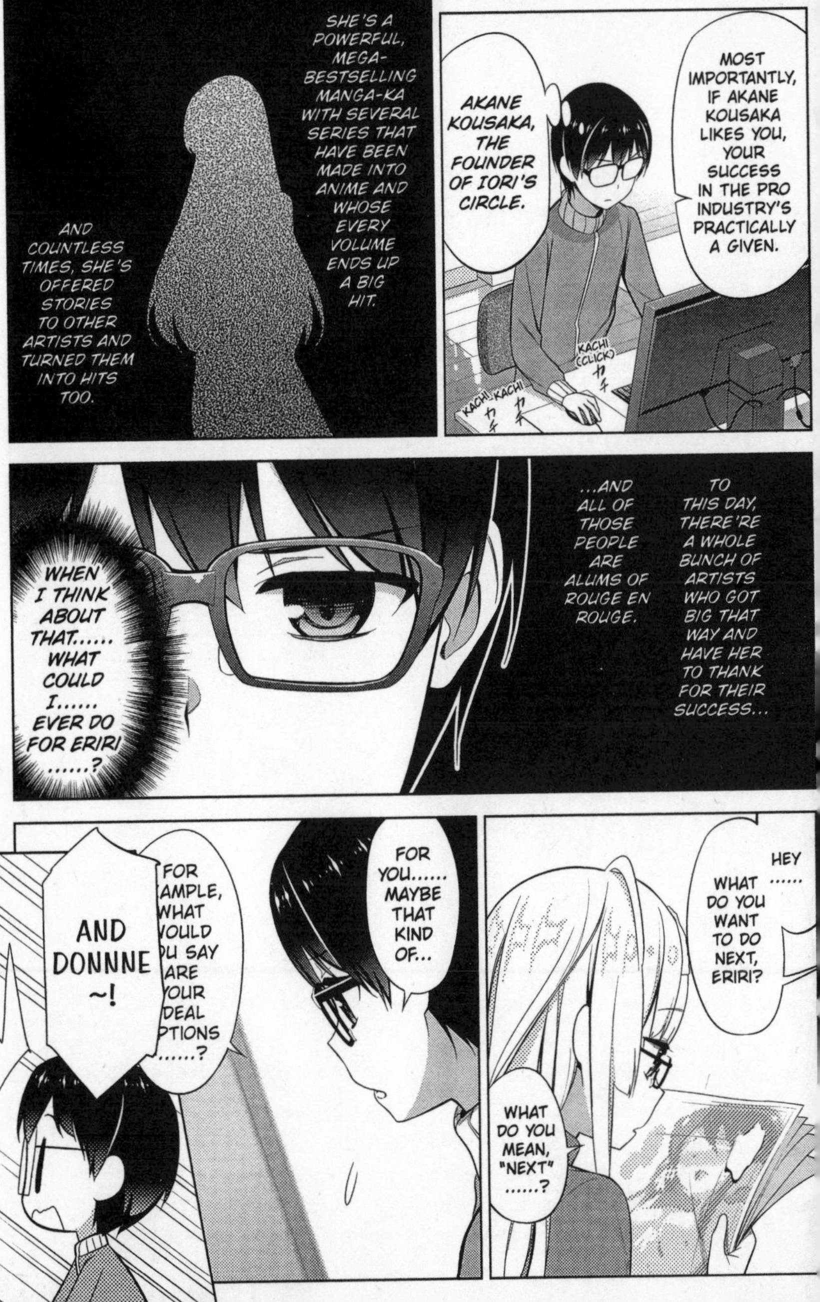
MOST IMPORTANTLY, IF AKANE KOUSAKA LIKES YOU, YOUR SUCCESS IN THE PRO INDUSTRY'S PRACTICALLY A GIVEN.
AKANE KOUSAKA, THE FOUNDER OF IORI'S CIRCLE.
KACHI (CLICK)
KACHI
KACHI
SHE'S A POWERFUL, MEGA-BESTSELLING MANGA-KA WITH SEVERAL SERIES THAT HAVE BEEN MADE INTO ANIME AND WHOSE EVERY VOLUME ENDS UP A BIG HIT.
AND COUNTLESS TIMES, SHE'S OFFERED STORIES TO OTHER ARTISTS AND TURNED THEM INTO HITS TOO.
TO THIS DAY, THERE'RE A WHOLE BUNCH OF ARTISTS WHO GOT BIG THAT WAY AND HAVE HER TO THANK FOR THEIR SUCCESS...
...AND ALL OF THOSE PEOPLE ARE ALUMS OF ROUGE EN ROUGE.
WHEN I THINK ABOUT THAT...... WHAT COULD I...... EVER DO FOR ERIRI ......?
HEY ......
WHAT DO YOU WANT TO DO NEXT, ERIRI?
WHAT DO YOU MEAN, "NEXT" ......?
FOR YOU...... MAYBE THAT KIND OF...
FOR AMPLE, WHAT VOULD U SAY ARE YOUR DEAL PTIONS ......?
AND DONNNE ~!

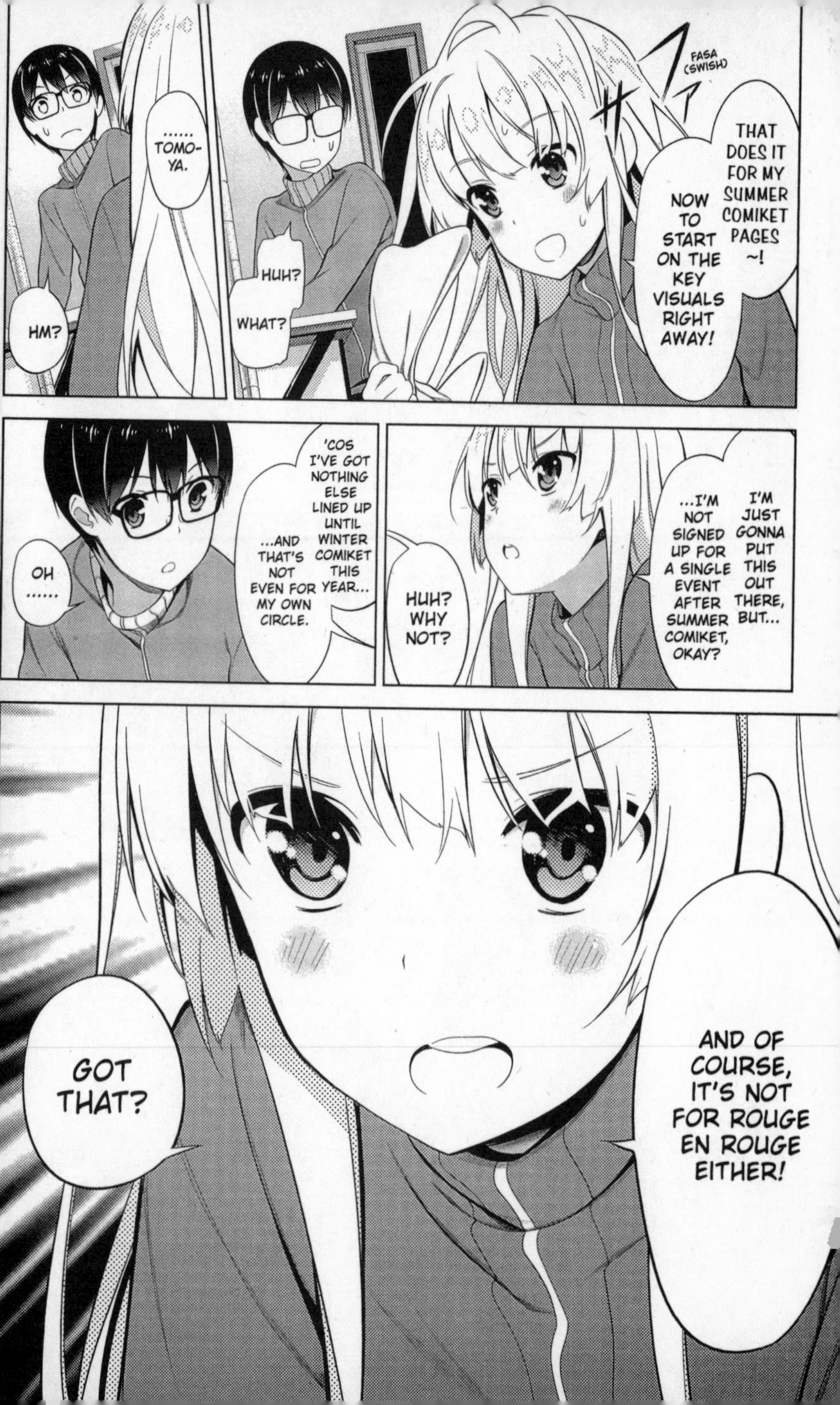
FASA (SWISH)
THAT DOES IT FOR MY SUMMER COMIKET PAGES ~!
NOW TO START ON THE KEY VISUALS RIGHT AWAY!
HUH?
WHAT?
...... TOMO-YA.
HM?
I'M JUST GONNA PUT THIS OUT THERE, BUT...
...I'M NOT SIGNED UP FOR A SINGLE EVENT AFTER SUMMER COMIKET, OKAY?
HUH? WHY NOT?
'COS I'VE GOT NOTHING ELSE LINED UP UNTIL WINTER COMIKET THIS YEAR...
...AND THAT'S NOT EVEN FOR MY OWN CIRCLE.
OH ......
AND OF COURSE, IT'S NOT FOR ROUGE EN ROUGE EITHER!
GOT THAT?

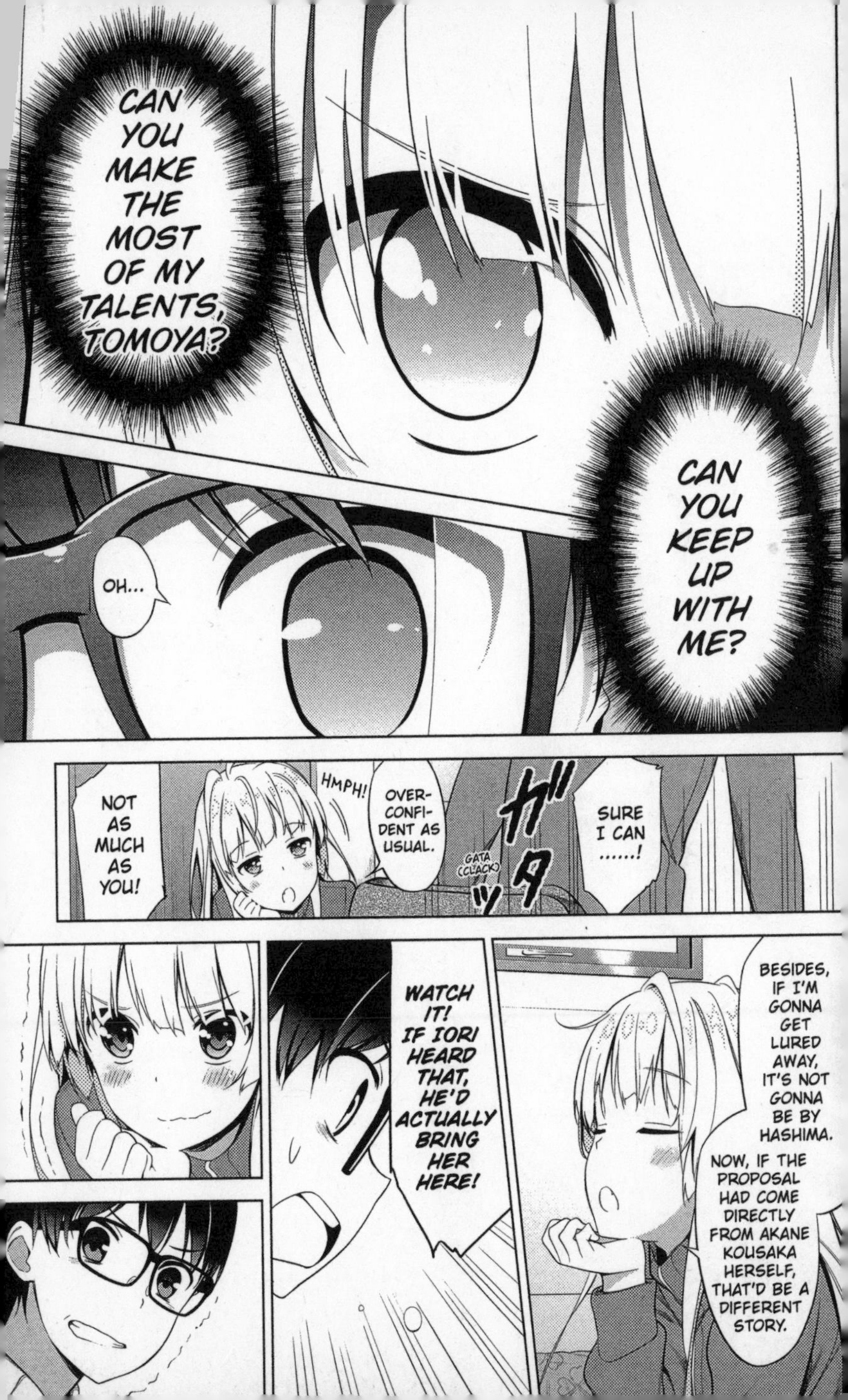
CAN YOU MAKE THE MOST OF MY TALENTS, TOMOYA?
CAN YOU KEEP UP WITH ME?
OH...
SURE I CAN ......!
GATA (CLACK)
OVER-CONFIDENT AS USUAL.
HMPH!
NOT AS MUCH AS YOU!
BESIDES, IF I'M GONNA GET LURED AWAY, IT'S NOT GONNA BE BY HASHIMA.
NOW, IF THE PROPOSAL HAD COME DIRECTLY FROM AKANE KOUSAKA HERSELF, THAT'D BE A DIFFERENT STORY.
WATCH IT! IF IORI HEARD THAT, HE'D ACTUALLY BRING HER HERE!

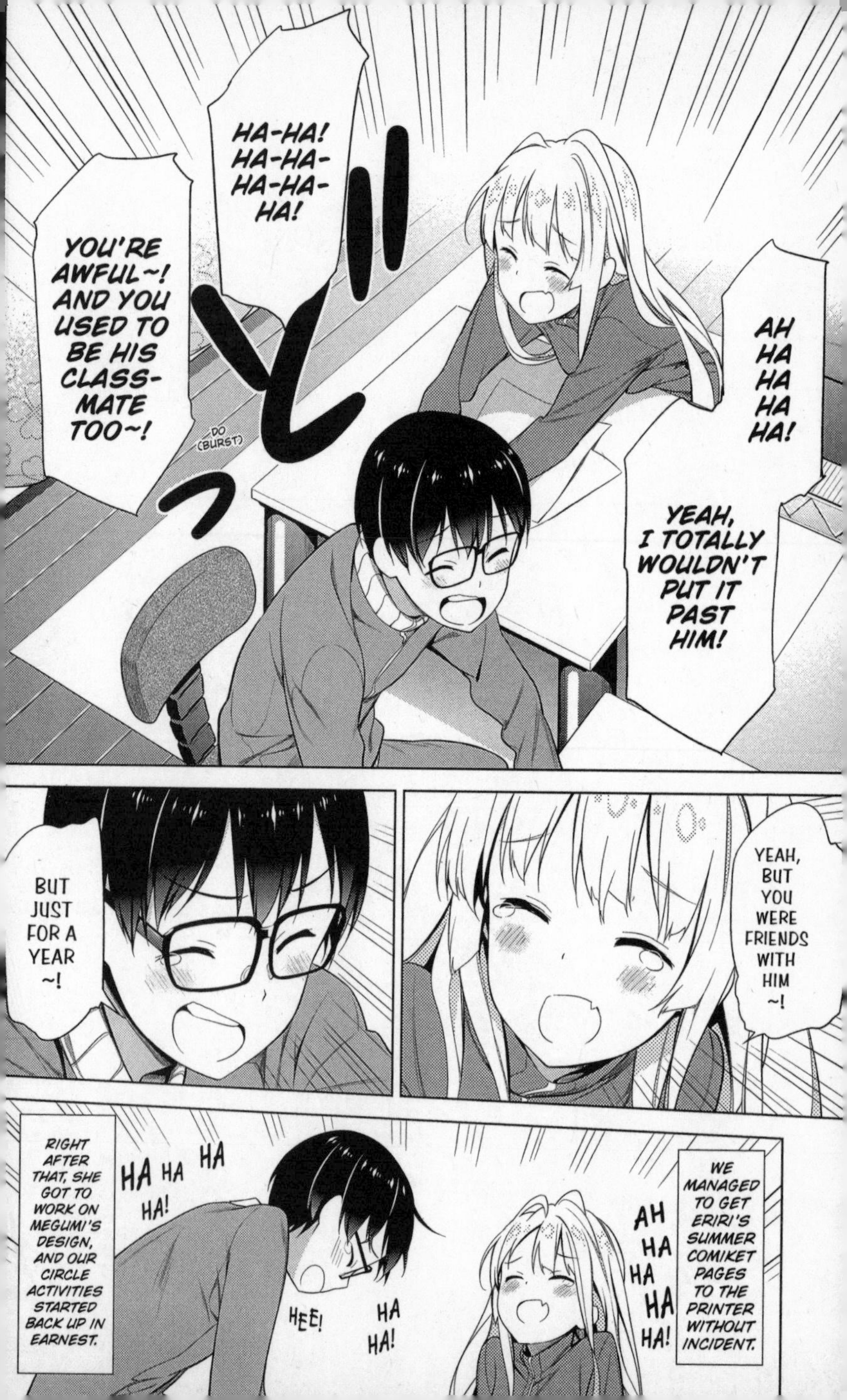
AH HA HA HA HA!
YEAH, I TOTALLY WOULDN'T PUT IT PAST HIM!
HA-HA! HA-HA-HA-HA-HA!
DO (BURST)
YOU'RE AWFUL~! AND YOU USED TO BE HIS CLASS-MATE TOO~!
YEAH, BUT YOU WERE FRIENDS WITH HIM ~!
BUT JUST FOR A YEAR ~!
WE MANAGED TO GET ERIRI'S SUMMER COMIKET PAGES TO THE PRINTER WITHOUT INCIDENT.
AH HA HA HA HA!
HA HA! HEE!
HA HA HA HA!
RIGHT AFTER THAT, SHE GOT TO WORK ON MEGUMI'S DESIGN, AND OUR CIRCLE ACTIVITIES STARTED BACK UP IN EARNEST.

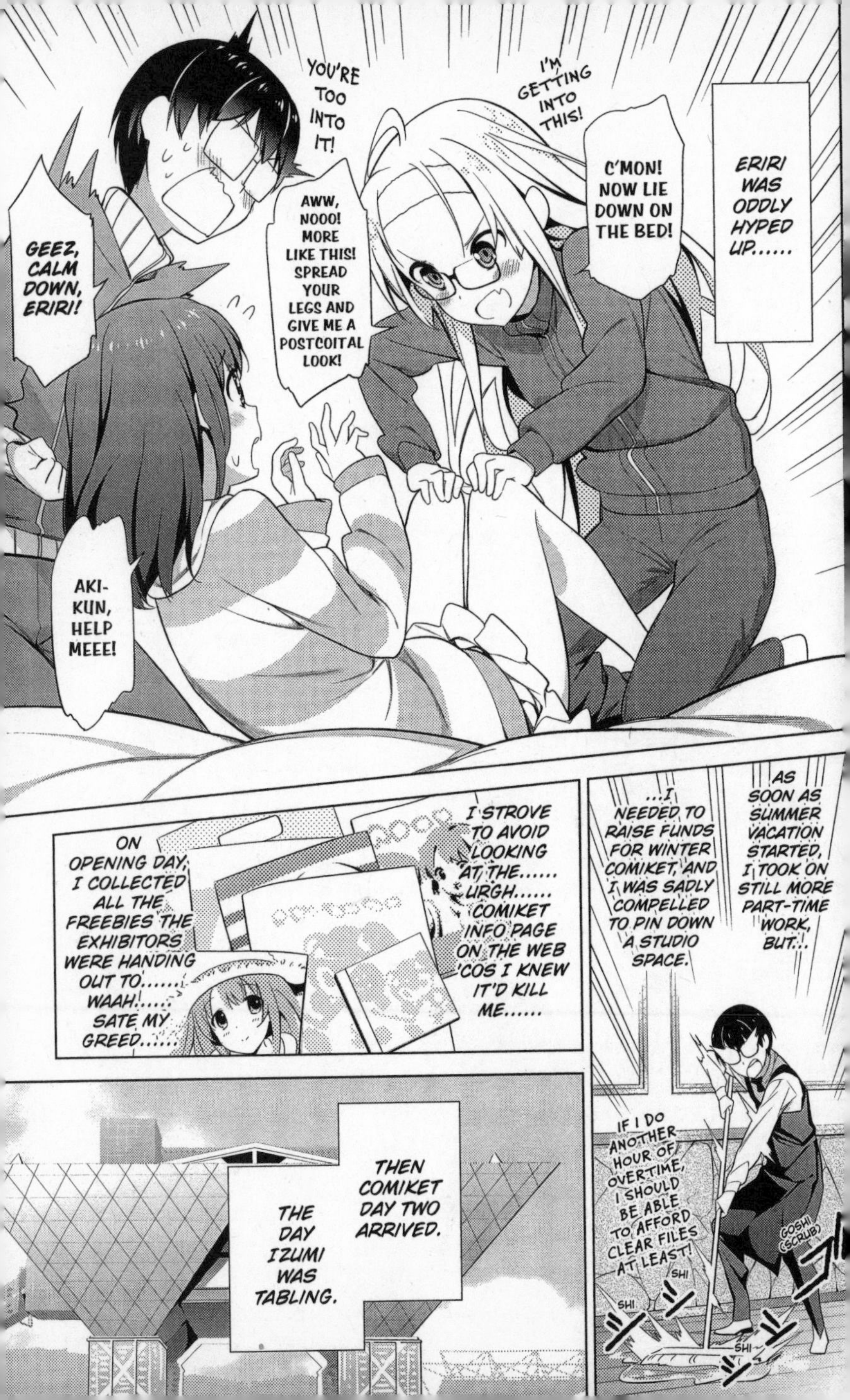
ERIRI WAS ODDLY HYPED UP......
I'M GETTING INTO THIS!
C'MON! NOW LIE DOWN ON THE BED!
YOU'RE TOO INTO IT!
AWW, NOOO! MORE LIKE THIS! SPREAD YOUR LEGS AND GIVE ME A POSTCOITAL LOOK!
GEEZ, CALM DOWN, ERIRI!
AKI-KUN, HELP MEEE!
AS SOON AS SUMMER VACATION STARTED, I TOOK ON STILL MORE PART-TIME WORK, BUT...
...I NEEDED TO RAISE FUNDS FOR WINTER COMIKET, AND I WAS SADLY COMPELLED TO PIN DOWN A STUDIO SPACE.
IF I DO ANOTHER HOUR OF OVERTIME, I SHOULD BE ABLE TO AFFORD CLEAR FILES AT LEAST!
GOSHI (SCRUB)
SHI
SHI
SHI
I STROVE TO AVOID LOOKING AT THE...... URGH...... COMIKET INFO PAGE ON THE WEB 'COS I KNEW IT'D KILL ME......
ON OPENING DAY, I COLLECTED ALL THE FREEBIES THE EXHIBITORS WERE HANDING OUT TO...... WAAH!...... SATE MY GREED......
THEN COMIKET DAY TWO ARRIVED.
THE DAY IZUMI WAS TABLING.

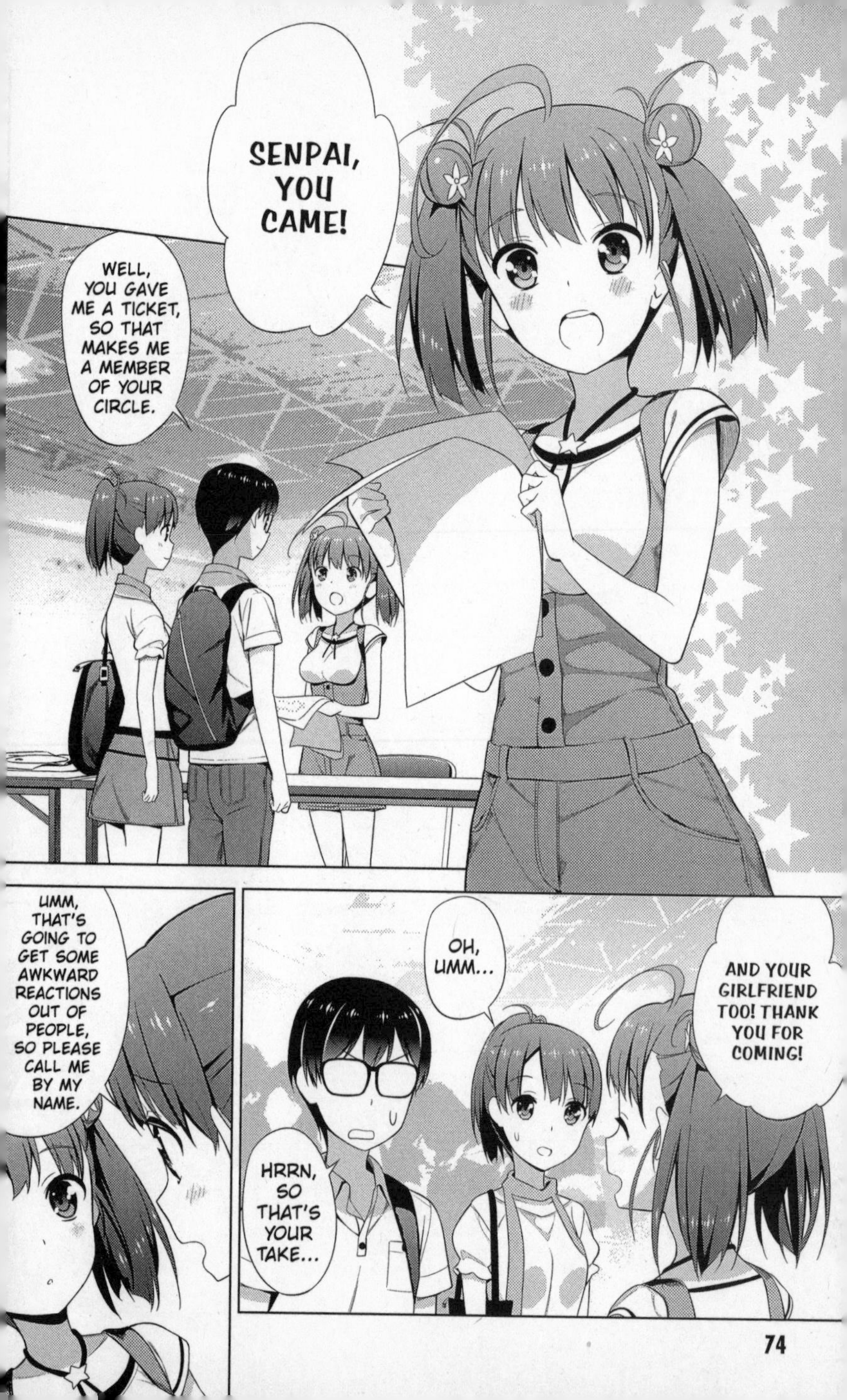
SENPAI, YOU CAME!
WELL, YOU GAVE ME A TICKET, SO THAT MAKES ME A MEMBER OF YOUR CIRCLE.
AND YOUR GIRLFRIEND TOO! THANK YOU FOR COMING!
OH, UMM...
HRRN, SO THAT'S YOUR TAKE...
UMM, THAT'S GOING TO GET SOME AWKWARD REACTIONS OUT OF PEOPLE, SO PLEASE CALL ME BY MY NAME.

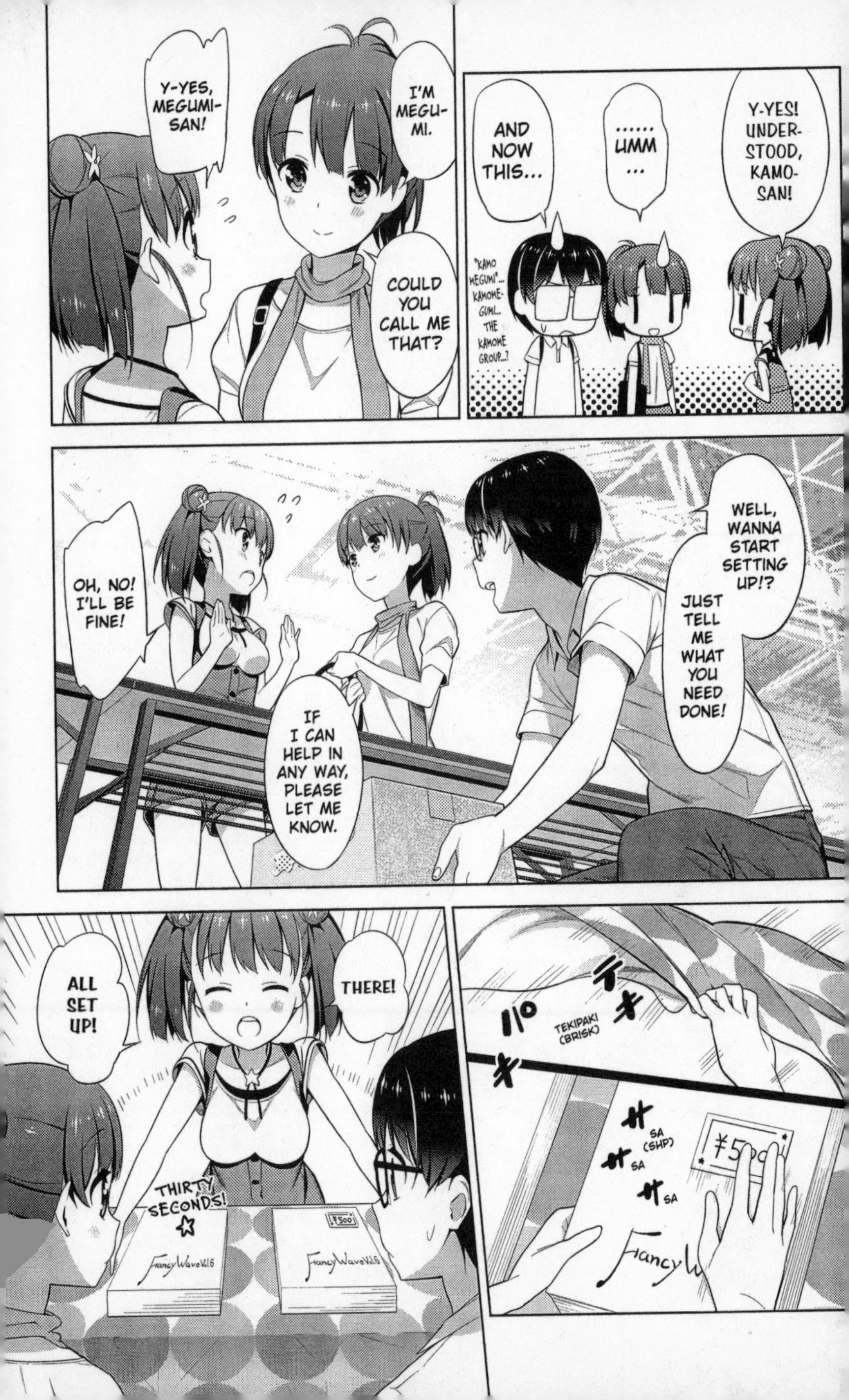
Y-YES! UNDERSTOOD, KAMO-SAN!
...... UMM ...
AND NOW THIS...
"KAMO MEGUMI"... KAMOME-GUMI... THE KAMOME GROUP...?
I'M MEGU-MI.
Y-YES, MEGUMI-SAN!
COULD YOU CALL ME THAT?
WELL, WANNA START SETTING UP!?
JUST TELL ME WHAT YOU NEED DONE!
IF I CAN HELP IN ANY WAY, PLEASE LET ME KNOW.
OH, NO! I'LL BE FINE!
TEKIPAKI (BRISK)
SA (SHP)
SA
SA
¥500
FancyW
THERE!
ALL SET UP!
THIRTY SECONDS!
¥500
FancyWave Vol.6
FancyWave Vol.6

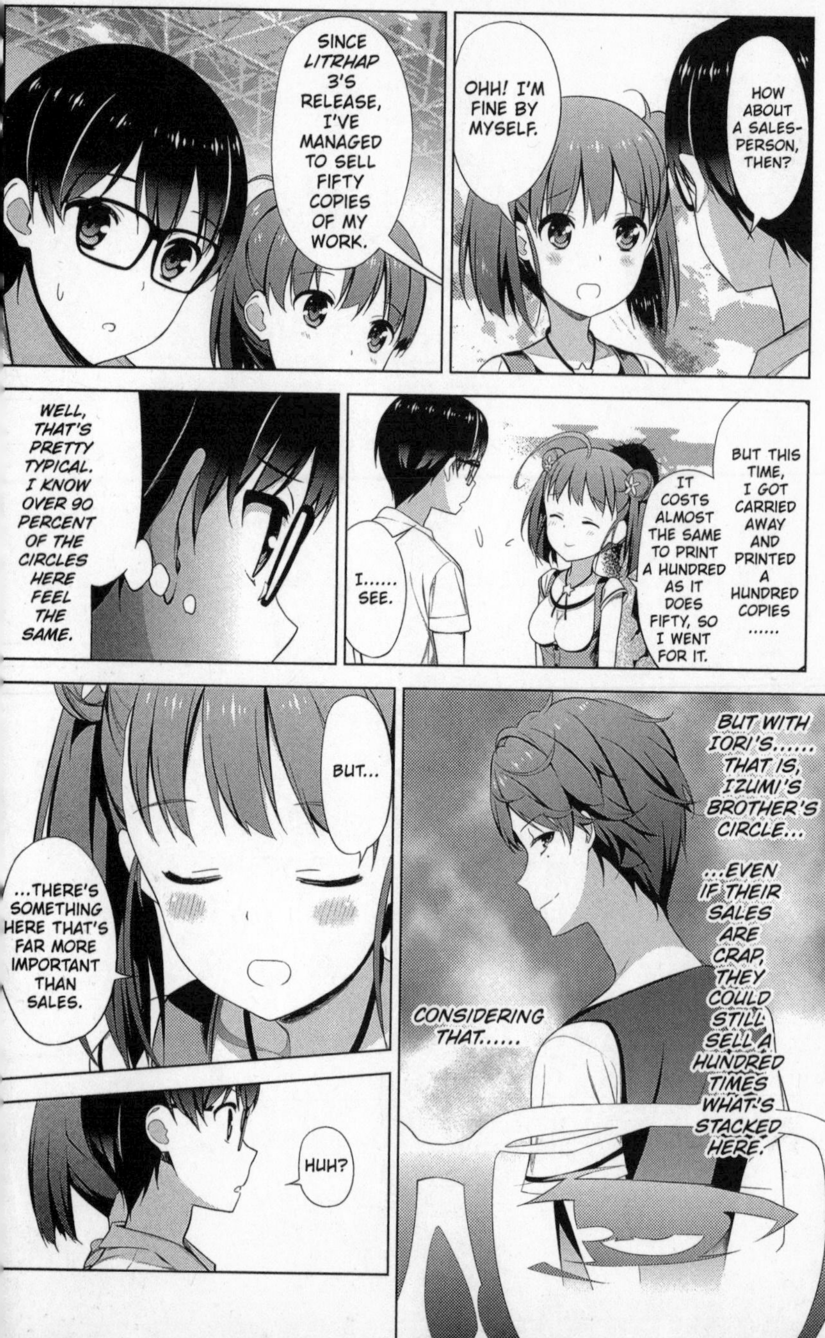
HOW ABOUT A SALES-PERSON, THEN?
OHH! I'M FINE BY MYSELF.
SINCE *LITRHAP* 3'S RELEASE, I'VE MANAGED TO SELL FIFTY COPIES OF MY WORK.
BUT THIS TIME, I GOT CARRIED AWAY AND PRINTED A HUNDRED COPIES......
IT COSTS ALMOST THE SAME TO PRINT A HUNDRED AS IT DOES FIFTY, SO I WENT FOR IT.
I...... SEE.
WELL, THAT'S PRETTY TYPICAL. I KNOW OVER 90 PERCENT OF THE CIRCLES HERE FEEL THE SAME.
BUT WITH IORI'S...... THAT IS, IZUMI'S BROTHER'S CIRCLE...
...EVEN IF THEIR SALES ARE CRAP, THEY COULD STILL SELL A HUNDRED TIMES WHAT'S STACKED HERE.
CONSIDERING THAT......
BUT...
...THERE'S SOMETHING HERE THAT'S FAR MORE IMPORTANT THAN SALES.
HUH?

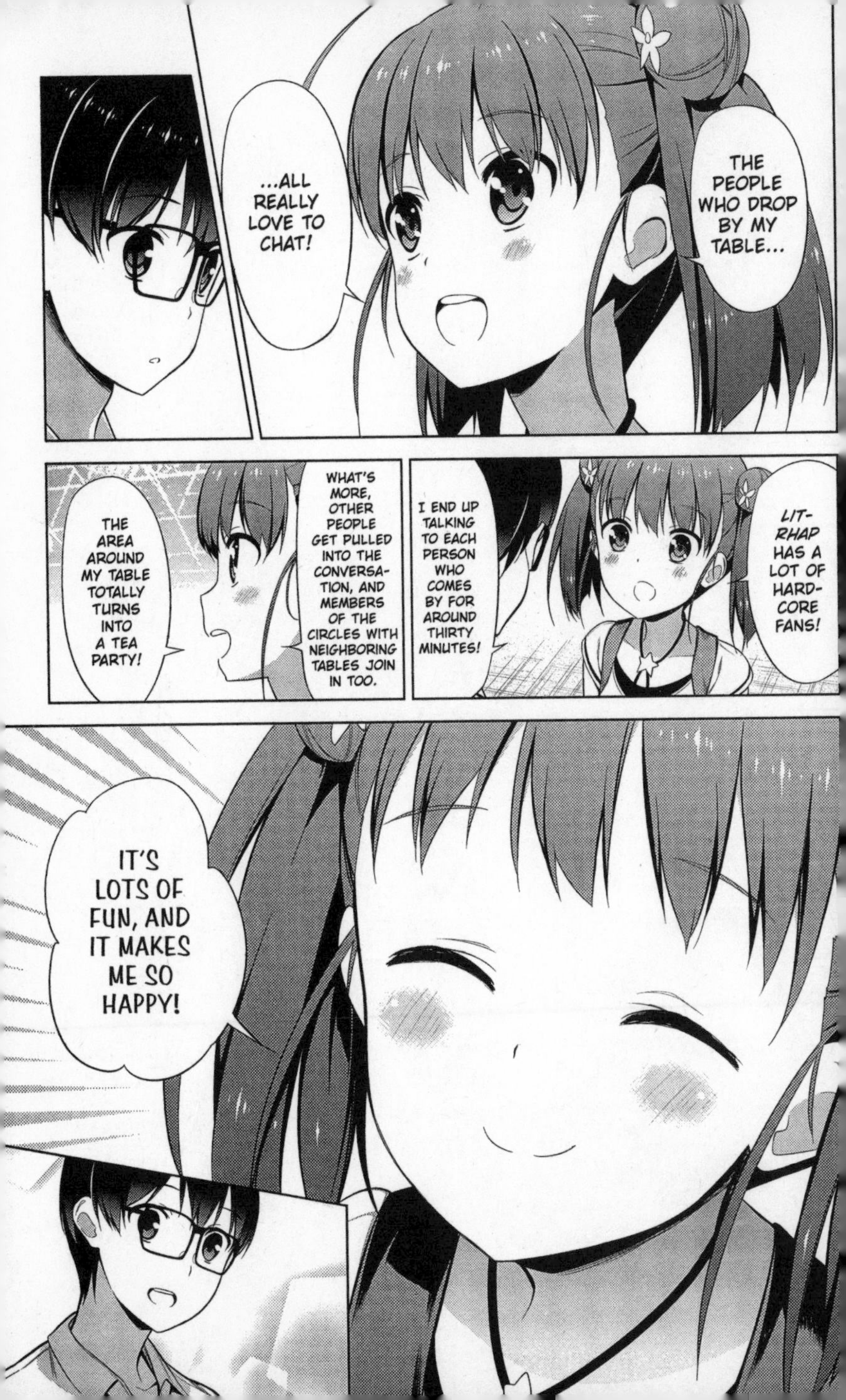
THE PEOPLE WHO DROP BY MY TABLE...
...ALL REALLY LOVE TO CHAT!
LIT-RHAP HAS A LOT OF HARD-CORE FANS!
I END UP TALKING TO EACH PERSON WHO COMES BY FOR AROUND THIRTY MINUTES!
WHAT'S MORE, OTHER PEOPLE GET PULLED INTO THE CONVERSA-TION, AND MEMBERS OF THE CIRCLES WITH NEIGHBORING TABLES JOIN IN TOO.
THE AREA AROUND MY TABLE TOTALLY TURNS INTO A TEA PARTY!
IT'S LOTS OF FUN, AND IT MAKES ME SO HAPPY!

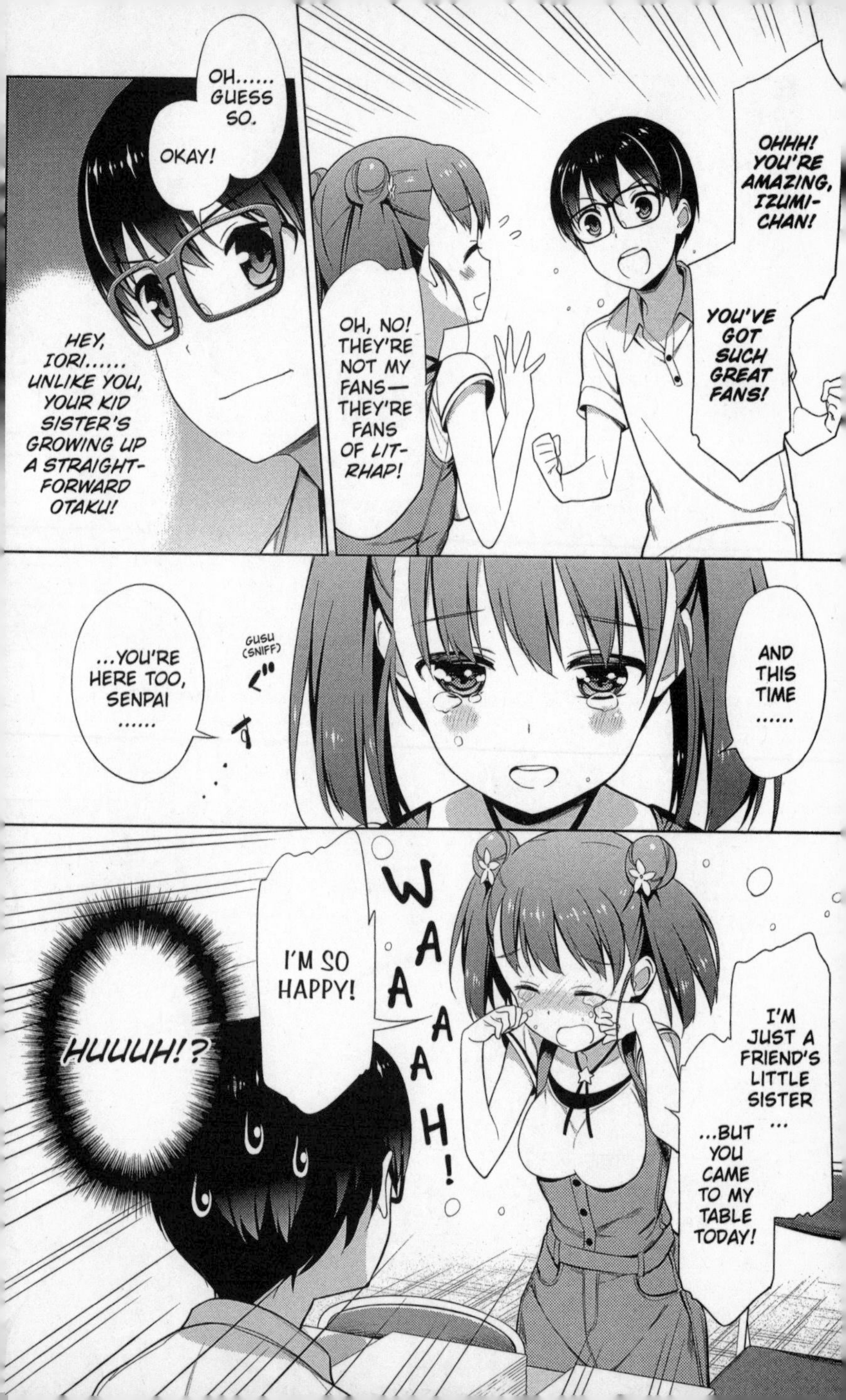
OHHH! YOU'RE AMAZING, IZUMI-CHAN!
YOU'VE GOT SUCH GREAT FANS!
OH, NO! THEY'RE NOT MY FANS— THEY'RE FANS OF LIT-RHAP!
OH...... GUESS SO.
OKAY!
HEY, IORI...... UNLIKE YOU, YOUR KID SISTER'S GROWING UP A STRAIGHT-FORWARD OTAKU!
AND THIS TIME ......
GUSU (SNIFF)
...YOU'RE HERE TOO, SENPAI ......
I'M JUST A FRIEND'S LITTLE SISTER ...
...BUT YOU CAME TO MY TABLE TODAY!
WAAAAH!
I'M SO HAPPY!
HUUUH!?

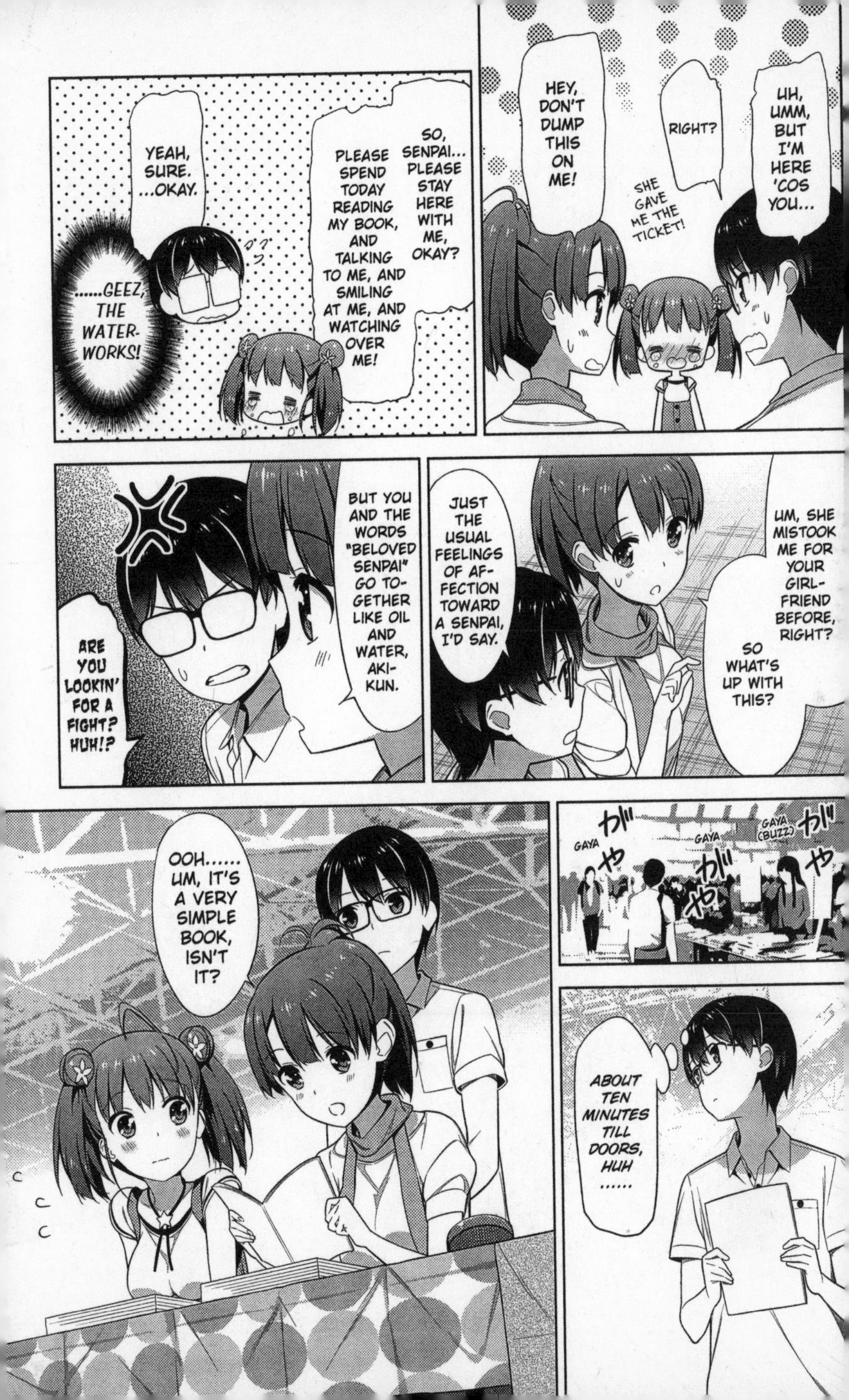
UH, UMM, BUT I'M HERE 'COS YOU...
RIGHT?
SHE GAVE ME THE TICKET!
HEY, DON'T DUMP THIS ON ME!
SO, SENPAI... PLEASE STAY HERE WITH ME, OKAY?
PLEASE SPEND TODAY READING MY BOOK, AND TALKING TO ME, AND SMILING AT ME, AND WATCHING OVER ME!
YEAH, SURE. ...OKAY.
......GEEZ, THE WATER-WORKS!
UM, SHE MISTOOK ME FOR YOUR GIRL-FRIEND BEFORE, RIGHT?
SO WHAT'S UP WITH THIS?
JUST THE USUAL FEELINGS OF AF-FECTION TOWARD A SENPAI, I'D SAY.
BUT YOU AND THE WORDS "BELOVED SENPAI" GO TO-GETHER LIKE OIL AND WATER, AKI-KUN.
ARE YOU LOOKIN' FOR A FIGHT? HUH!?
GAYA (BUZZ) ガヤ
GAYA ガヤ
GAYA ガヤ
ABOUT TEN MINUTES TILL DOORS, HUH ......
OOH...... UM, IT'S A VERY SIMPLE BOOK, ISN'T IT?

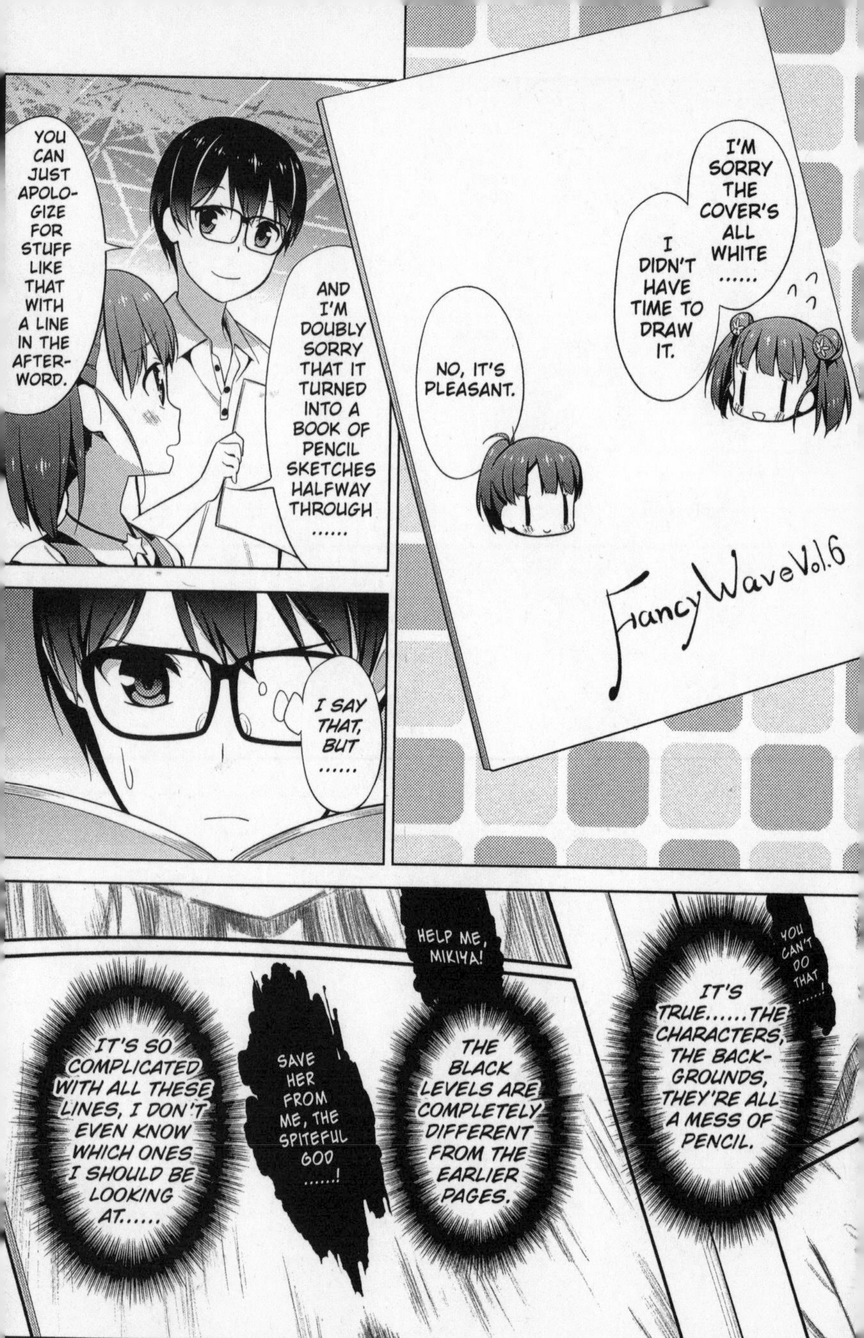
I'M SORRY THE COVER'S ALL WHITE......
I DIDN'T HAVE TIME TO DRAW IT.
NO, IT'S PLEASANT.
FancyWave Vol.6
AND I'M DOUBLY SORRY THAT IT TURNED INTO A BOOK OF PENCIL SKETCHES HALFWAY THROUGH......
YOU CAN JUST APOLOGIZE FOR STUFF LIKE THAT WITH A LINE IN THE AFTERWORD.
I SAY THAT, BUT......
YOU CAN'T DO THAT......!
IT'S TRUE......THE CHARACTERS, THE BACKGROUNDS, THEY'RE ALL A MESS OF PENCIL.
HELP ME, MIKIYA!
THE BLACK LEVELS ARE COMPLETELY DIFFERENT FROM THE EARLIER PAGES.
SAVE HER FROM ME, THE SPITEFUL GOD......!
IT'S SO COMPLICATED WITH ALL THESE LINES, I DON'T EVEN KNOW WHICH ONES I SHOULD BE LOOKING AT......

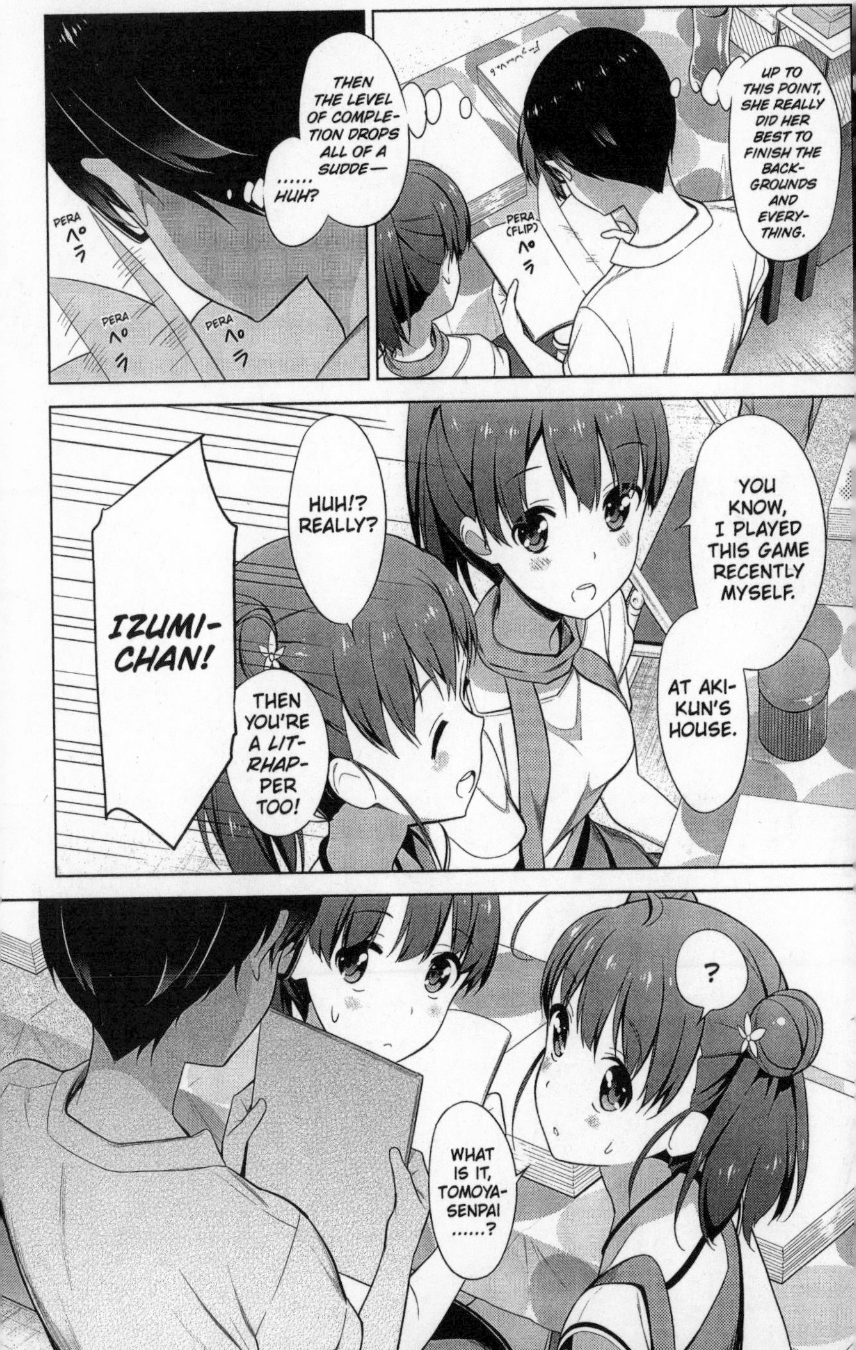

UP TO THIS POINT, SHE REALLY DID HER BEST TO FINISH THE BACK-GROUNDS AND EVERY-THING.
PERA (FLIP) ぺら
THEN THE LEVEL OF COMPLE-TION DROPS ALL OF A SUDDE—
...... HUH?
PERA ぺら
PERA ぺら
PERA ぺら
YOU KNOW, I PLAYED THIS GAME RECENTLY MYSELF.
AT AKI-KUN'S HOUSE.
HUH!? REALLY?
THEN YOU'RE A LIT-RHAP-PER TOO!
IZUMI-CHAN!
?
WHAT IS IT, TOMOYA-SENPAI ......?

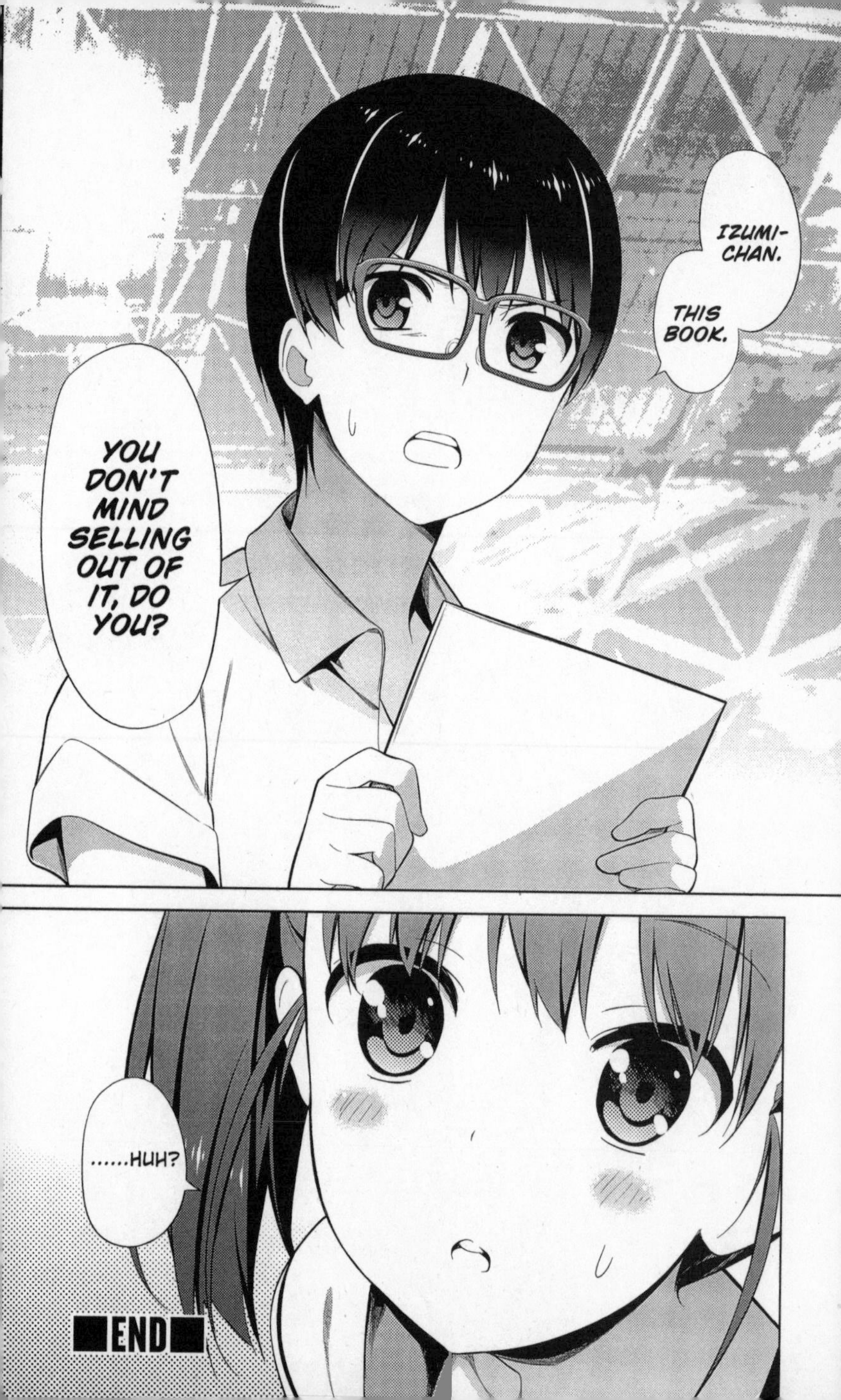
IZUMI-CHAN.
THIS BOOK.
YOU DON'T MIND SELLING OUT OF IT, DO YOU?
......HUH?
END

# CHAPTER 14

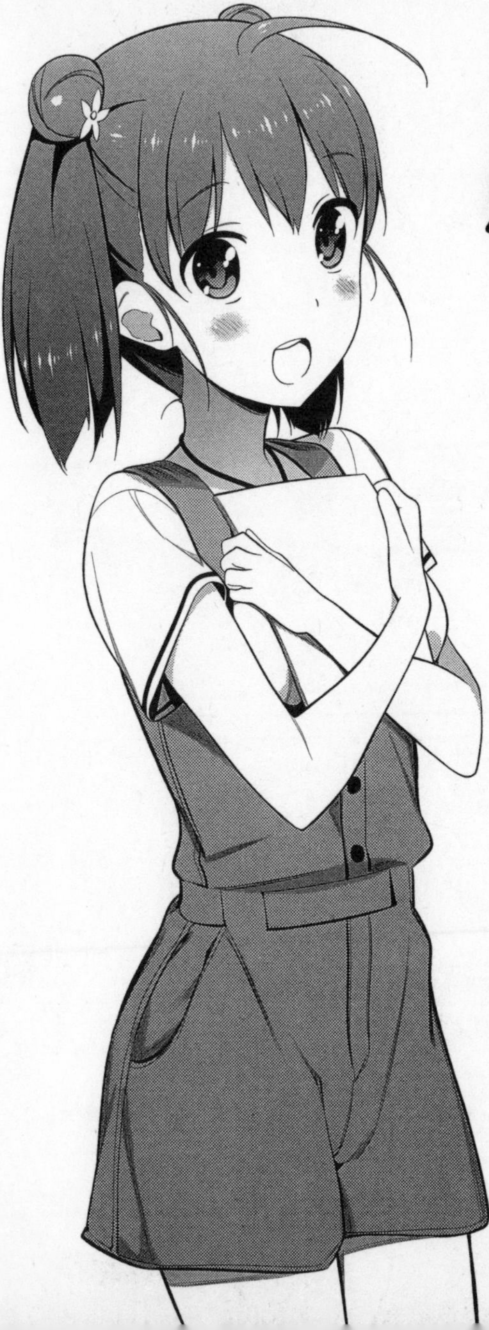

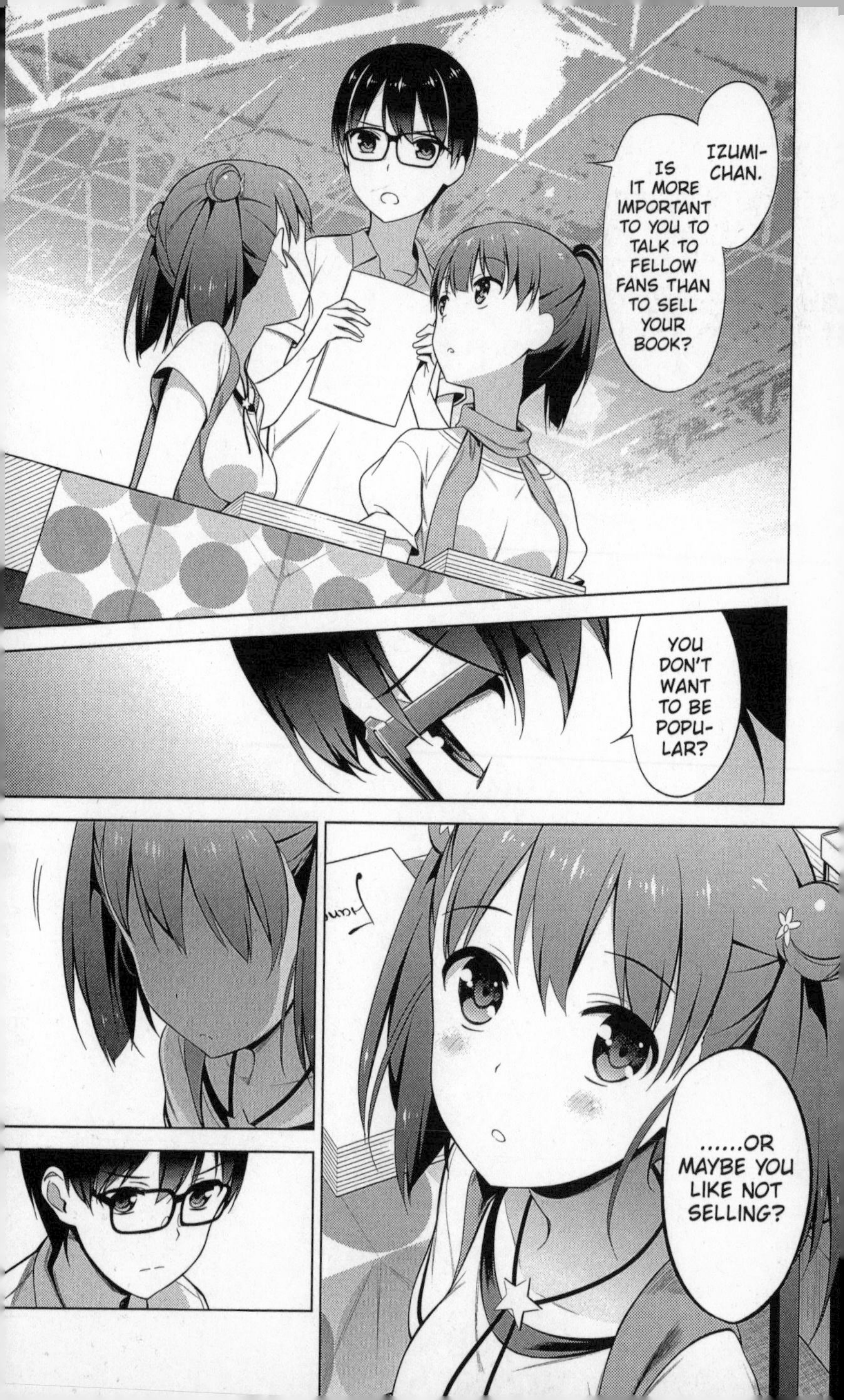
IZUMI-CHAN. IS IT MORE IMPORTANT TO YOU TO TALK TO FELLOW FANS THAN TO SELL YOUR BOOK?
YOU DON'T WANT TO BE POPU-LAR?
......OR MAYBE YOU LIKE NOT SELLING?

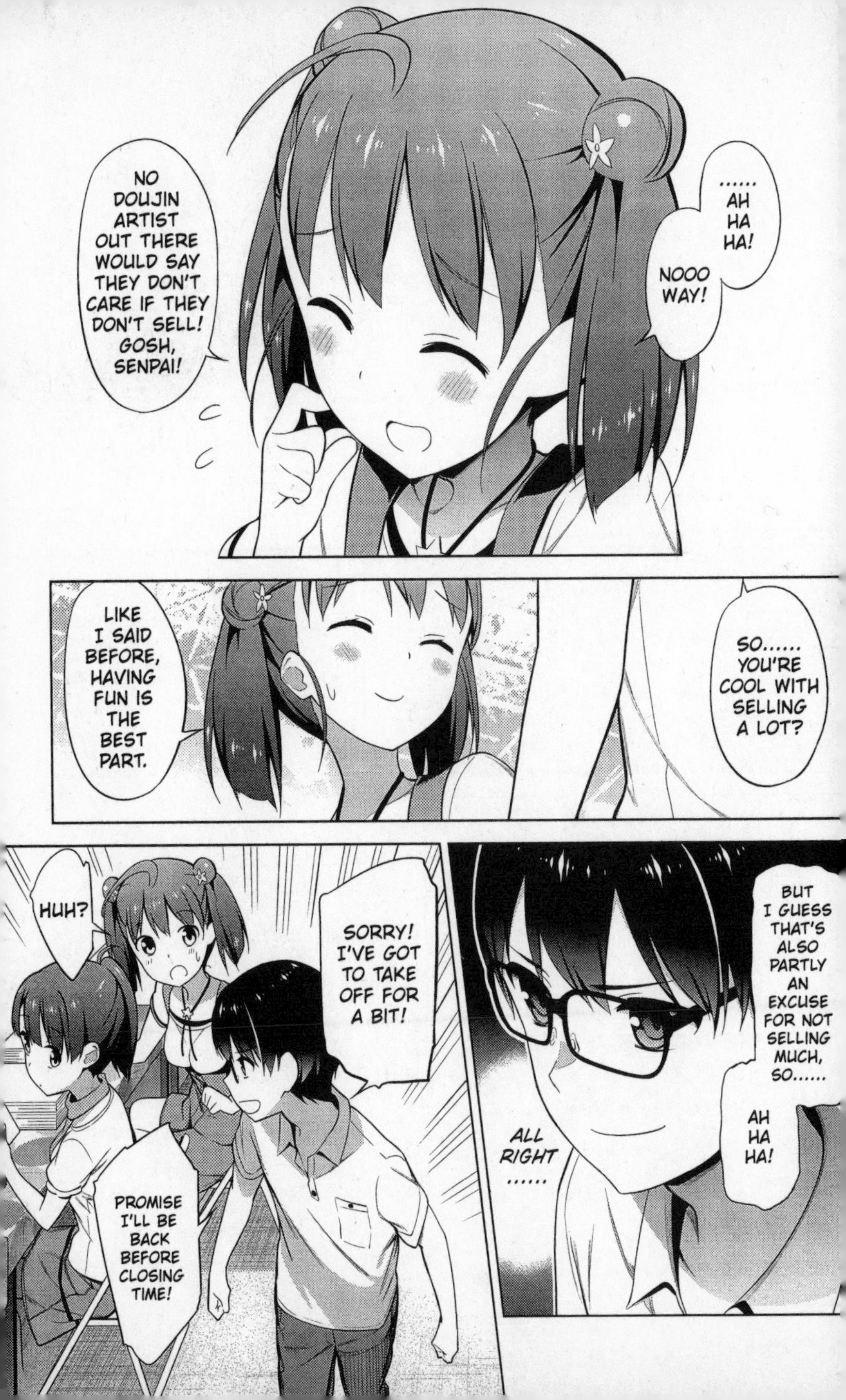
...... AH HA HA! NOOO WAY!
NO DOUJIN ARTIST OUT THERE WOULD SAY THEY DON'T CARE IF THEY DON'T SELL! GOSH, SENPAI!
SO...... YOU'RE COOL WITH SELLING A LOT?
LIKE I SAID BEFORE, HAVING FUN IS THE BEST PART.
BUT I GUESS THAT'S ALSO PARTLY AN EXCUSE FOR NOT SELLING MUCH, SO......
AH HA HA!
ALL RIGHT ......
SORRY! I'VE GOT TO TAKE OFF FOR A BIT!
HUH?
PROMISE I'LL BE BACK BEFORE CLOSING TIME!

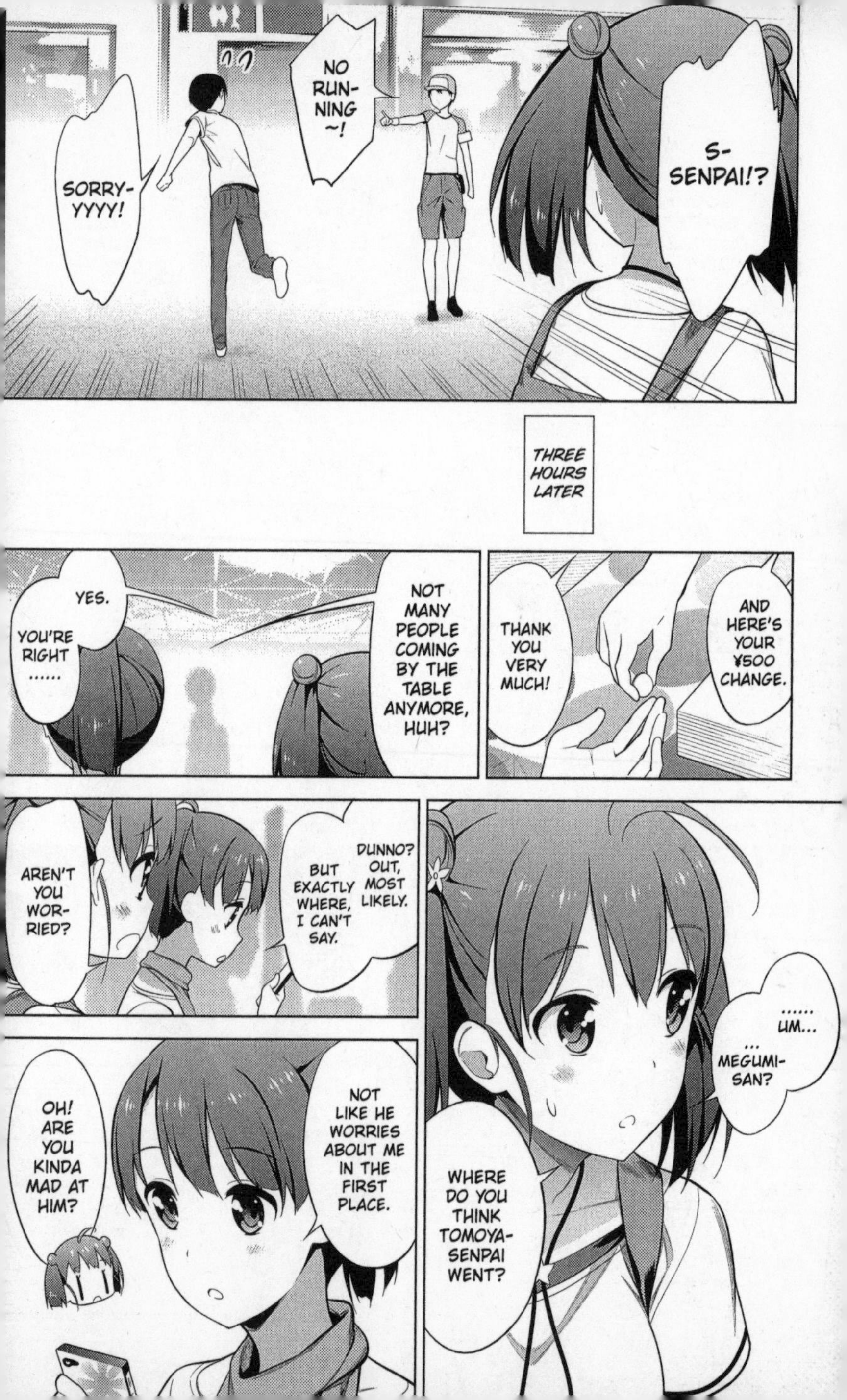
S-SENPAI!?
NO RUNNING~!
SORRY-YYYY!
THREE HOURS LATER
AND HERE'S YOUR ¥500 CHANGE.
THANK YOU VERY MUCH!
NOT MANY PEOPLE COMING BY THE TABLE ANYMORE, HUH?
YES. YOU'RE RIGHT ......
...... UM... ... MEGUMI-SAN?
WHERE DO YOU THINK TOMOYA-SENPAI WENT?
DUNNO? OUT, MOST LIKELY.
BUT EXACTLY WHERE, I CAN'T SAY.
AREN'T YOU WORRIED?
NOT LIKE HE WORRIES ABOUT ME IN THE FIRST PLACE.
OH! ARE YOU KINDA MAD AT HIM?

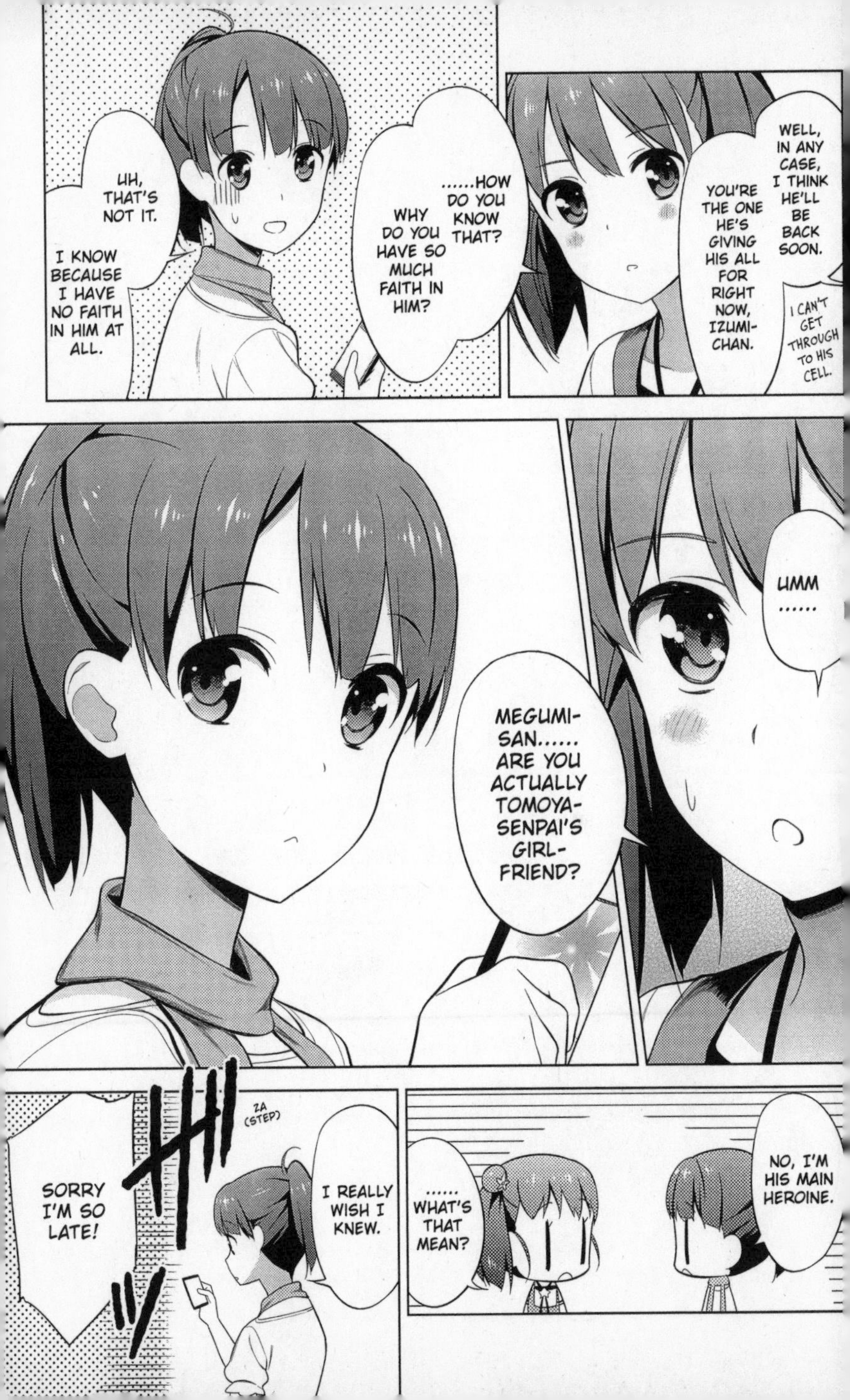
WELL, IN ANY CASE, I THINK HE'LL BE BACK SOON.
I CAN'T GET THROUGH TO HIS CELL.
YOU'RE THE ONE HE'S GIVING HIS ALL FOR RIGHT NOW, IZUMI-CHAN.
......HOW DO YOU KNOW THAT?
WHY DO YOU HAVE SO MUCH FAITH IN HIM?
UH, THAT'S NOT IT.
I KNOW BECAUSE I HAVE NO FAITH IN HIM AT ALL.
UMM......
MEGUMI-SAN...... ARE YOU ACTUALLY TOMOYA-SENPAI'S GIRLFRIEND?
NO, I'M HIS MAIN HEROINE.
......WHAT'S THAT MEAN?
I REALLY WISH I KNEW.
ZA (STEP)
SORRY I'M SO LATE!

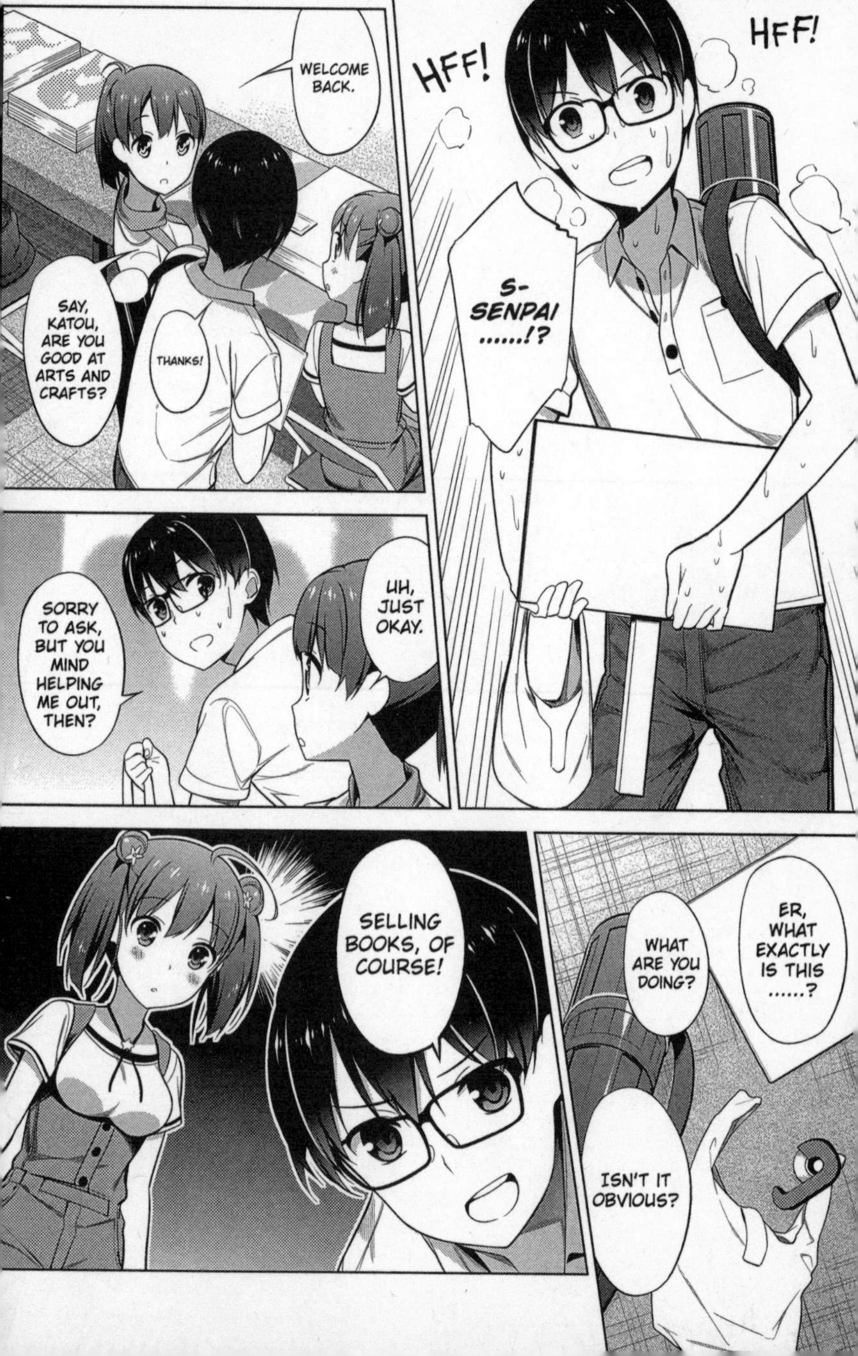
HFF!
HFF!
S-SENPAI ......!?
WELCOME BACK.
THANKS!
SAY, KATOU, ARE YOU GOOD AT ARTS AND CRAFTS?
UH, JUST OKAY.
SORRY TO ASK, BUT YOU MIND HELPING ME OUT, THEN?
ER, WHAT EXACTLY IS THIS ......?
WHAT ARE YOU DOING?
ISN'T IT OBVIOUS?
SELLING BOOKS, OF COURSE!

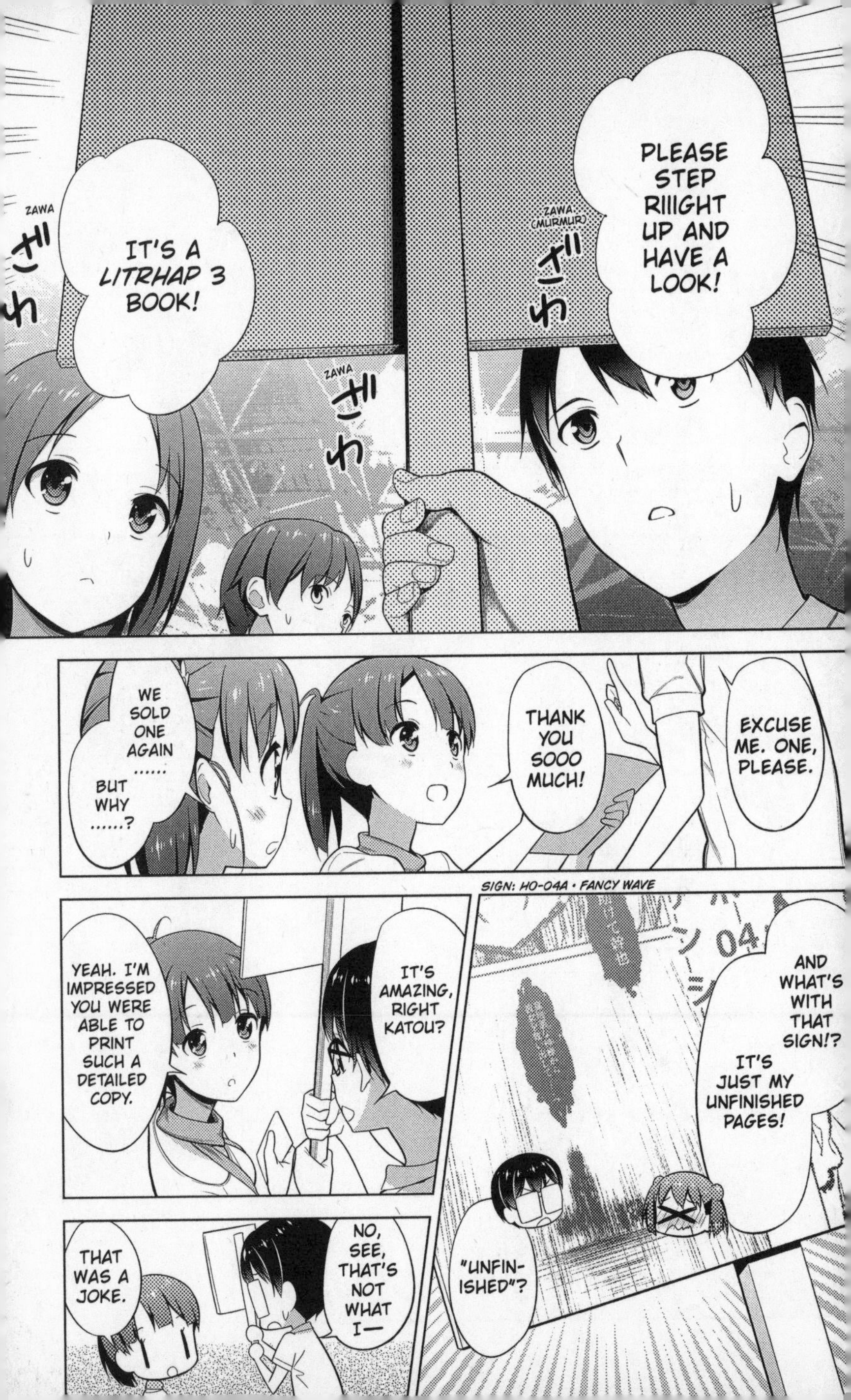
PLEASE STEP RIIIGHT UP AND HAVE A LOOK!
ZAWA (MURMUR)
ざわ
ZAWA
ざわ
IT'S A *LITRHAP 3* BOOK!
ZAWA
ざわ
EXCUSE ME. ONE, PLEASE.
THANK YOU SOOO MUCH!
WE SOLD ONE AGAIN...... BUT WHY......?
SIGN: HO-04A • FANCY WAVE
AND WHAT'S WITH THAT SIGN!?
IT'S JUST MY UNFINISHED PAGES!
"UNFINISHED"?
IT'S AMAZING, RIGHT KATOU?
YEAH. I'M IMPRESSED YOU WERE ABLE TO PRINT SUCH A DETAILED COPY.
NO, SEE, THAT'S NOT WHAT I—
THAT WAS A JOKE.

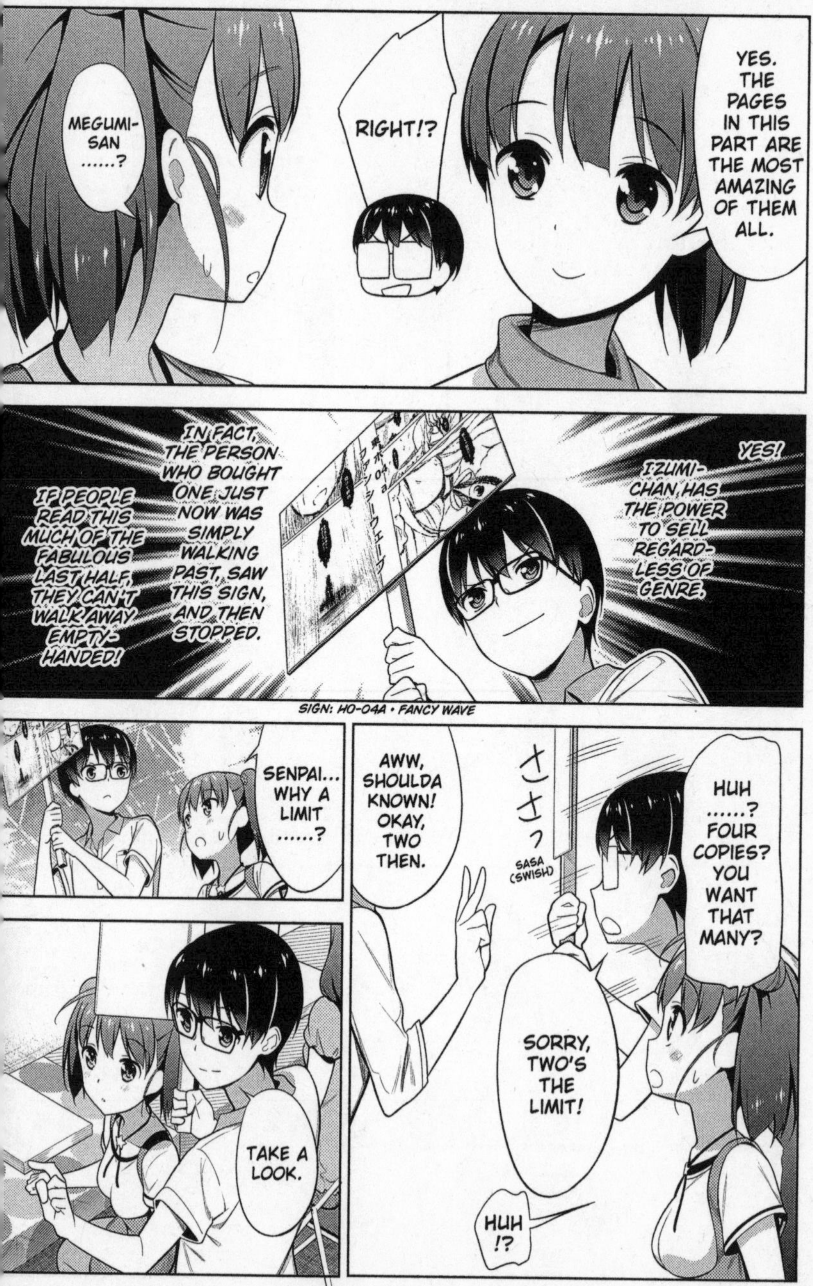
YES. THE PAGES IN THIS PART ARE THE MOST AMAZING OF THEM ALL.
RIGHT!?
MEGUMI-SAN ......?
YES!
IZUMI-CHAN HAS THE POWER TO SELL REGARDLESS OF GENRE.
IN FACT, THE PERSON WHO BOUGHT ONE JUST NOW WAS SIMPLY WALKING PAST, SAW THIS SIGN, AND THEN STOPPED.
IF PEOPLE READ THIS MUCH OF THE FABULOUS LAST HALF, THEY CAN'T WALK AWAY EMPTY-HANDED!
SIGN: HO-04A • FANCY WAVE
HUH ......? FOUR COPIES? YOU WANT THAT MANY?
ささっ
SASA (SWISH)
AWW, SHOULDA KNOWN! OKAY, TWO THEN.
SORRY, TWO'S THE LIMIT!
HUH !?
SENPAI... WHY A LIMIT ......?
TAKE A LOOK.

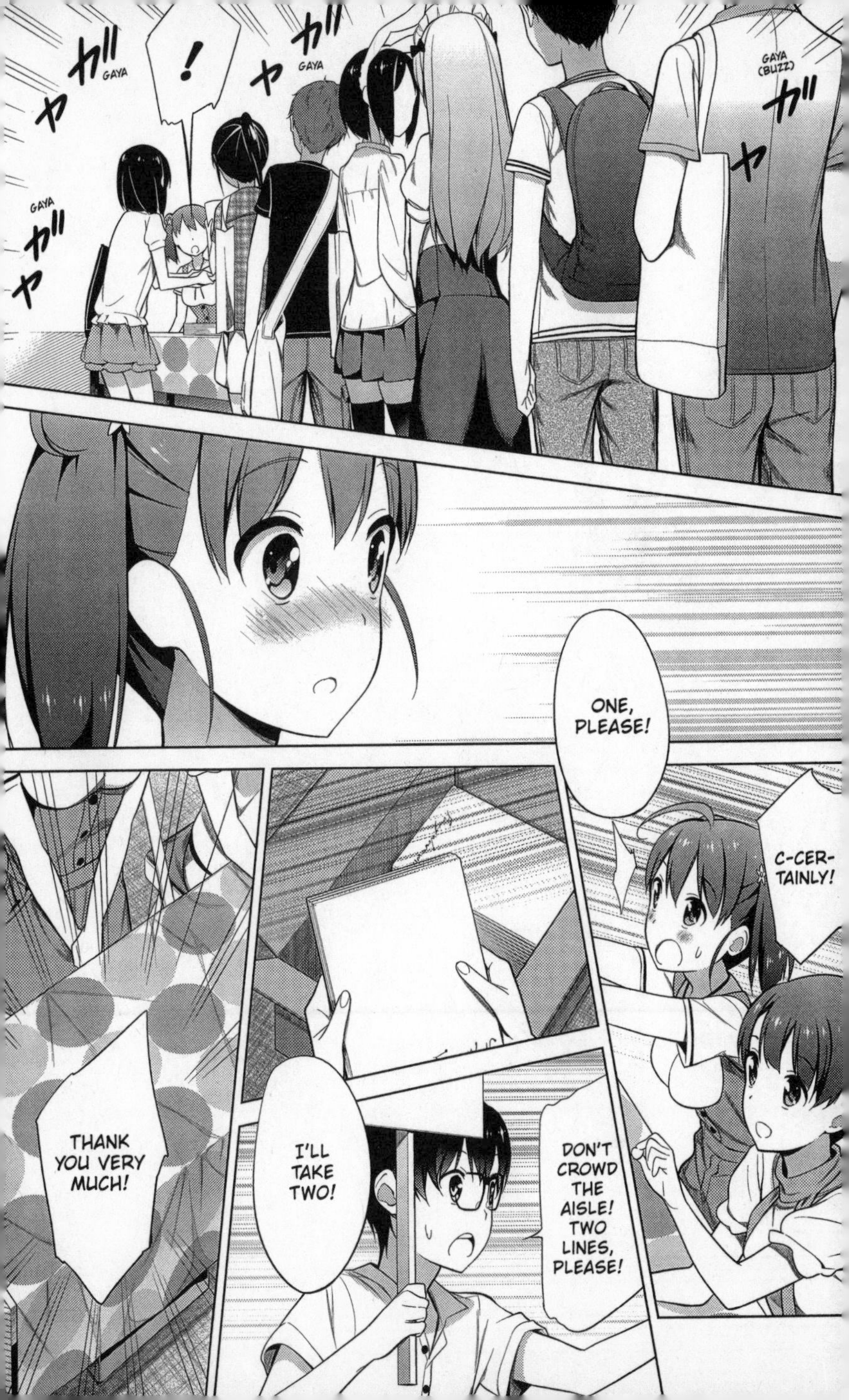

ガヤ
GAYA (BUZZ)
ガヤ
GAYA
!
ガヤ
GAYA
ガヤ
GAYA
ONE, PLEASE!
C-CER-TAINLY!
DON'T CROWD THE AISLE! TWO LINES, PLEASE!
I'LL TAKE TWO!
THANK YOU VERY MUCH!

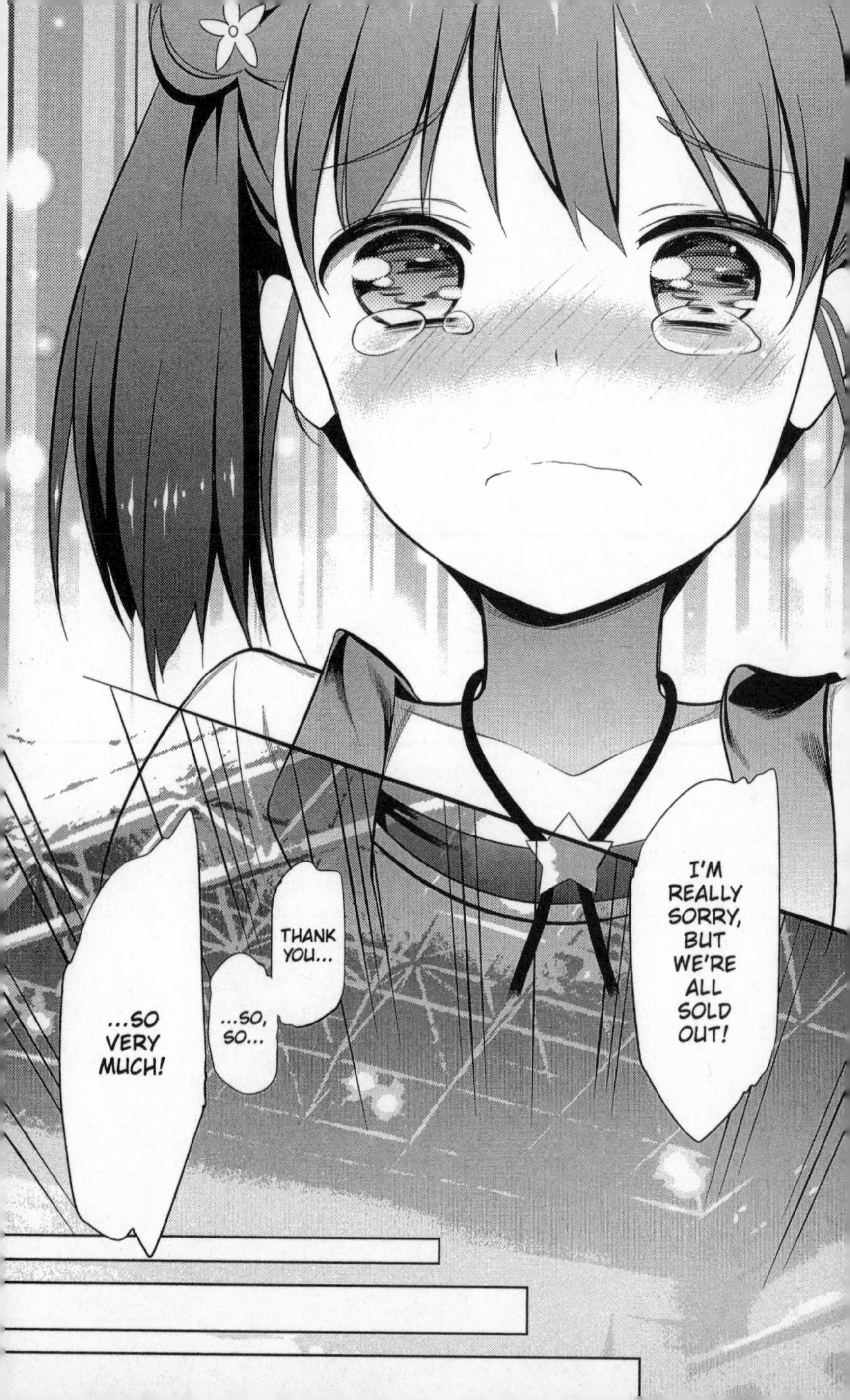
I'M REALLY SORRY, BUT WE'RE ALL SOLD OUT!
THANK YOU...
...SO, SO...
...SO VERY MUCH!

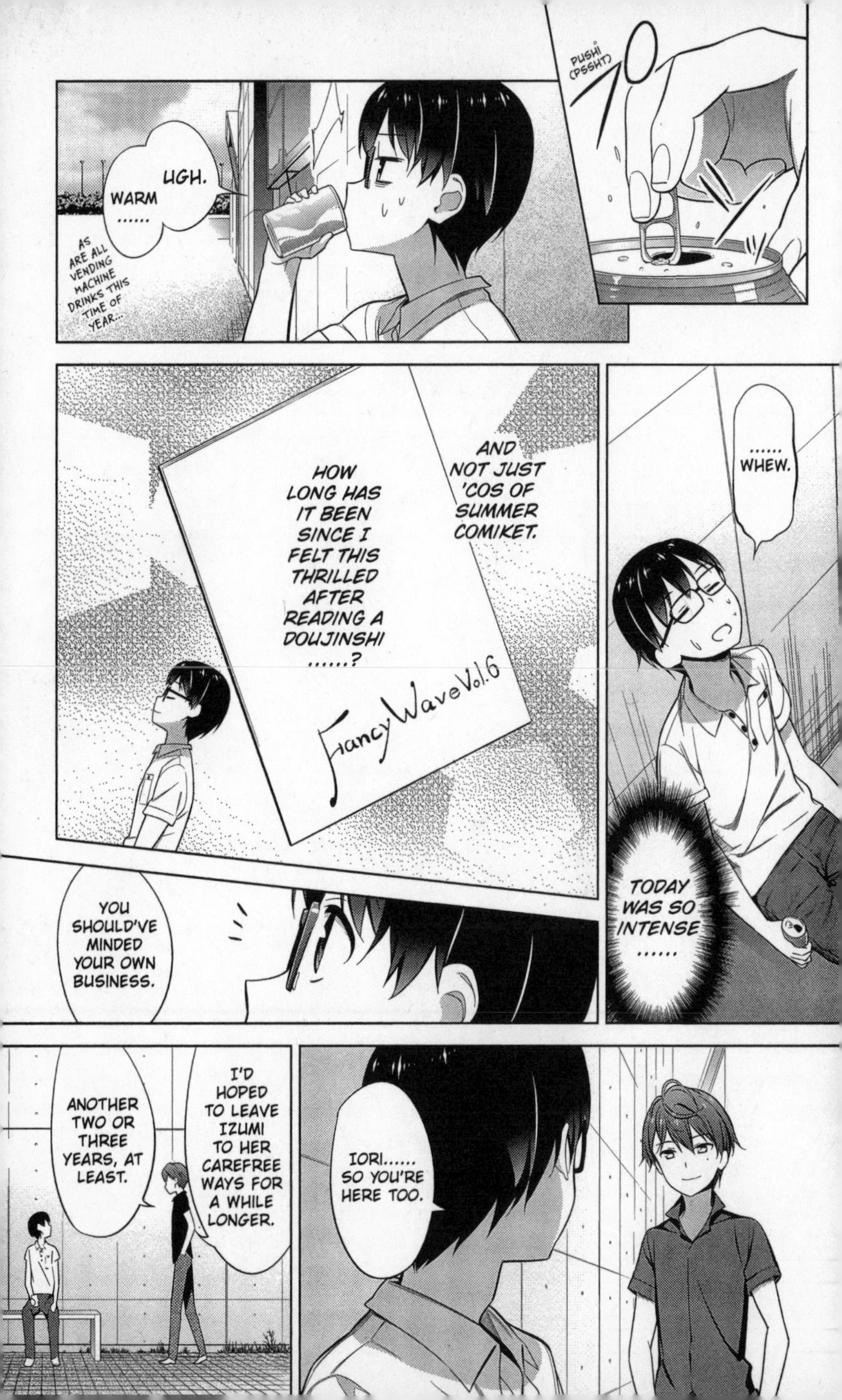
PUSHI (PSSHT)
UGH.
WARM ......
AS ARE ALL VENDING MACHINE DRINKS THIS TIME OF YEAR...
...... WHEW.
TODAY WAS SO INTENSE ......
AND NOT JUST 'COS OF SUMMER COMIKET.
HOW LONG HAS IT BEEN SINCE I FELT THIS THRILLED AFTER READING A DOUJINSHI ......?
Fancy Wave Vol.6
YOU SHOULD'VE MINDED YOUR OWN BUSINESS.
IORI...... SO YOU'RE HERE TOO.
I'D HOPED TO LEAVE IZUMI TO HER CAREFREE WAYS FOR A WHILE LONGER.
ANOTHER TWO OR THREE YEARS, AT LEAST.

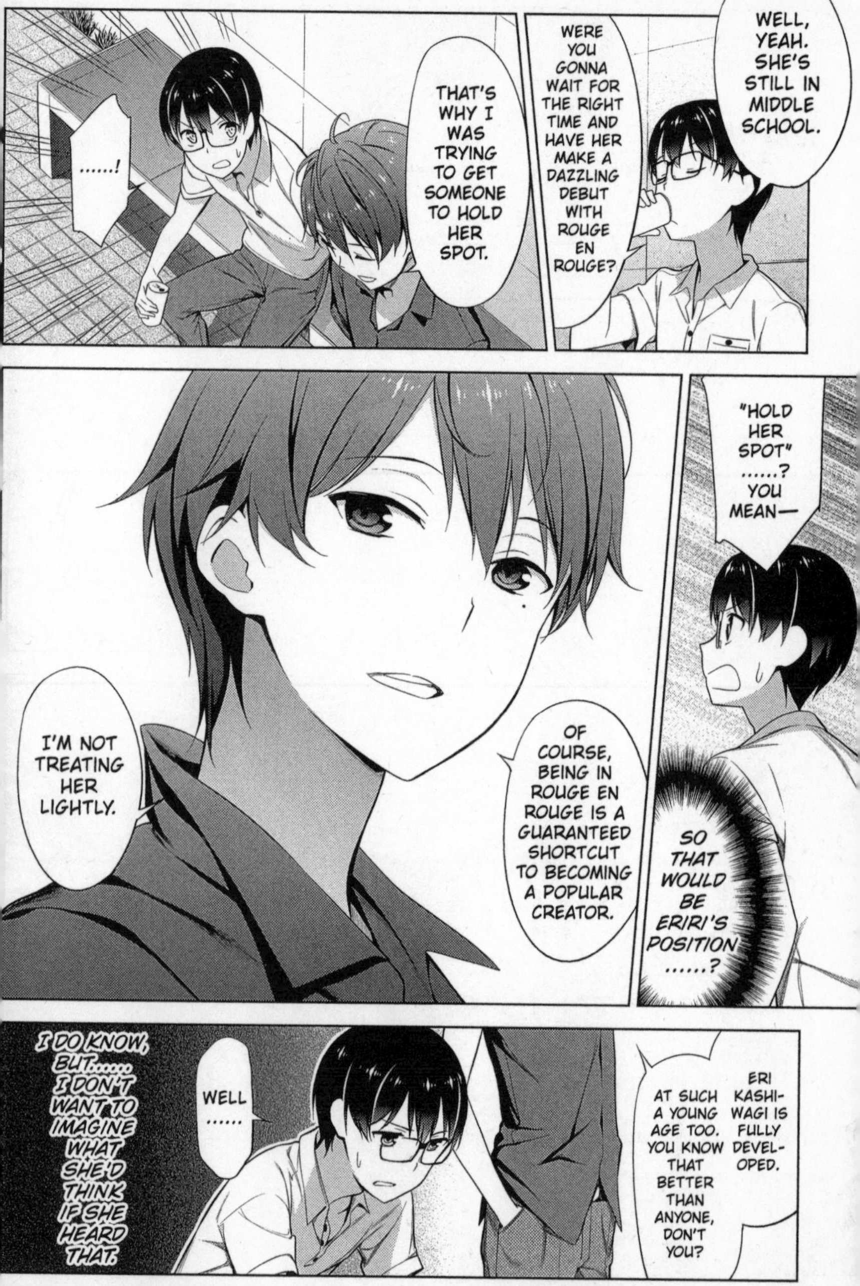
WELL, YEAH. SHE'S STILL IN MIDDLE SCHOOL.
WERE YOU GONNA WAIT FOR THE RIGHT TIME AND HAVE HER MAKE A DAZZLING DEBUT WITH ROUGE EN ROUGE?
THAT'S WHY I WAS TRYING TO GET SOMEONE TO HOLD HER SPOT.
......!
"HOLD HER SPOT" ......? YOU MEAN—
SO THAT WOULD BE ERIRI'S POSITION ......?
OF COURSE, BEING IN ROUGE EN ROUGE IS A GUARANTEED SHORTCUT TO BECOMING A POPULAR CREATOR.
I'M NOT TREATING HER LIGHTLY.
ERI KASHIWAGI IS FULLY DEVELOPED. AT SUCH A YOUNG AGE TOO. YOU KNOW THAT BETTER THAN ANYONE, DON'T YOU?
WELL ......
I DO KNOW, BUT...... I DON'T WANT TO IMAGINE WHAT SHE'D THINK IF SHE HEARD THAT.

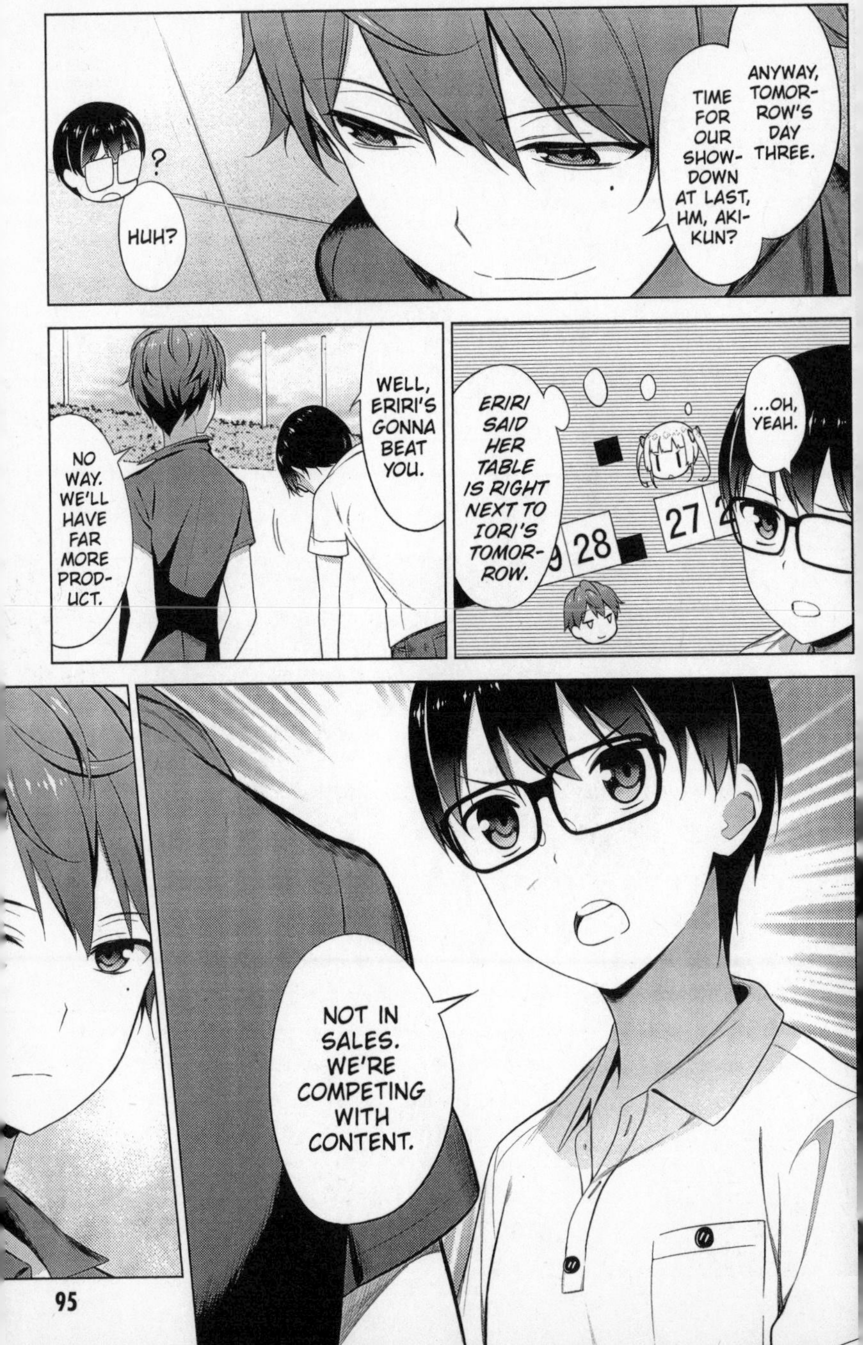
ANYWAY, TOMORROW'S DAY THREE.
TIME FOR OUR SHOWDOWN AT LAST, HM, AKI-KUN?
?
HUH?
...OH, YEAH.
ERIRI SAID HER TABLE IS RIGHT NEXT TO IORI'S TOMORROW.
27
28
WELL, ERIRI'S GONNA BEAT YOU.
NO WAY. WE'LL HAVE FAR MORE PRODUCT.
NOT IN SALES. WE'RE COMPETING WITH CONTENT.

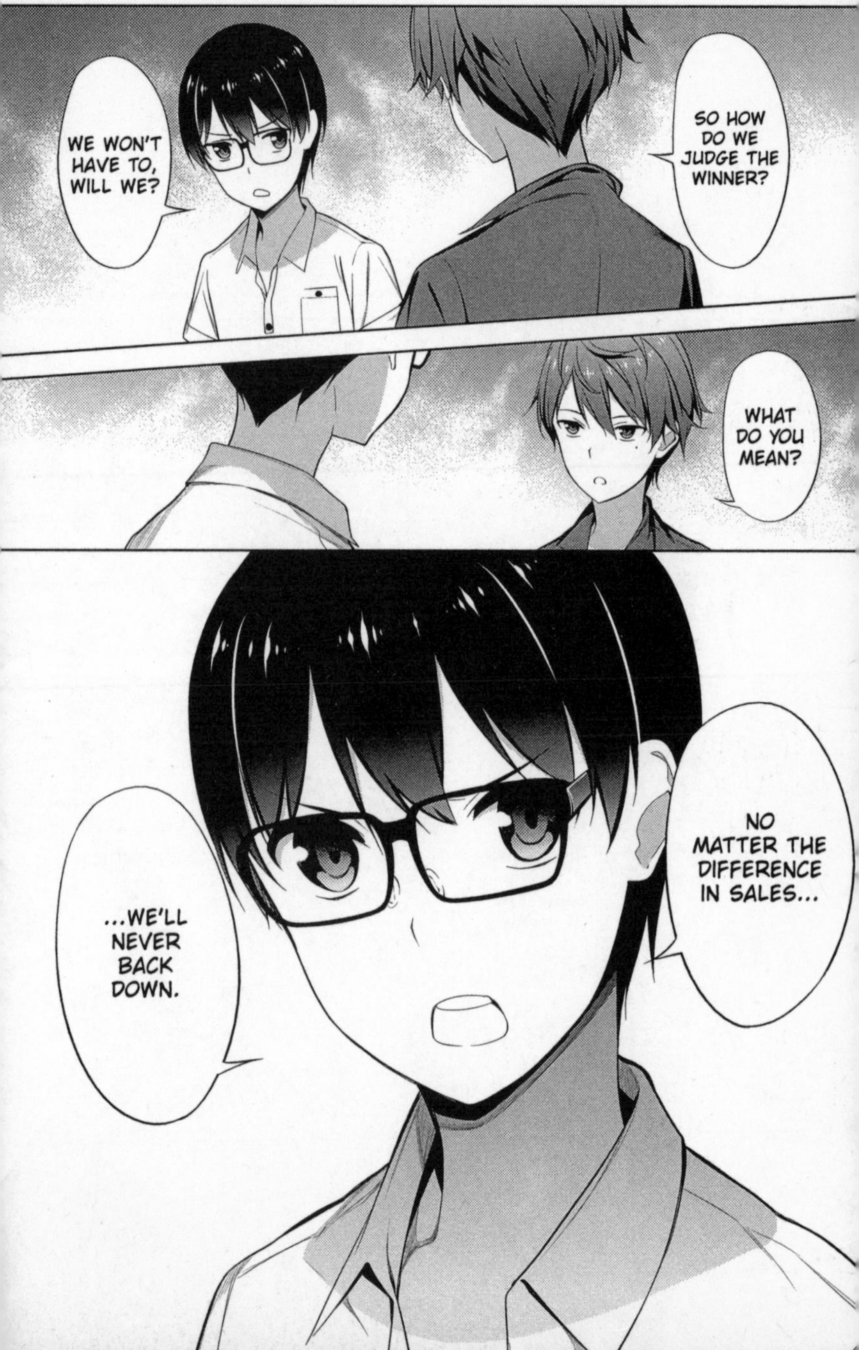
SO HOW DO WE JUDGE THE WINNER?
WE WON'T HAVE TO, WILL WE?
WHAT DO YOU MEAN?
NO MATTER THE DIFFERENCE IN SALES...
...WE'LL NEVER BACK DOWN.

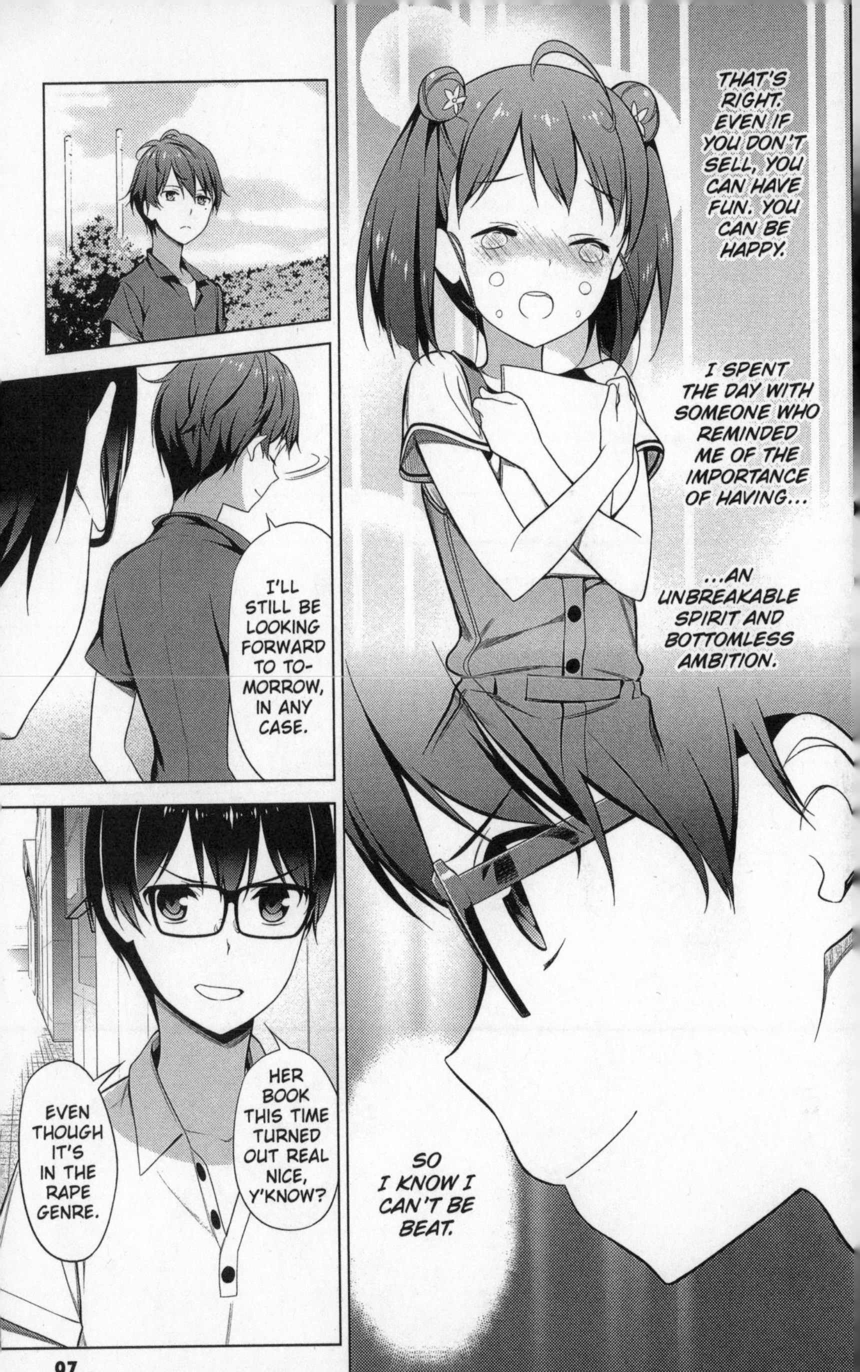
THAT'S RIGHT. EVEN IF YOU DON'T SELL, YOU CAN HAVE FUN. YOU CAN BE HAPPY.
I SPENT THE DAY WITH SOMEONE WHO REMINDED ME OF THE IMPORTANCE OF HAVING...
...AN UNBREAKABLE SPIRIT AND BOTTOMLESS AMBITION.
SO I KNOW I CAN'T BE BEAT.
I'LL STILL BE LOOKING FORWARD TO TO-MORROW, IN ANY CASE.
HER BOOK THIS TIME TURNED OUT REAL NICE, Y'KNOW?
EVEN THOUGH IT'S IN THE RAPE GENRE.

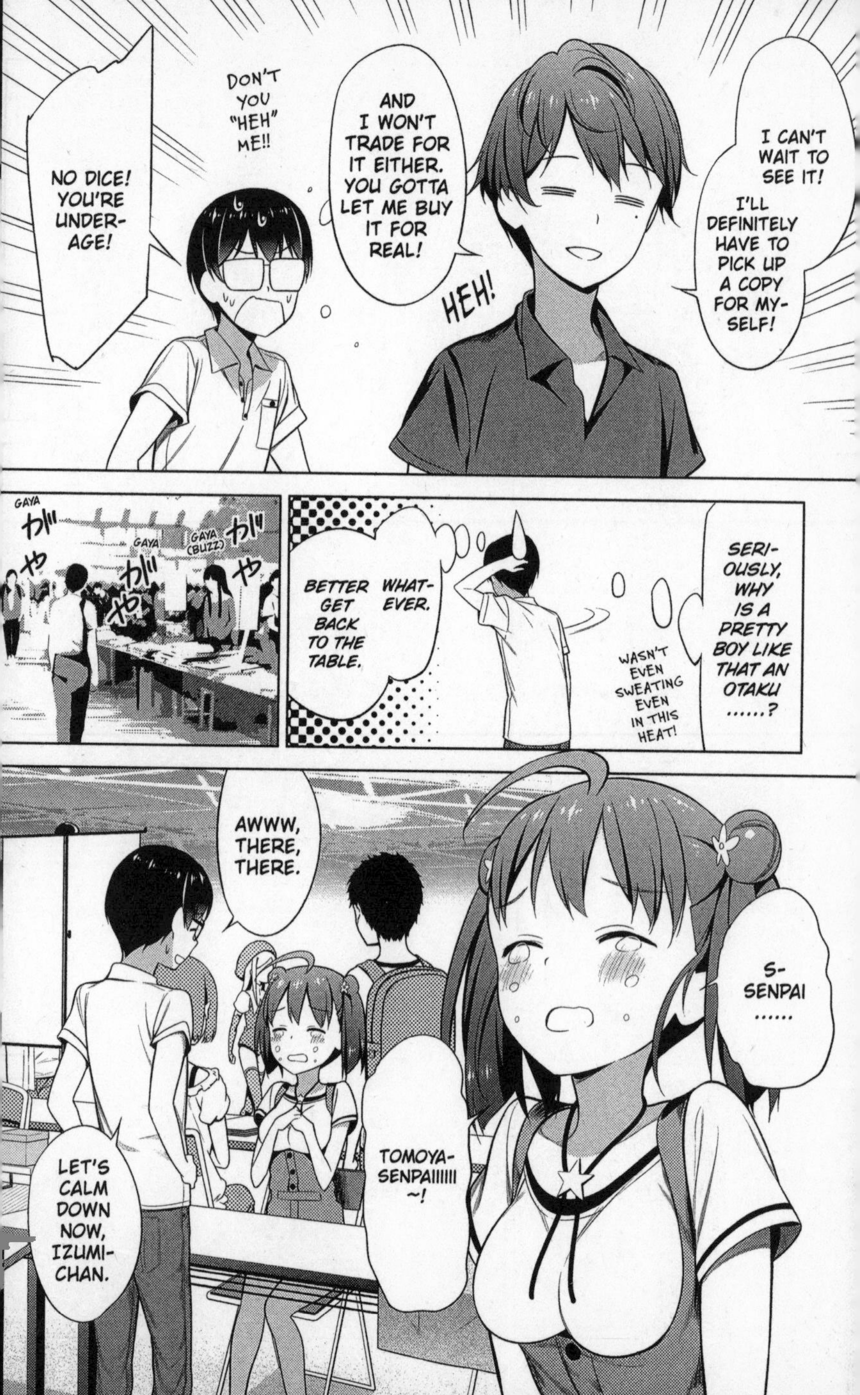
I CAN'T WAIT TO SEE IT!
I'LL DEFINITELY HAVE TO PICK UP A COPY FOR MYSELF!
HEH!
AND I WON'T TRADE FOR IT EITHER. YOU GOTTA LET ME BUY IT FOR REAL!
DON'T YOU "HEH" ME!!
NO DICE! YOU'RE UNDER-AGE!
SERI-OUSLY, WHY IS A PRETTY BOY LIKE THAT AN OTAKU ......?
WASN'T EVEN SWEATING EVEN IN THIS HEAT!
WHAT-EVER.
BETTER GET BACK TO THE TABLE.
GAYA (BUZZ)
GAYA
GAYA
S-SENPAI ......
TOMOYA-SENPAIIIIII ~!
AWWW, THERE, THERE.
LET'S CALM DOWN NOW, IZUMI-CHAN.

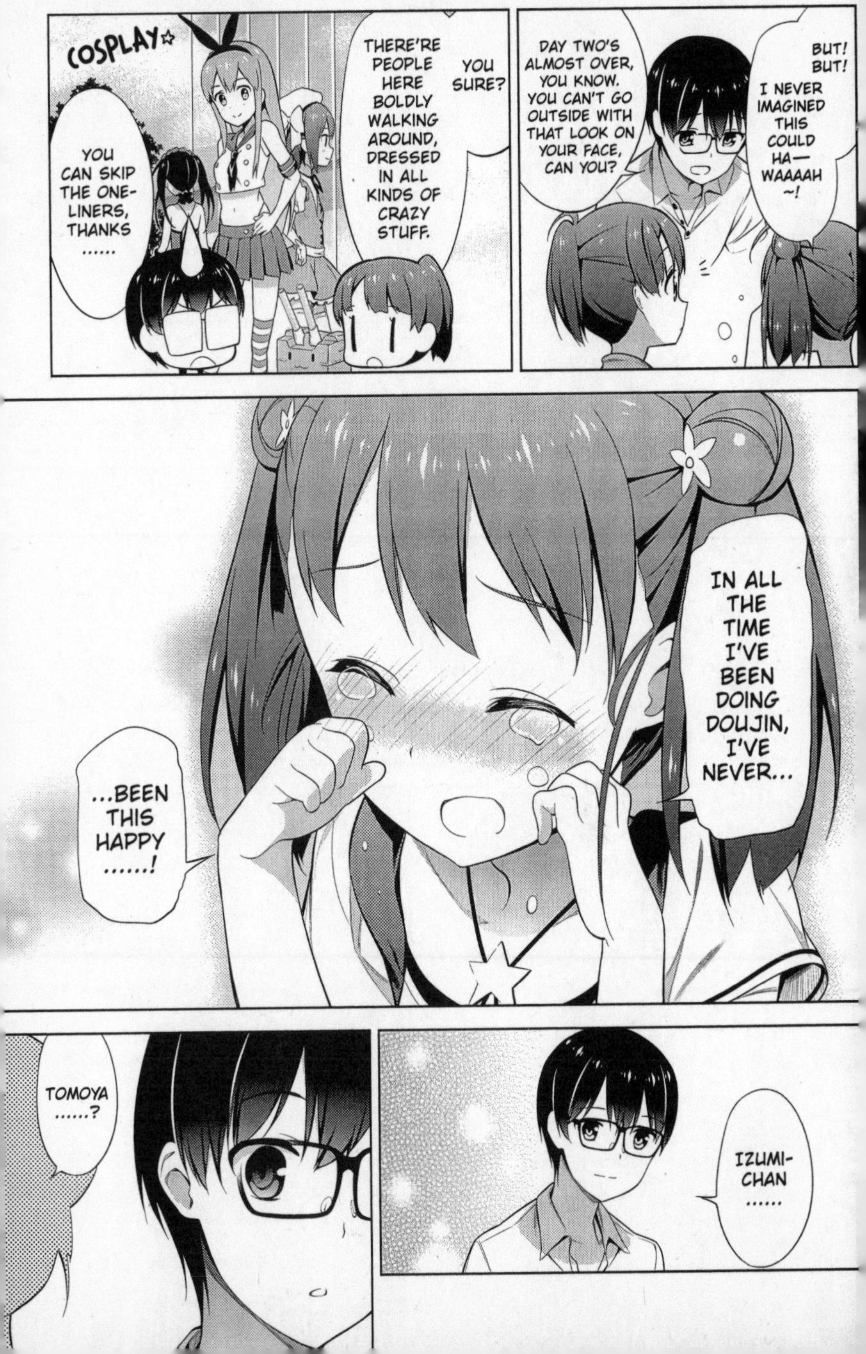
BUT! BUT! I NEVER IMAGINED THIS COULD HA—WAAAAH~!
DAY TWO'S ALMOST OVER, YOU KNOW. YOU CAN'T GO OUTSIDE WITH THAT LOOK ON YOUR FACE, CAN YOU?
YOU SURE?
THERE'RE PEOPLE HERE BOLDLY WALKING AROUND, DRESSED IN ALL KINDS OF CRAZY STUFF.
COSPLAY☆
YOU CAN SKIP THE ONE-LINERS, THANKS......
IN ALL THE TIME I'VE BEEN DOING DOUJIN, I'VE NEVER...
...BEEN THIS HAPPY......!
IZUMI-CHAN......
TOMOYA......?

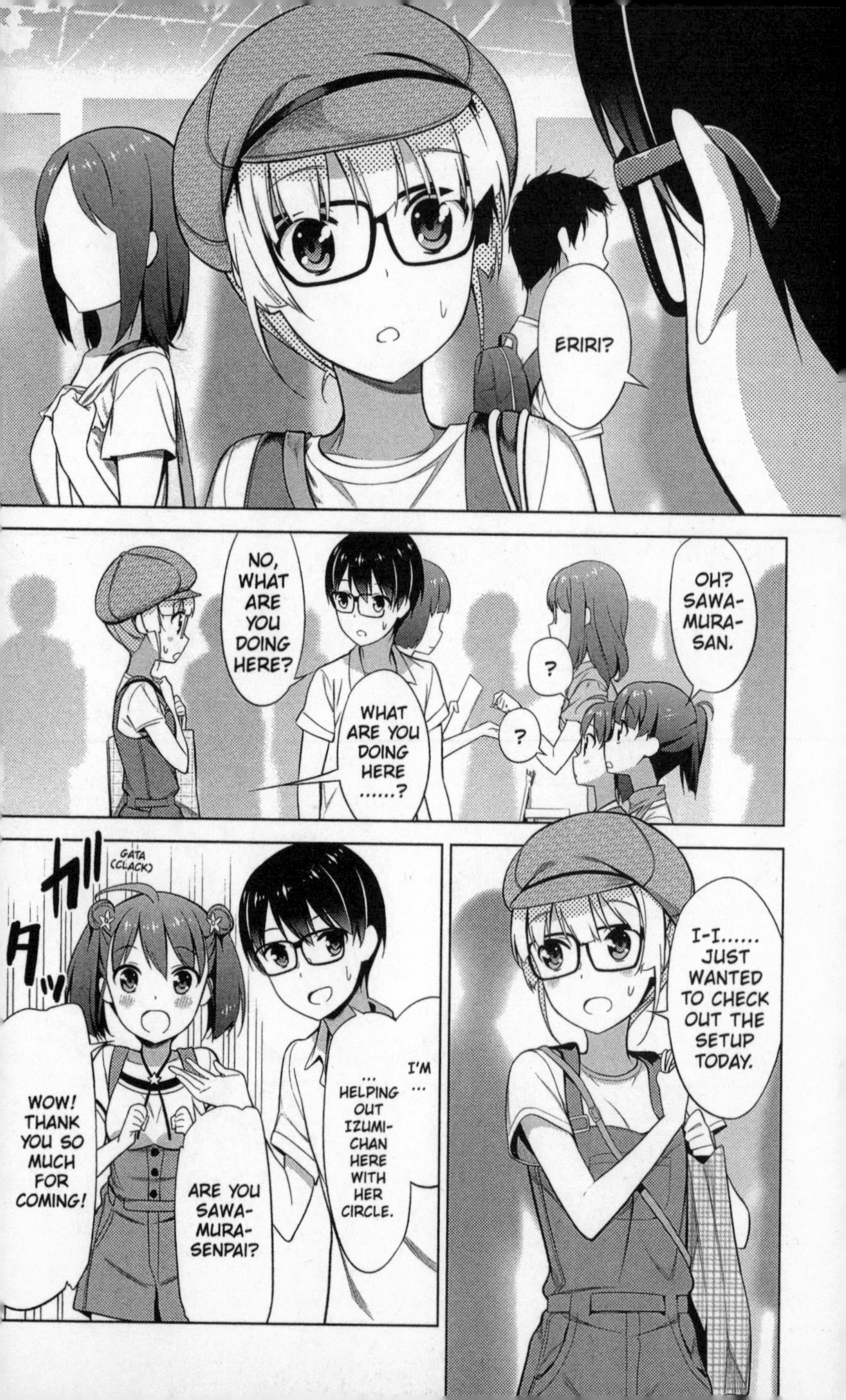
ERIRI?
OH? SAWAMURA-SAN.
?
?
NO, WHAT ARE YOU DOING HERE?
WHAT ARE YOU DOING HERE ......?
I-I...... JUST WANTED TO CHECK OUT THE SETUP TODAY.
I'M ... HELPING OUT IZUMI-CHAN HERE WITH HER CIRCLE.
GATA (CLACK)
ガタッ
ARE YOU SAWAMURA-SENPAI?
WOW! THANK YOU SO MUCH FOR COMING!

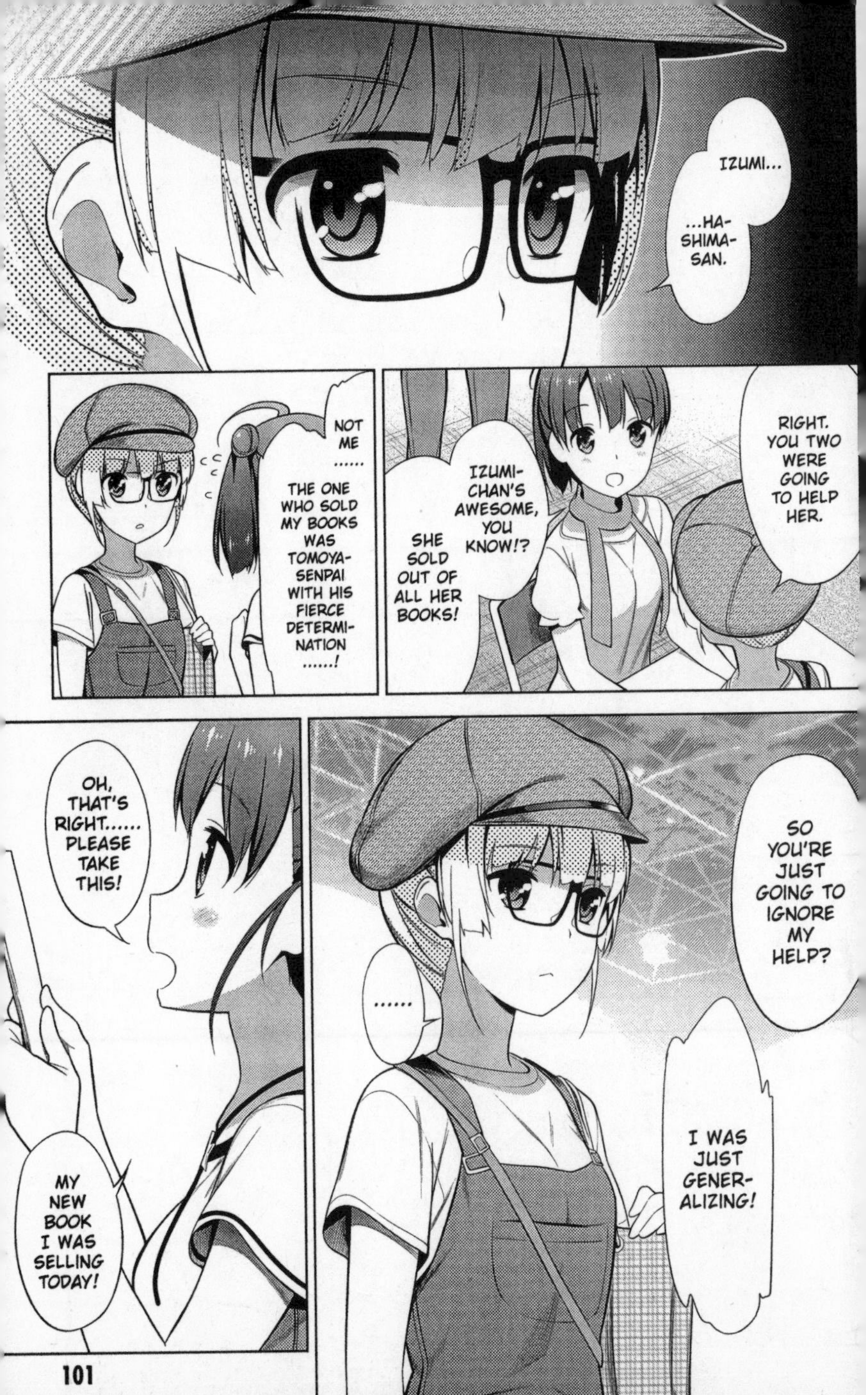
IZUMI...
...HASHIMA-SAN.
RIGHT. YOU TWO WERE GOING TO HELP HER.
IZUMI-CHAN'S AWESOME, YOU KNOW!?
SHE SOLD OUT OF ALL HER BOOKS!
NOT ME ......
THE ONE WHO SOLD MY BOOKS WAS TOMOYA-SENPAI WITH HIS FIERCE DETERMINATION ......!
SO YOU'RE JUST GOING TO IGNORE MY HELP?
......
I WAS JUST GENERALIZING!
OH, THAT'S RIGHT...... PLEASE TAKE THIS!
MY NEW BOOK I WAS SELLING TODAY!

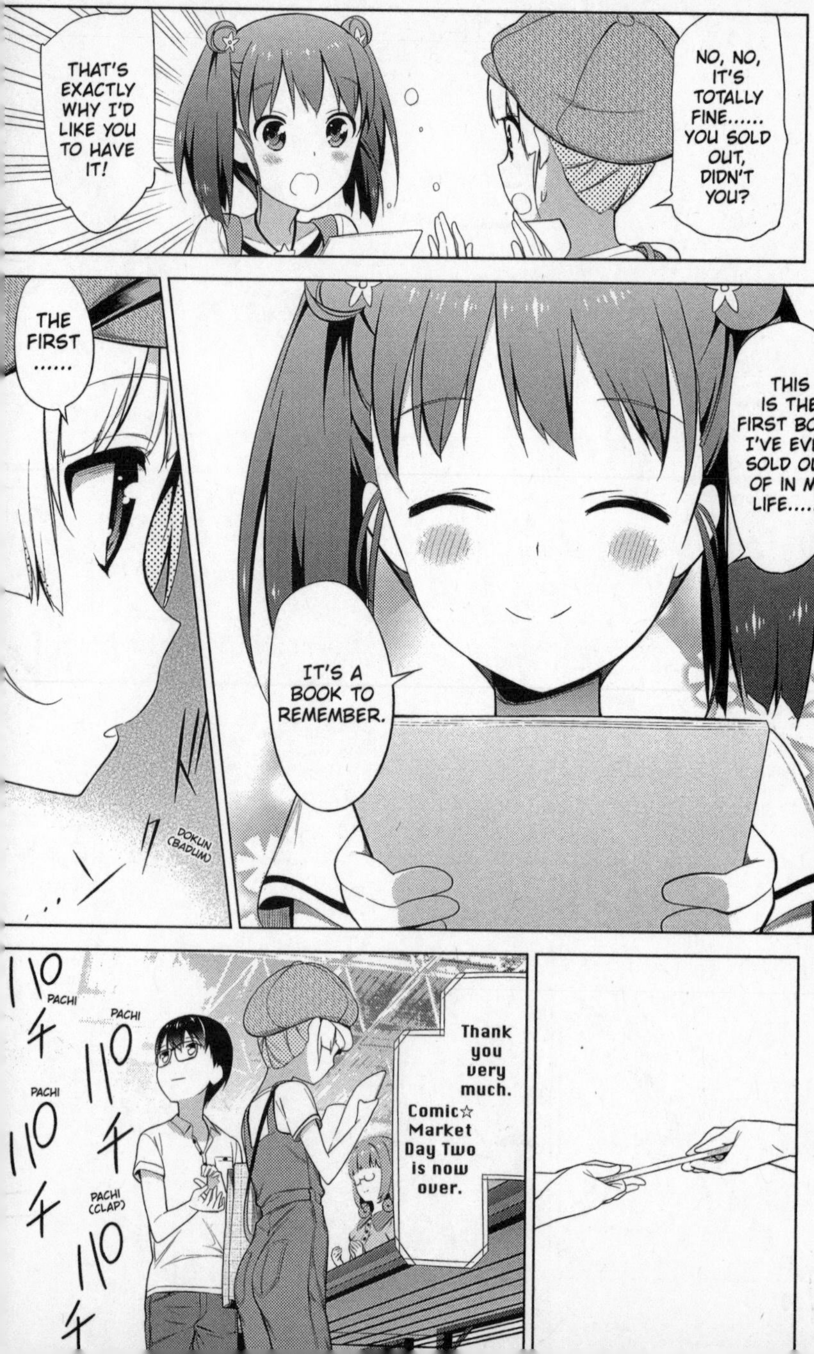
NO, NO, IT'S TOTALLY FINE...... YOU SOLD OUT, DIDN'T YOU?
THAT'S EXACTLY WHY I'D LIKE YOU TO HAVE IT!
THIS IS THE FIRST BOOK I'VE EVER SOLD OUT OF IN MY LIFE......
IT'S A BOOK TO REMEMBER.
THE FIRST ......
DOKUN (BADUM)
Thank you very much. Comic☆ Market Day Two is now over.
PACHI
PACHI
PACHI
PACHI (CLAP)

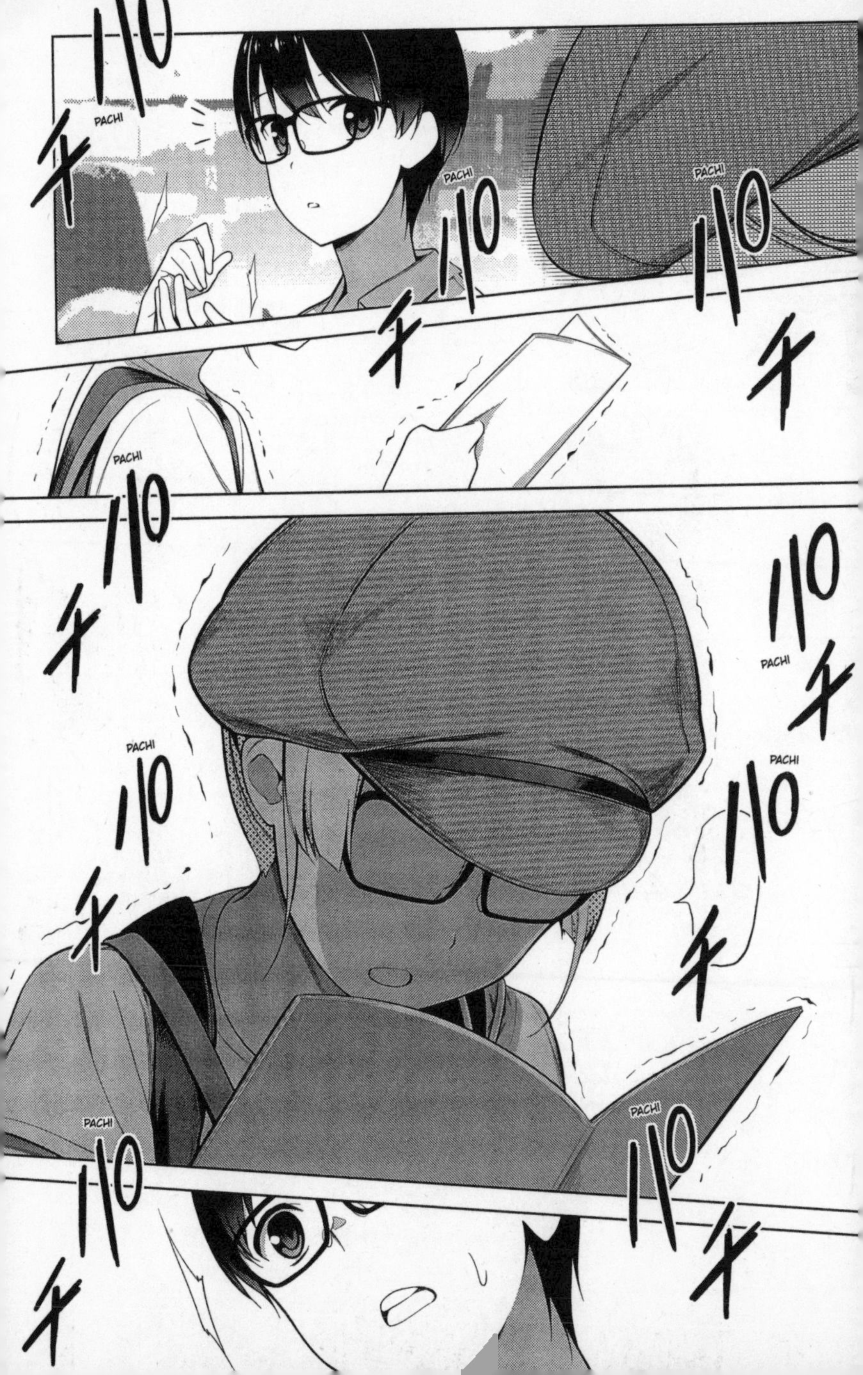
パチ PACHI
パチ PACHI
パチ PACHI
パチ PACHI
パチ PACHI
パチ PACHI
パチ PACHI
パチ PACHI
パチ PACHI
パチ PACHI

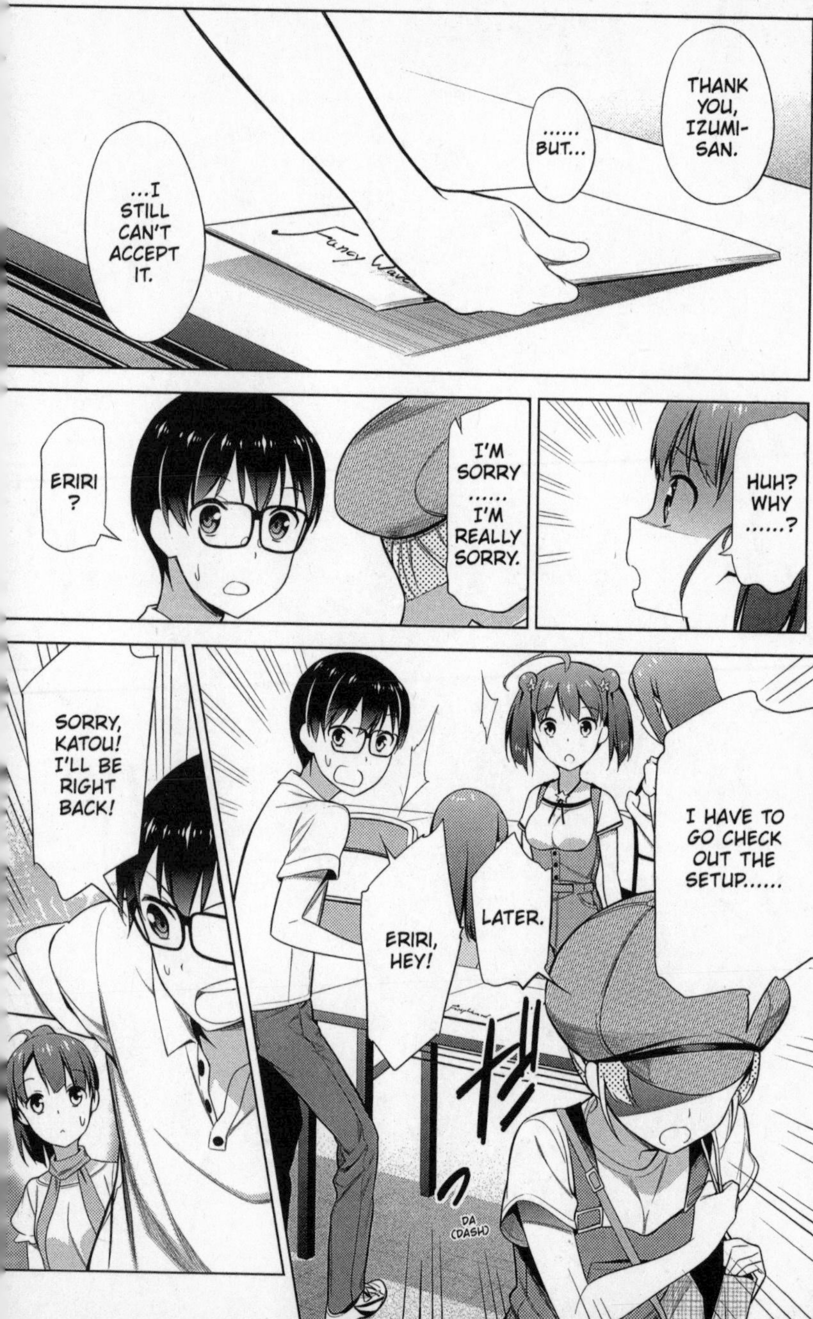
THANK YOU, IZUMI-SAN.
......BUT...
...I STILL CAN'T ACCEPT IT.
HUH? WHY ......?
I'M SORRY ...... I'M REALLY SORRY.
ERIRI?
I HAVE TO GO CHECK OUT THE SETUP......
LATER.
ERIRI, HEY!
DA (DASH)
SORRY, KATOU! I'LL BE RIGHT BACK!

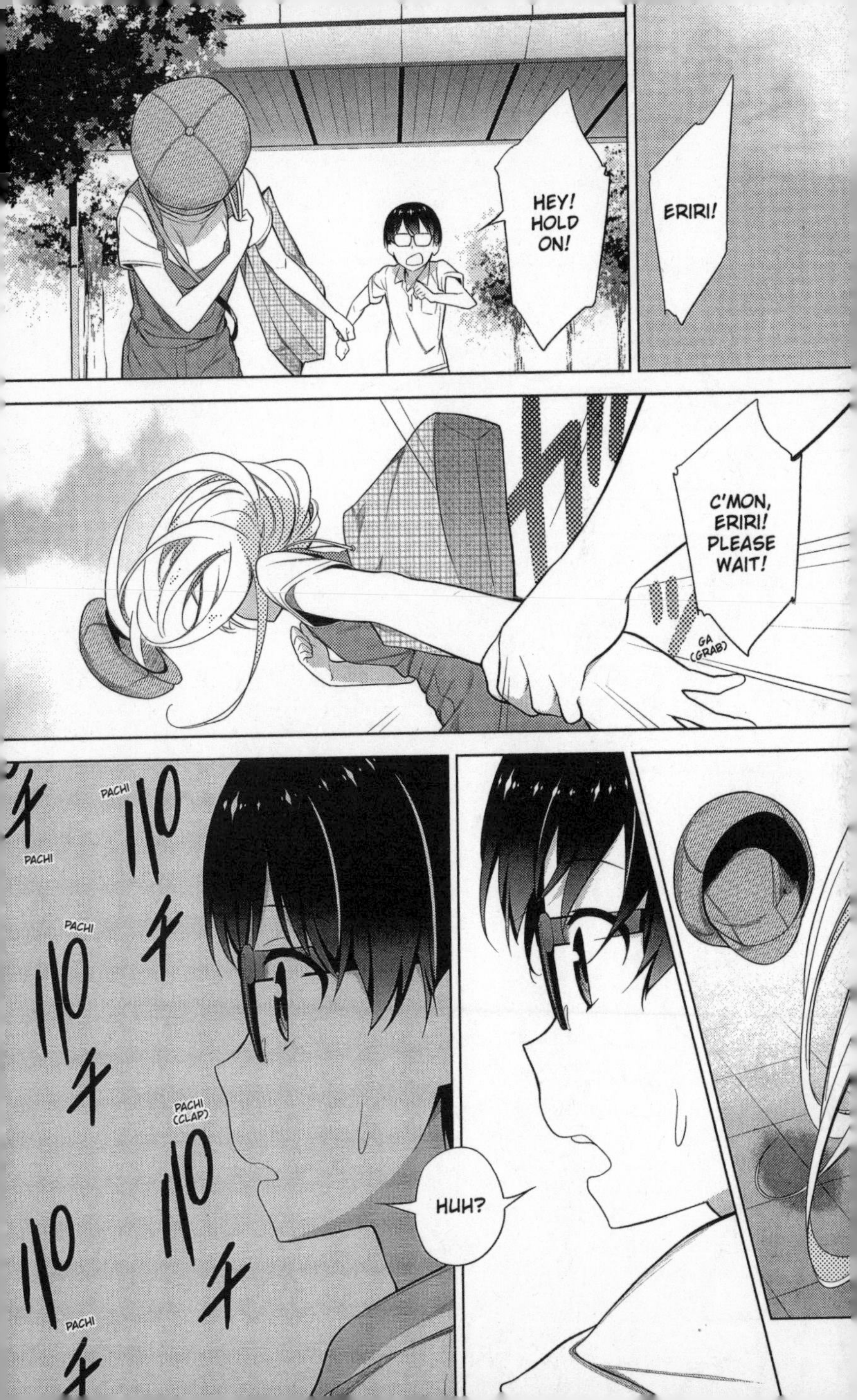
ERIRI!
HEY! HOLD ON!
C'MON, ERIRI! PLEASE WAIT!
GA (GRAB)
HUH?
PACHI
PACHI
PACHI
PACHI (CLAP)
PACHI

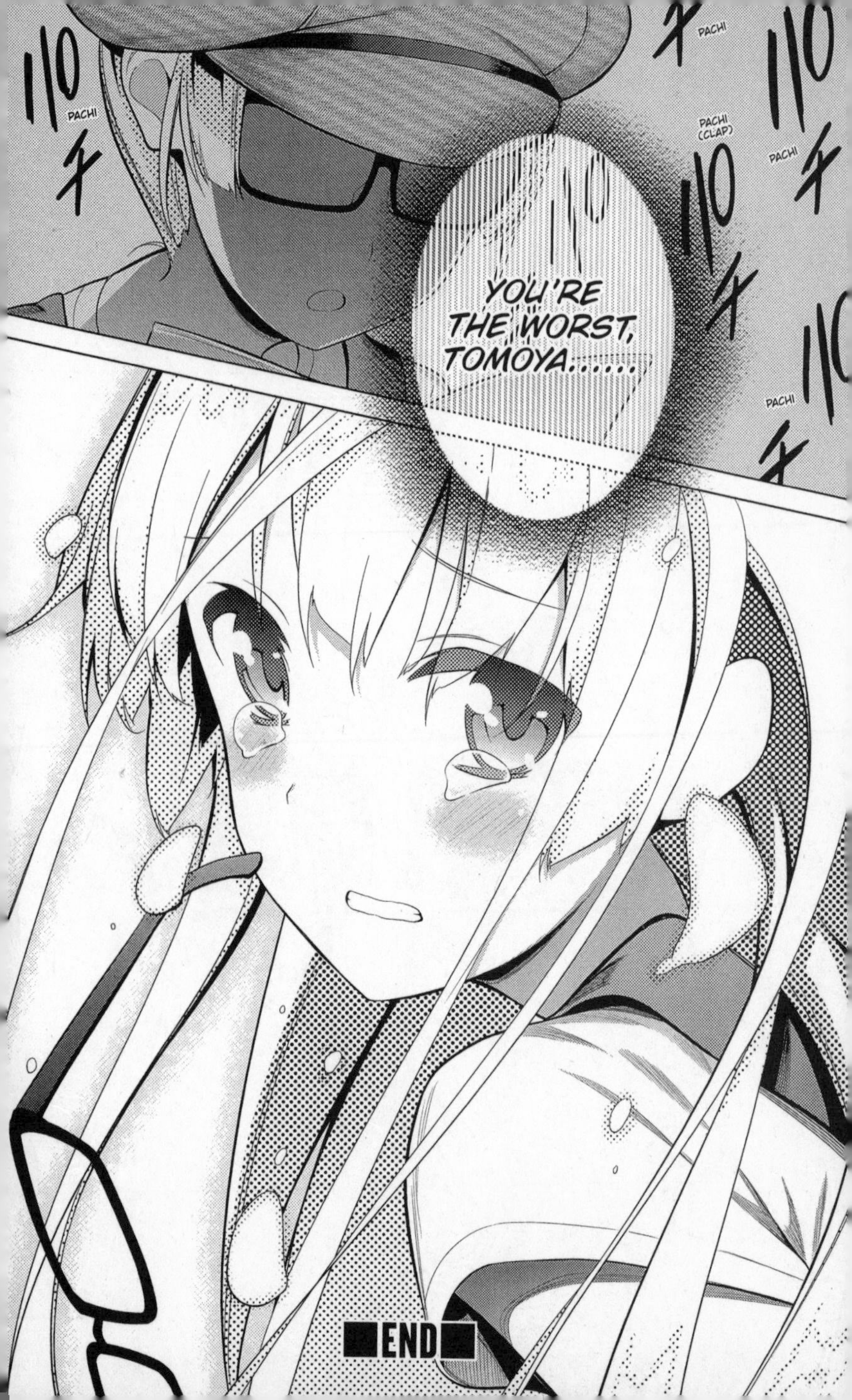
PACHI
PACHI (CLAP)
PACHI
PACHI
PACHI
YOU'RE THE WORST, TOMOYA......
END

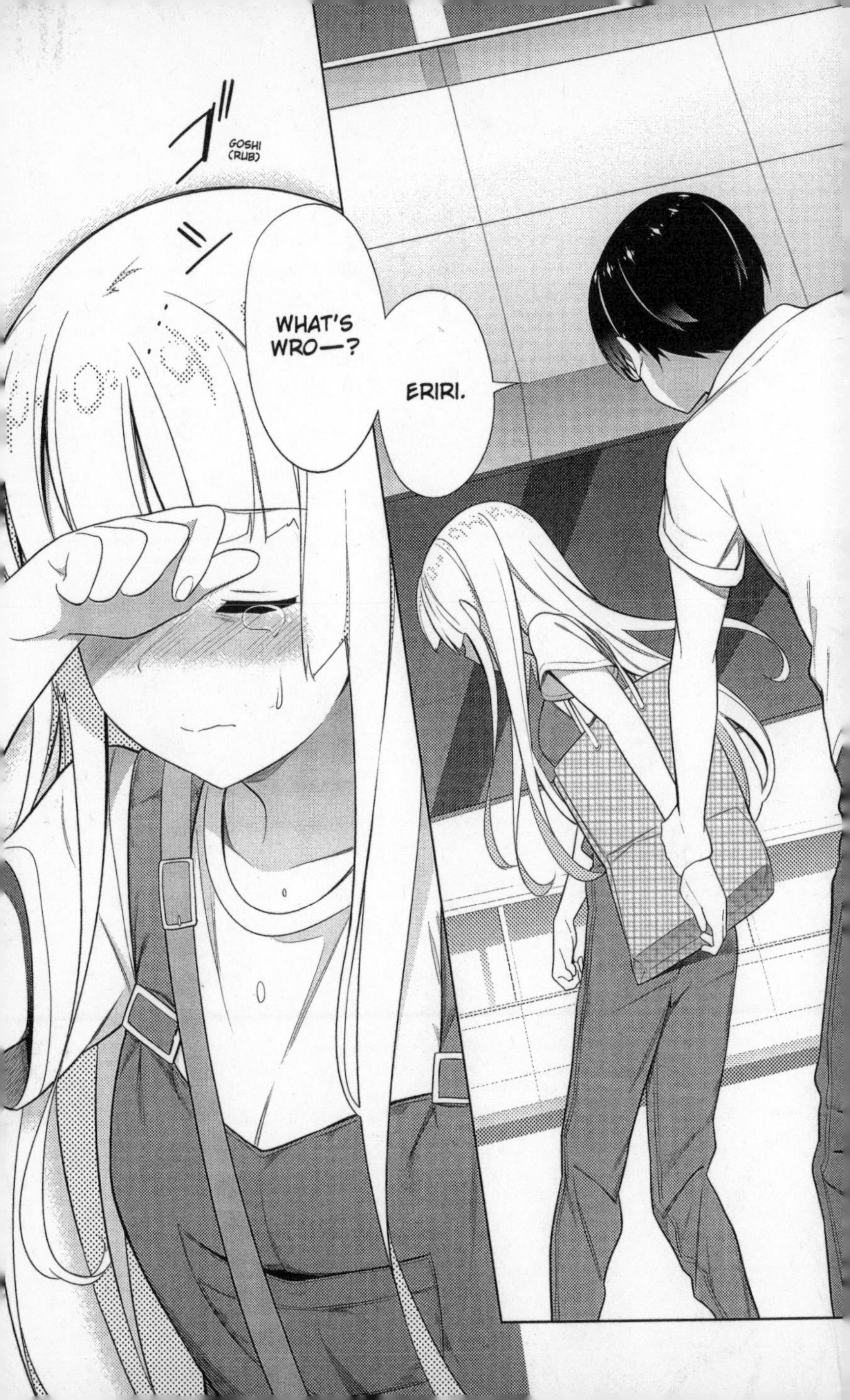
ERIRI.
WHAT'S WRO—?
GOSHI (RUB)

# CHAPTER 15

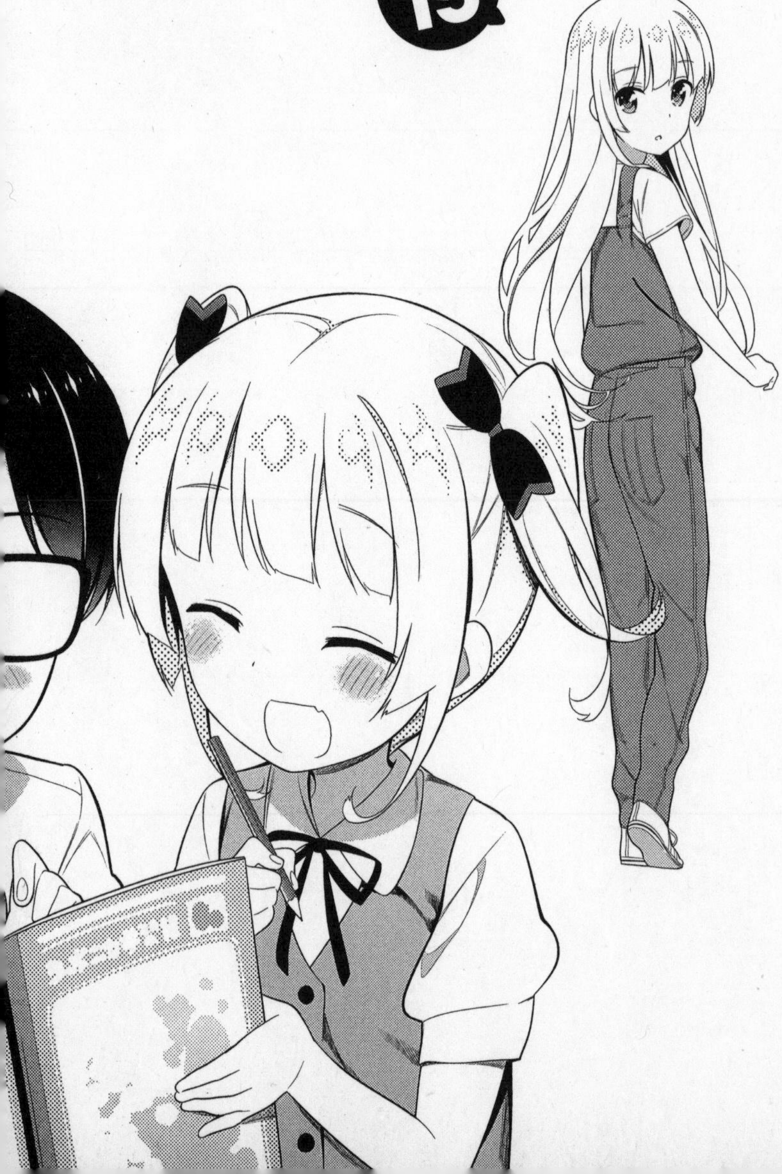

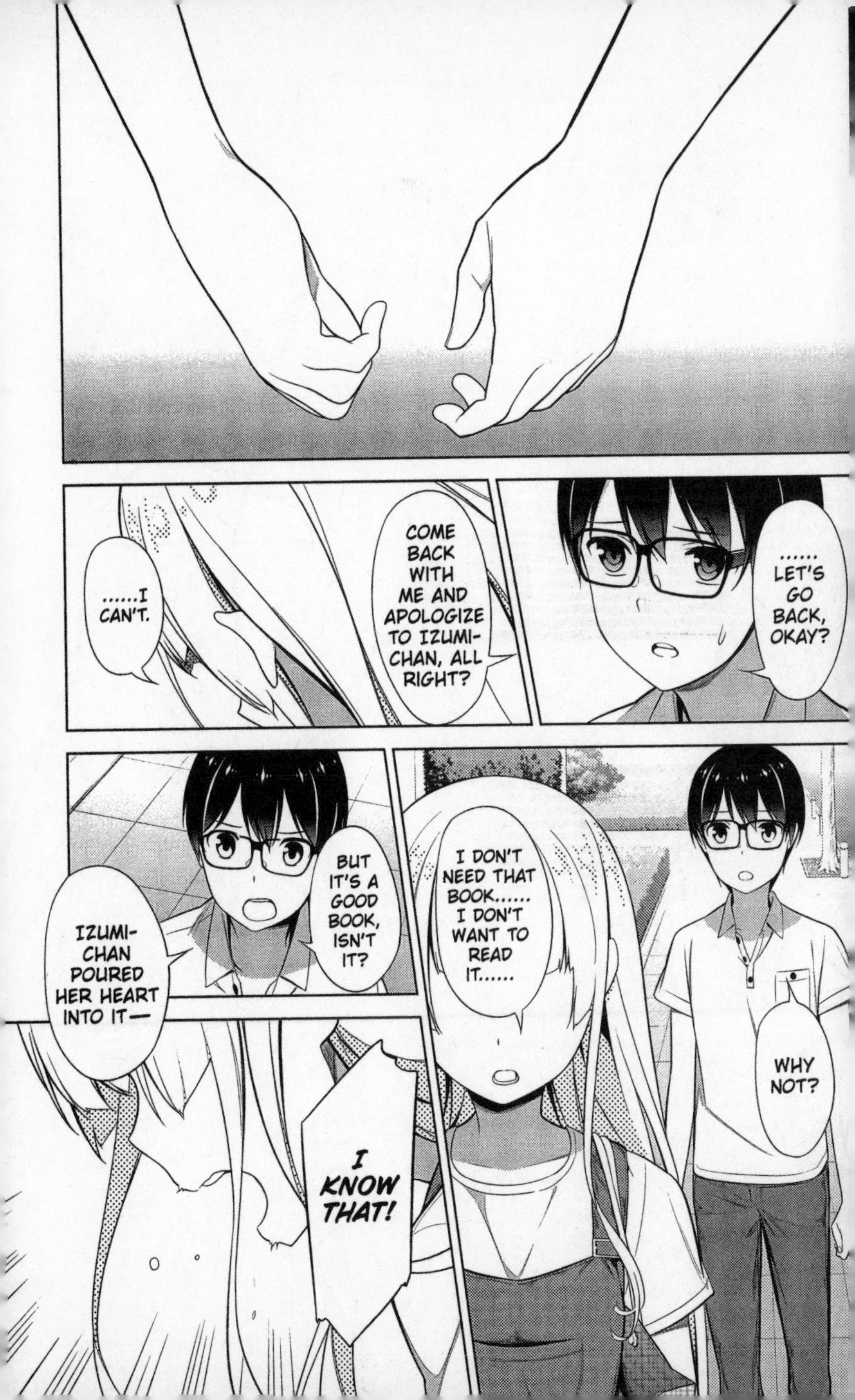

......LET'S GO BACK, OKAY?
COME BACK WITH ME AND APOLOGIZE TO IZUMI-CHAN, ALL RIGHT?
......I CAN'T.
I DON'T NEED THAT BOOK...... I DON'T WANT TO READ IT......
WHY NOT?
BUT IT'S A GOOD BOOK, ISN'T IT?
IZUMI-CHAN POURED HER HEART INTO IT—
I KNOW THAT!

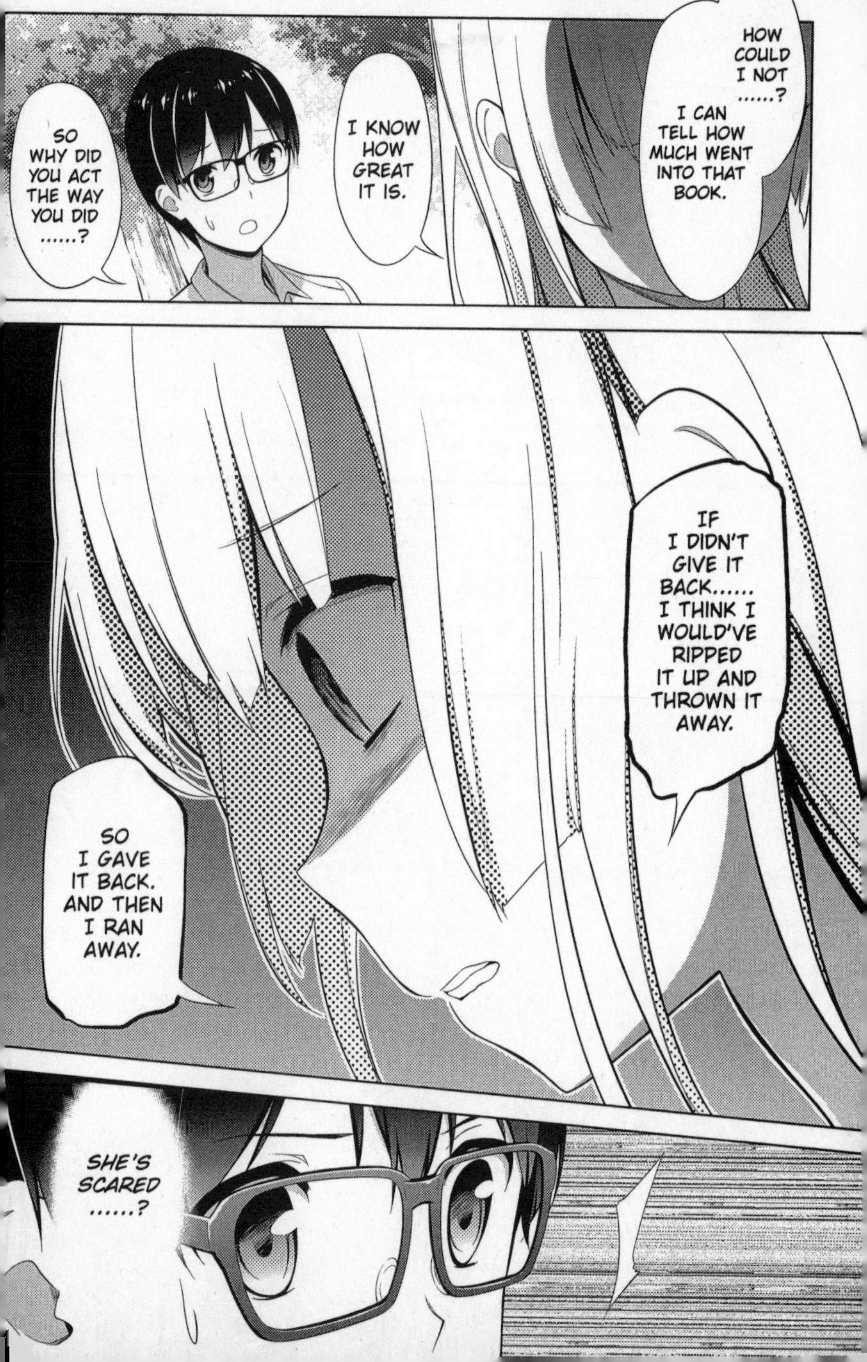
HOW COULD I NOT ......? I CAN TELL HOW MUCH WENT INTO THAT BOOK.
I KNOW HOW GREAT IT IS.
SO WHY DID YOU ACT THE WAY YOU DID ......?
IF I DIDN'T GIVE IT BACK...... I THINK I WOULD'VE RIPPED IT UP AND THROWN IT AWAY.
SO I GAVE IT BACK. AND THEN I RAN AWAY.
SHE'S SCARED ......?

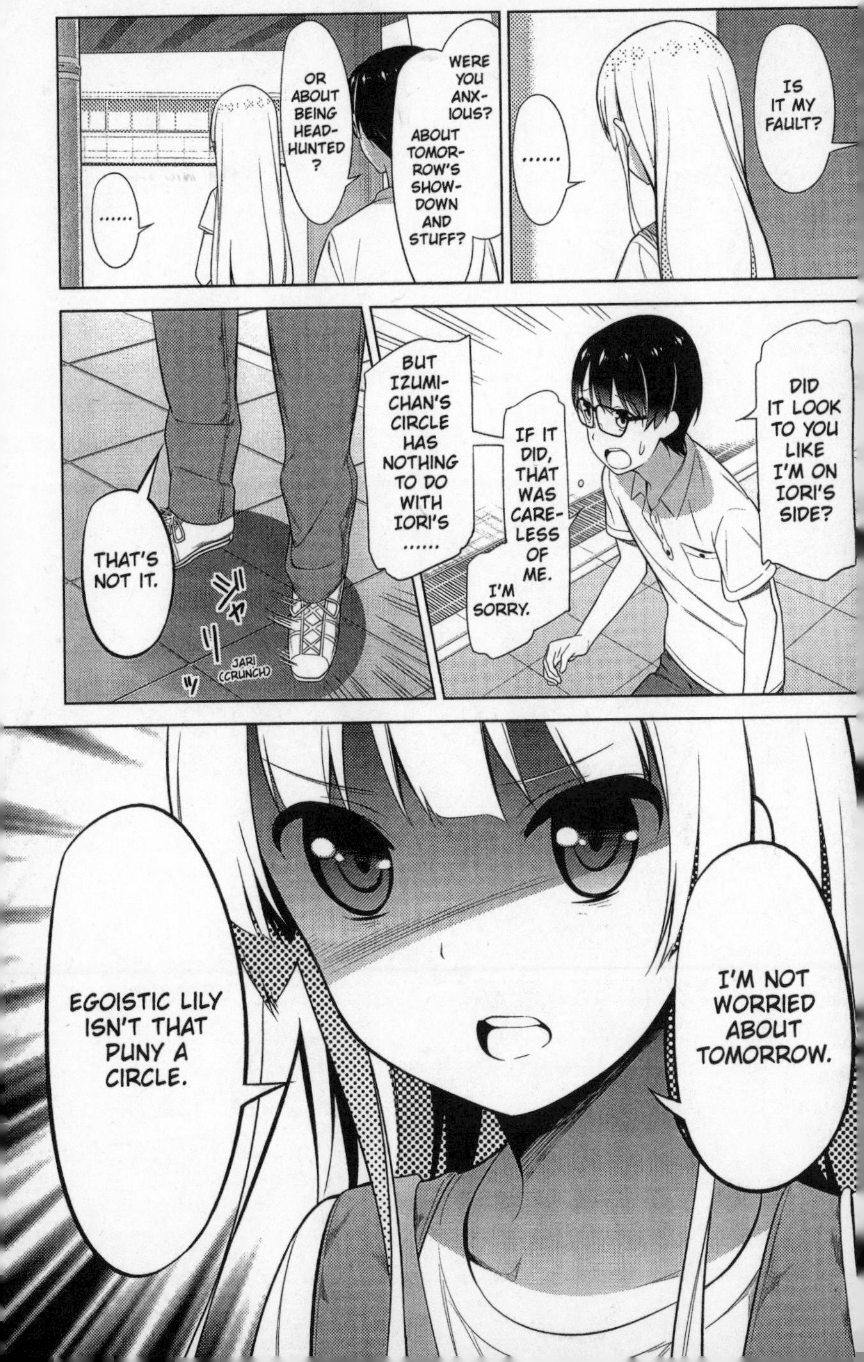
IS IT MY FAULT?
......
WERE YOU ANXIOUS? ABOUT TOMORROW'S SHOWDOWN AND STUFF?
OR ABOUT BEING HEADHUNTED?
......
DID IT LOOK TO YOU LIKE I'M ON IORI'S SIDE?
IF IT DID, THAT WAS CARELESS OF ME. I'M SORRY.
BUT IZUMI-CHAN'S CIRCLE HAS NOTHING TO DO WITH IORI'S ......
THAT'S NOT IT.
JARI (CRUNCH)
I'M NOT WORRIED ABOUT TOMORROW.
EGOISTIC LILY ISN'T THAT PUNY A CIRCLE.

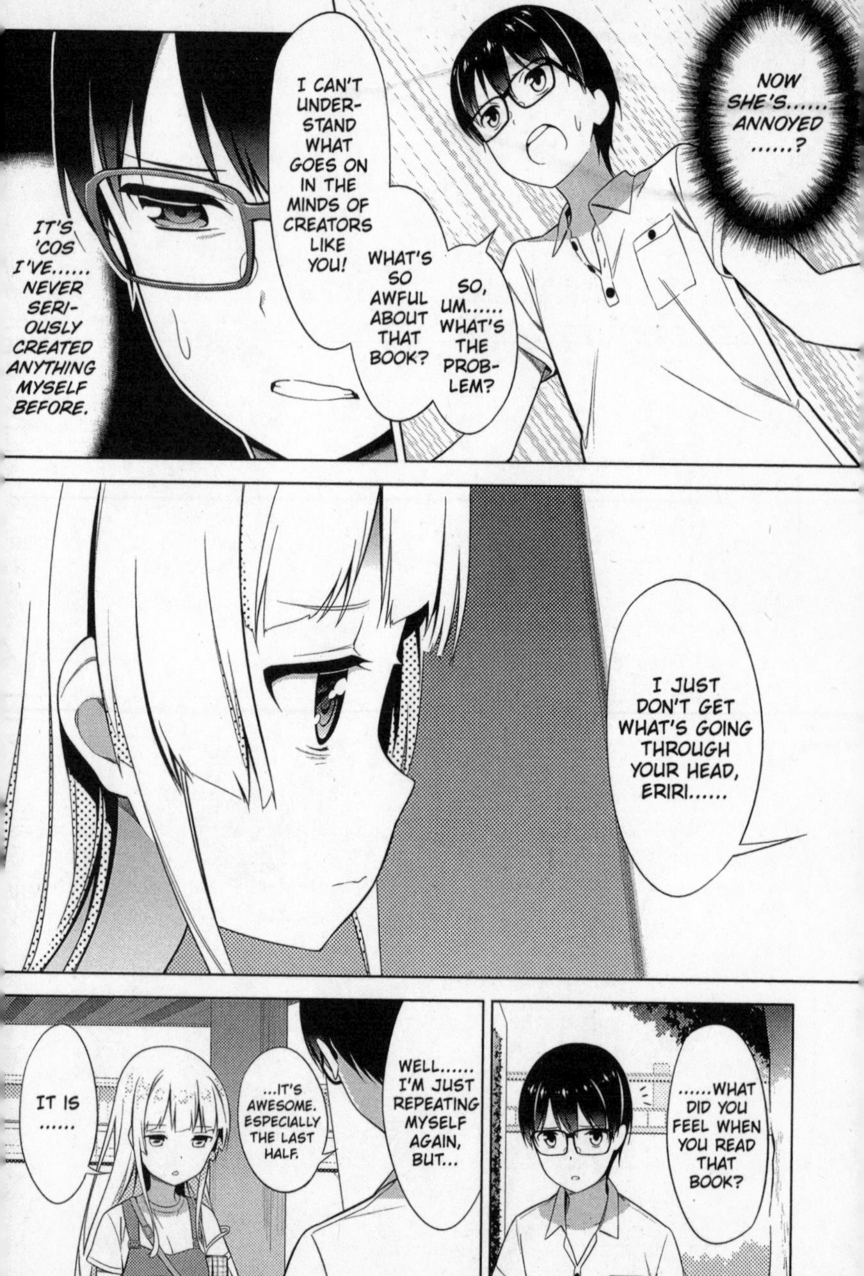
NOW SHE'S...... ANNOYED ......?
SO, UM...... WHAT'S THE PROB-LEM?
WHAT'S SO AWFUL ABOUT THAT BOOK?
I CAN'T UNDER-STAND WHAT GOES ON IN THE MINDS OF CREATORS LIKE YOU!
IT'S 'COS I'VE...... NEVER SERI-OUSLY CREATED ANYTHING MYSELF BEFORE.
I JUST DON'T GET WHAT'S GOING THROUGH YOUR HEAD, ERIRI......
......WHAT DID YOU FEEL WHEN YOU READ THAT BOOK?
WELL...... I'M JUST REPEATING MYSELF AGAIN, BUT...
...IT'S AWESOME. ESPECIALLY THE LAST HALF.
IT IS ......

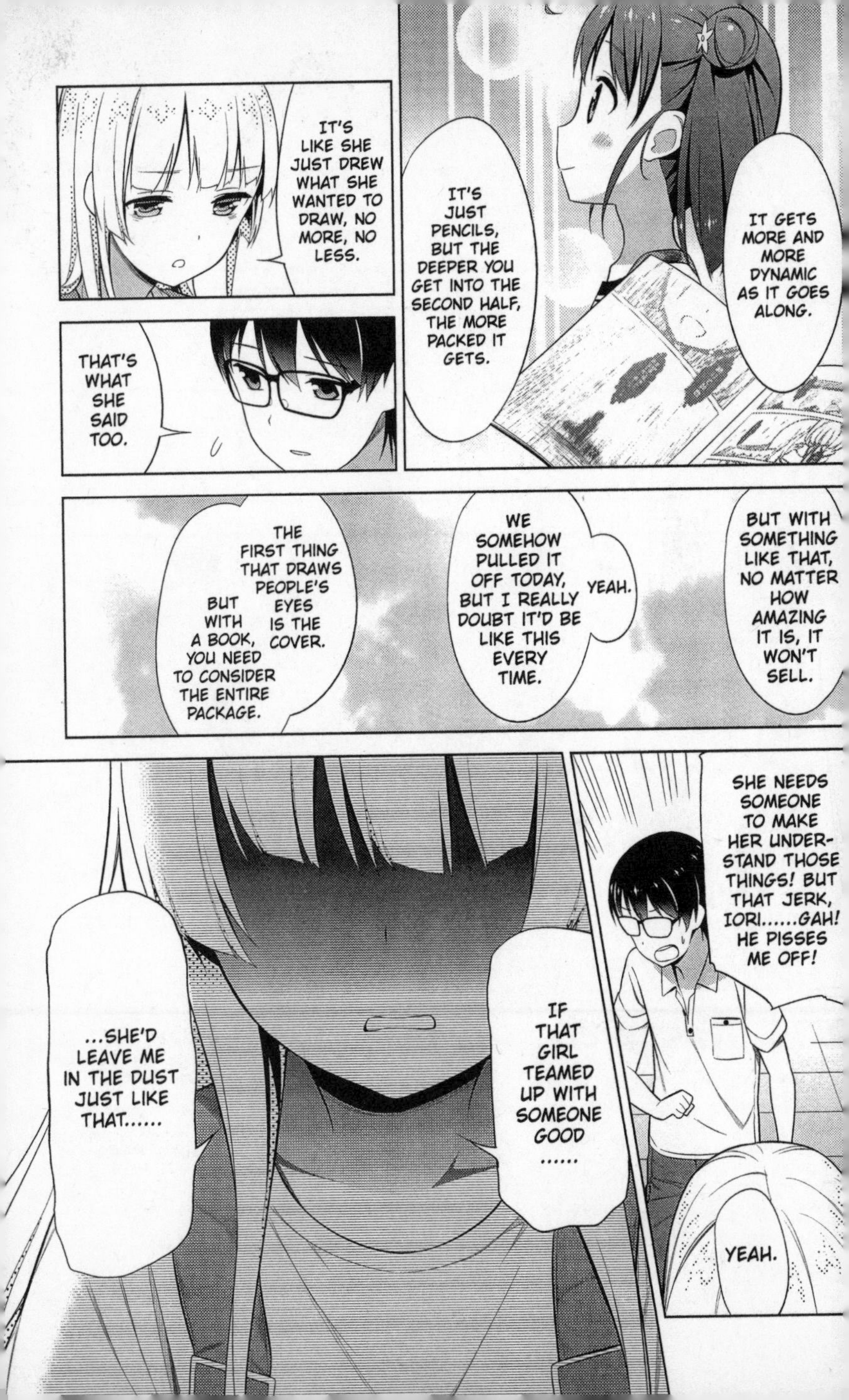
IT GETS MORE AND MORE DYNAMIC AS IT GOES ALONG.
IT'S JUST PENCILS, BUT THE DEEPER YOU GET INTO THE SECOND HALF, THE MORE PACKED IT GETS.
IT'S LIKE SHE JUST DREW WHAT SHE WANTED TO DRAW, NO MORE, NO LESS.
THAT'S WHAT SHE SAID TOO.
BUT WITH SOMETHING LIKE THAT, NO MATTER HOW AMAZING IT IS, IT WON'T SELL.
YEAH.
WE SOMEHOW PULLED IT OFF TODAY, BUT I REALLY DOUBT IT'D BE LIKE THIS EVERY TIME.
THE FIRST THING THAT DRAWS PEOPLE'S EYES IS THE COVER. BUT WITH A BOOK, YOU NEED TO CONSIDER THE ENTIRE PACKAGE.
SHE NEEDS SOMEONE TO MAKE HER UNDER-STAND THOSE THINGS! BUT THAT JERK, IORI......GAH! HE PISSES ME OFF!
YEAH.
IF THAT GIRL TEAMED UP WITH SOMEONE GOOD ......
...SHE'D LEAVE ME IN THE DUST JUST LIKE THAT......

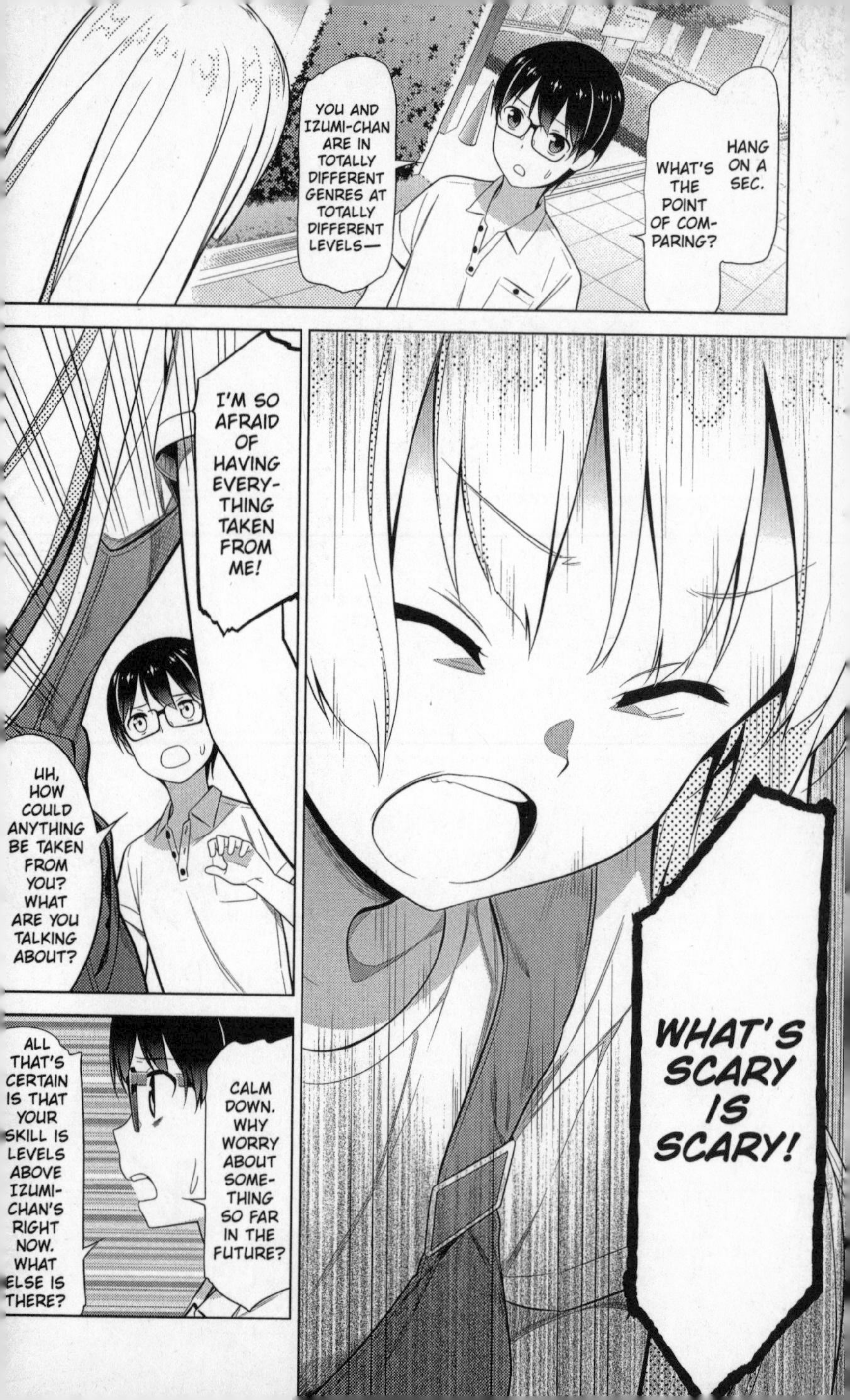
HANG ON A SEC.
WHAT'S THE POINT OF COMPARING?
YOU AND IZUMI-CHAN ARE IN TOTALLY DIFFERENT GENRES AT TOTALLY DIFFERENT LEVELS—
WHAT'S SCARY IS SCARY!
I'M SO AFRAID OF HAVING EVERYTHING TAKEN FROM ME!
UH, HOW COULD ANYTHING BE TAKEN FROM YOU? WHAT ARE YOU TALKING ABOUT?
CALM DOWN. WHY WORRY ABOUT SOMETHING SO FAR IN THE FUTURE?
ALL THAT'S CERTAIN IS THAT YOUR SKILL IS LEVELS ABOVE IZUMI-CHAN'S RIGHT NOW. WHAT ELSE IS THERE?

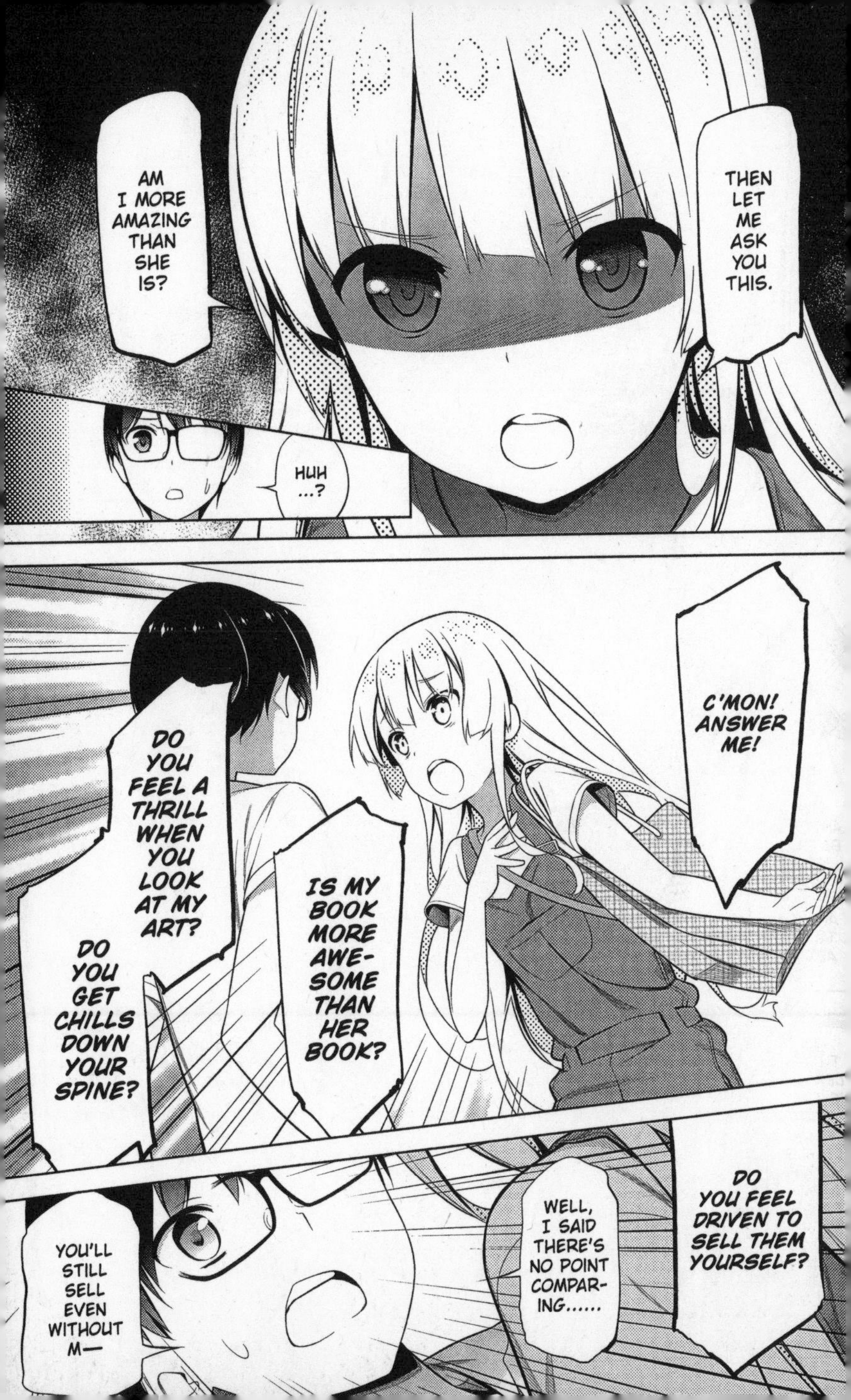
THEN LET ME ASK YOU THIS.
AM I MORE AMAZING THAN SHE IS?
HUH ...?
C'MON! ANSWER ME!
IS MY BOOK MORE AWE-SOME THAN HER BOOK?
DO YOU FEEL A THRILL WHEN YOU LOOK AT MY ART?
DO YOU GET CHILLS DOWN YOUR SPINE?
DO YOU FEEL DRIVEN TO SELL THEM YOURSELF?
WELL, I SAID THERE'S NO POINT COMPAR-ING......
YOU'LL STILL SELL EVEN WITHOUT M—

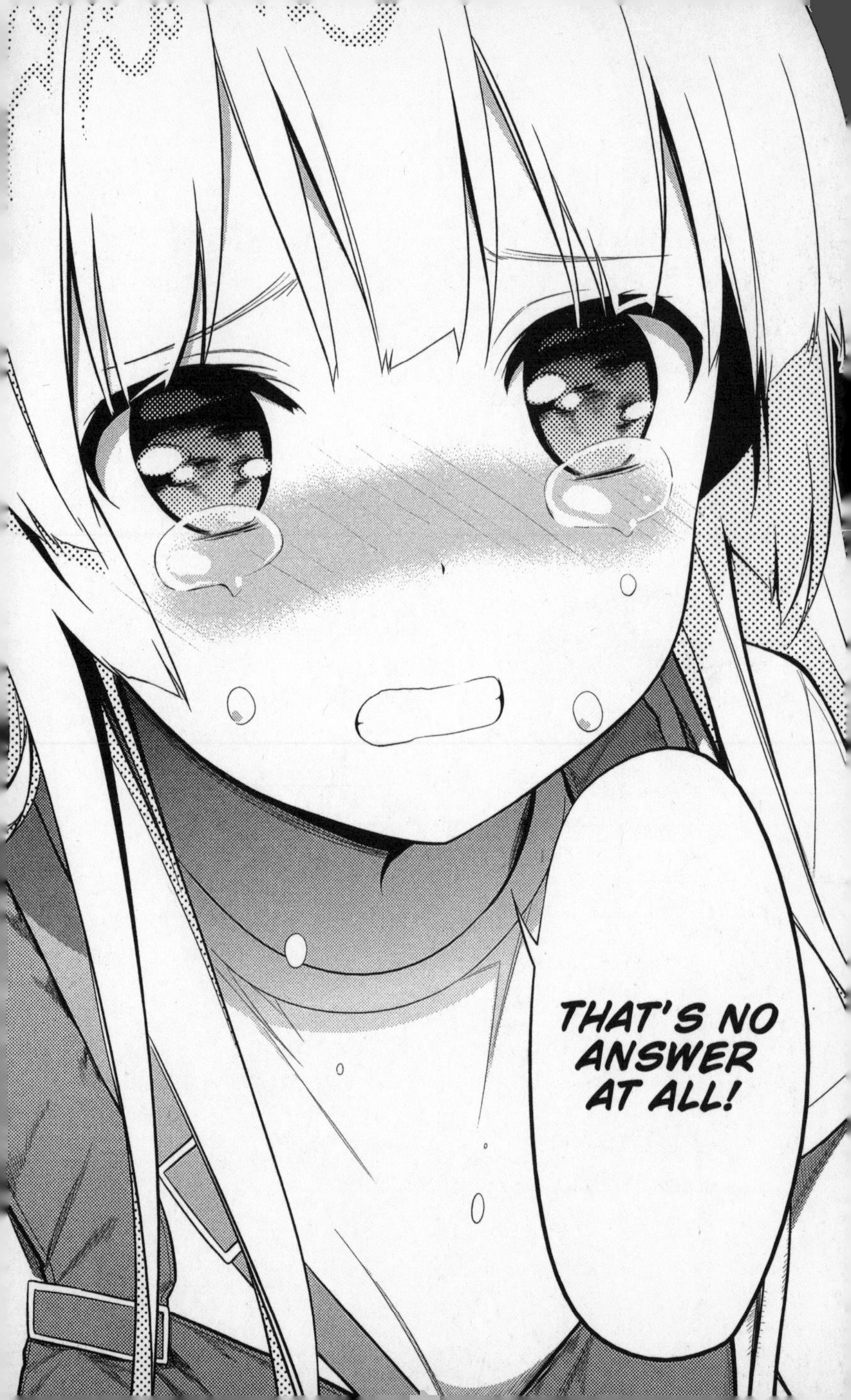
THAT'S NO ANSWER AT ALL!

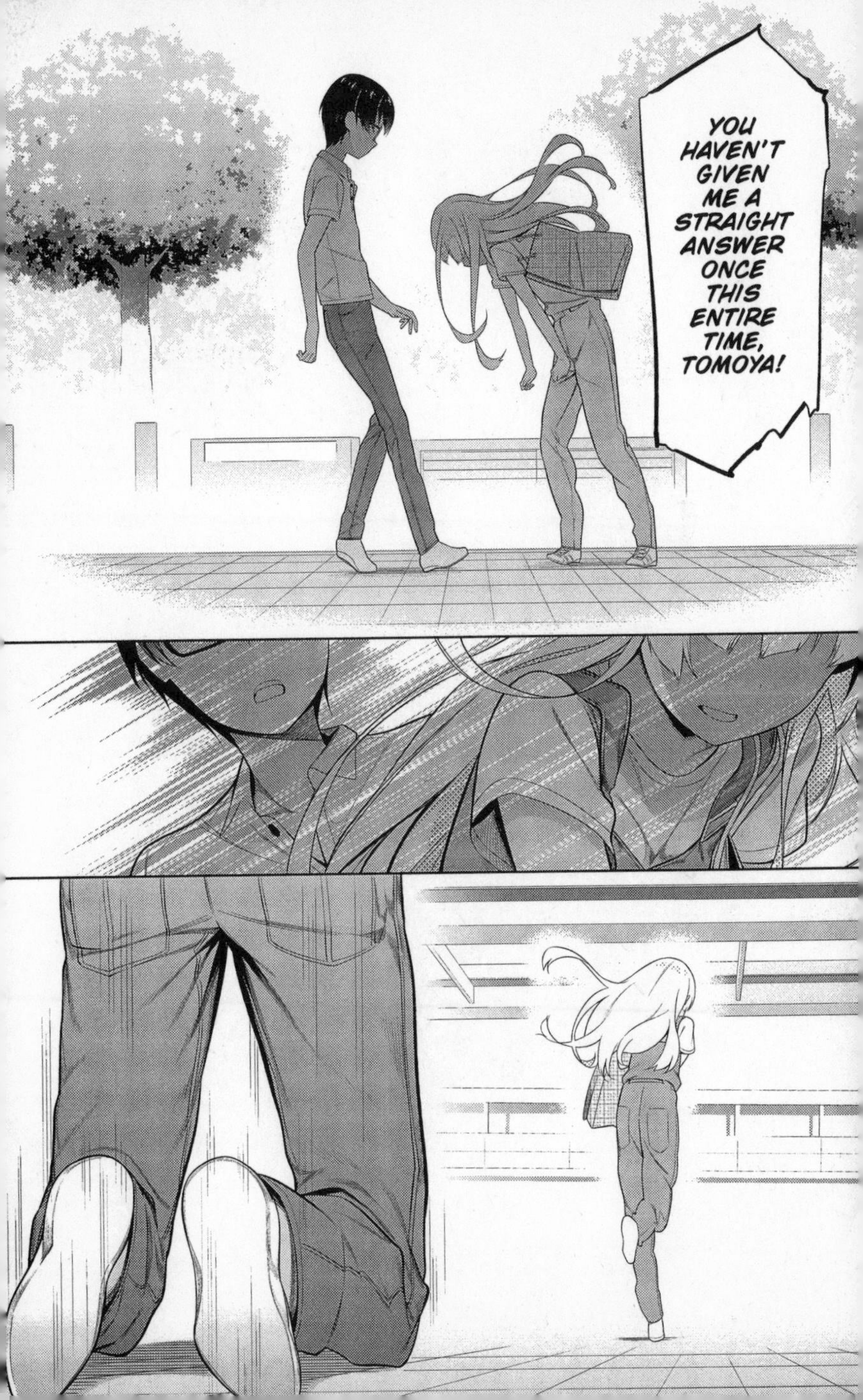
YOU HAVEN'T GIVEN ME A STRAIGHT ANSWER ONCE THIS ENTIRE TIME, TOMOYA!

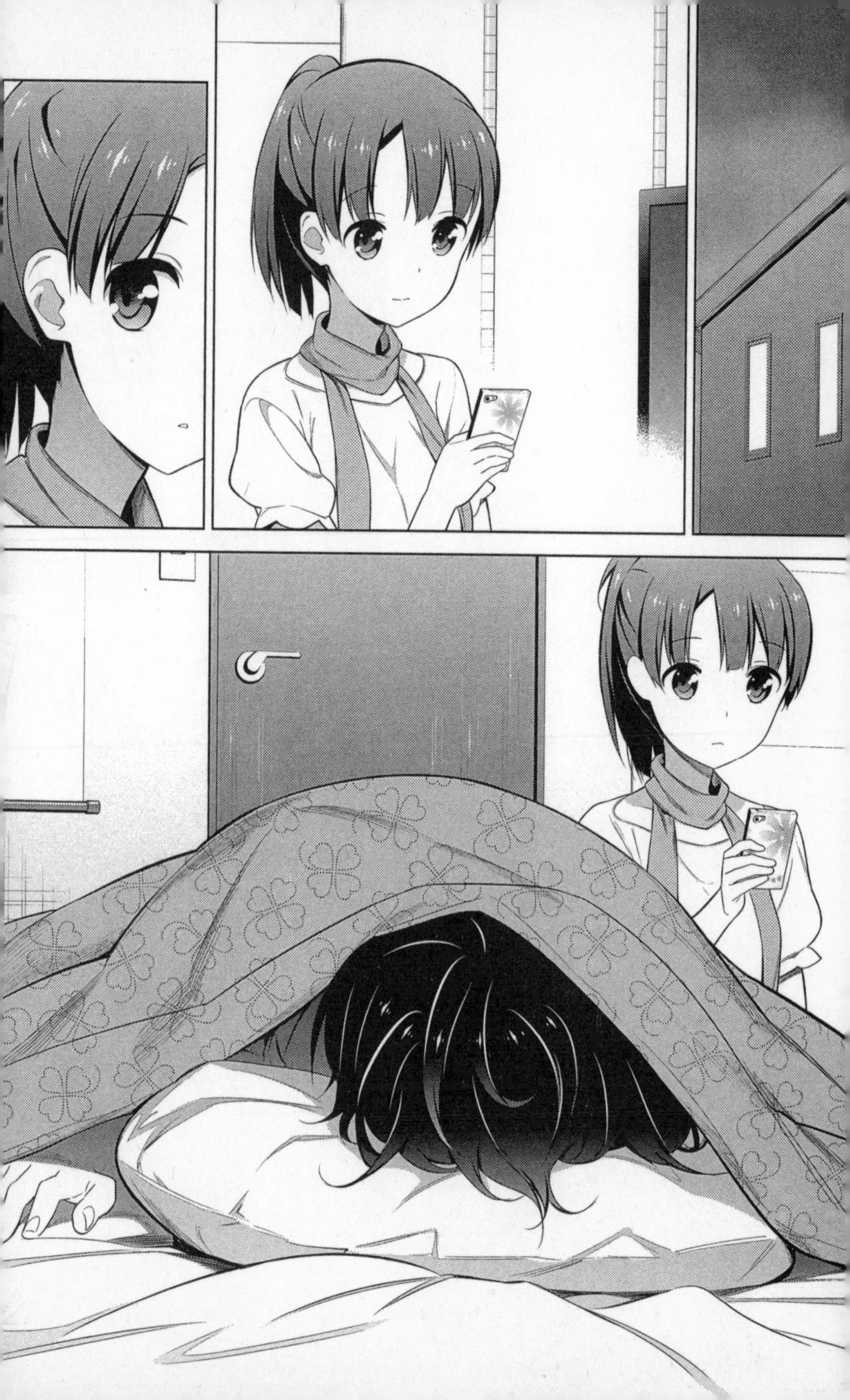

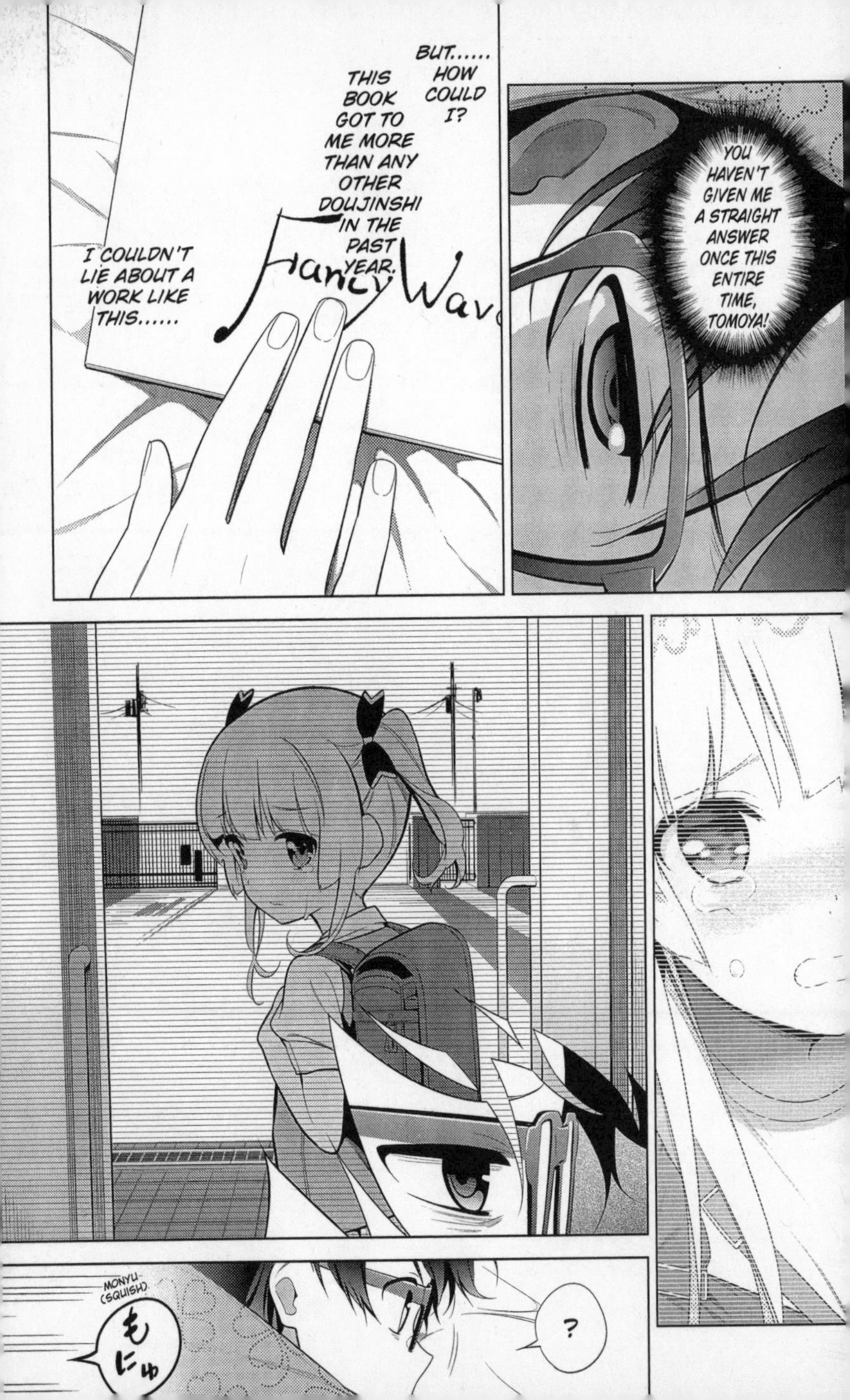
YOU HAVEN'T GIVEN ME A STRAIGHT ANSWER ONCE THIS ENTIRE TIME, TOMOYA!
BUT...... HOW COULD I?
THIS BOOK GOT TO ME MORE THAN ANY OTHER DOUJINSHI IN THE PAST YEAR.
I COULDN'T LIE ABOUT A WORK LIKE THIS......
?
MONYU- (SQUISH)
もにゅ

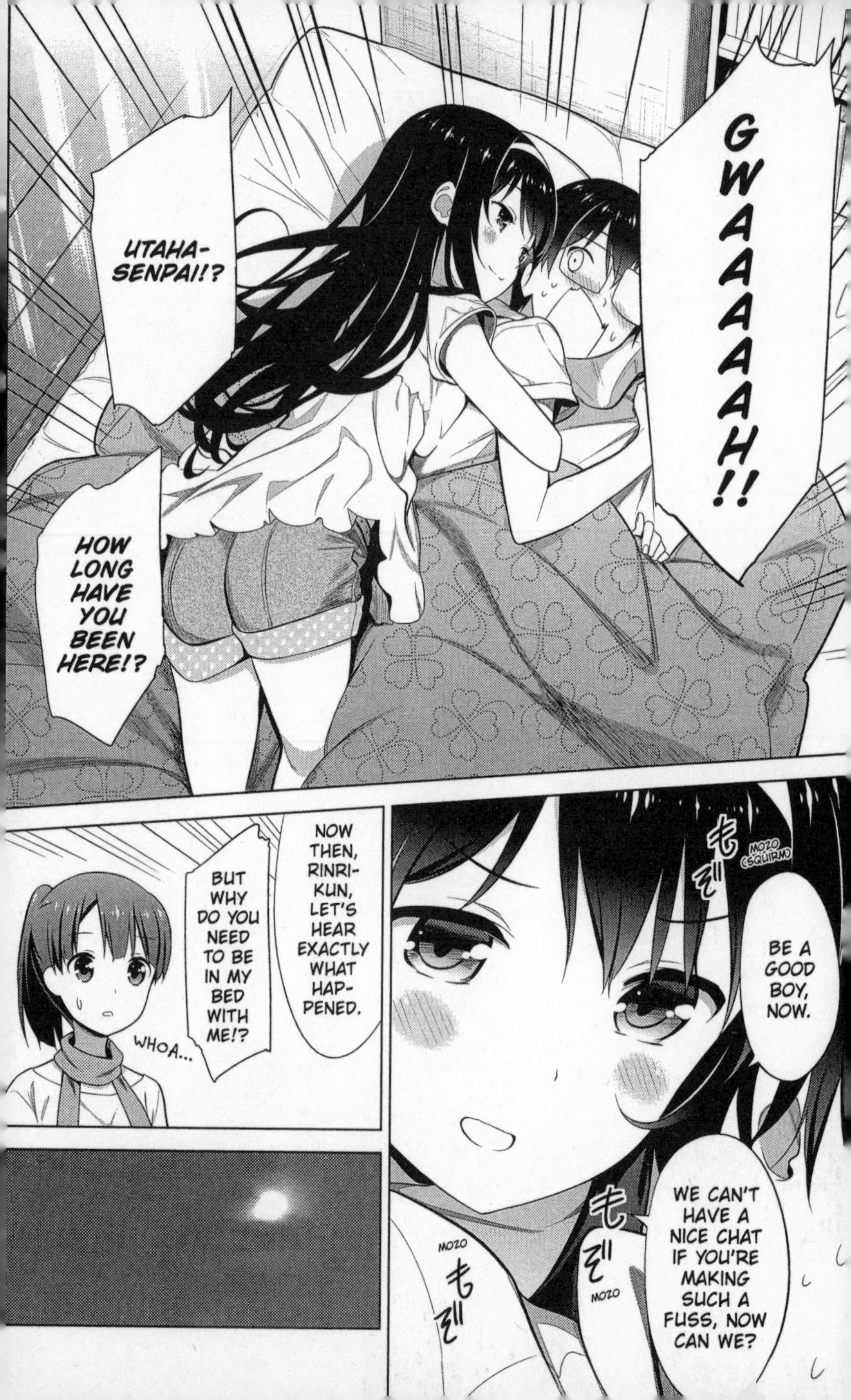
GWAAAAAAAH!!
UTAHA-SENPAI!?
HOW LONG HAVE YOU BEEN HERE!?
もぞ
MOZO (SQUIRM)
BE A GOOD BOY, NOW.
WE CAN'T HAVE A NICE CHAT IF YOU'RE MAKING SUCH A FUSS, NOW CAN WE?
もぞ
MOZO
もぞ
MOZO
NOW THEN, RINRI-KUN, LET'S HEAR EXACTLY WHAT HAPPENED.
BUT WHY DO YOU NEED TO BE IN MY BED WITH ME!?
WHOA...

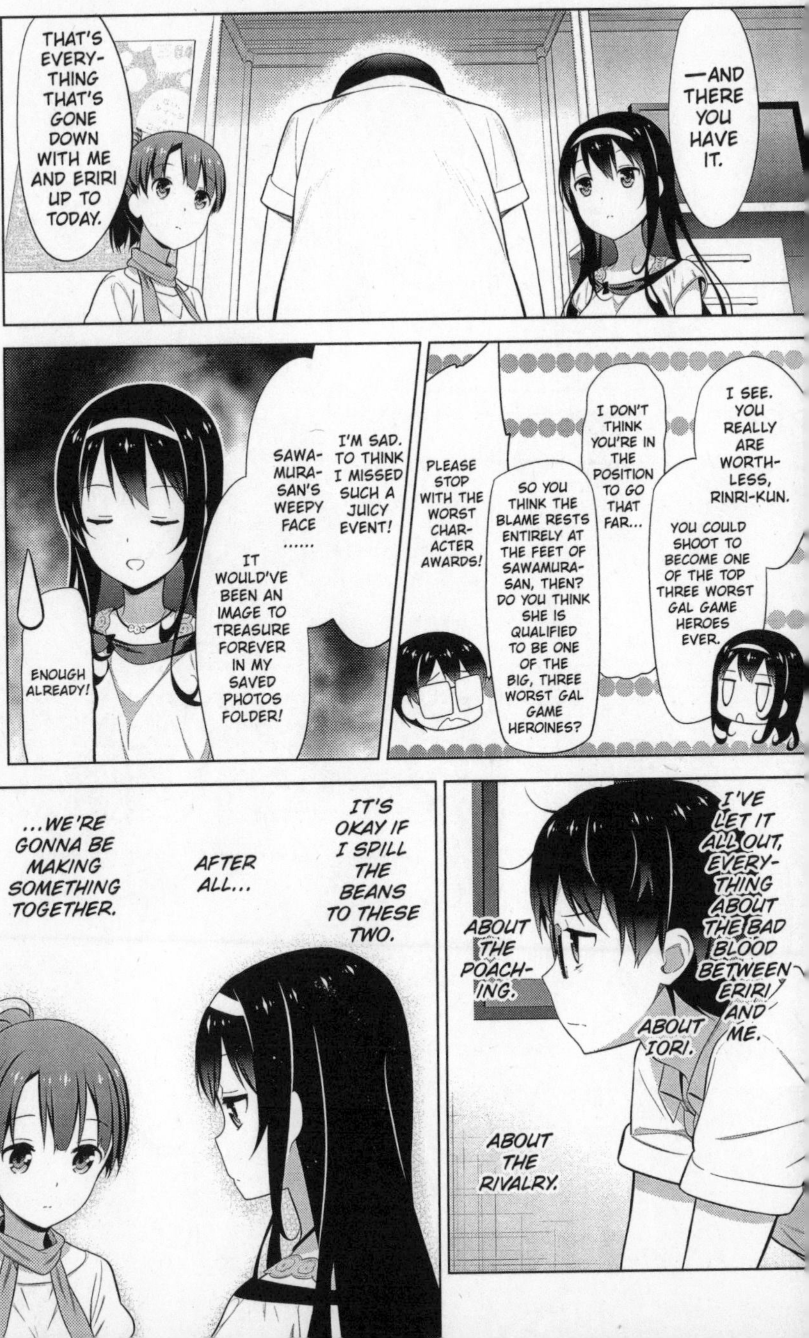
—AND THERE YOU HAVE IT.
THAT'S EVERYTHING THAT'S GONE DOWN WITH ME AND ERIRI UP TO TODAY.
I SEE. YOU REALLY ARE WORTHLESS, RINRI-KUN.
YOU COULD SHOOT TO BECOME ONE OF THE TOP THREE WORST GAL GAME HEROES EVER.
I DON'T THINK YOU'RE IN THE POSITION TO GO THAT FAR...
SO YOU THINK THE BLAME RESTS ENTIRELY AT THE FEET OF SAWAMURA-SAN, THEN? DO YOU THINK SHE IS QUALIFIED TO BE ONE OF THE BIG, THREE WORST GAL GAME HEROINES?
PLEASE STOP WITH THE WORST CHARACTER AWARDS!
I'M SAD. TO THINK I MISSED SUCH A JUICY EVENT!
SAWAMURA-SAN'S WEEPY FACE......
IT WOULD'VE BEEN AN IMAGE TO TREASURE FOREVER IN MY SAVED PHOTOS FOLDER!
ENOUGH ALREADY!
I'VE LET IT ALL OUT, EVERYTHING ABOUT THE BAD BLOOD BETWEEN ERIRI AND ME.
ABOUT IORI.
ABOUT THE POACHING.
ABOUT THE RIVALRY.
IT'S OKAY IF I SPILL THE BEANS TO THESE TWO.
AFTER ALL...
...WE'RE GONNA BE MAKING SOMETHING TOGETHER.

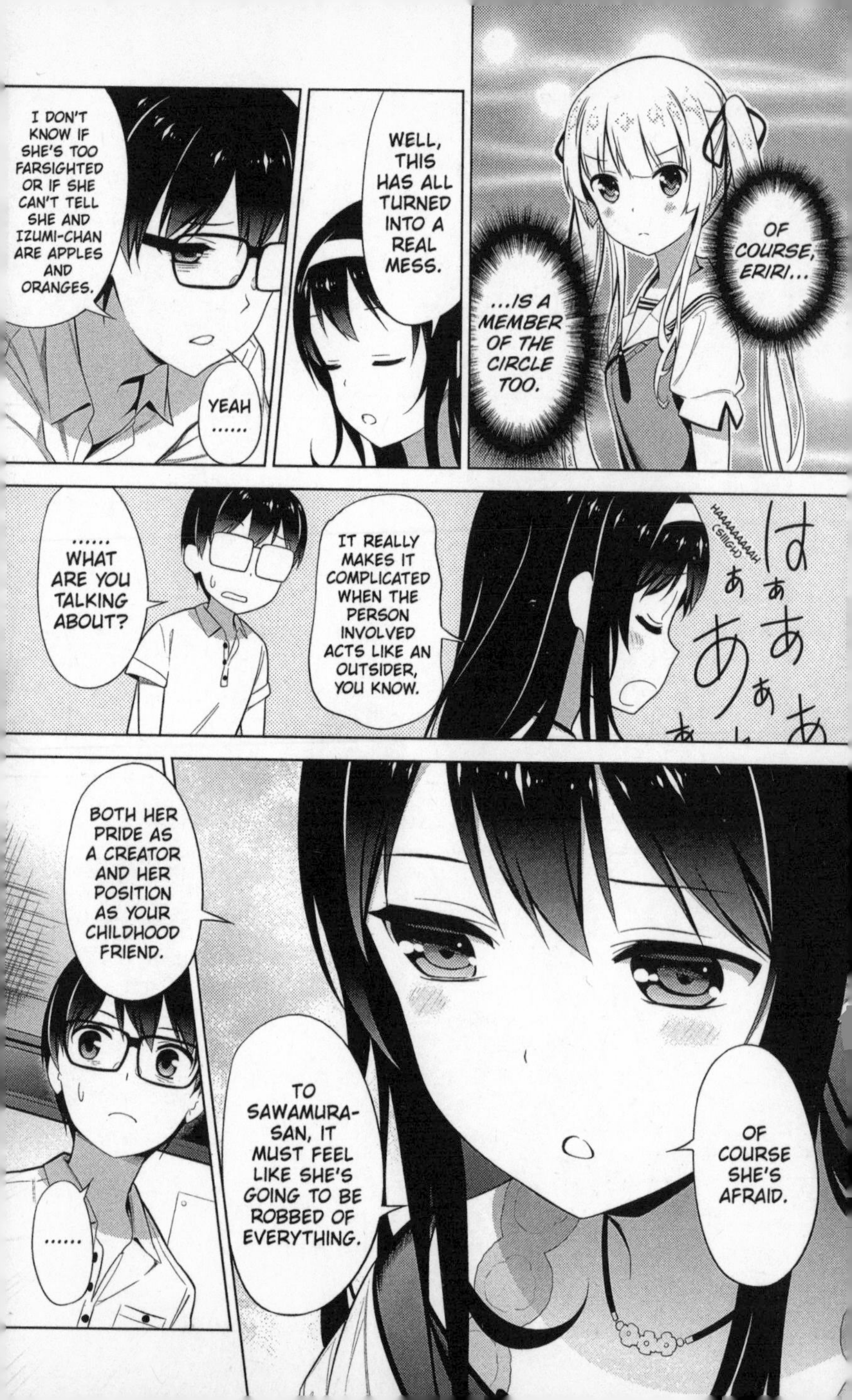
OF COURSE, ERIRI…
…IS A MEMBER OF THE CIRCLE TOO.
WELL, THIS HAS ALL TURNED INTO A REAL MESS.
I DON'T KNOW IF SHE'S TOO FARSIGHTED OR IF SHE CAN'T TELL SHE AND IZUMI-CHAN ARE APPLES AND ORANGES.
YEAH ……
HAAAAAAAAH (SIIIGH)
IT REALLY MAKES IT COMPLICATED WHEN THE PERSON INVOLVED ACTS LIKE AN OUTSIDER, YOU KNOW.
…… WHAT ARE YOU TALKING ABOUT?
OF COURSE SHE'S AFRAID.
TO SAWAMURA-SAN, IT MUST FEEL LIKE SHE'S GOING TO BE ROBBED OF EVERYTHING.
BOTH HER PRIDE AS A CREATOR AND HER POSITION AS YOUR CHILDHOOD FRIEND.
……

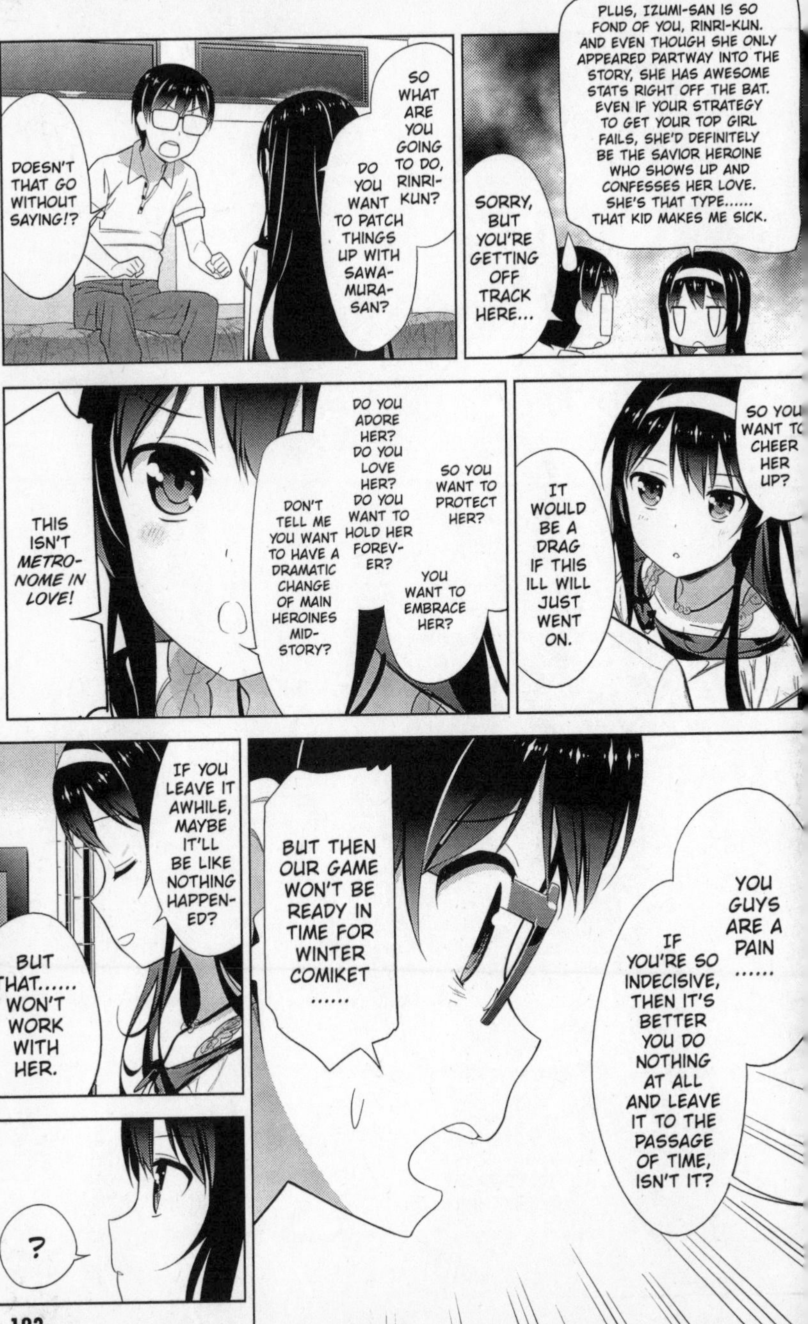

PLUS, IZUMI-SAN IS SO FOND OF YOU, RINRI-KUN. AND EVEN THOUGH SHE ONLY APPEARED PARTWAY INTO THE STORY, SHE HAS AWESOME STATS RIGHT OFF THE BAT. EVEN IF YOUR STRATEGY TO GET YOUR TOP GIRL FAILS, SHE'D DEFINITELY BE THE SAVIOR HEROINE WHO SHOWS UP AND CONFESSES HER LOVE. SHE'S THAT TYPE...... THAT KID MAKES ME SICK.
SORRY, BUT YOU'RE GETTING OFF TRACK HERE...
SO WHAT ARE YOU GOING TO DO, RINRI-KUN?
DO YOU WANT TO PATCH THINGS UP WITH SAWAMURA-SAN?
DOESN'T THAT GO WITHOUT SAYING!?
SO YOU WANT TO CHEER HER UP?
IT WOULD BE A DRAG IF THIS ILL WILL JUST WENT ON.
SO YOU WANT TO PROTECT HER?
DO YOU ADORE HER? DO YOU LOVE HER? DO YOU WANT TO HOLD HER FOREVER?
YOU WANT TO EMBRACE HER?
DON'T TELL ME YOU WANT TO HAVE A DRAMATIC CHANGE OF MAIN HEROINES MID-STORY?
THIS ISN'T *METRONOME IN LOVE!*
YOU GUYS ARE A PAIN......
IF YOU'RE SO INDECISIVE, THEN IT'S BETTER YOU DO NOTHING AT ALL AND LEAVE IT TO THE PASSAGE OF TIME, ISN'T IT?
BUT THEN OUR GAME WON'T BE READY IN TIME FOR WINTER COMIKET......
IF YOU LEAVE IT AWHILE, MAYBE IT'LL BE LIKE NOTHING HAPPENED?
BUT THAT...... WON'T WORK WITH HER.
?

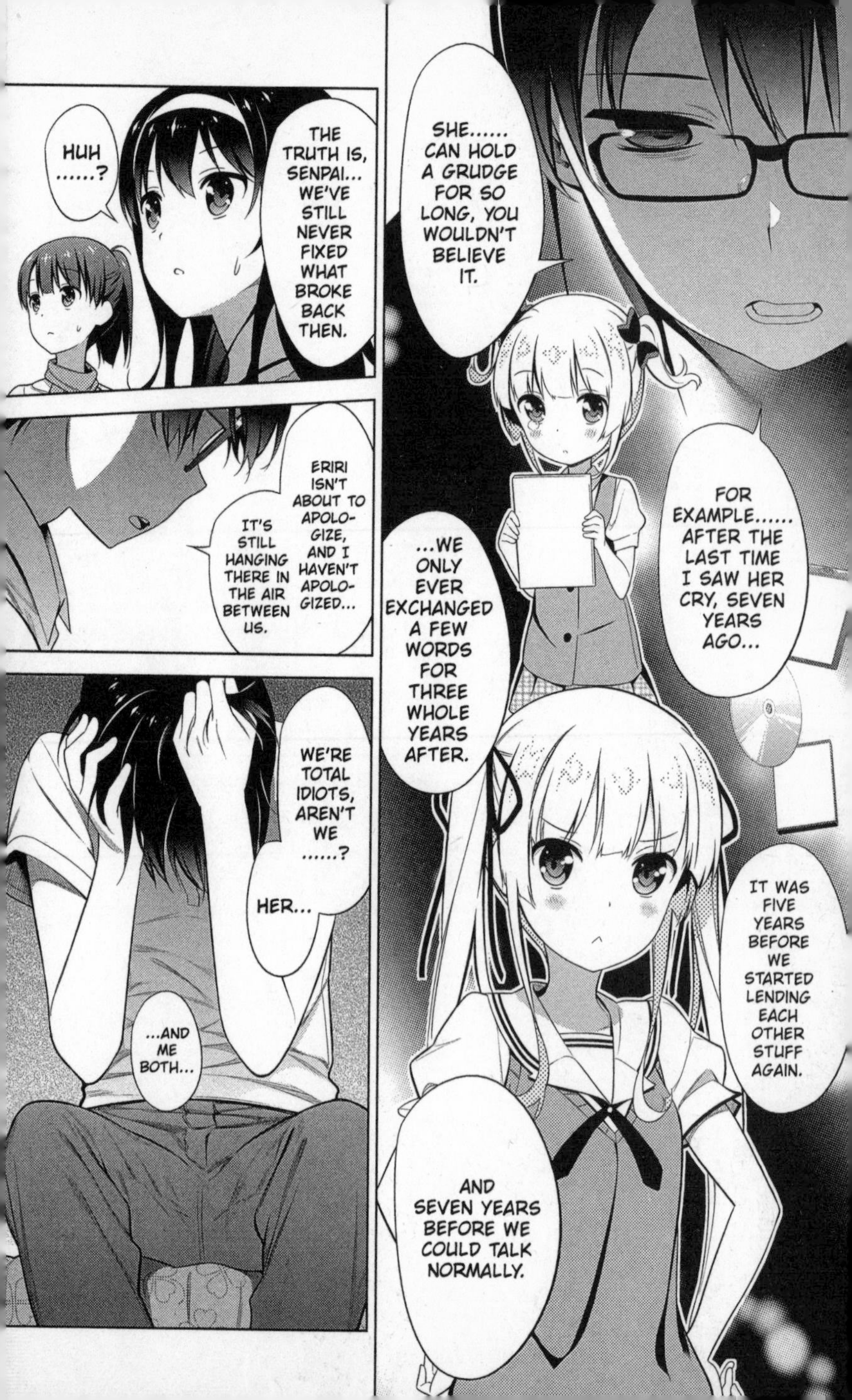
SHE...... CAN HOLD A GRUDGE FOR SO LONG, YOU WOULDN'T BELIEVE IT.
FOR EXAMPLE...... AFTER THE LAST TIME I SAW HER CRY, SEVEN YEARS AGO...
...WE ONLY EVER EXCHANGED A FEW WORDS FOR THREE WHOLE YEARS AFTER.
IT WAS FIVE YEARS BEFORE WE STARTED LENDING EACH OTHER STUFF AGAIN.
AND SEVEN YEARS BEFORE WE COULD TALK NORMALLY.
THE TRUTH IS, SENPAI... WE'VE STILL NEVER FIXED WHAT BROKE BACK THEN.
HUH ......?
ERIRI ISN'T ABOUT TO APOLOGIZE, AND I HAVEN'T APOLOGIZED...
IT'S STILL HANGING THERE IN THE AIR BETWEEN US.
WE'RE TOTAL IDIOTS, AREN'T WE ......?
HER...
...AND ME BOTH...

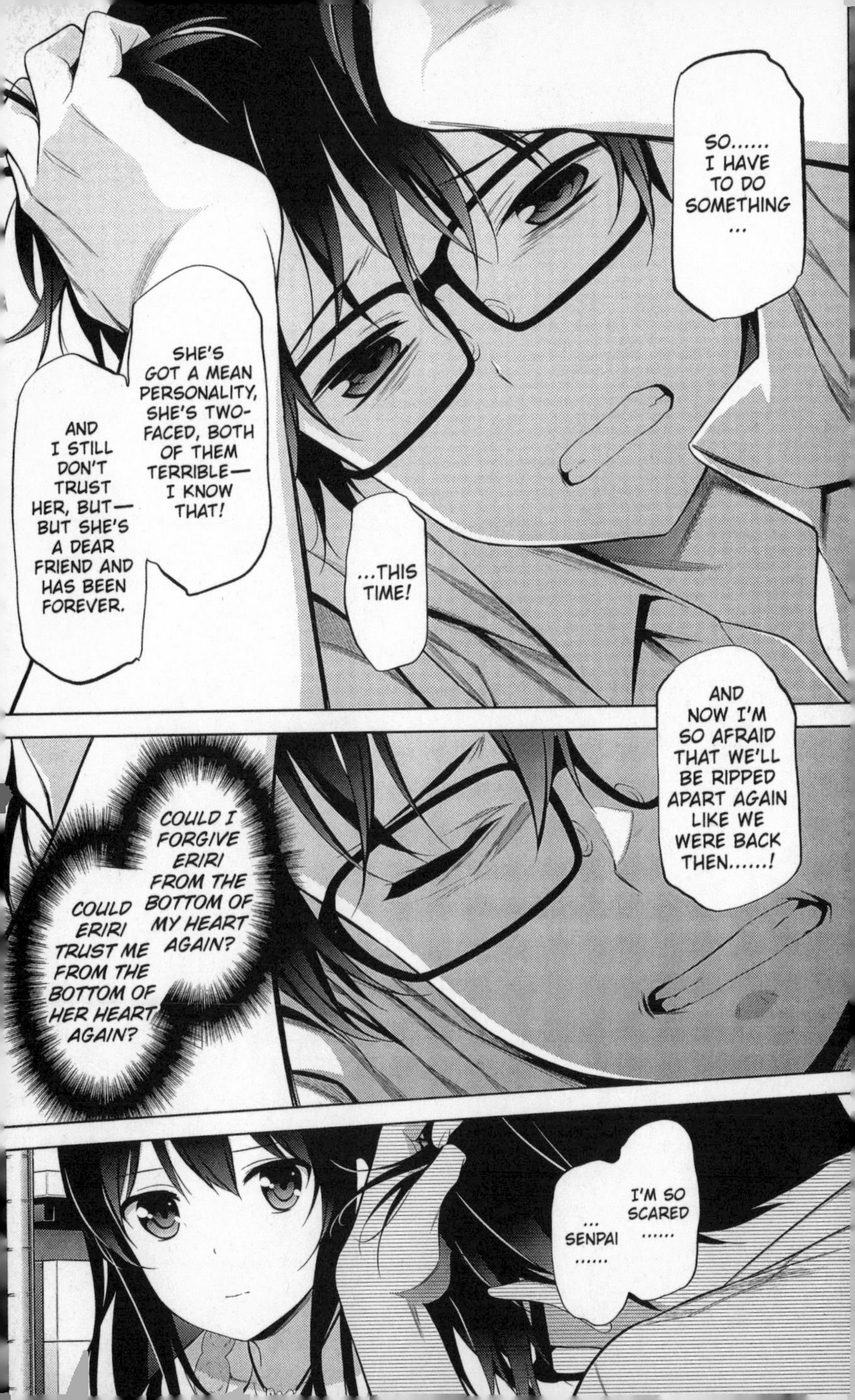
SO...... I HAVE TO DO SOMETHING ...
...THIS TIME!
SHE'S GOT A MEAN PERSONALITY, SHE'S TWO-FACED, BOTH OF THEM TERRIBLE— I KNOW THAT!
AND I STILL DON'T TRUST HER, BUT— BUT SHE'S A DEAR FRIEND AND HAS BEEN FOREVER.
AND NOW I'M SO AFRAID THAT WE'LL BE RIPPED APART AGAIN LIKE WE WERE BACK THEN......!
COULD I FORGIVE ERIRI FROM THE BOTTOM OF MY HEART AGAIN?
COULD ERIRI TRUST ME FROM THE BOTTOM OF HER HEART AGAIN?
I'M SO SCARED ......
... SENPAI ......

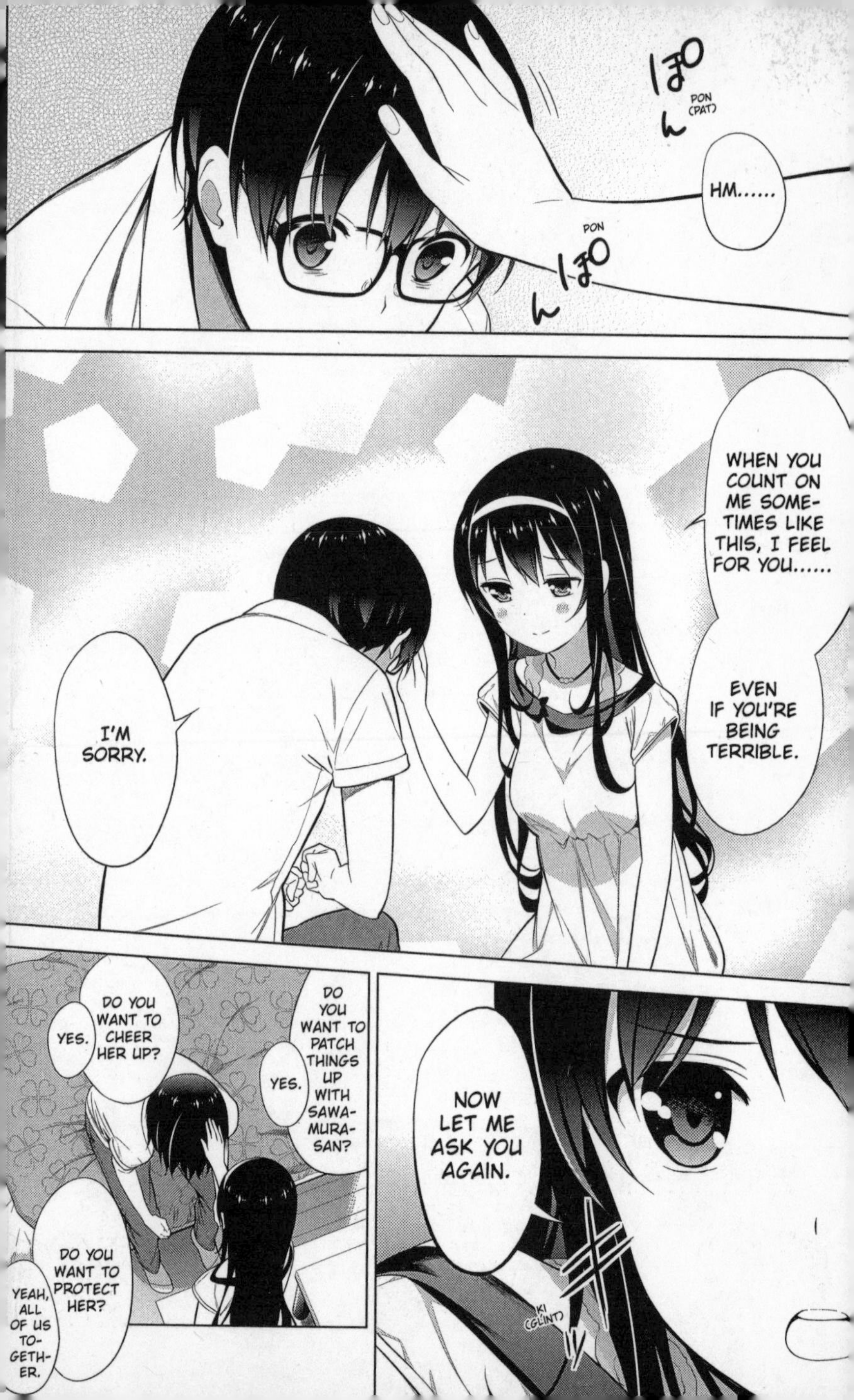
ぽん
PON (PAT)
HM......
PON
ぽん
WHEN YOU COUNT ON ME SOME-TIMES LIKE THIS, I FEEL FOR YOU......
EVEN IF YOU'RE BEING TERRIBLE.
I'M SORRY.
NOW LET ME ASK YOU AGAIN.
KI (GLINT)
DO YOU WANT TO PATCH THINGS UP WITH SAWA-MURA-SAN?
YES.
DO YOU WANT TO CHEER HER UP?
YES.
DO YOU WANT TO PROTECT HER?
YEAH, ALL OF US TO-GETH-ER.

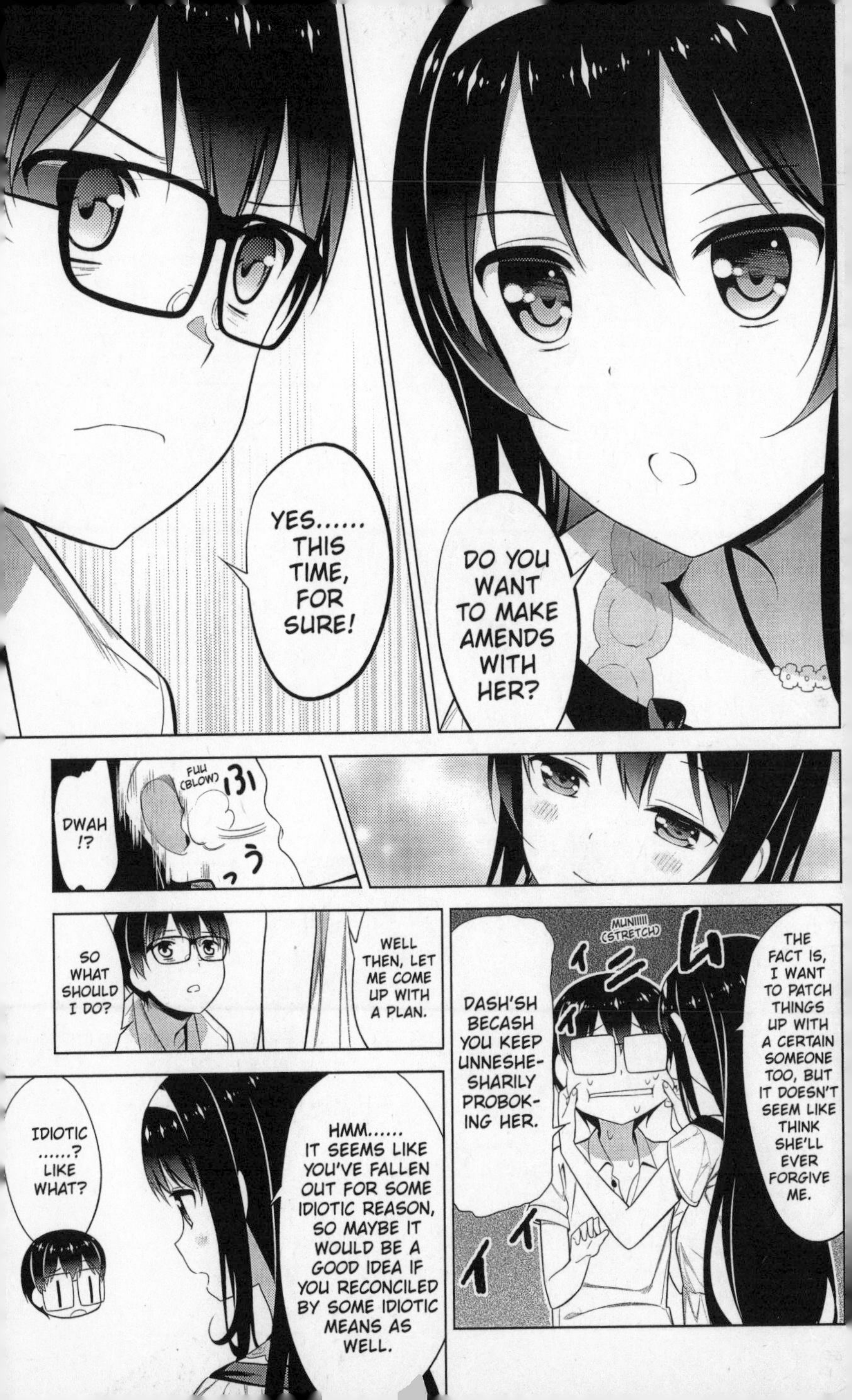
DO YOU WANT TO MAKE AMENDS WITH HER?
YES...... THIS TIME, FOR SURE!
FUU (BLOW)
DWAH !?
THE FACT IS, I WANT TO PATCH THINGS UP WITH A CERTAIN SOMEONE TOO, BUT IT DOESN'T SEEM LIKE THINK SHE'LL EVER FORGIVE ME.
MUNIIIII (STRETCH)
DASH'SH BECASH YOU KEEP UNNESHE-SHARILY PROBOK-ING HER.
WELL THEN, LET ME COME UP WITH A PLAN.
SO WHAT SHOULD I DO?
HMM...... IT SEEMS LIKE YOU'VE FALLEN OUT FOR SOME IDIOTIC REASON, SO MAYBE IT WOULD BE A GOOD IDEA IF YOU RECONCILED BY SOME IDIOTIC MEANS AS WELL.
IDIOTIC ......? LIKE WHAT?

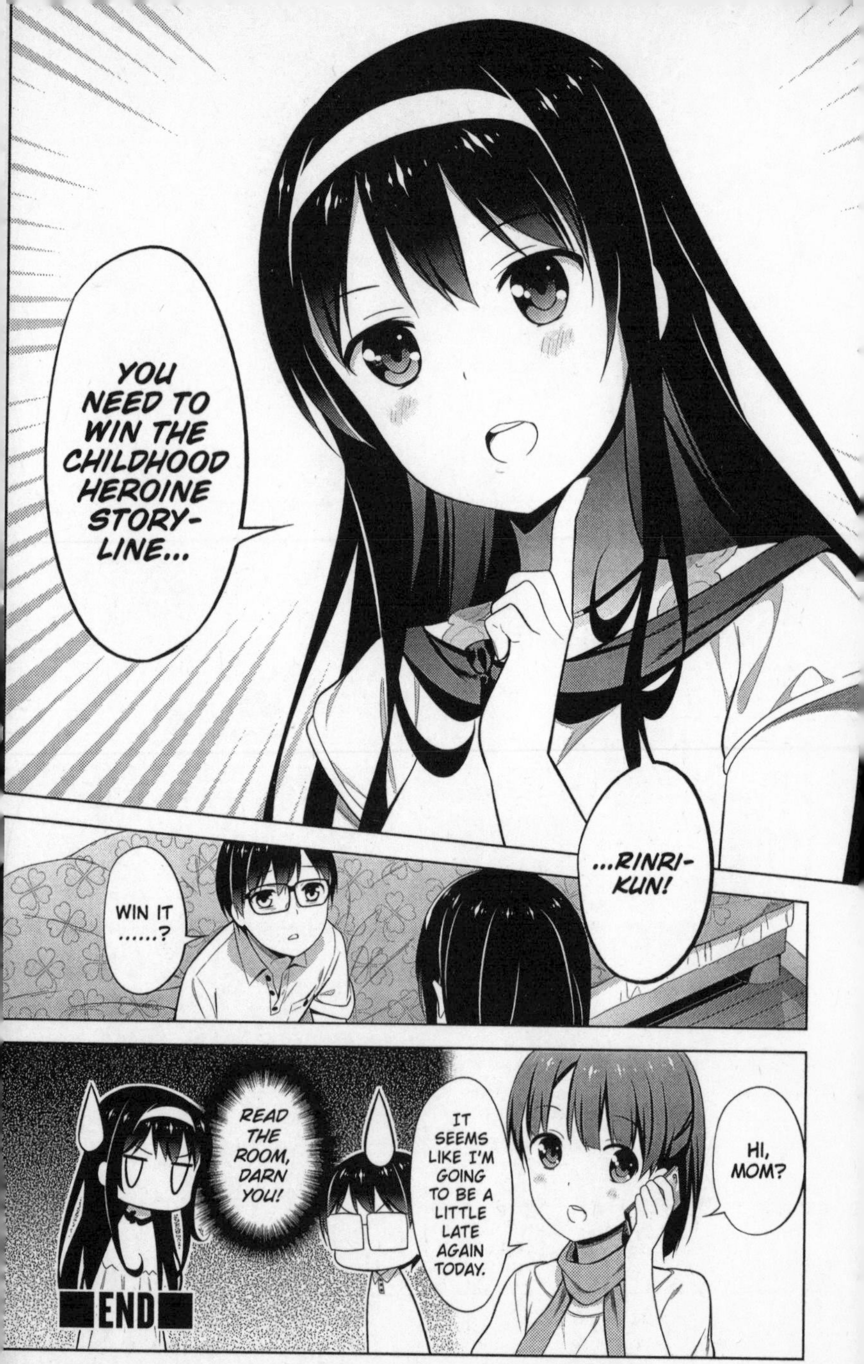
YOU NEED TO WIN THE CHILDHOOD HEROINE STORY-LINE...
...RINRI-KUN!
WIN IT ......?
HI, MOM?
IT SEEMS LIKE I'M GOING TO BE A LITTLE LATE AGAIN TODAY.
READ THE ROOM, DARN YOU!
END

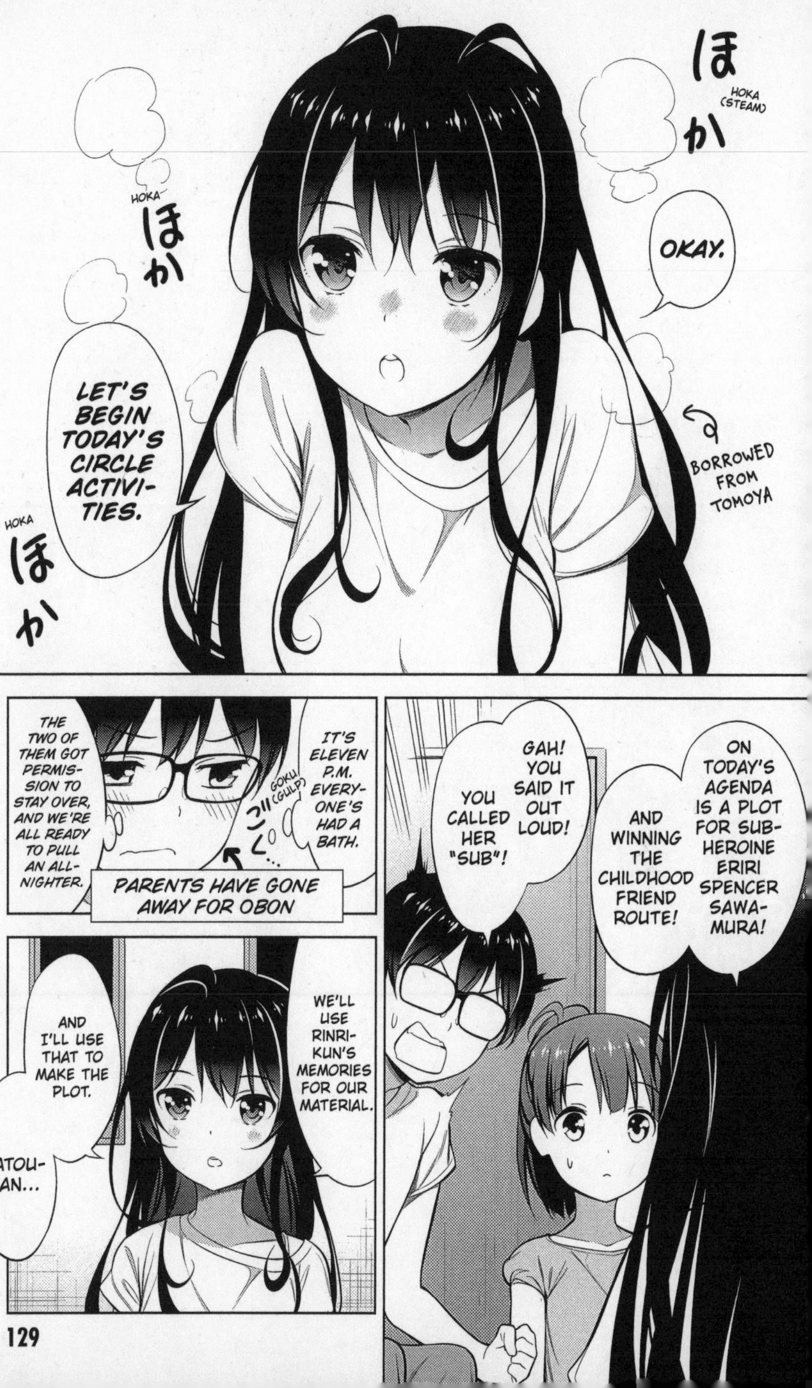

ほか
HOKA (STEAM)
OKAY.
BORROWED FROM TOMOYA
HOKA
ほか
LET'S BEGIN TODAY'S CIRCLE ACTIVITIES.
HOKA
ほか
ON TODAY'S AGENDA IS A PLOT FOR SUB-HEROINE ERIRI SPENCER SAWAMURA!
AND WINNING THE CHILDHOOD FRIEND ROUTE!
GAH! YOU SAID IT OUT LOUD!
YOU CALLED HER "SUB"!
IT'S ELEVEN P.M. EVERYONE'S HAD A BATH.
ごくっ…
GOKU (GULP)
THE TWO OF THEM GOT PERMISSION TO STAY OVER, AND WE'RE ALL READY TO PULL AN ALL-NIGHTER.
PARENTS HAVE GONE AWAY FOR OBON
WE'LL USE RINRI-KUN'S MEMORIES FOR OUR MATERIAL.
AND I'LL USE THAT TO MAKE THE PLOT.
KATOU-SAN...

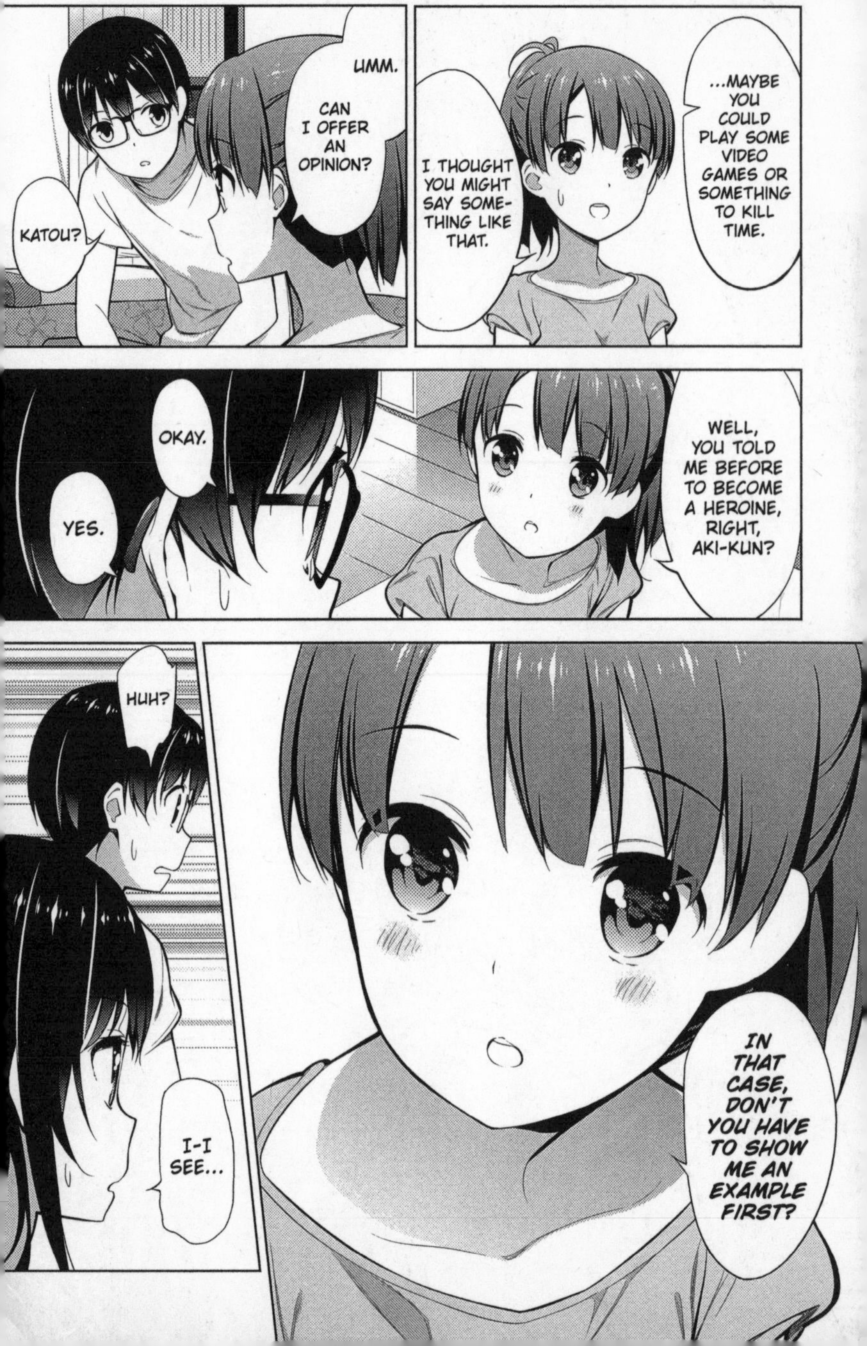
...MAYBE YOU COULD PLAY SOME VIDEO GAMES OR SOMETHING TO KILL TIME.
I THOUGHT YOU MIGHT SAY SOME-THING LIKE THAT.
UMM.
CAN I OFFER AN OPINION?
KATOU?
WELL, YOU TOLD ME BEFORE TO BECOME A HEROINE, RIGHT, AKI-KUN?
OKAY.
YES.
IN THAT CASE, DON'T YOU HAVE TO SHOW ME AN EXAMPLE FIRST?
HUH?
I-I SEE...

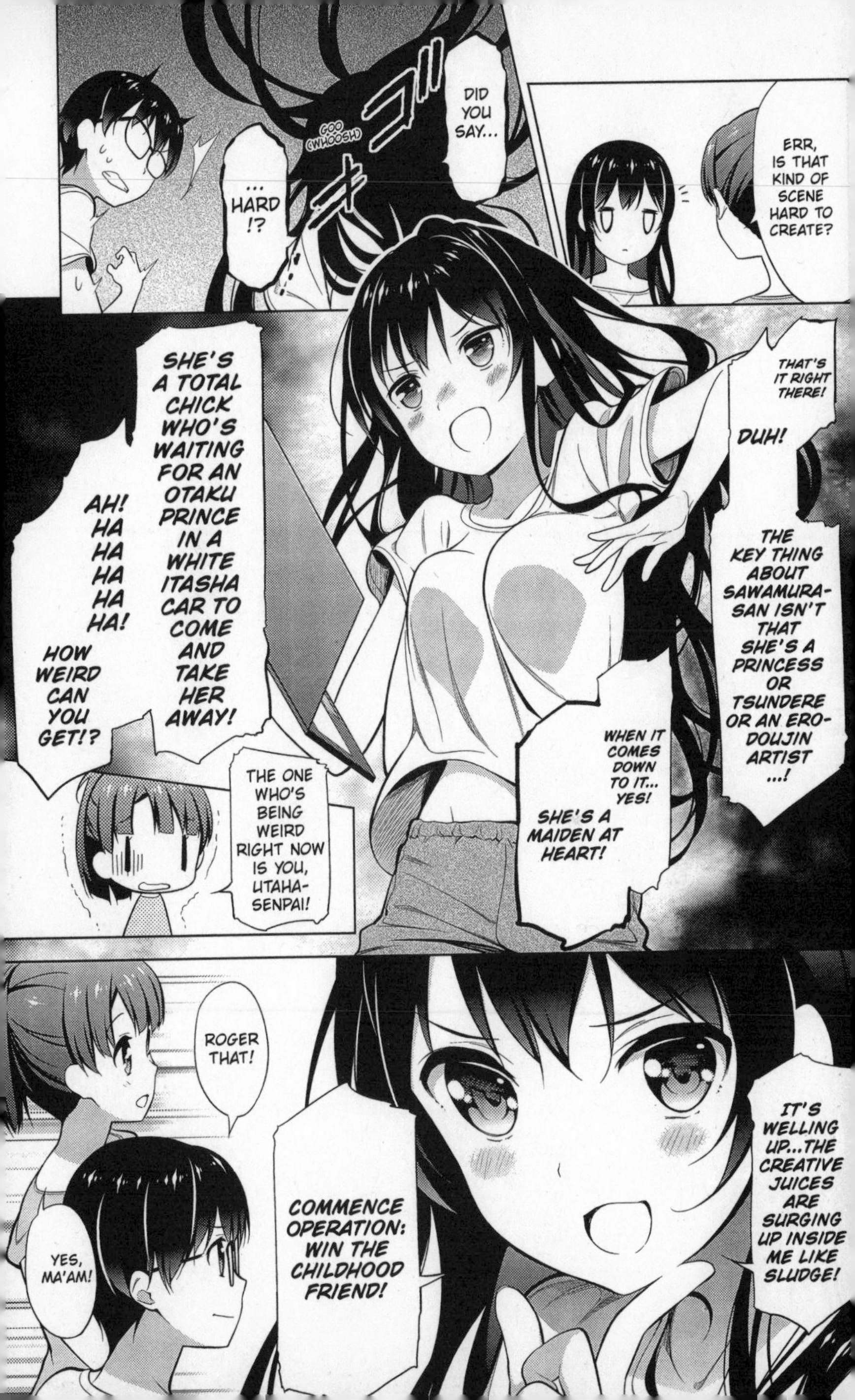
ERR, IS THAT KIND OF SCENE HARD TO CREATE?
DID YOU SAY...
GOO (WHOOSH)
...HARD!?
THAT'S IT RIGHT THERE!
DUH!
THE KEY THING ABOUT SAWAMURA-SAN ISN'T THAT SHE'S A PRINCESS OR TSUNDERE OR AN ERO-DOUJIN ARTIST ...!
WHEN IT COMES DOWN TO IT... YES!
SHE'S A MAIDEN AT HEART!
SHE'S A TOTAL CHICK WHO'S WAITING FOR AN OTAKU PRINCE IN A WHITE ITASHA CAR TO COME AND TAKE HER AWAY!
AH! HA HA HA HA HA!
HOW WEIRD CAN YOU GET!?
THE ONE WHO'S BEING WEIRD RIGHT NOW IS YOU, UTAHA-SENPAI!
IT'S WELLING UP...THE CREATIVE JUICES ARE SURGING UP INSIDE ME LIKE SLUDGE!
COMMENCE OPERATION: WIN THE CHILDHOOD FRIEND!
ROGER THAT!
YES, MA'AM!

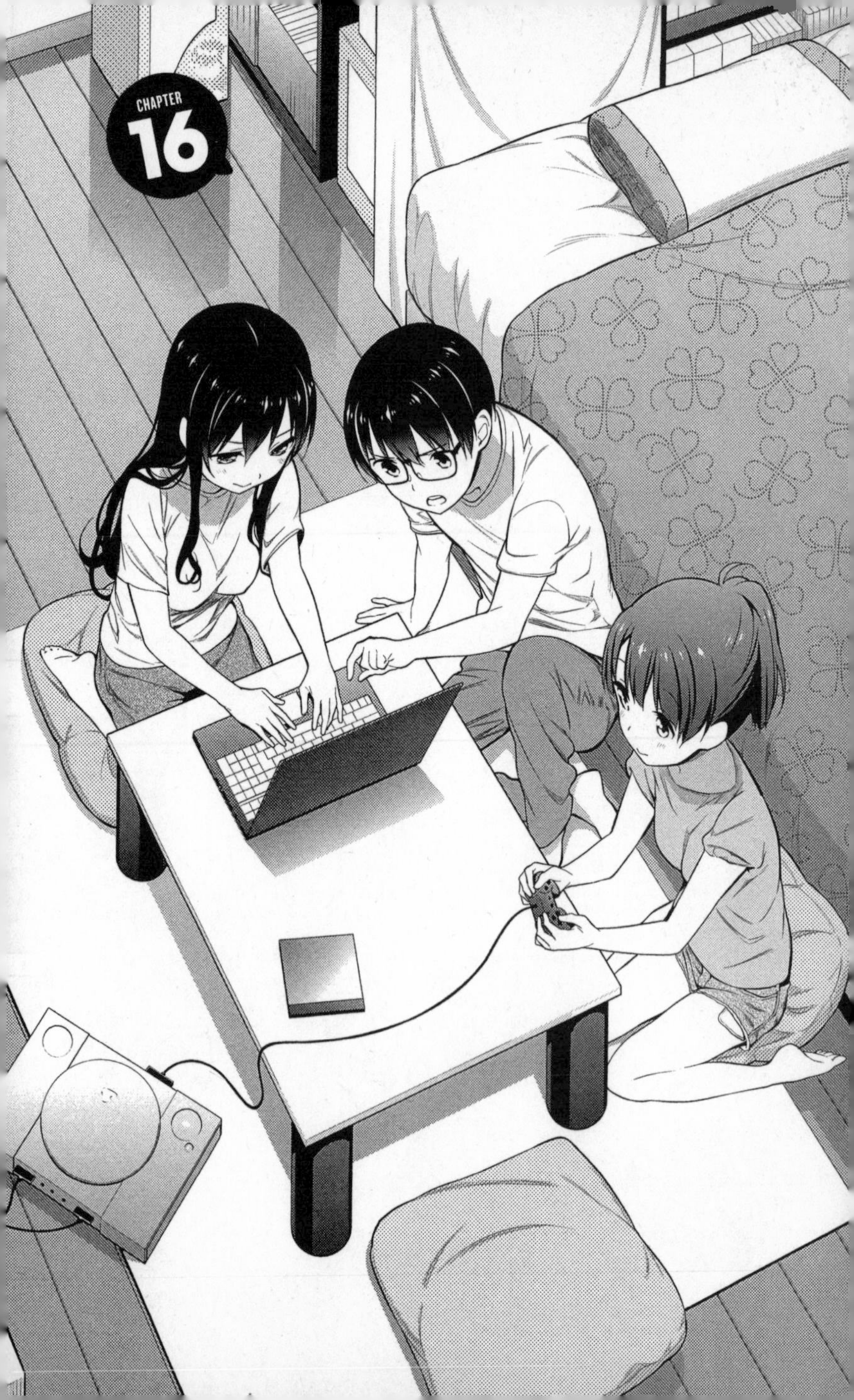
CHAPTER
16

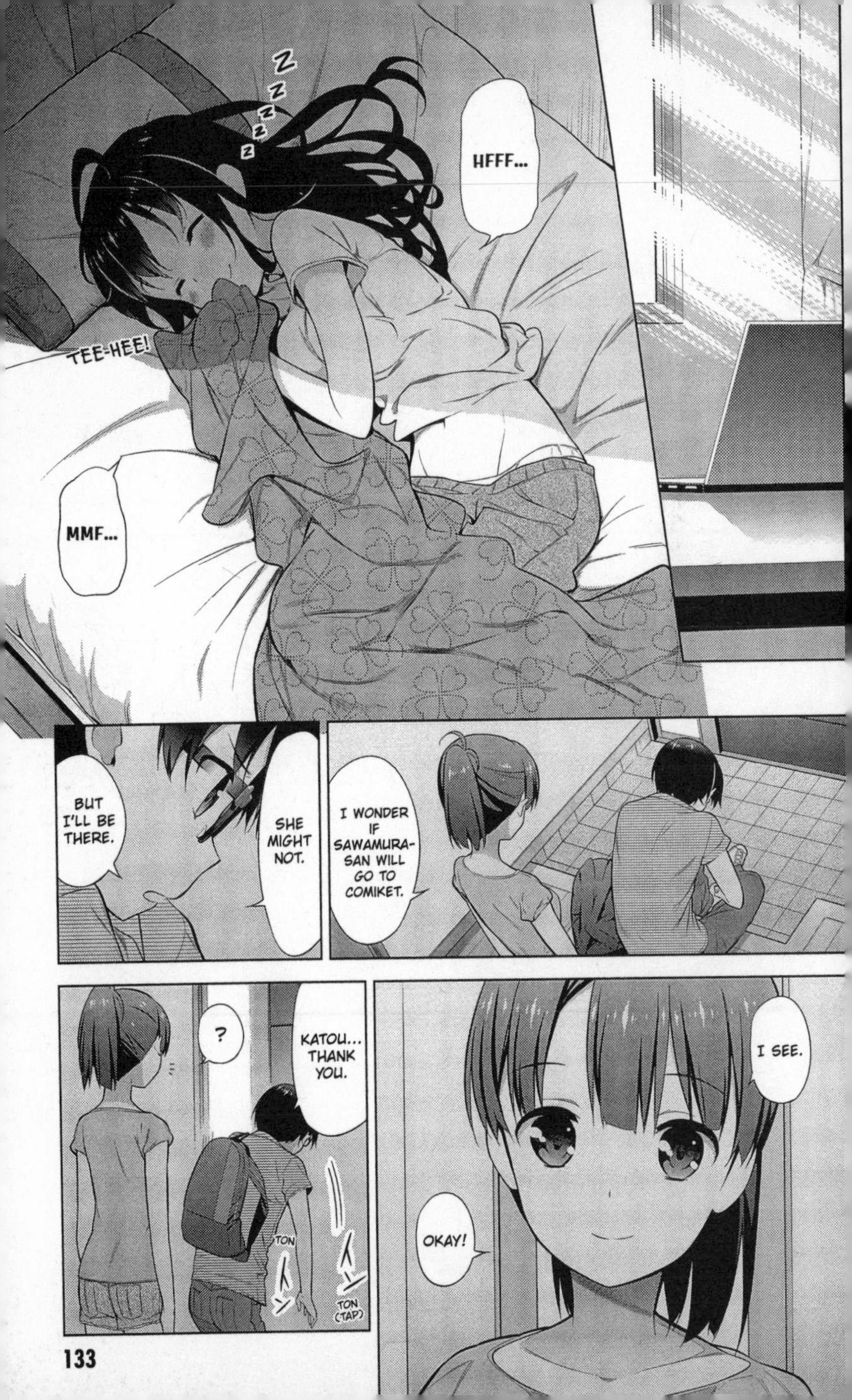
HFFF...
ZZZZZ
TEE-HEE!
MMF...
I WONDER IF SAWAMURA-SAN WILL GO TO COMIKET.
SHE MIGHT NOT.
BUT I'LL BE THERE.
I SEE.
OKAY!
KATOU... THANK YOU.
?
TON
TON (TAP)

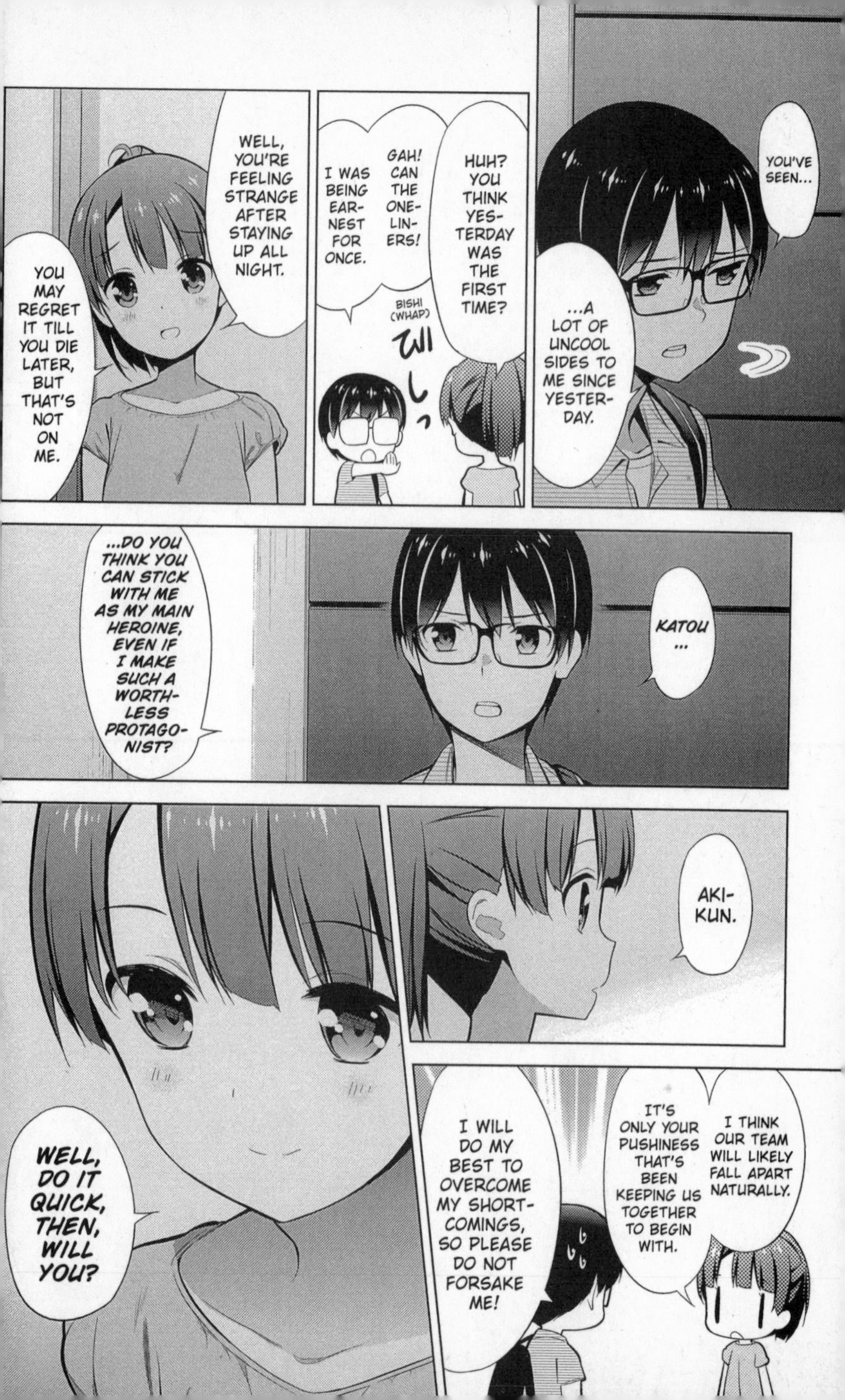
YOU'VE SEEN...
...A LOT OF UNCOOL SIDES TO ME SINCE YESTERDAY.
HUH? YOU THINK YESTERDAY WAS THE FIRST TIME?
GAH! CAN THE ONE-LINERS!
I WAS BEING EARNEST FOR ONCE.
BISHI (WHAP)
WELL, YOU'RE FEELING STRANGE AFTER STAYING UP ALL NIGHT.
YOU MAY REGRET IT TILL YOU DIE LATER, BUT THAT'S NOT ON ME.
KATOU...
...DO YOU THINK YOU CAN STICK WITH ME AS MY MAIN HEROINE, EVEN IF I MAKE SUCH A WORTHLESS PROTAGONIST?
AKI-KUN.
I THINK OUR TEAM WILL LIKELY FALL APART NATURALLY.
IT'S ONLY YOUR PUSHINESS THAT'S BEEN KEEPING US TOGETHER TO BEGIN WITH.
I WILL DO MY BEST TO OVERCOME MY SHORTCOMINGS, SO PLEASE DO NOT FORSAKE ME!
WELL, DO IT QUICK, THEN, WILL YOU?

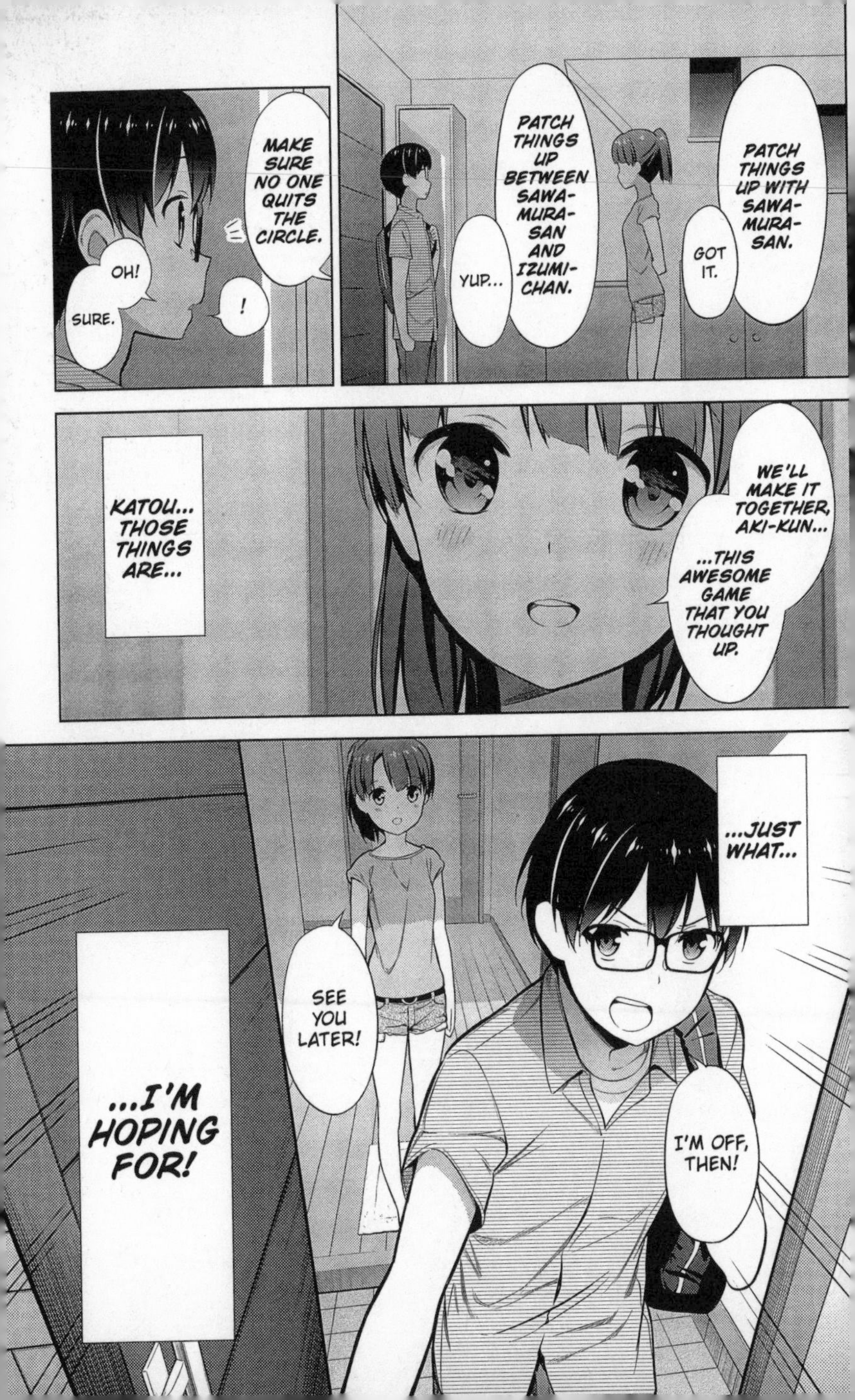
PATCH THINGS UP WITH SAWA-MURA-SAN.
GOT IT.
PATCH THINGS UP BETWEEN SAWA-MURA-SAN AND IZUMI-CHAN.
YUP...
MAKE SURE NO ONE QUITS THE CIRCLE.
!
OH!
SURE.
WE'LL MAKE IT TOGETHER, AKI-KUN...
...THIS AWESOME GAME THAT YOU THOUGHT UP.
KATOU... THOSE THINGS ARE...
...JUST WHAT...
I'M OFF, THEN!
SEE YOU LATER!
...I'M HOPING FOR!

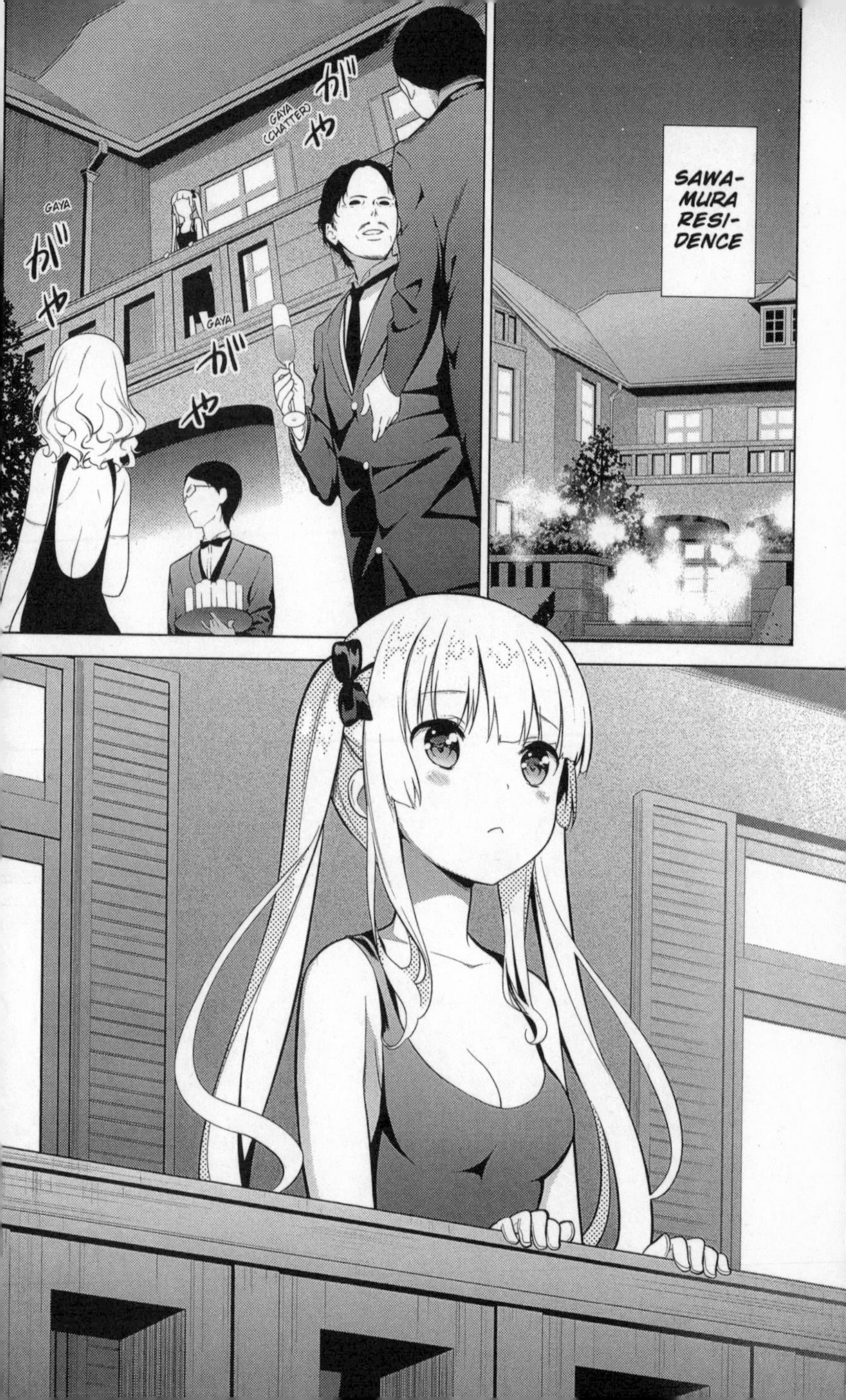
SAWA-MURA RESI-DENCE
GAYA (CHATTER)
がや
GAYA
がや
GAYA
がや

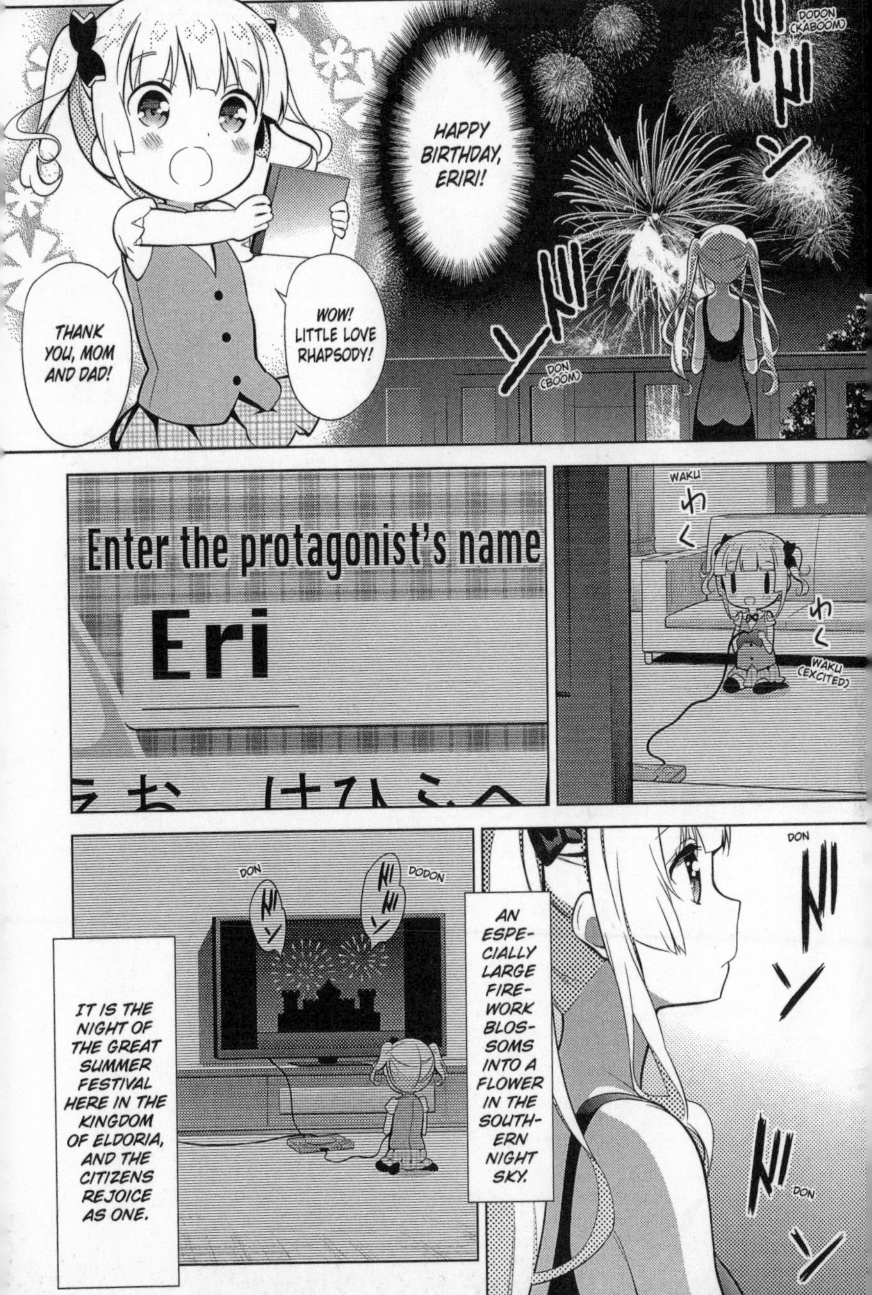
DODON (KABOOM)
HAPPY BIRTHDAY, ERIRI!
DON (BOOM)
WOW! LITTLE LOVE RHAPSODY!
THANK YOU, MOM AND DAD!
WAKU
WAKU (EXCITED)
Enter the protagonist's name
Eri
DON
AN ESPECIALLY LARGE FIREWORK BLOSSOMS INTO A FLOWER IN THE SOUTHERN NIGHT SKY.
DON
DODON
DON
IT IS THE NIGHT OF THE GREAT SUMMER FESTIVAL HERE IN THE KINGDOM OF ELDORIA, AND THE CITIZENS REJOICE AS ONE.

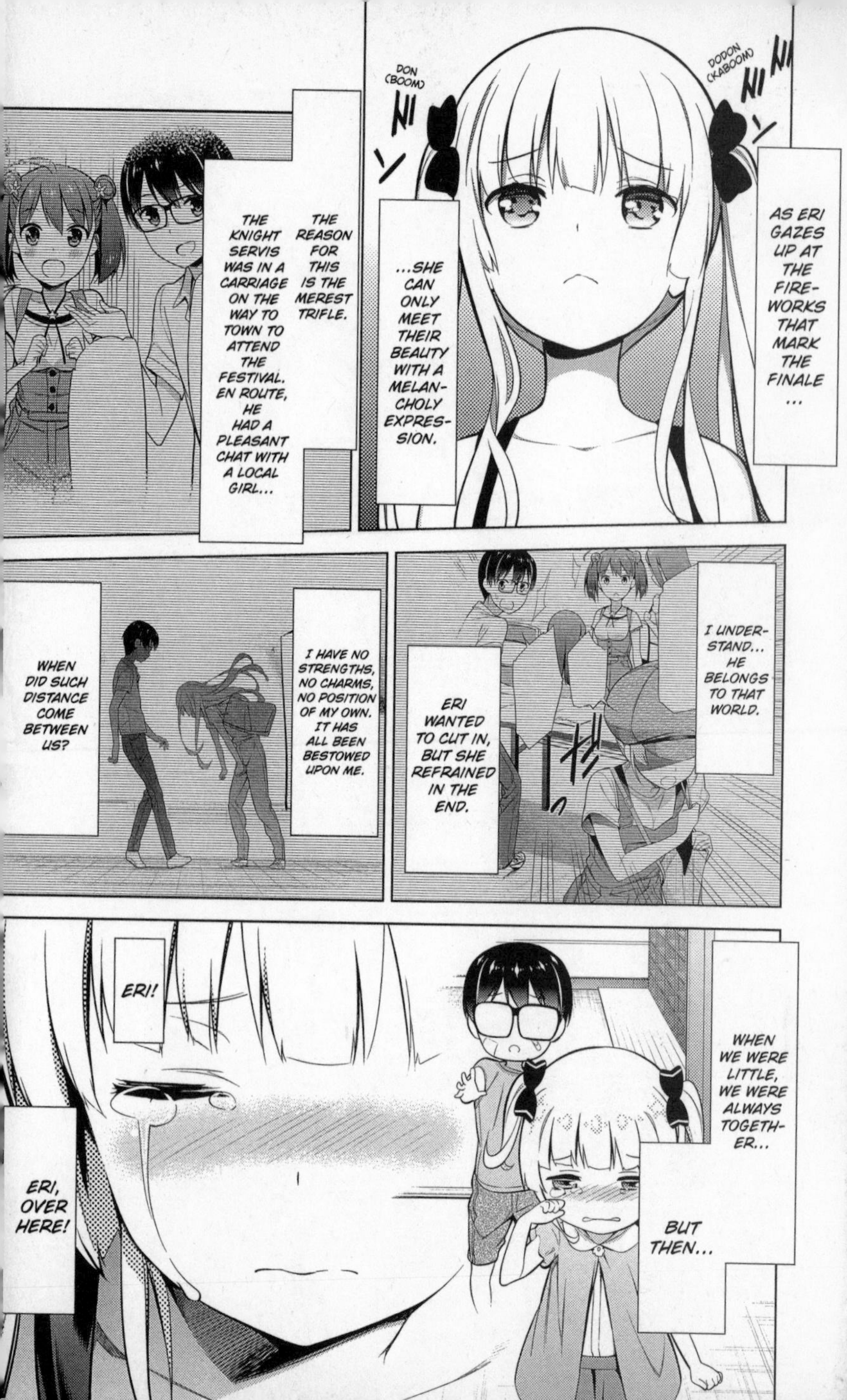
DODON (KABOOM)
DON (BOOM)
AS ERI GAZES UP AT THE FIRE-WORKS THAT MARK THE FINALE...
...SHE CAN ONLY MEET THEIR BEAUTY WITH A MELAN-CHOLY EXPRES-SION.
THE REASON FOR THIS IS THE MEREST TRIFLE.
THE KNIGHT SERVIS WAS IN A CARRIAGE ON THE WAY TO TOWN TO ATTEND THE FESTIVAL. EN ROUTE, HE HAD A PLEASANT CHAT WITH A LOCAL GIRL...
I UNDER-STAND... HE BELONGS TO THAT WORLD.
ERI WANTED TO CUT IN, BUT SHE REFRAINED IN THE END.
I HAVE NO STRENGTHS, NO CHARMS, NO POSITION OF MY OWN. IT HAS ALL BEEN BESTOWED UPON ME.
WHEN DID SUCH DISTANCE COME BETWEEN US?
WHEN WE WERE LITTLE, WE WERE ALWAYS TOGETH-ER...
BUT THEN...
ERI!
ERI, OVER HERE!

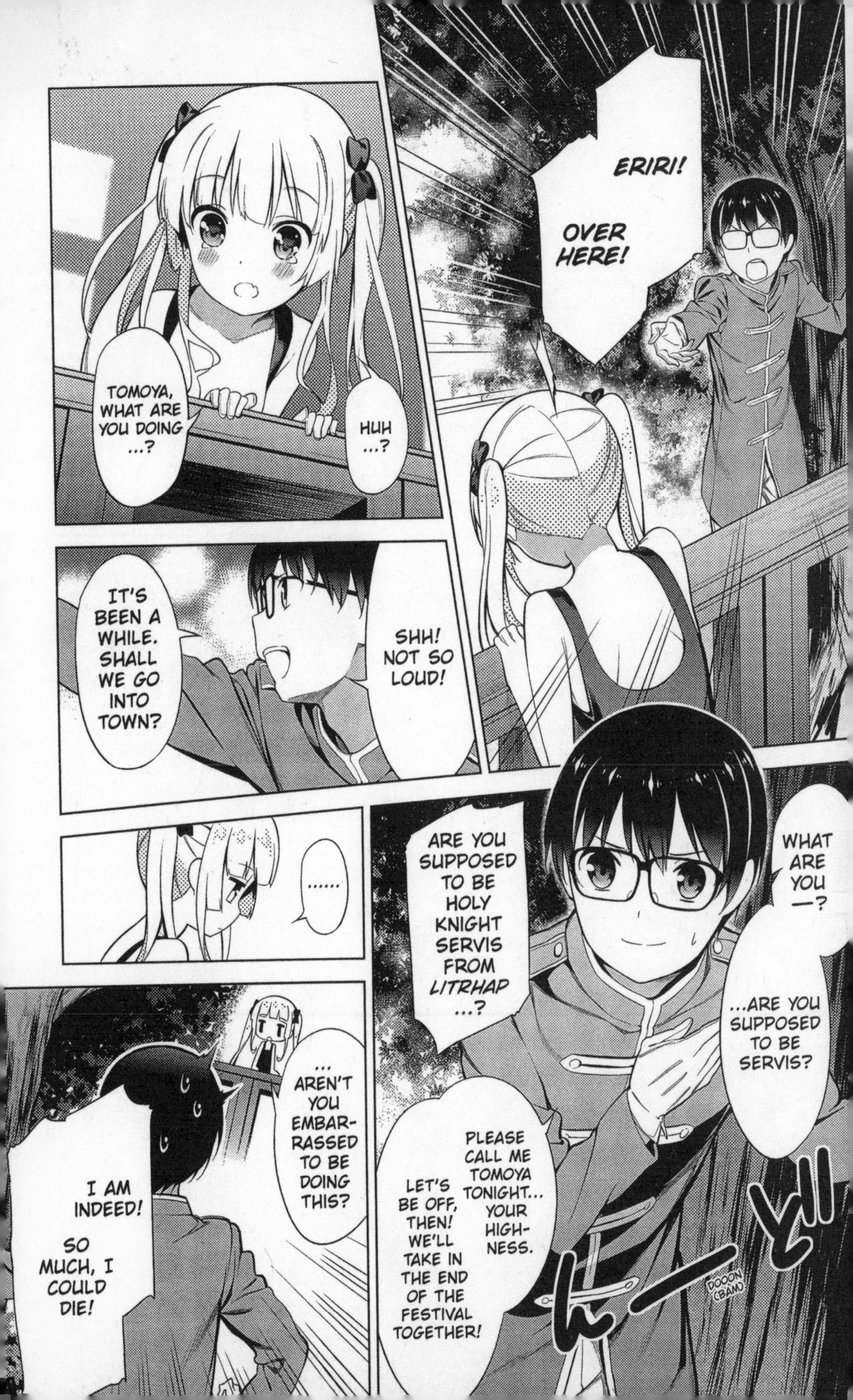
ERIRI!
OVER HERE!
HUH ...?
TOMOYA, WHAT ARE YOU DOING ...?
IT'S BEEN A WHILE. SHALL WE GO INTO TOWN?
SHH! NOT SO LOUD!
WHAT ARE YOU—?
...ARE YOU SUPPOSED TO BE SERVIS?
ARE YOU SUPPOSED TO BE HOLY KNIGHT SERVIS FROM *LITRHAP* ...?
PLEASE CALL ME TOMOYA TONIGHT... YOUR HIGHNESS.
LET'S BE OFF, THEN! WE'LL TAKE IN THE END OF THE FESTIVAL TOGETHER!
DOOON (BAM)
.......
... AREN'T YOU EMBARRASSED TO BE DOING THIS?
I AM INDEED!
SO MUCH, I COULD DIE!

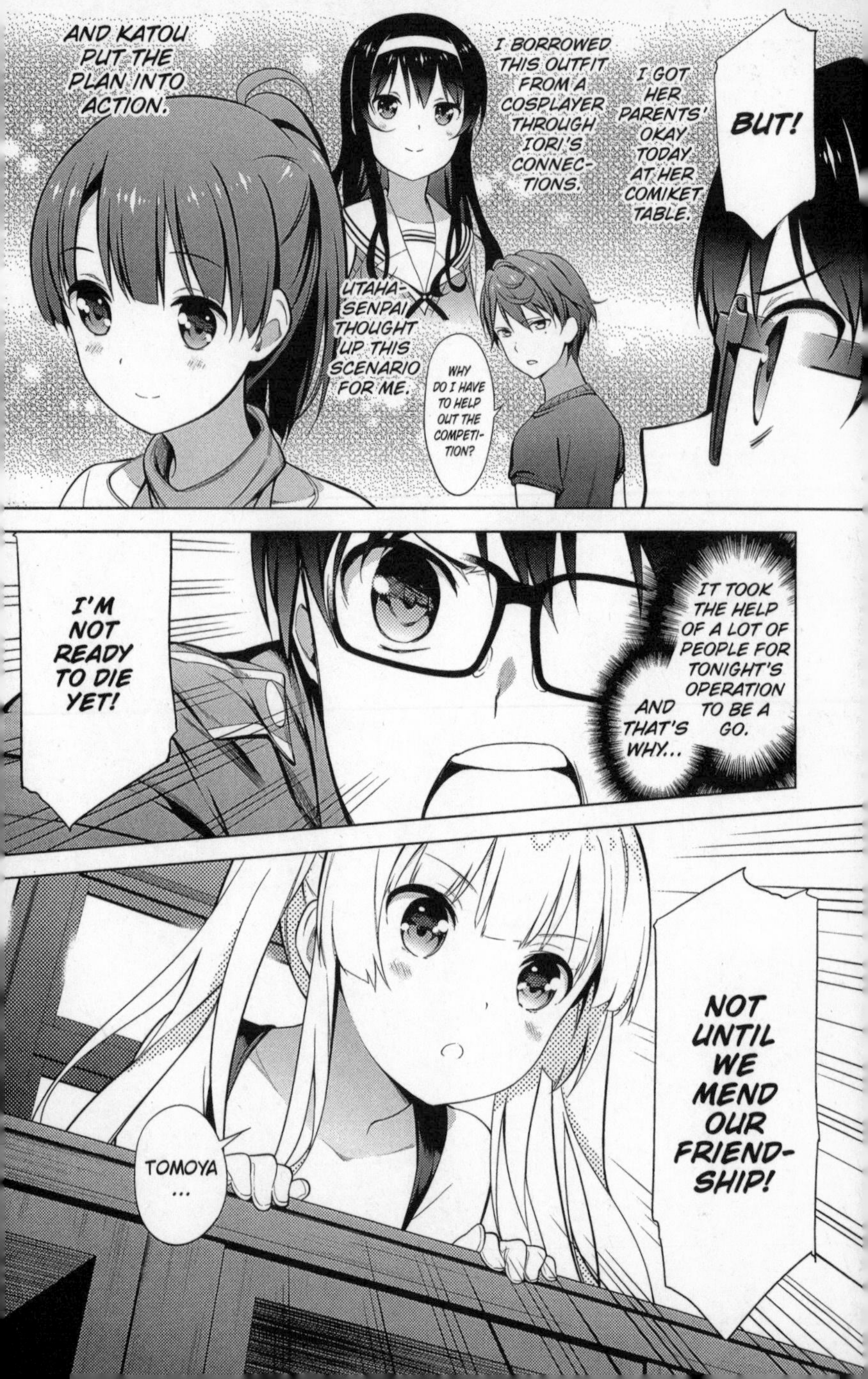
BUT!
I GOT HER PARENTS' OKAY TODAY AT HER COMIKET TABLE.
I BORROWED THIS OUTFIT FROM A COSPLAYER THROUGH IORI'S CONNECTIONS.
AND KATOU PUT THE PLAN INTO ACTION.
UTAHA-SENPAI THOUGHT UP THIS SCENARIO FOR ME.
WHY DO I HAVE TO HELP OUT THE COMPETITION?
IT TOOK THE HELP OF A LOT OF PEOPLE FOR TONIGHT'S OPERATION TO BE A GO.
AND THAT'S WHY...
I'M NOT READY TO DIE YET!
NOT UNTIL WE MEND OUR FRIEND-SHIP!
TOMOYA ...

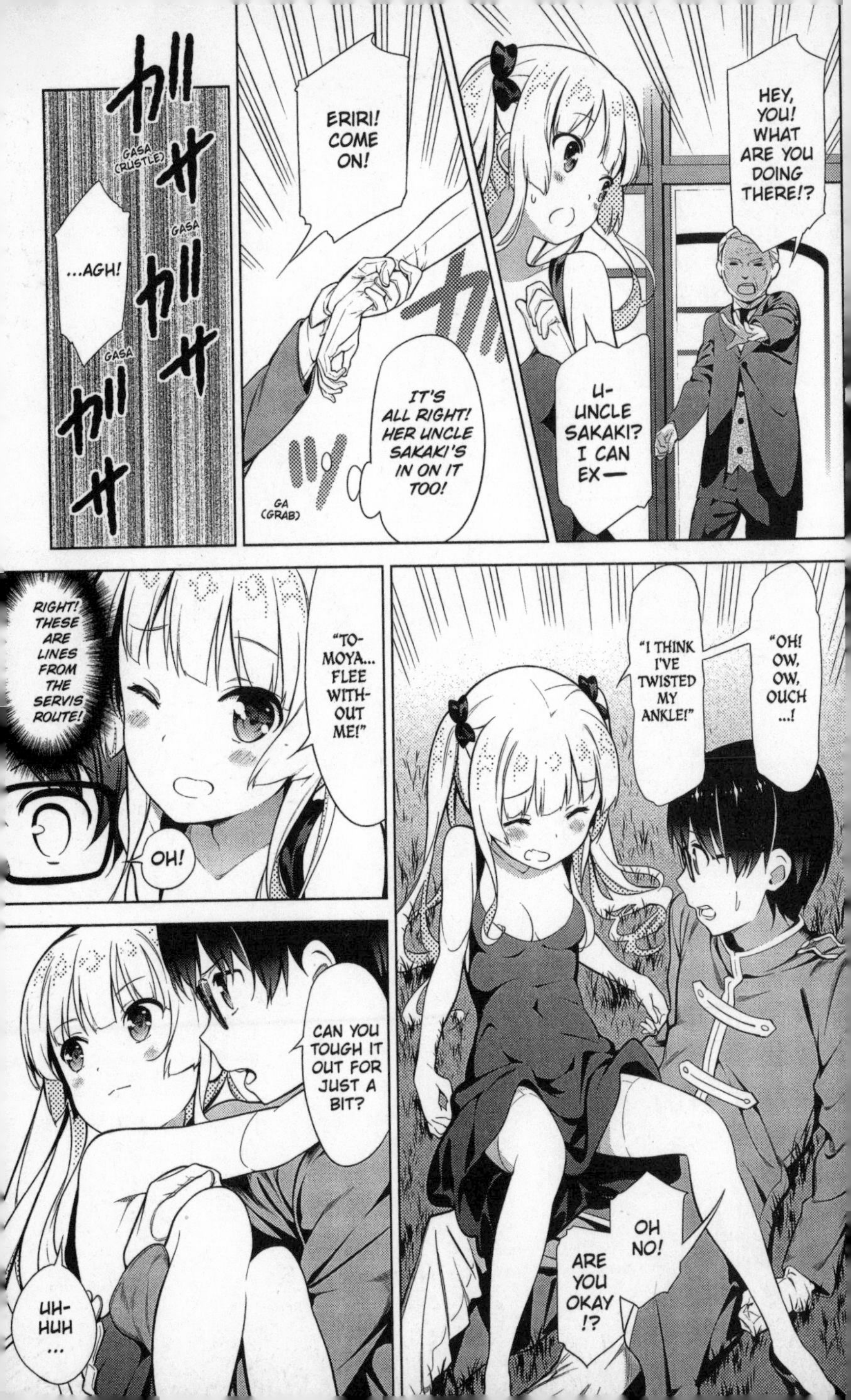
HEY, YOU! WHAT ARE YOU DOING THERE!?
U-UNCLE SAKAKI? I CAN EX—
ERIRI! COME ON!
IT'S ALL RIGHT! HER UNCLE SAKAKI'S IN ON IT TOO!
GA (GRAB)
GASA (RUSTLE)
GASA
GASA
...AGH!
"OH! OW, OW, OUCH ...!
"I THINK I'VE TWISTED MY ANKLE!"
OH NO!
ARE YOU OKAY !?
"TO-MOYA... FLEE WITH-OUT ME!"
RIGHT! THESE ARE LINES FROM THE SERVIS ROUTE!
OH!
CAN YOU TOUGH IT OUT FOR JUST A BIT?
UH-HUH ...

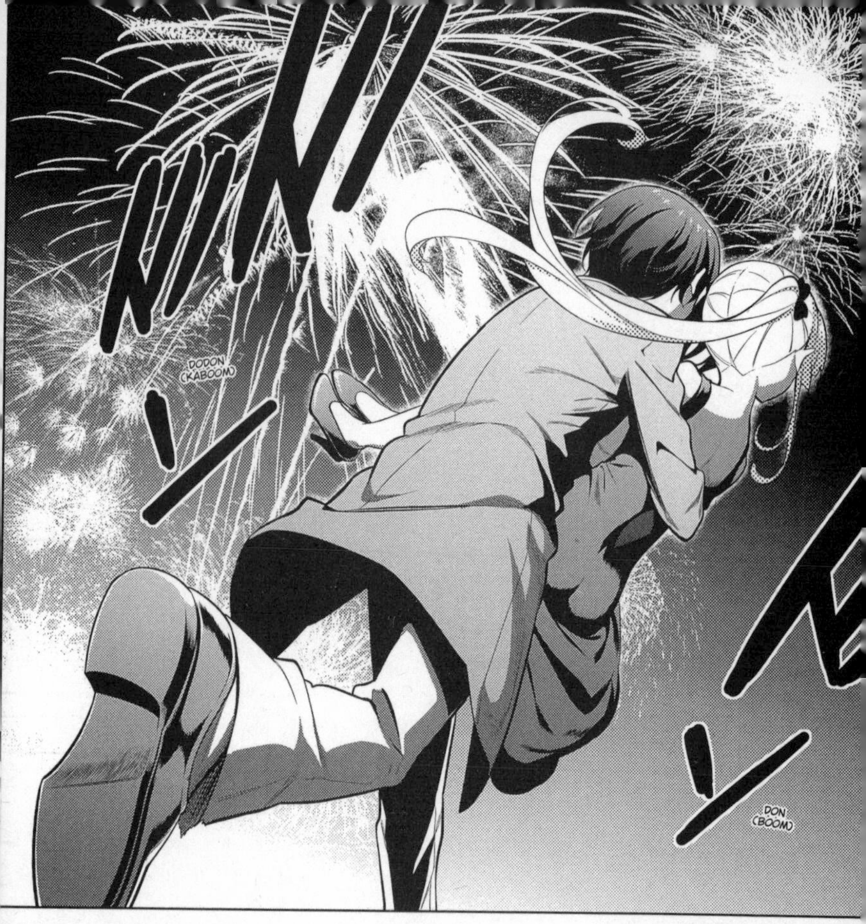
DODON (KABOOM)
DON (BOOM)

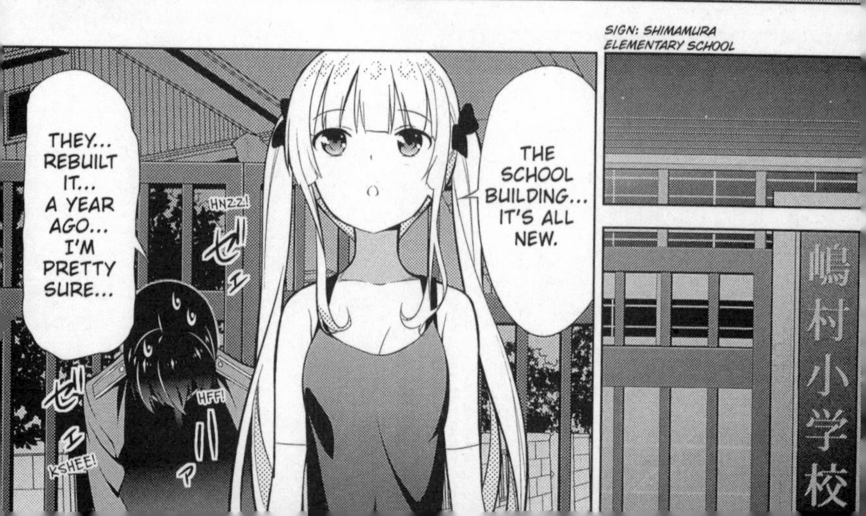
SIGN: SHIMAMURA ELEMENTARY SCHOOL
嶋村小学校
THE SCHOOL BUILDING... IT'S ALL NEW.
THEY... REBUILT IT... A YEAR AGO... I'M PRETTY SURE...
HNZ-Z!
HFF!
KSHEE!

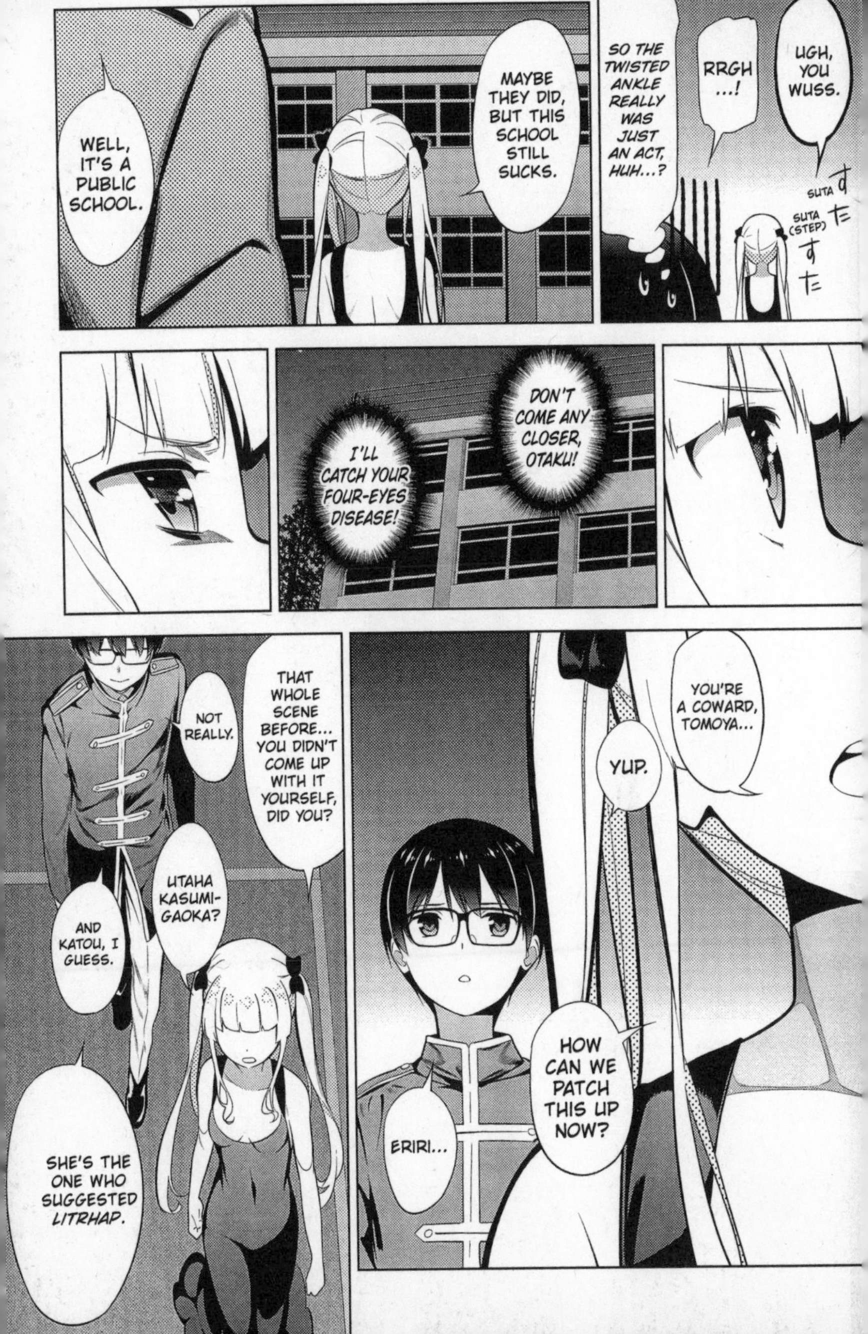
UGH, YOU WUSS.
RRGH...!
SO THE TWISTED ANKLE REALLY WAS JUST AN ACT, HUH...?
SUTA す
SUTA (STEP) た
す
た
MAYBE THEY DID, BUT THIS SCHOOL STILL SUCKS.
WELL, IT'S A PUBLIC SCHOOL.
DON'T COME ANY CLOSER, OTAKU!
I'LL CATCH YOUR FOUR-EYES DISEASE!
YOU'RE A COWARD, TOMOYA...
YUP.
HOW CAN WE PATCH THIS UP NOW?
ERIRI...
THAT WHOLE SCENE BEFORE... YOU DIDN'T COME UP WITH IT YOURSELF, DID YOU?
NOT REALLY.
UTAHA KASUMI-GAOKA?
AND KATOU, I GUESS.
SHE'S THE ONE WHO SUGGESTED *LITRHAP*.

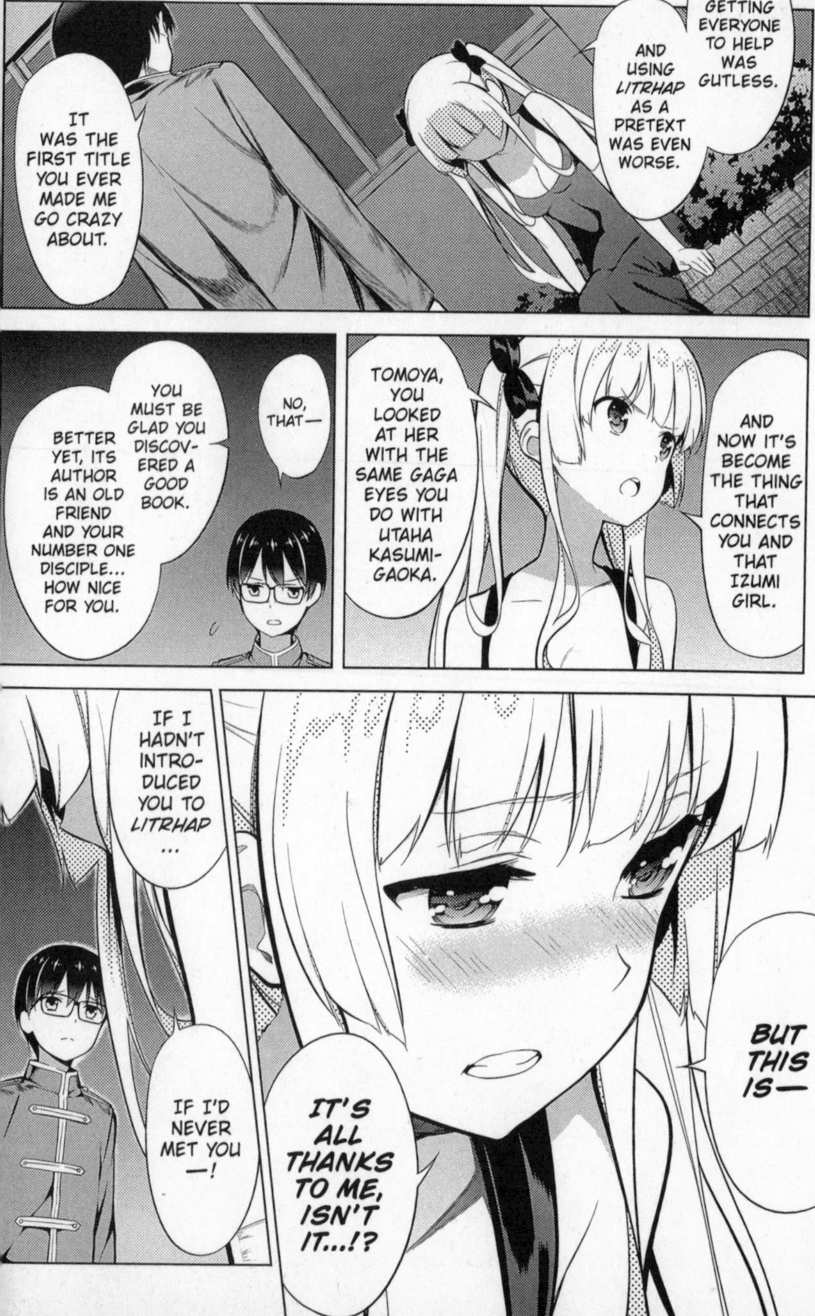

GETTING EVERYONE TO HELP WAS GUTLESS.
AND USING *LITRHAP* AS A PRETEXT WAS EVEN WORSE.
IT WAS THE FIRST TITLE YOU EVER MADE ME GO CRAZY ABOUT.
AND NOW IT'S BECOME THE THING THAT CONNECTS YOU AND THAT IZUMI GIRL.
TOMOYA, YOU LOOKED AT HER WITH THE SAME GAGA EYES YOU DO WITH UTAHA KASUMIGAOKA.
NO, THAT—
YOU MUST BE GLAD YOU DISCOVERED A GOOD BOOK.
BETTER YET, ITS AUTHOR IS AN OLD FRIEND AND YOUR NUMBER ONE DISCIPLE... HOW NICE FOR YOU.
BUT THIS IS—
IT'S ALL THANKS TO ME, ISN'T IT...!?
IF I HADN'T INTRODUCED YOU TO *LITRHAP*...
IF I'D NEVER MET YOU—!

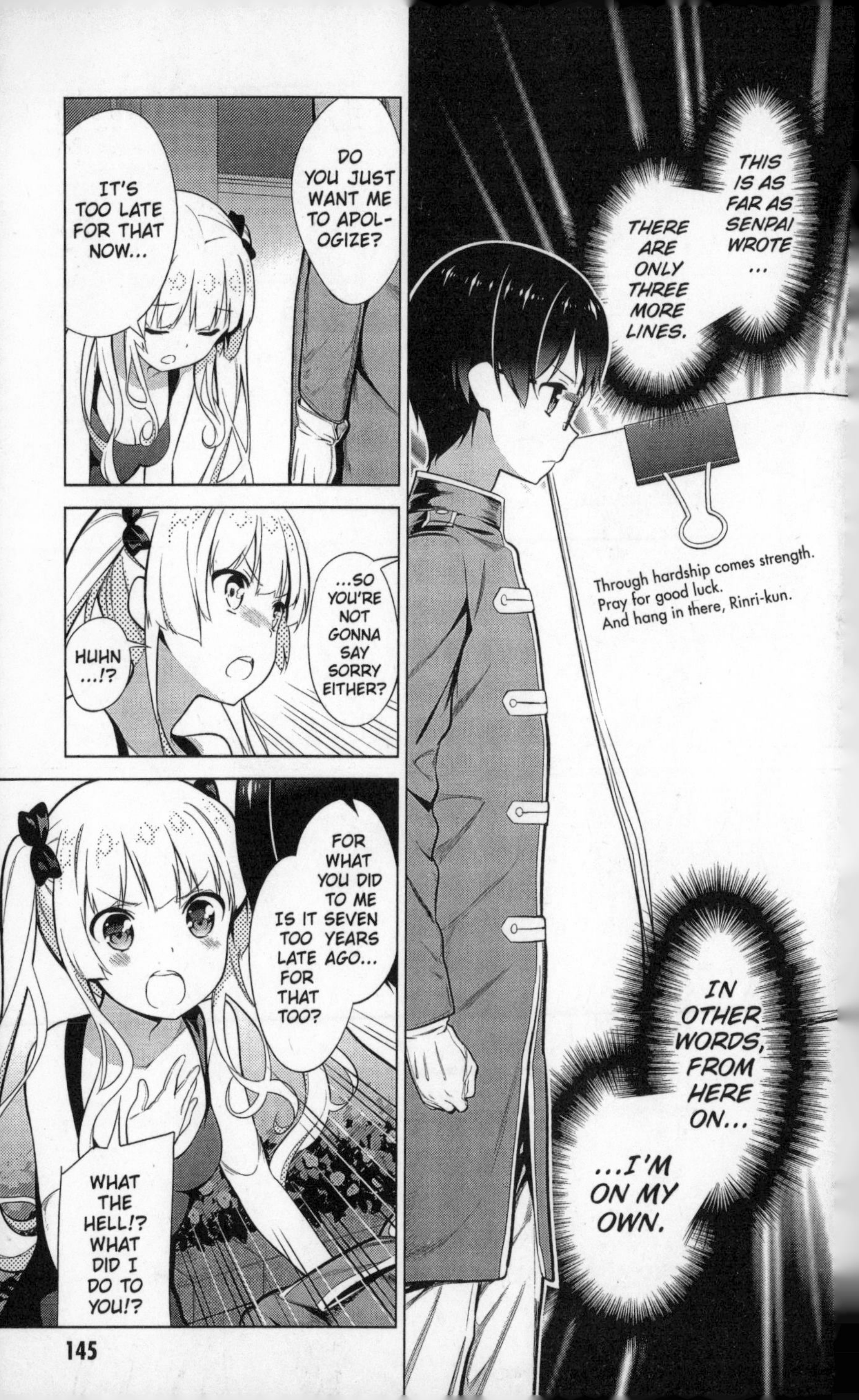
THIS IS AS FAR AS SENPAI WROTE...
THERE ARE ONLY THREE MORE LINES.
Through hardship comes strength.
Pray for good luck.
And hang in there, Rinri-kun.
IN OTHER WORDS, FROM HERE ON...
...I'M ON MY OWN.
DO YOU JUST WANT ME TO APOLOGIZE?
IT'S TOO LATE FOR THAT NOW...
...SO YOU'RE NOT GONNA SAY SORRY EITHER?
HUHN...!?
FOR WHAT YOU DID TO ME SEVEN YEARS AGO...
IS IT TOO LATE FOR THAT TOO?
WHAT THE HELL!? WHAT DID I DO TO YOU!?

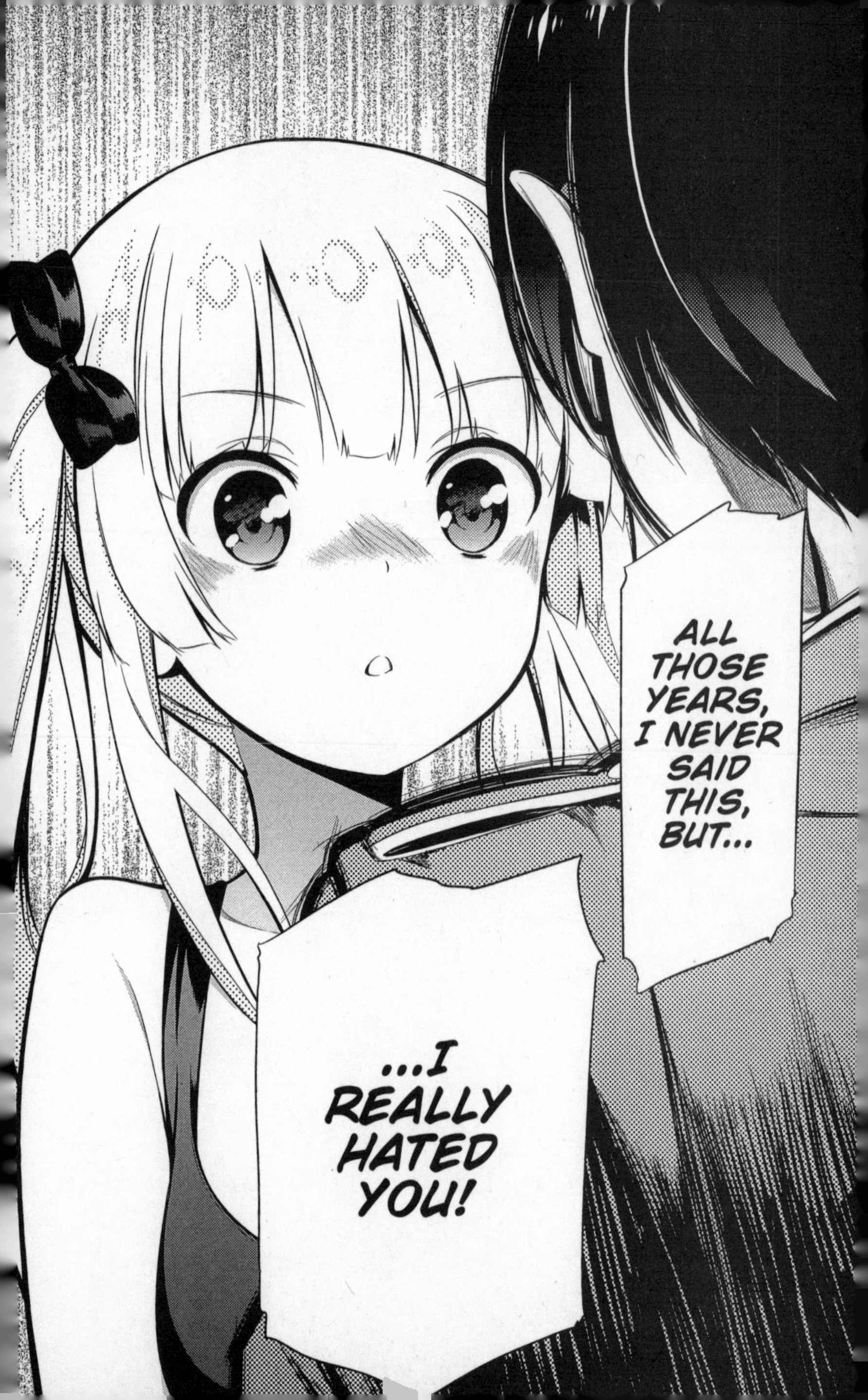
ALL THOSE YEARS, I NEVER SAID THIS, BUT...
...I REALLY HATED YOU!

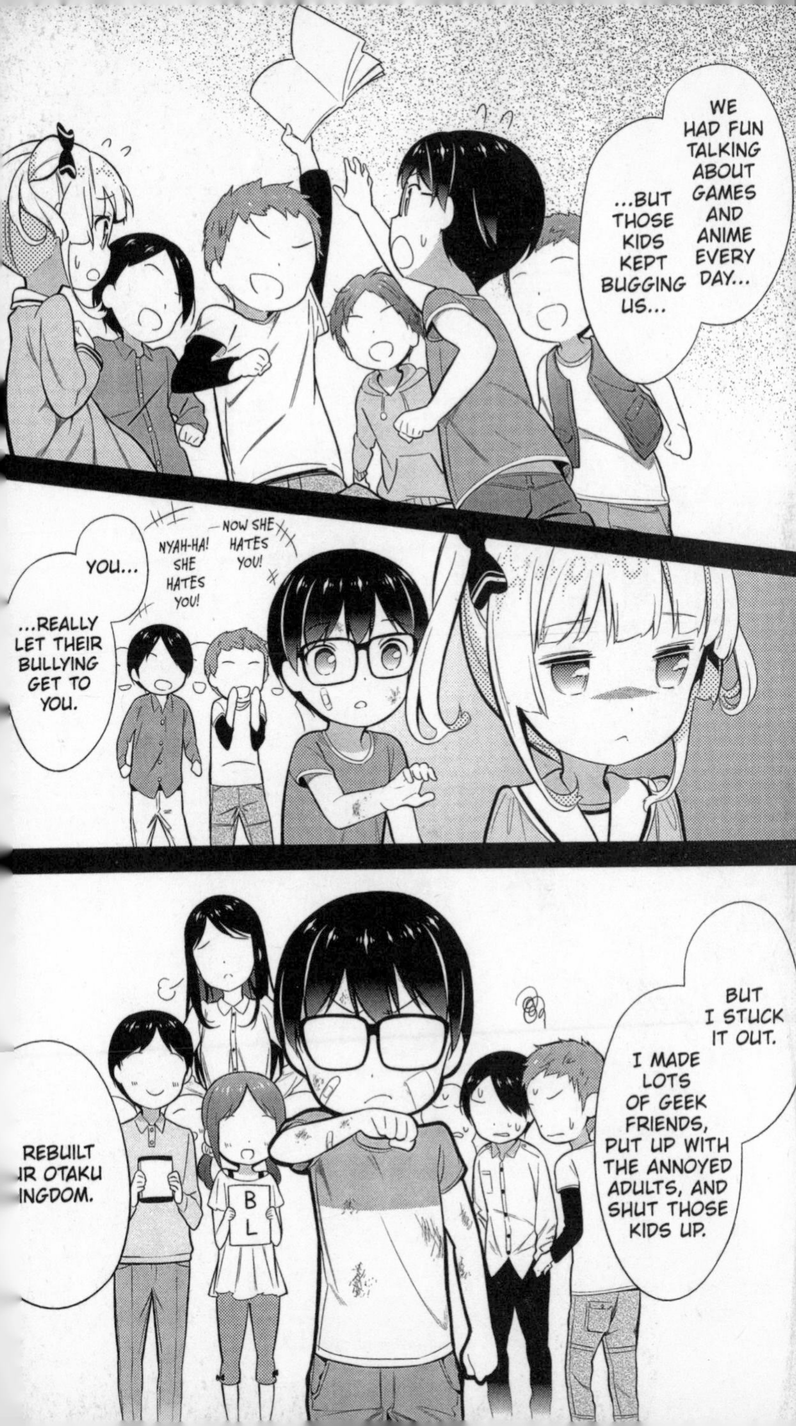
WE HAD FUN TALKING ABOUT GAMES AND ANIME EVERY DAY...
...BUT THOSE KIDS KEPT BUGGING US...
NOW SHE HATES YOU!
NYAH-HA! SHE HATES YOU!
YOU...
...REALLY LET THEIR BULLYING GET TO YOU.
BUT I STUCK IT OUT.
I MADE LOTS OF GEEK FRIENDS, PUT UP WITH THE ANNOYED ADULTS, AND SHUT THOSE KIDS UP.
REBUILT IR OTAKU INGDOM.
BL

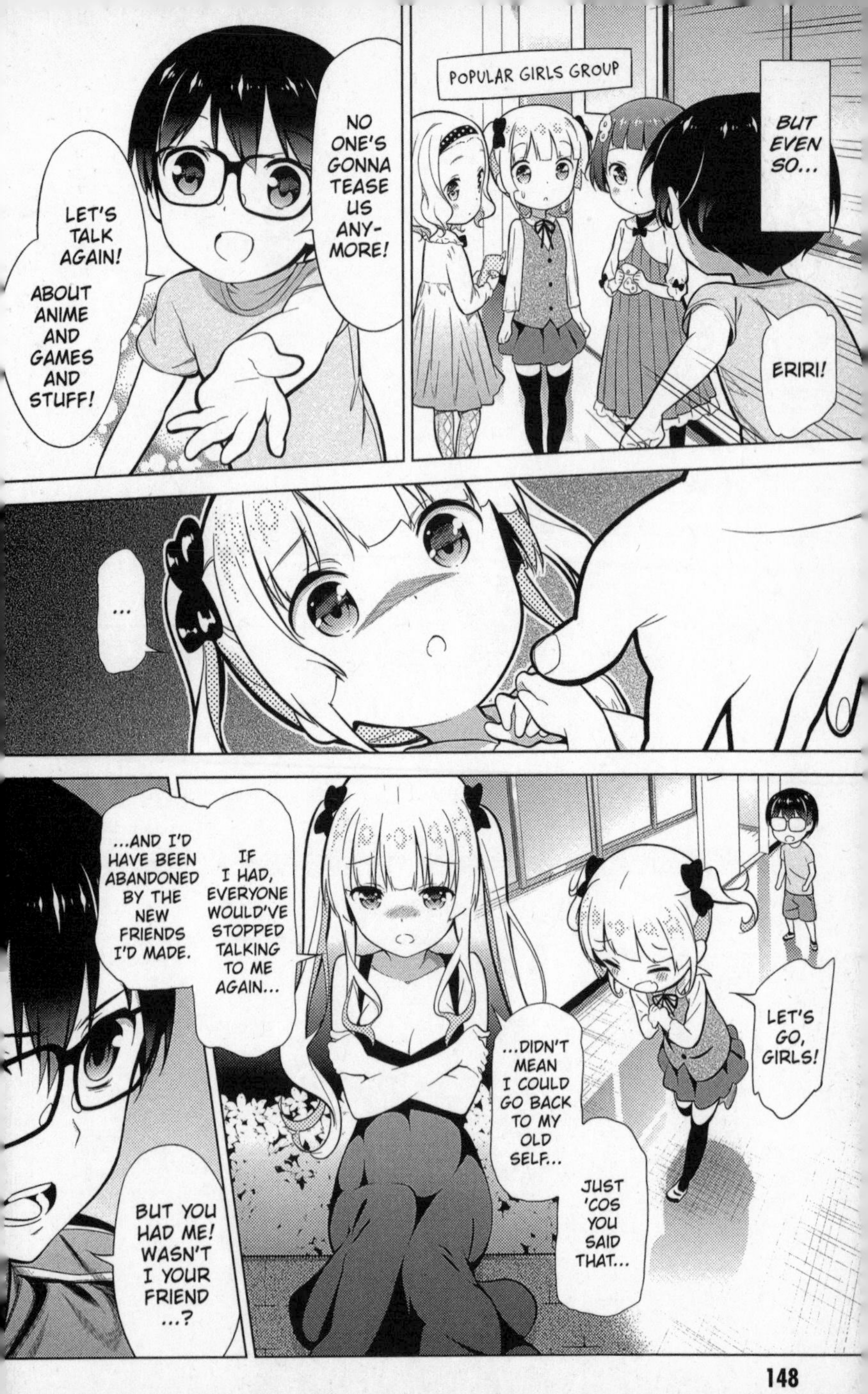
BUT EVEN SO...
POPULAR GIRLS GROUP
ERIRI!
NO ONE'S GONNA TEASE US ANYMORE!
LET'S TALK AGAIN!
ABOUT ANIME AND GAMES AND STUFF!
...
LET'S GO, GIRLS!
JUST 'COS YOU SAID THAT...
...DIDN'T MEAN I COULD GO BACK TO MY OLD SELF...
IF I HAD, EVERYONE WOULD'VE STOPPED TALKING TO ME AGAIN...
...AND I'D HAVE BEEN ABANDONED BY THE NEW FRIENDS I'D MADE.
BUT YOU HAD ME! WASN'T I YOUR FRIEND ...?

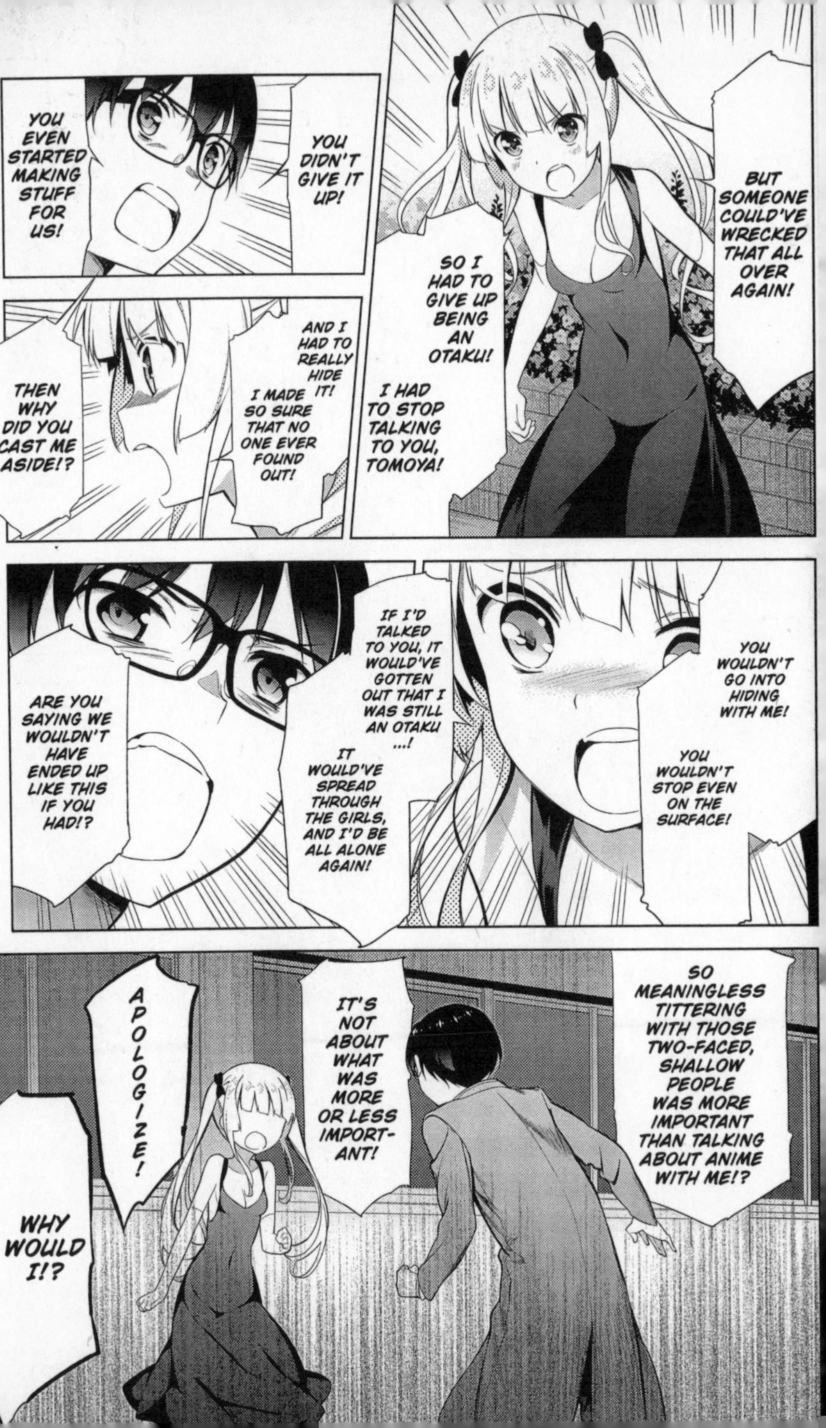
BUT SOMEONE COULD'VE WRECKED THAT ALL OVER AGAIN!
SO I HAD TO GIVE UP BEING AN OTAKU!
I HAD TO STOP TALKING TO YOU, TOMOYA!
YOU DIDN'T GIVE IT UP!
YOU EVEN STARTED MAKING STUFF FOR US!
AND I HAD TO REALLY HIDE IT!
I MADE SO SURE THAT NO ONE EVER FOUND OUT!
THEN WHY DID YOU CAST ME ASIDE!?
YOU WOULDN'T GO INTO HIDING WITH ME!
YOU WOULDN'T STOP EVEN ON THE SURFACE!
IF I'D TALKED TO YOU, IT WOULD'VE GOTTEN OUT THAT I WAS STILL AN OTAKU ...!
IT WOULD'VE SPREAD THROUGH THE GIRLS, AND I'D BE ALL ALONE AGAIN!
ARE YOU SAYING WE WOULDN'T HAVE ENDED UP LIKE THIS IF YOU HAD!?
SO MEANINGLESS TITTERING WITH THOSE TWO-FACED, SHALLOW PEOPLE WAS MORE IMPORTANT THAN TALKING ABOUT ANIME WITH ME!?
IT'S NOT ABOUT WHAT WAS MORE OR LESS IMPORT-ANT!
APOLOGIZE!
WHY WOULD I!?

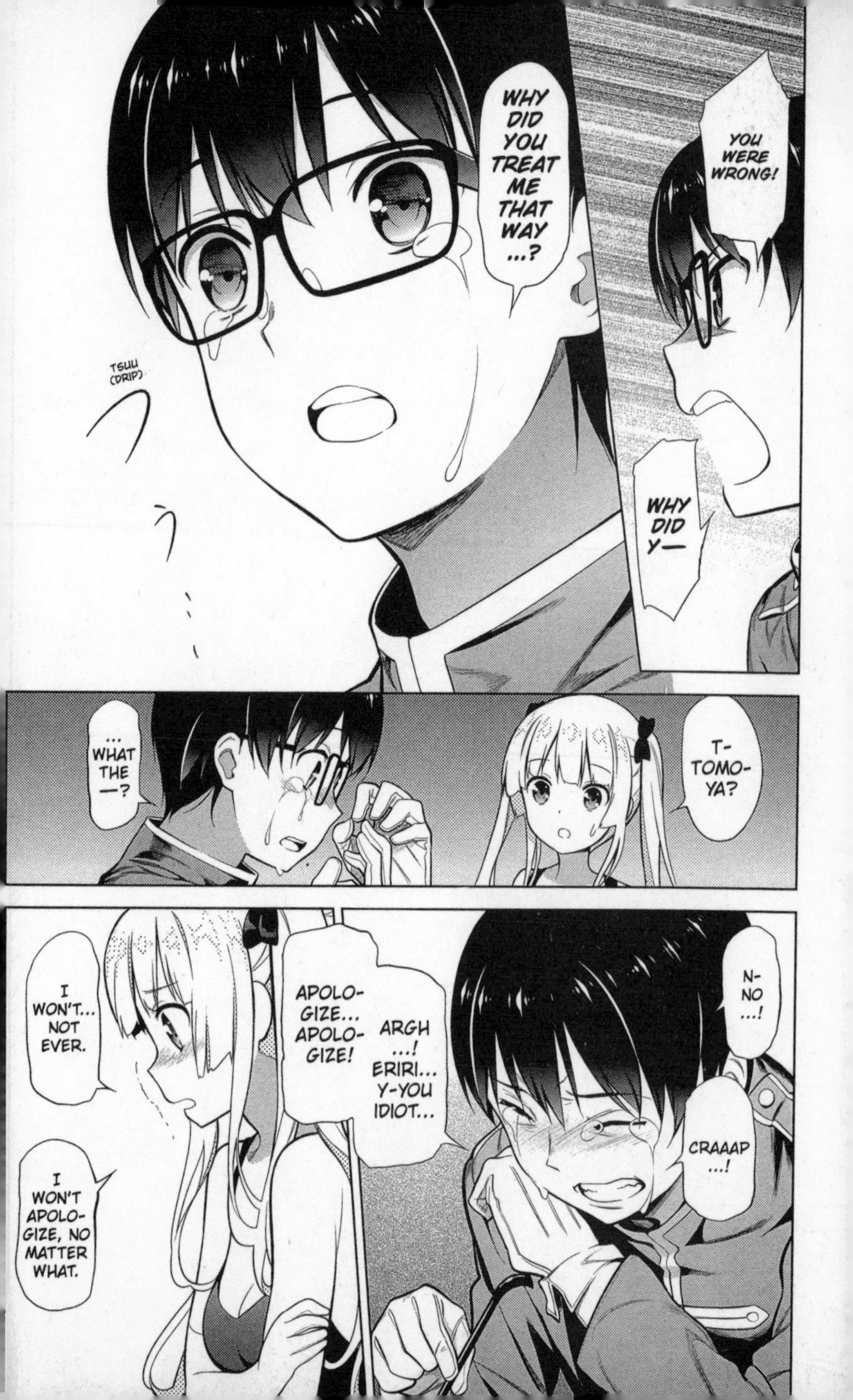
YOU WERE WRONG!
WHY DID Y—
WHY DID YOU TREAT ME THAT WAY ...?
TSUU (DRIP)
T-TOMO-YA?
... WHAT THE —?
N-NO ...!
CRAAAP ...!
ARGH ...! ERIRI... Y-YOU IDIOT...
APOLO-GIZE... APOLO-GIZE!
I WON'T... NOT EVER.
I WON'T APOLO-GIZE, NO MATTER WHAT.

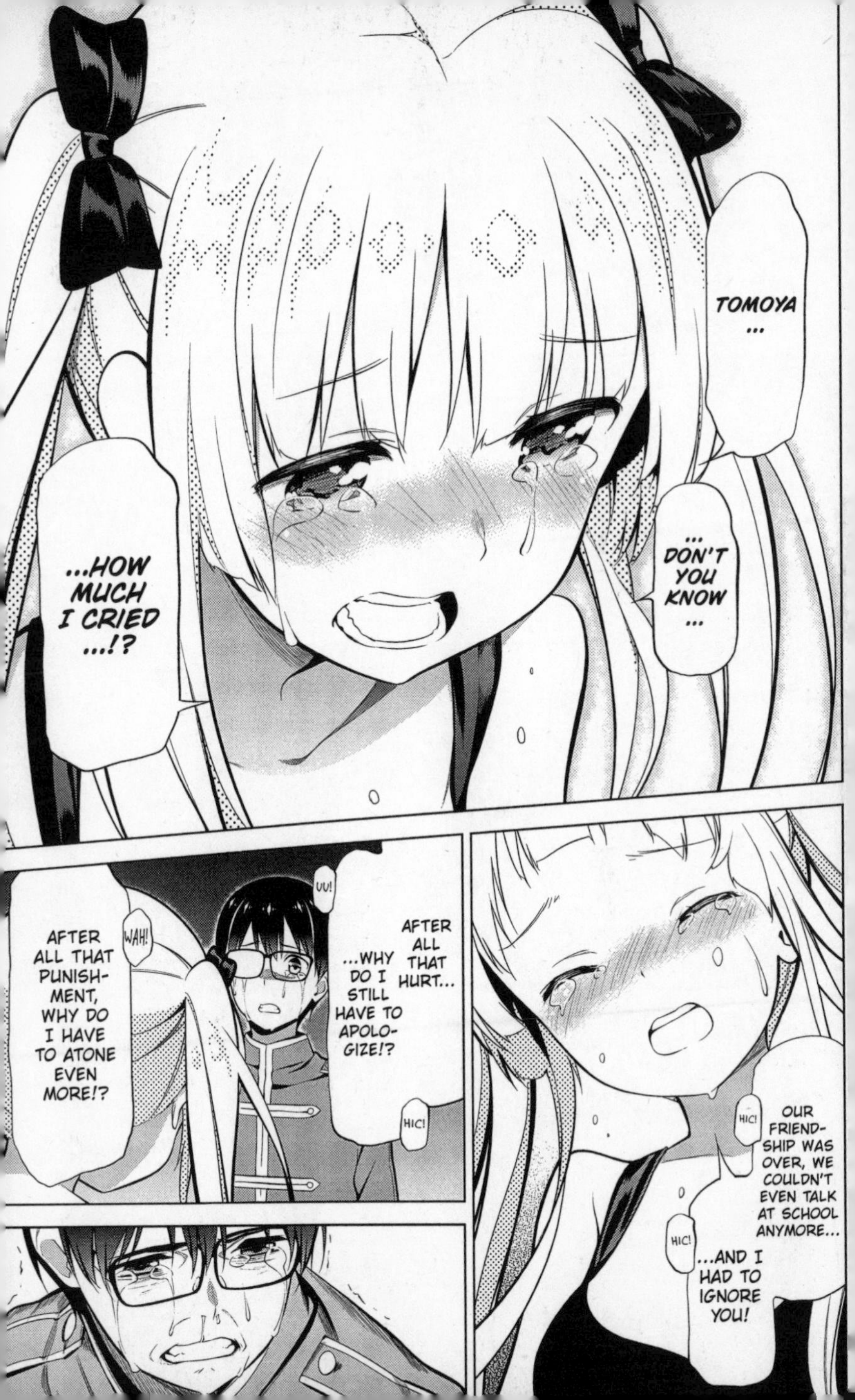
TOMOYA ...
... DON'T YOU KNOW ...
...HOW MUCH I CRIED ...!?
OUR FRIEND-SHIP WAS OVER, WE COULDN'T EVEN TALK AT SCHOOL ANYMORE...
HIC!
HIC!
...AND I HAD TO IGNORE YOU!
UU!
AFTER ALL THAT HURT...
...WHY DO I STILL HAVE TO APOLO-GIZE!?
WAH!
AFTER ALL THAT PUNISH-MENT, WHY DO I HAVE TO ATONE EVEN MORE!?
HIC!

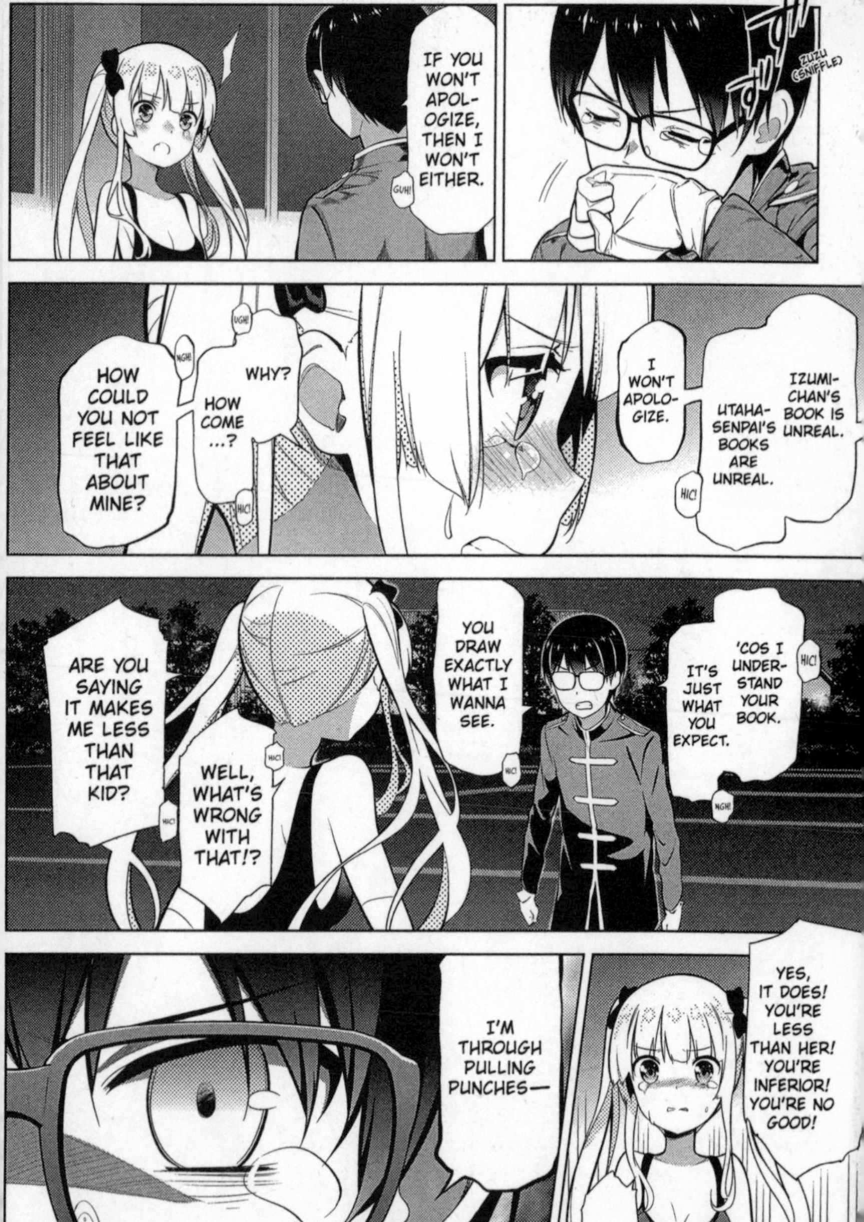
ZUZU (SNIFFLE)
IF YOU WON'T APOLOGIZE, THEN I WON'T EITHER.
GUH!
IZUMI-CHAN'S BOOK IS UNREAL.
UTAHA-SENPAI'S BOOKS ARE UNREAL.
HIC!
I WON'T APOLOGIZE.
UGH!
WHY?
HOW COME ...?
HIC!
NGH!
HOW COULD YOU NOT FEEL LIKE THAT ABOUT MINE?
'COS I UNDERSTAND YOUR BOOK.
HIC!
IT'S JUST WHAT YOU EXPECT.
NGH!
YOU DRAW EXACTLY WHAT I WANNA SEE.
HIC!
HIC!
WELL, WHAT'S WRONG WITH THAT!?
ARE YOU SAYING IT MAKES ME LESS THAN THAT KID?
HIC!
YES, IT DOES! YOU'RE LESS THAN HER! YOU'RE INFERIOR! YOU'RE NO GOOD!
WHA—!?
I'M THROUGH PULLING PUNCHES—

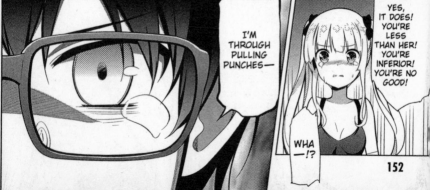

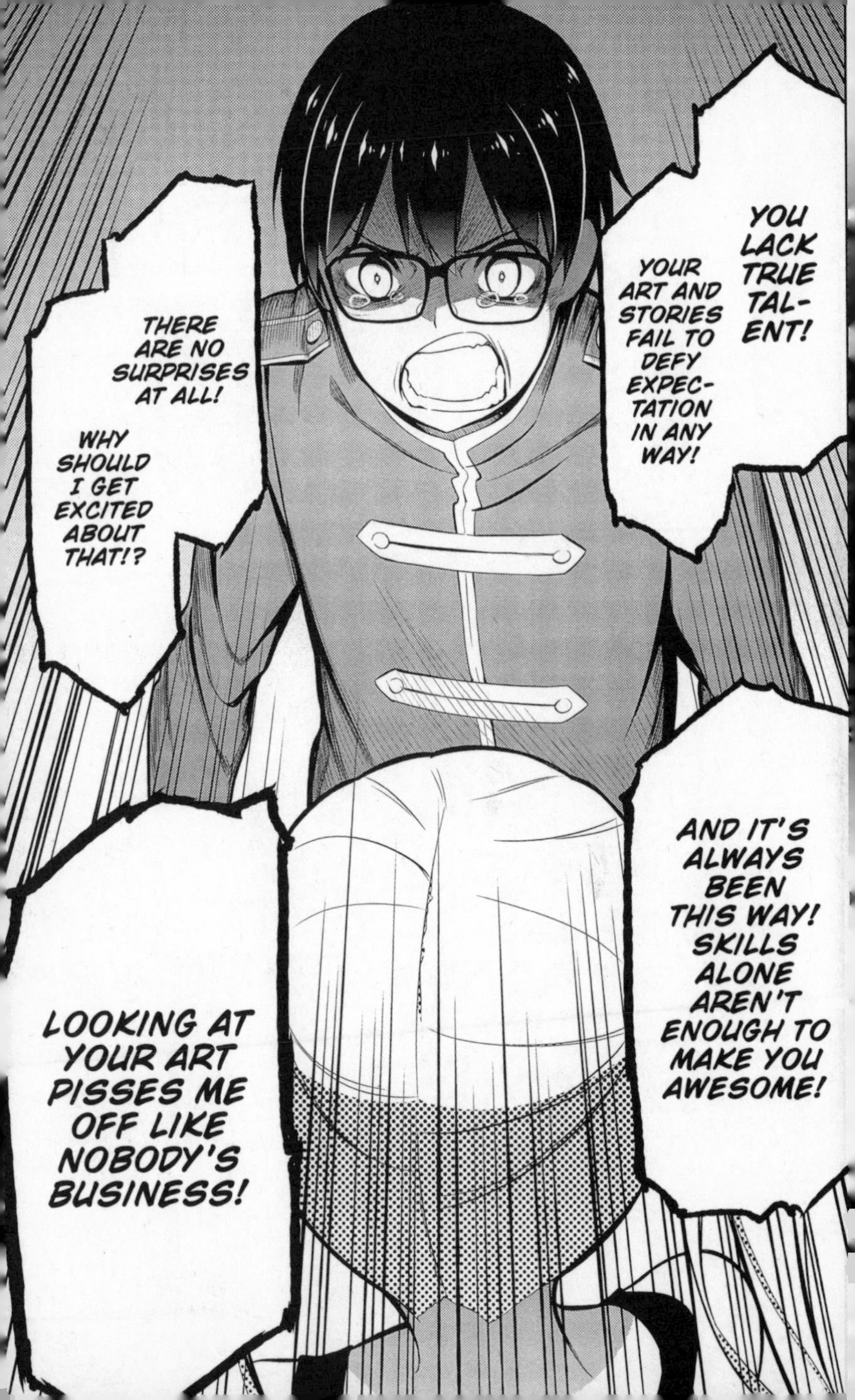
YOU LACK TRUE TAL- ENT!
YOUR ART AND STORIES FAIL TO DEFY EXPEC- TATION IN ANY WAY!
THERE ARE NO SURPRISES AT ALL!
WHY SHOULD I GET EXCITED ABOUT THAT!?
AND IT'S ALWAYS BEEN THIS WAY! SKILLS ALONE AREN'T ENOUGH TO MAKE YOU AWESOME!
LOOKING AT YOUR ART PISSES ME OFF LIKE NOBODY'S BUSINESS!

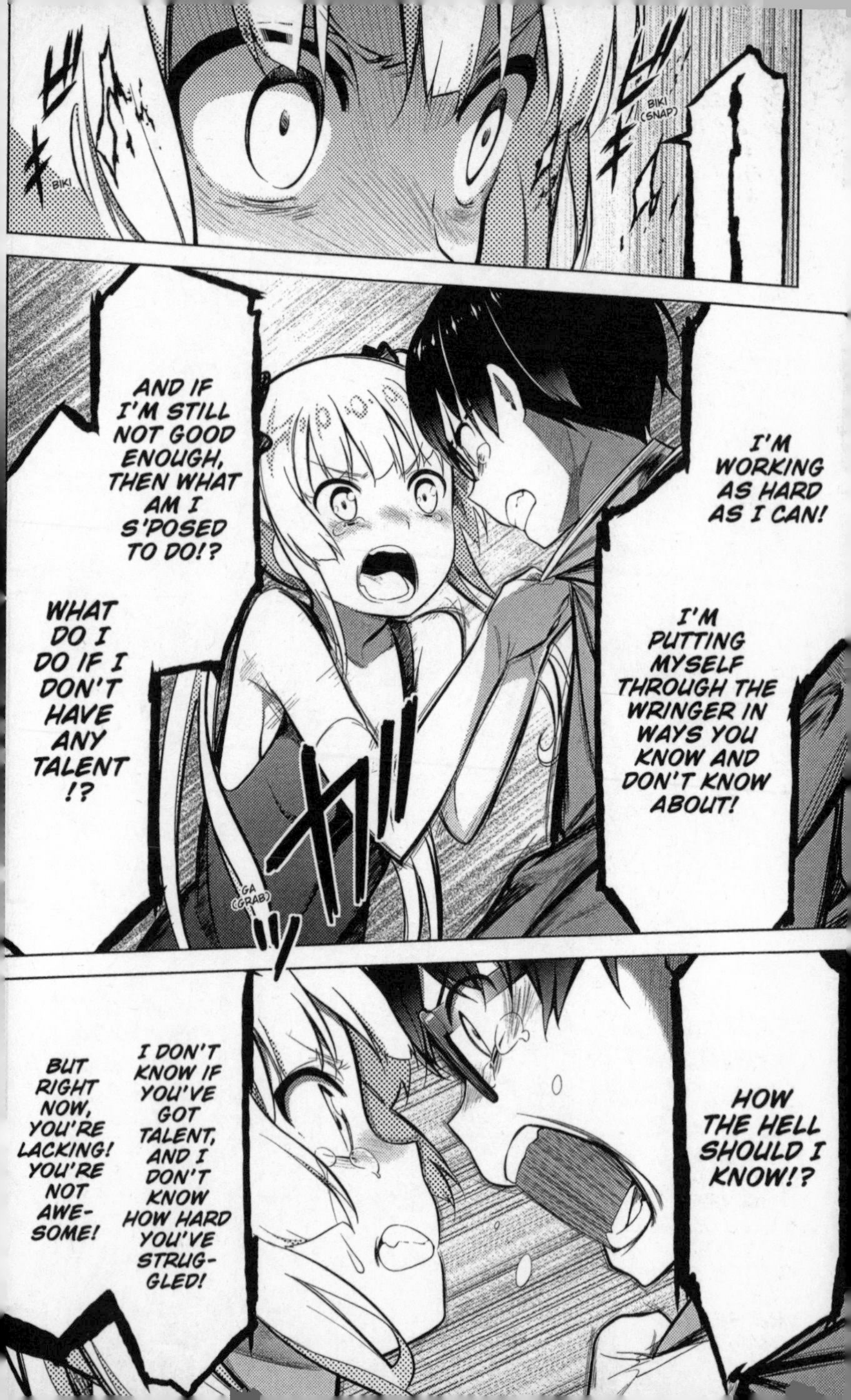
BIKI (SNAP)
BIKI
I'M WORKING AS HARD AS I CAN!
I'M PUTTING MYSELF THROUGH THE WRINGER IN WAYS YOU KNOW AND DON'T KNOW ABOUT!
AND IF I'M STILL NOT GOOD ENOUGH, THEN WHAT AM I S'POSED TO DO!?
WHAT DO I DO IF I DON'T HAVE ANY TALENT !?
GA (GRAB)
HOW THE HELL SHOULD I KNOW!?
I DON'T KNOW IF YOU'VE GOT TALENT, AND I DON'T KNOW HOW HARD YOU'VE STRUG-GLED!
BUT RIGHT NOW, YOU'RE LACKING! YOU'RE NOT AWE-SOME!

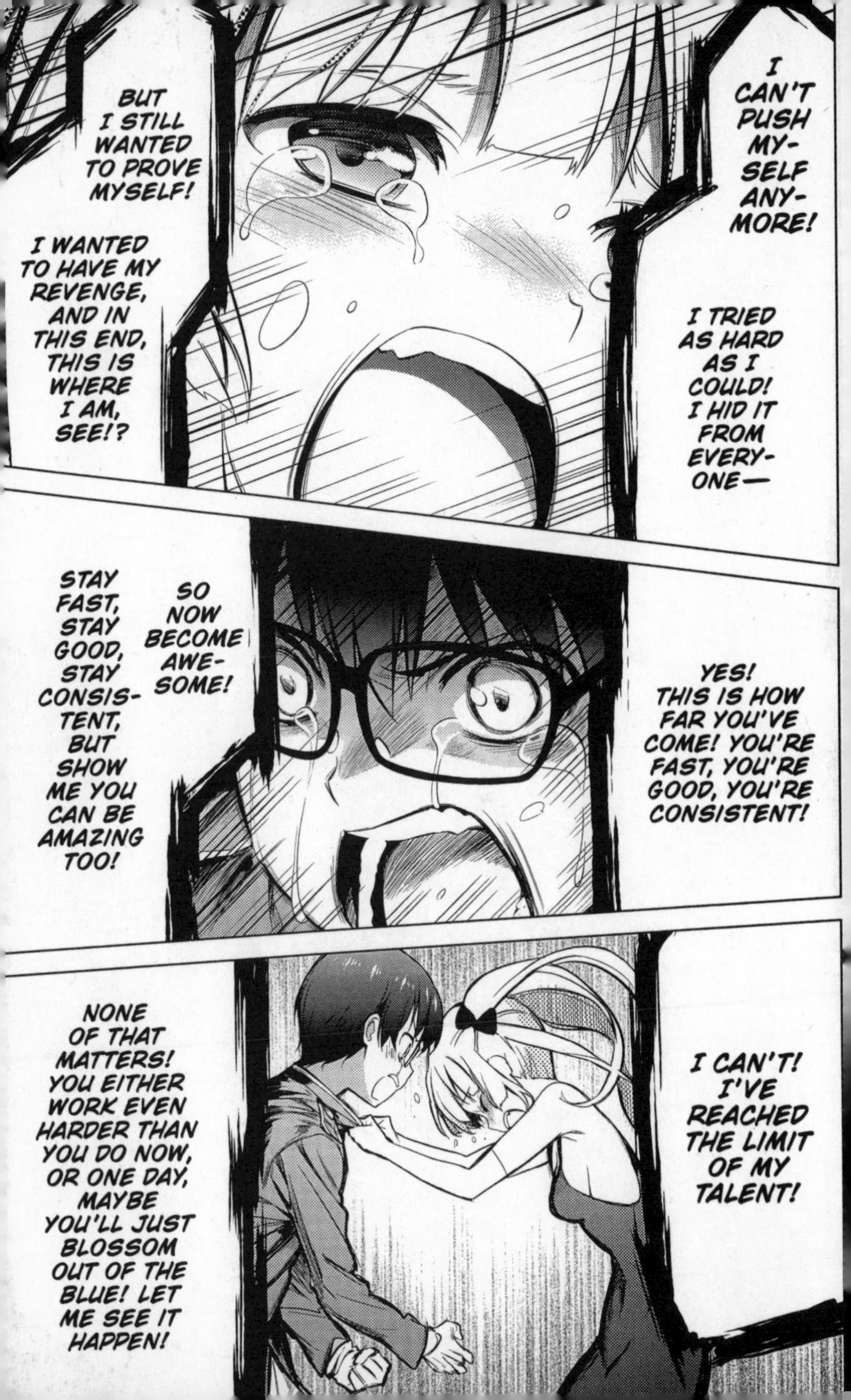
I CAN'T PUSH MYSELF ANYMORE!
I TRIED AS HARD AS I COULD! I HID IT FROM EVERYONE—
BUT I STILL WANTED TO PROVE MYSELF!
I WANTED TO HAVE MY REVENGE, AND IN THIS END, THIS IS WHERE I AM, SEE!?
YES! THIS IS HOW FAR YOU'VE COME! YOU'RE FAST, YOU'RE GOOD, YOU'RE CONSISTENT!
SO NOW BECOME AWESOME!
STAY FAST, STAY GOOD, STAY CONSISTENT, BUT SHOW ME YOU CAN BE AMAZING TOO!
I CAN'T! I'VE REACHED THE LIMIT OF MY TALENT!
NONE OF THAT MATTERS! YOU EITHER WORK EVEN HARDER THAN YOU DO NOW, OR ONE DAY, MAYBE YOU'LL JUST BLOSSOM OUT OF THE BLUE! LET ME SEE IT HAPPEN!

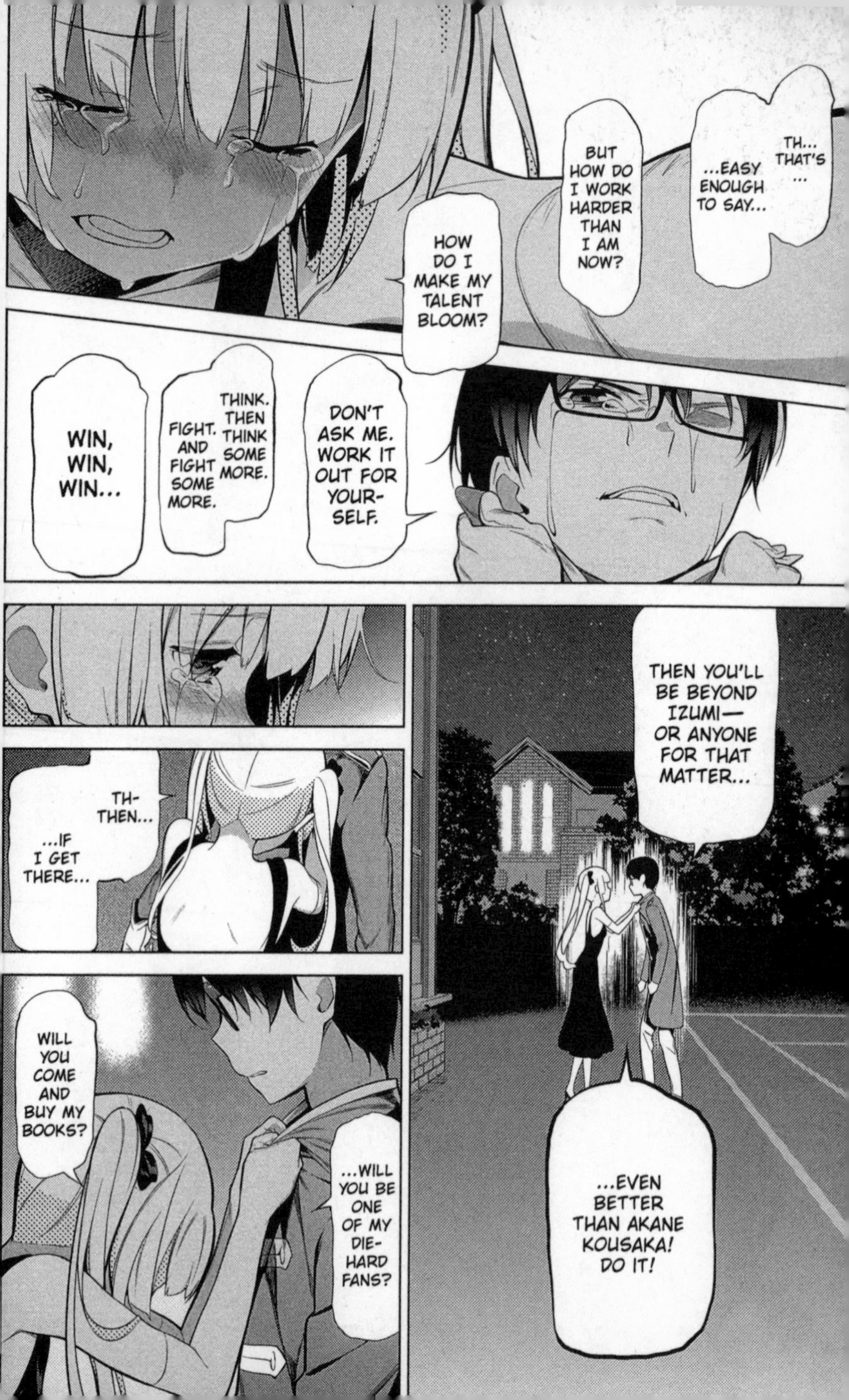
TH... THAT'S...
...EASY ENOUGH TO SAY...
BUT HOW DO I WORK HARDER THAN I AM NOW?
HOW DO I MAKE MY TALENT BLOOM?
DON'T ASK ME. WORK IT OUT FOR YOURSELF.
THINK. THEN THINK SOME MORE.
FIGHT. AND FIGHT SOME MORE.
WIN, WIN, WIN...
THEN YOU'LL BE BEYOND IZUMI— OR ANYONE FOR THAT MATTER...
...EVEN BETTER THAN AKANE KOUSAKA! DO IT!
TH-THEN...
...IF I GET THERE...
WILL YOU COME AND BUY MY BOOKS?
...WILL YOU BE ONE OF MY DIE-HARD FANS?

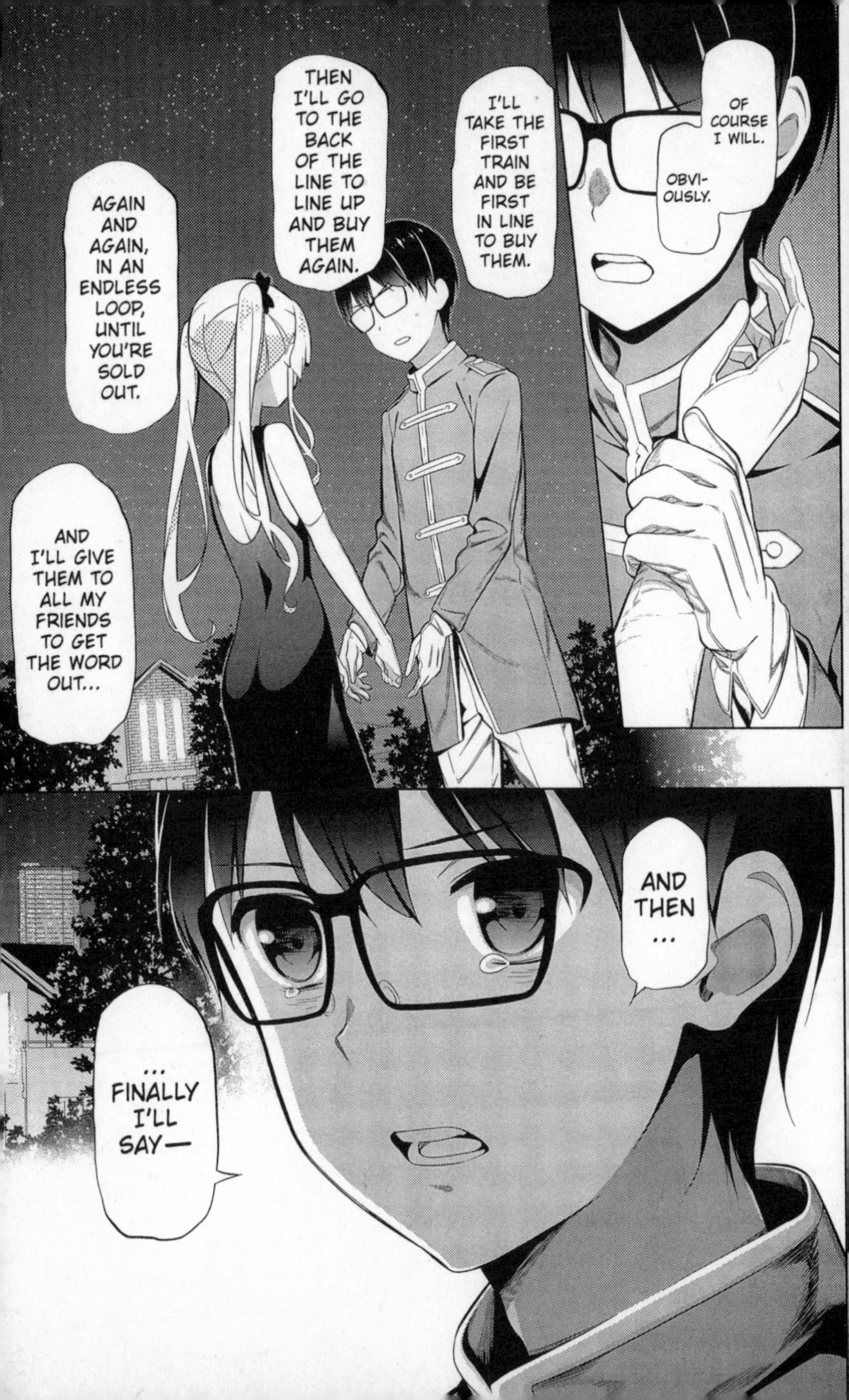
OF COURSE I WILL.
OBVIOUSLY.
I'LL TAKE THE FIRST TRAIN AND BE FIRST IN LINE TO BUY THEM.
THEN I'LL GO TO THE BACK OF THE LINE TO LINE UP AND BUY THEM AGAIN.
AGAIN AND AGAIN, IN AN ENDLESS LOOP, UNTIL YOU'RE SOLD OUT.
AND I'LL GIVE THEM TO ALL MY FRIENDS TO GET THE WORD OUT...
AND THEN...
...FINALLY I'LL SAY—

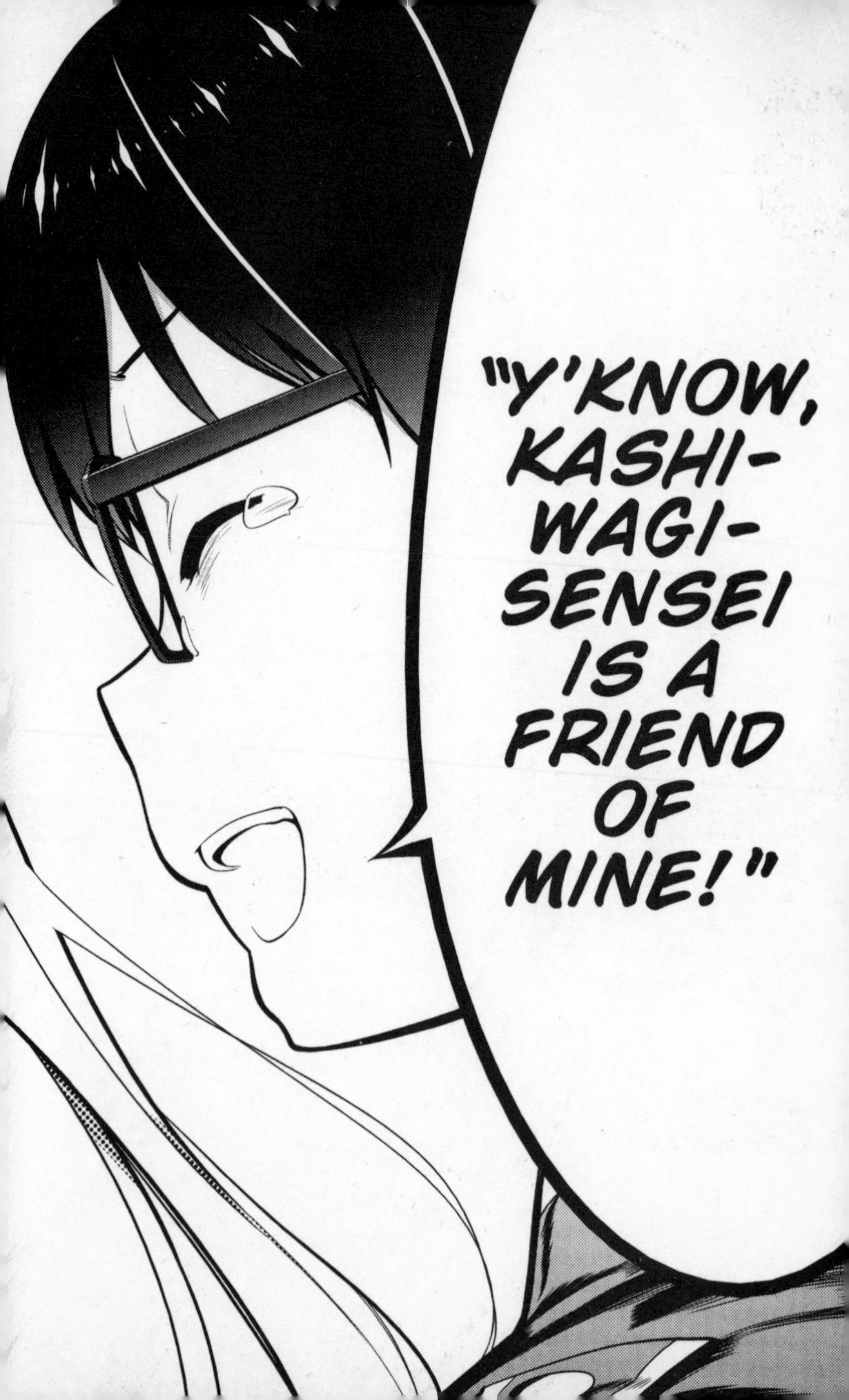
"Y'KNOW, KASHI-WAGI-SENSEI IS A FRIEND OF MINE!"

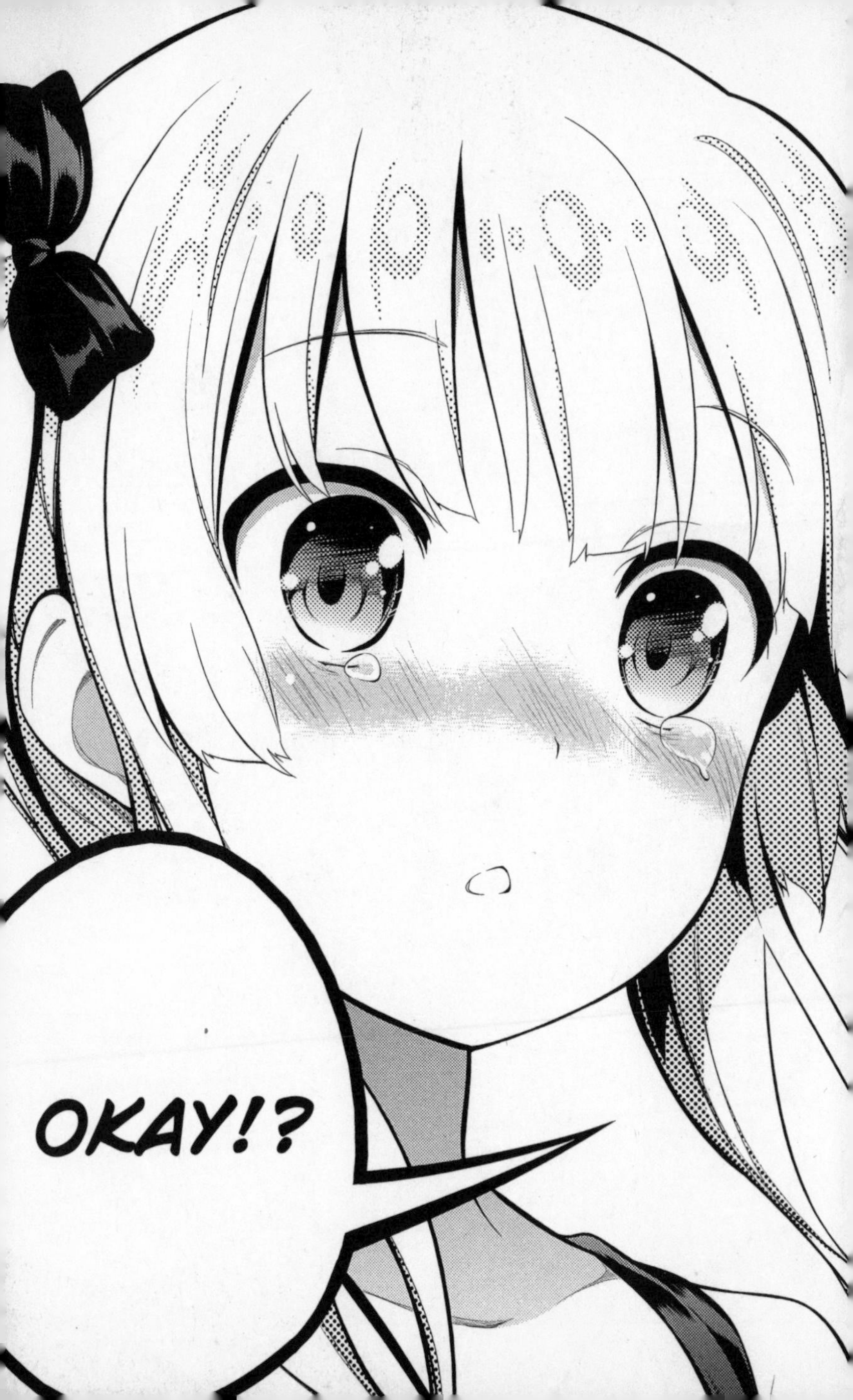
OKAY!?

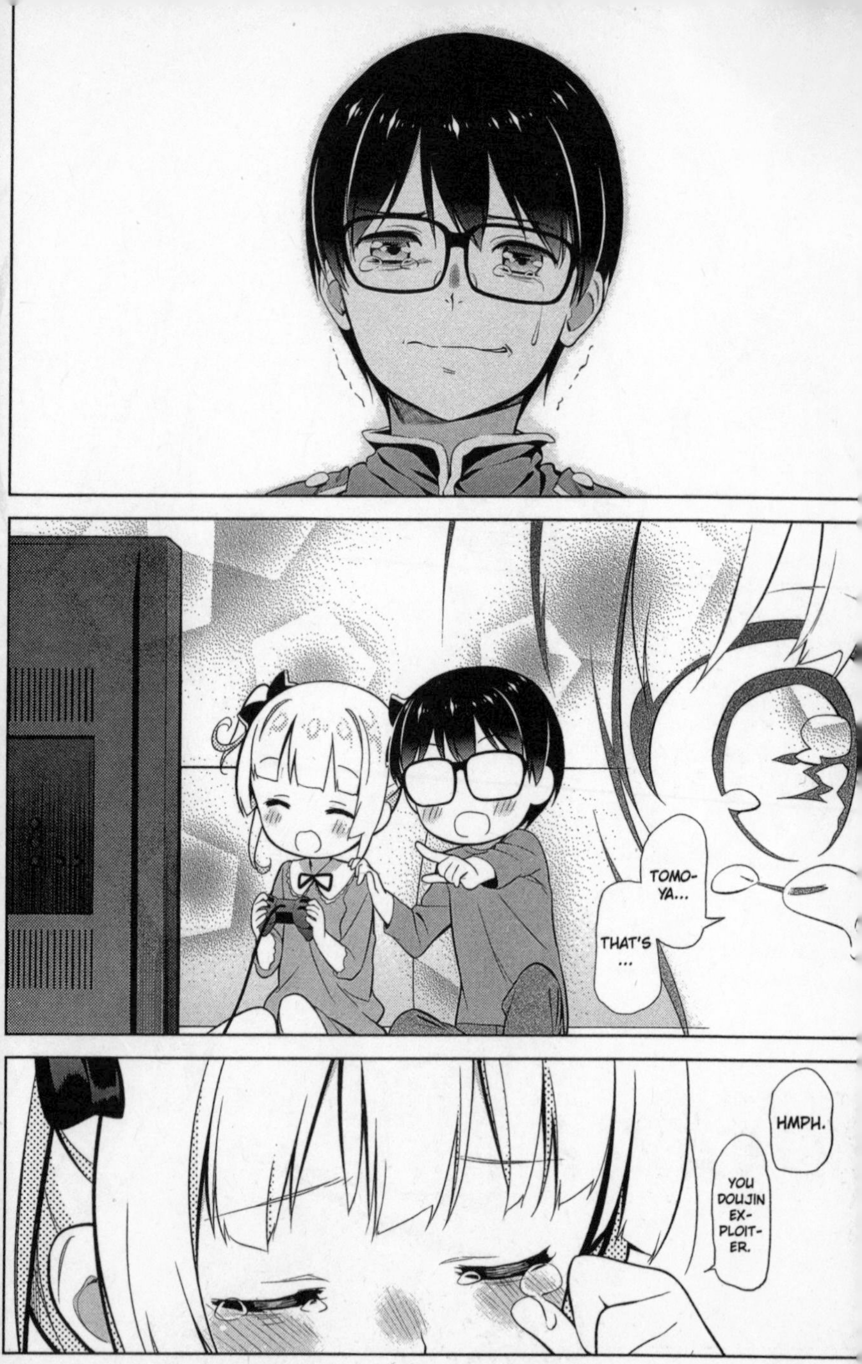
TOMO-YA...
THAT'S ...
HMPH.
YOU DOUJIN EX-PLOIT-ER.

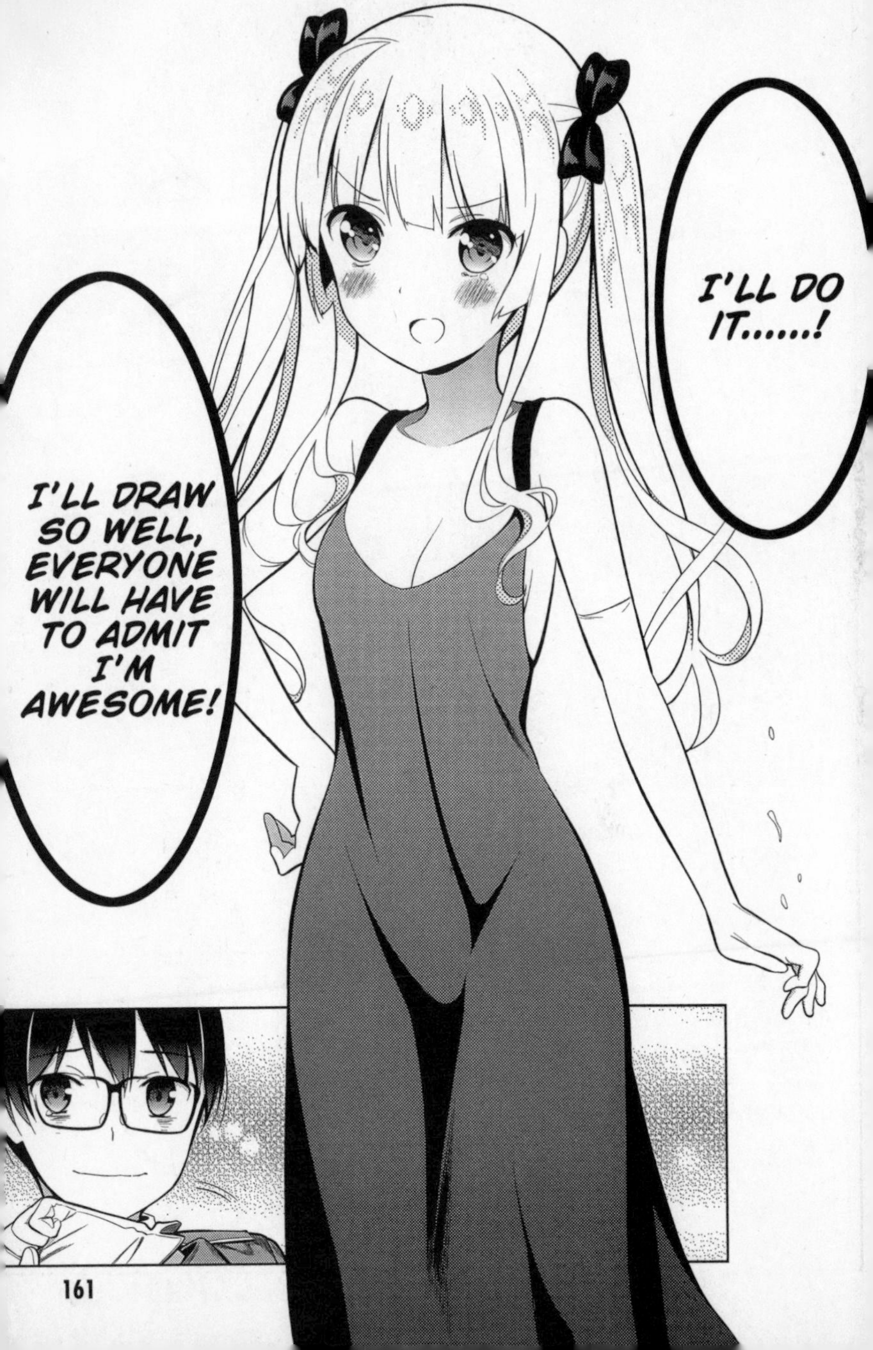
I'LL DO IT......!
I'LL DRAW SO WELL, EVERYONE WILL HAVE TO ADMIT I'M AWESOME!

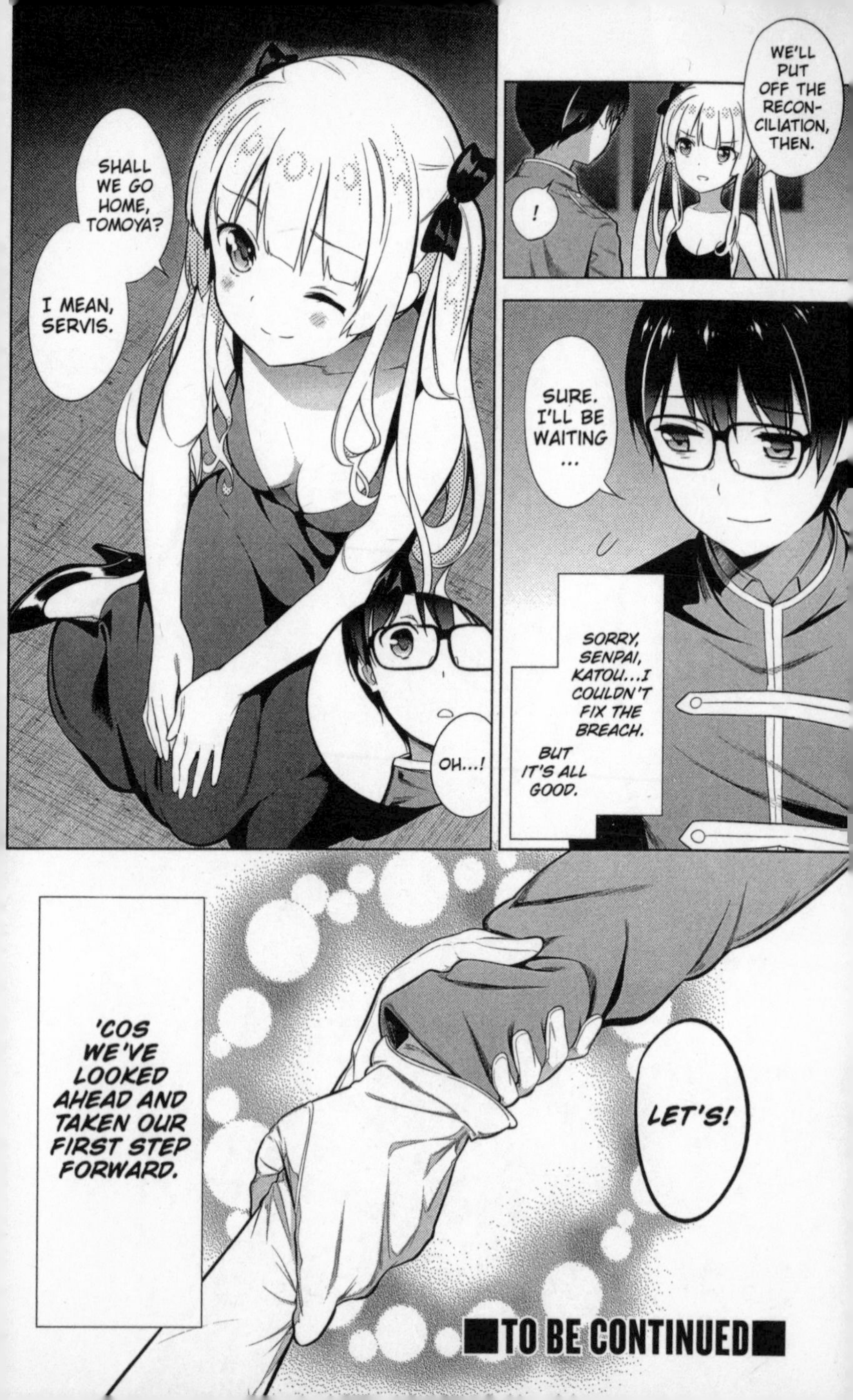
WE'LL PUT OFF THE RECON-CILIATION, THEN.
!
SURE. I'LL BE WAITING ...
SORRY, SENPAI, KATOU...I COULDN'T FIX THE BREACH.
BUT IT'S ALL GOOD.
SHALL WE GO HOME, TOMOYA?
I MEAN, SERVIS.
OH...!
LET'S!
'COS WE'VE LOOKED AHEAD AND TAKEN OUR FIRST STEP FORWARD.
TO BE CONTINUED

# How to Raise a Boring Girlfriend

# How to Raise a Boring Girlfriend

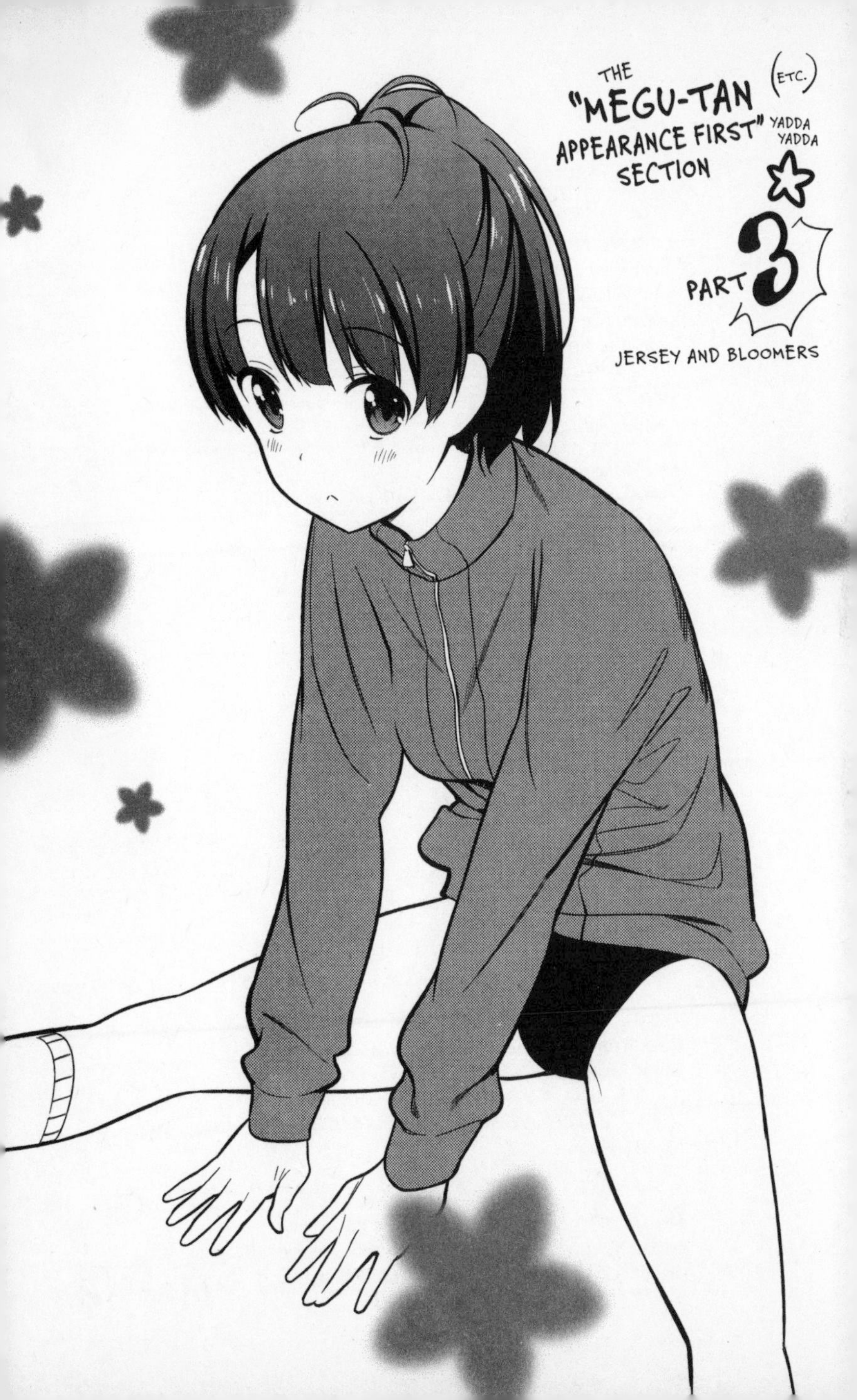
THE "MEGU-TAN (ETC.) APPEARANCE FIRST" YADDA YADDA SECTION
PART 3
JERSEY AND BLOOMERS

**COMMON HONORIFICS**

no honorific: Indicates familiarity or closeness; if used without permission or reason, addressing someone in this manner would constitute an insult.

-san: The Japanese equivalent of Mr./Mrs./Miss. If a situation calls for politeness, this is the fail-safe honorific.

-sama: Conveys great respect; may also indicate that the social status of the speaker is lower than that of the addressee.

-kun: Used most often when referring to boys, this indicates affection or familiarity. Occasionally used by older men among their peers, but it may also be used by anyone referring to a person of lower standing.

-chan (also -tan): An affectionate honorific indicating familiarity used mostly in reference to girls; also used in reference to cute persons or animals of either gender.

-senpai: An honorific used to address upperclassmen or more experienced coworkers.

-sensei: A respectful honorific for teachers, artists, or high-level professionals.

### PAGE 38
The **mock trial** here is an homage to the *Phoenix Wright: Ace Attorney* video game franchise from Capcom, from the jabbing objections to the brushy interjection balloons that continue up to the appearance of Izumi.

### PAGE 43
**Comiket**, a portmanteau of Comic Market, is the world's largest *doujinshi* fair. Founded in 1975, it is now held twice a year (August and December) in Tokyo and draws crowds exceeding 500,000 heads per show.

### PAGE 43
**Doujinshi** (*doujin*, for short) is self-published art, comics, video games, or novels produced (usually) by amateurs and derivative of existing properties.

**PAGE 45**
**Kouhai**, a companion word to *senpai*, is used when talking about one's underclassman, junior, or protégé. It can be used in academic, business, or team settings.

**PAGE 46**
**Miiin** is the sound effect for the chirping or buzzing of cicadas, the presence of which is very evocative of summer in Japan.

**PAGE 66**
A **ward** (*ku*) is a subdivision of a Japanese city as decided by the government.

**PAGE 73**
**Clear files** are folders made from durable plastic sealed on two sides for housing a few sheets of paper (standard size is A4). They are often sold as fan goods for anime and manga series and feature key art from those series.

**PAGE 75**
When Izumi mistakenly refers to Megumi as **Kamo-san**, Tomoya starts thinking wordplay. In Japanese name order, Megumi is Katou Megumi. Taking Izumi's blooper into account, it becomes Kamo Megumi, which sounds just like *kamome-gumi*. This means "sea gull group" and could be either a company or circle name, or the name given to a kindergarten class (often named after animals and plants).

**PAGE 98**
The **age of legal adulthood in Japan** is twenty years old, and pornographic material is often restricted from those under eighteen, so pretty much everyone in the story is too young to be reading Eriri's *doujinshi*, including Eriri herself! She would also not be allowed to sell her work, but she has help from her dad, as she mentioned in Volume 1.

### PAGE 99

The **cosplay outfit** shown here belongs to Shimakaze from *Kantai* ("Fleet") *Collection* (*KanColle*), a Japanese web game that involves collecting cards of sailing vessels—anthropomorphized as pretty girls—in order to build squadrons. The character is based on the one-of-a-kind Japanese destroyer of the same name built by the Imperial Japanese Army in World War II.

### PAGE 129

**Obon** is a Buddhist festival to celebrate the spirits of one's ancestors. It lasts three days and typically falls in July.

### PAGE 131

*Tsundere* is a compound term derived from the words *tsuntsun* ("disdainful, prickly") and *deredere* ("affectionate, fawning") that refers to a person who is initially abrasive or combative but softens over time or reveals a warm inner nature.

### PAGE 131

*Itasha* is the word for a car that has been decorated all over with anime decals and so on.

# How to Raise a Boring Girlfriend

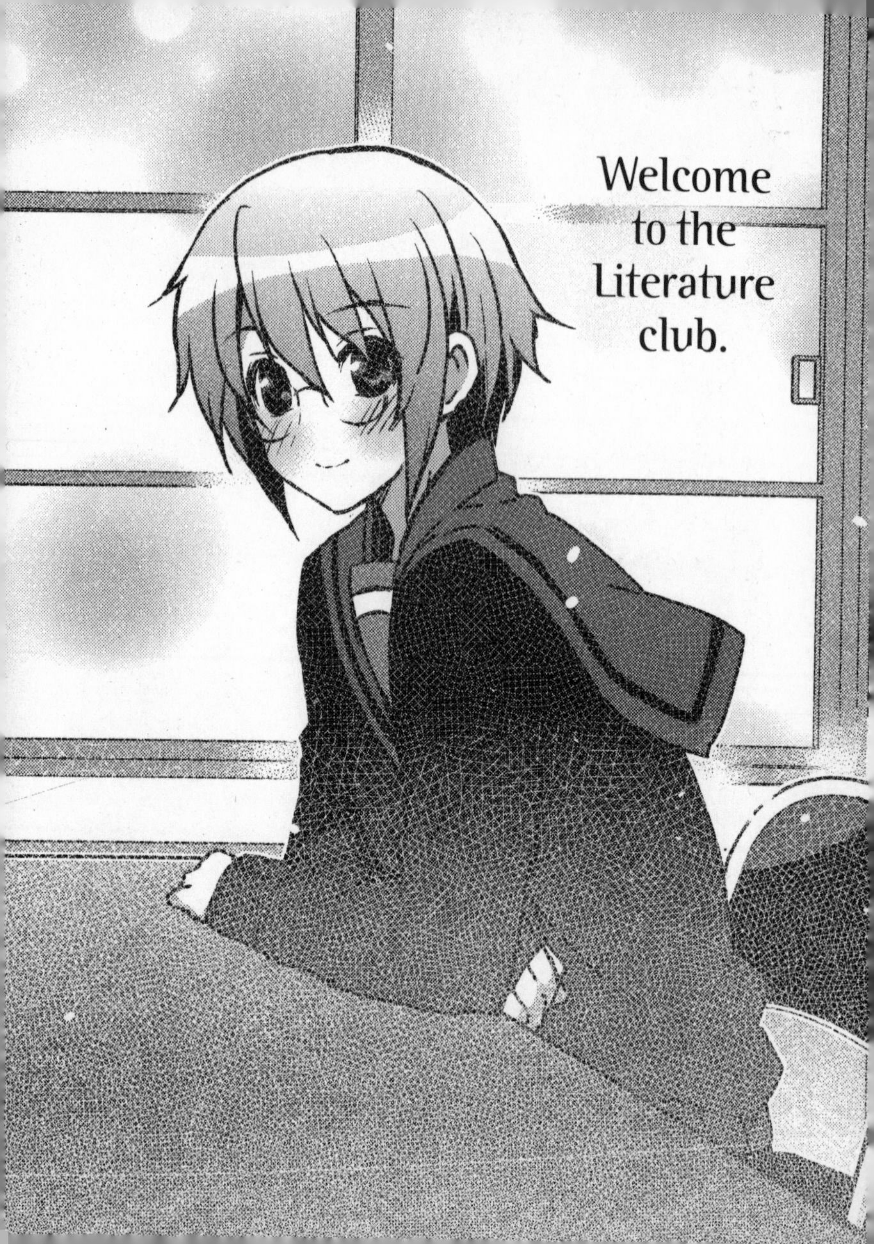
Welcome to the Literature club.

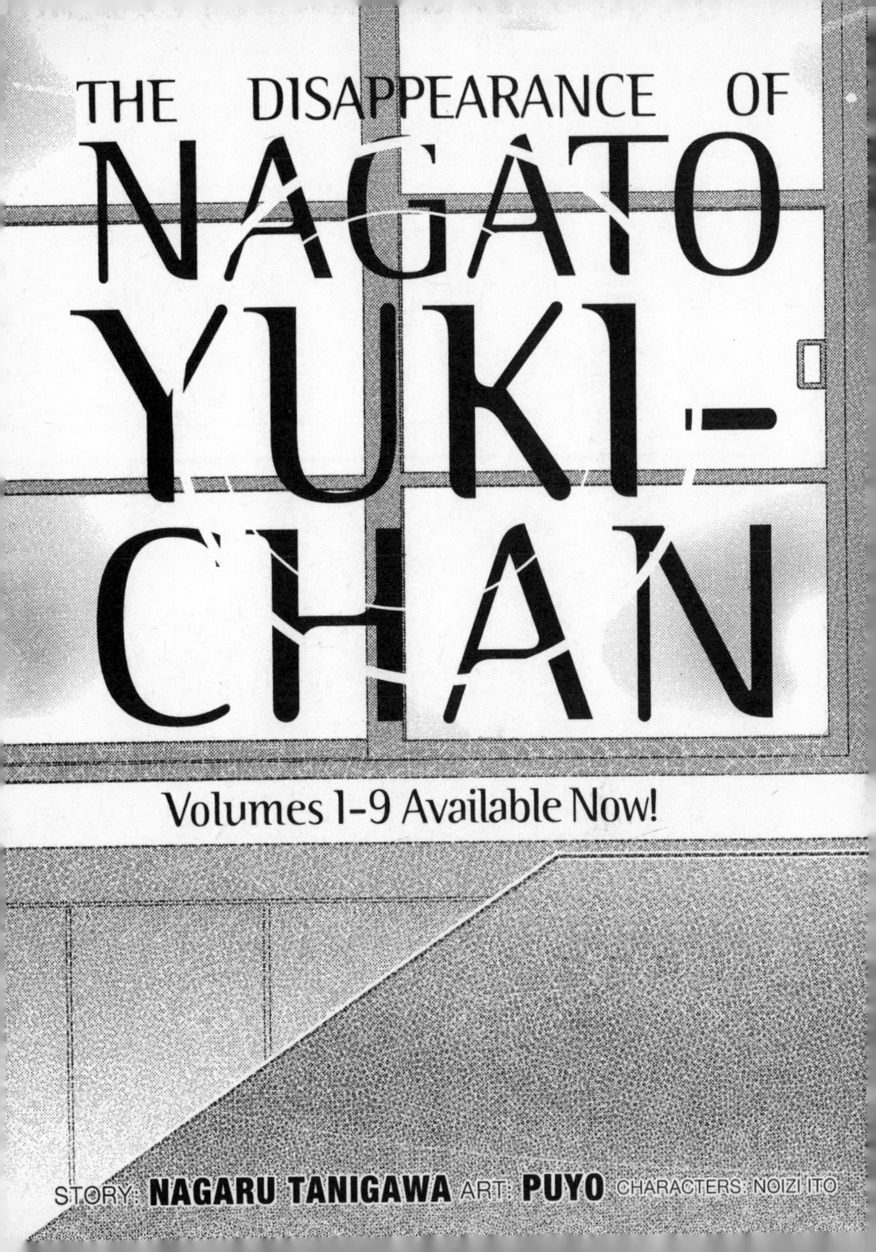
THE DISAPPEARANCE OF
NAGATO YUKI-CHAN
Volumes 1-9 Available Now!
STORY: NAGARU TANIGAWA ART: PUYO CHARACTERS: NOIZI ITO

# Hello! This is YOTSUBA!

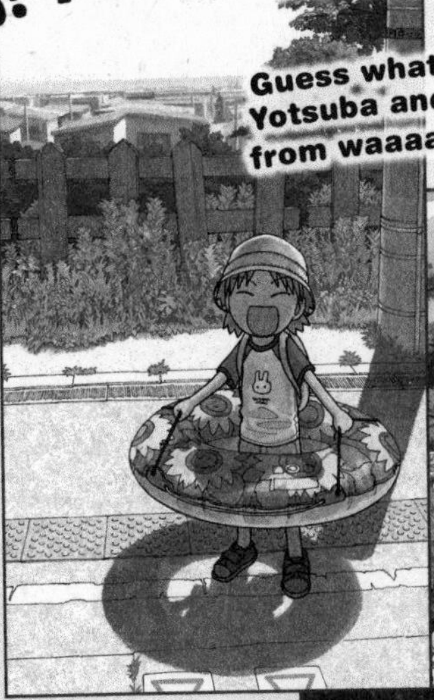

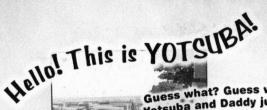

Guess what? Guess what?
Yotsuba and Daddy just moved here from waaaay over there!

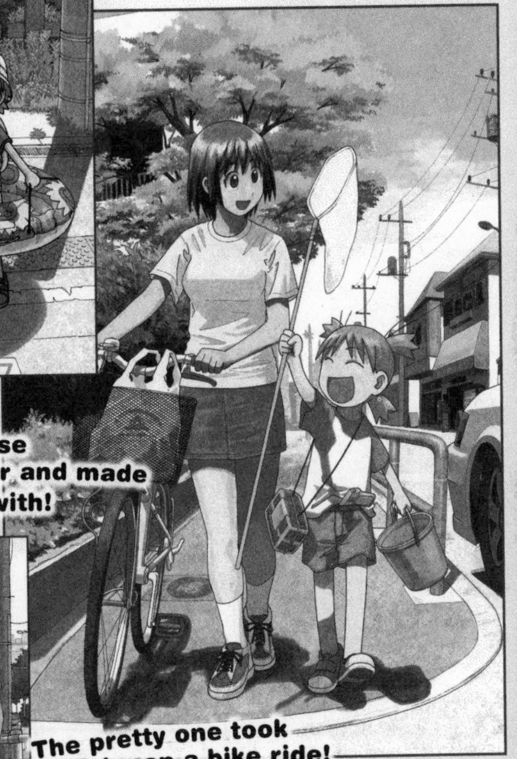

And Yotsuba met these nice people next door and made new friends to play with!

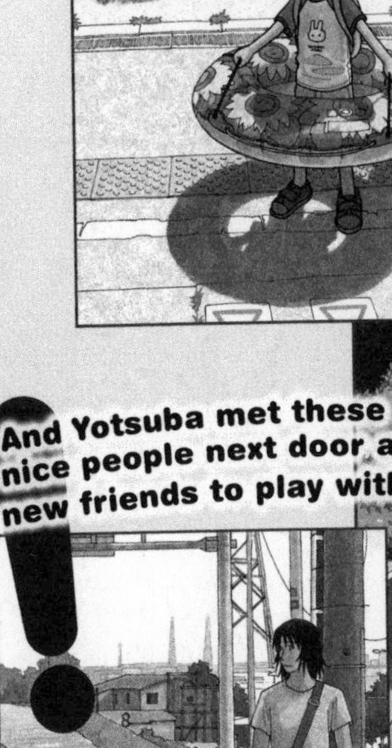

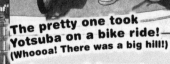

The pretty one took Yotsuba on a bike ride!
(Whoooa! There was a big hill!)

And Ena's a good drawer!
(Almost as good as Yotsuba!)

And their mom always gives Yotsuba ice cream!
(Yummy!)

And...

And...

OHHHH!

# HOW TO RAISE A BORING GIRLFRIEND ❸

**TAKESHI MORIKI**
Original Story: **FUMIAKI MARUTO**
Character Design: **KUREHITO MISAKI**

Translation: **Kumar Sivasubramanian**
Translation Consultant: **Chitoku Teshima**
Lettering: **Phil Christie**

SAENAI HEROINE NO SODATE-KATA Volume 3
©TAKESHI MORIKI 2014
©FUMIAKI MARUTO, KUREHITO MISAKI 2014.
First published in Japan in 2014 by KADOKAWA CORPORATION, Tokyo.
English translation rights reserved by YEN PRESS, LLC under the license
from KADOKAWA COPORATION, Tokyo through TUTTLE-MORI AGENCY, Inc., Tokyo.

English translation © 2016 by Yen Press, LLC

Yen Press
1290 Avenue of the Americas
New York, NY 10104

Visit us at yenpress.com
facebook.com/yenpress
twitter.com/yenpress
yenpress.tumblr.com

First Yen Press Edition: July 2016

Yen Press is an imprint of Yen Press, LLC.
The Yen Press name and logo are trademarks of Yen Press, LLC.

The publisher is not responsible for websites (or their content) that are not owned by the publisher.

Library of Congress Control Number: 2015952583

ISBNs: 978-0-316-31081-9 (paperback)
          978-0-316-31082-6 (ebook)
          978-0-316-31084-0 (app)

10 9 8 7 6 5 4 3 2 1

BVG

Printed in the United States of America

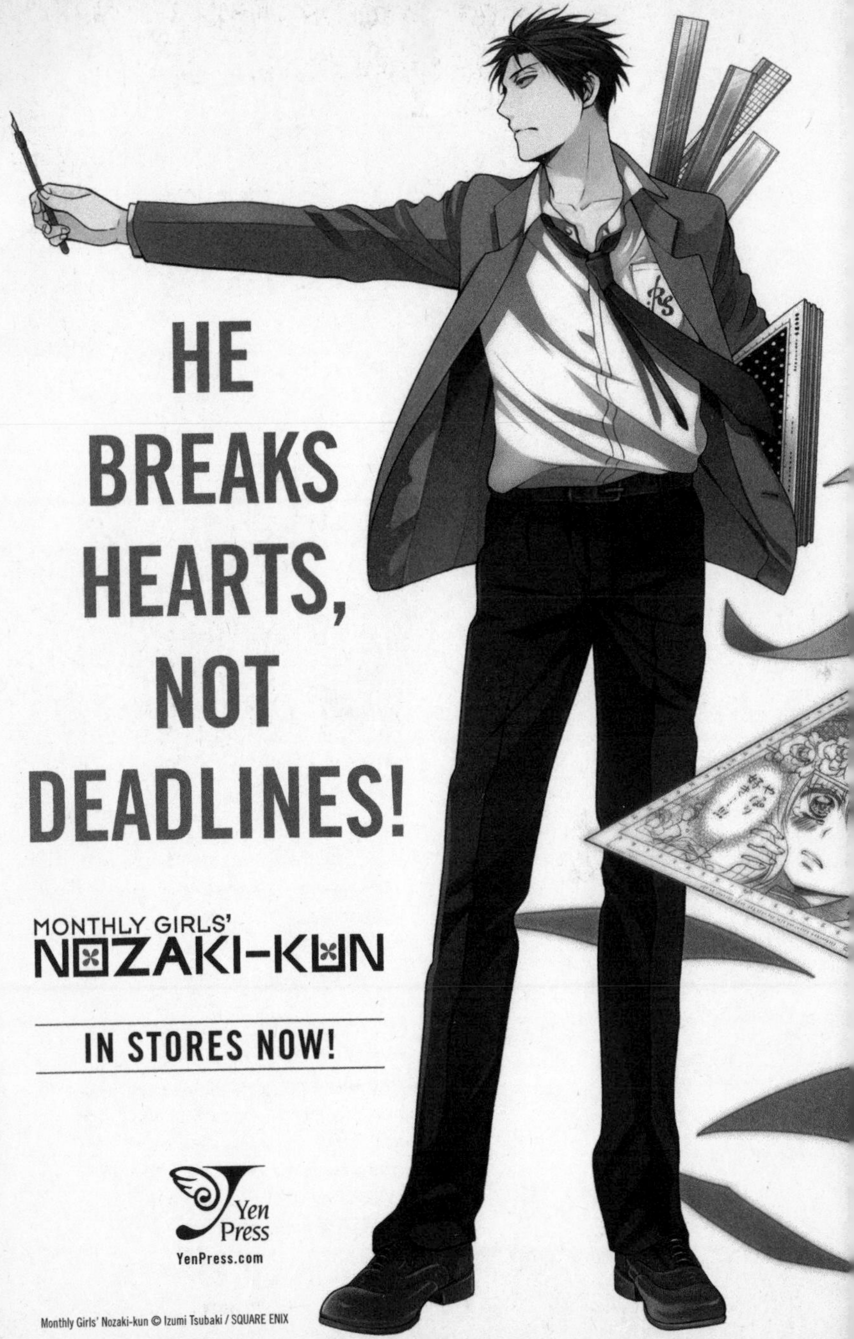
HE BREAKS HEARTS, NOT DEADLINES!
MONTHLY GIRLS'
NOZAKI-KUN
IN STORES NOW!
Yen Press
YenPress.com
Monthly Girls' Nozaki-kun © Izumi Tsubaki / SQUARE ENIX